Internet Newspapers

The Making of a Mainstream Medium

Edited by

XIGEN LI
Southern Illinois University Carbondale

LEA   LAWRENCE ERLBAUM ASSOCIATES, PUBLISHERS
2006   Mahwah, New Jersey   London

Lawrence Erlbaum Associates, Inc., Publishers
10 Industrial Avenue
Mahwah, New Jersey 07430
www.erlbaum.com

Cover design by Kathryn Houghtaling Lacey

Library of Congress Cataloging-in-Publication Data

Internet newspapers : the making of a mainstream medium / edited
by Xigen Li.
    p.   cm.
  Includes bibliographical references and indexes.
  ISBN 0–8058–5416–9 (alk. paper) — ISBN 0–8058–5417–7
(pbk. : alk. paper)
  1. Electronic newspapers. 2. Online journalism. I. Li, Xigen.
PN4833.I62 2005
0701'72—dc22   2005040575

Books published by Lawrence Erlbaum Associates are printed on acid-free
paper, and their bindings are chosen for strength and durability.

Printed in the United States of America
10 9 8 7 6 5 4 3 2

Contents

Part II: Emerging Medium in an Interactive Process

Part III: Internet Newspapers and the Public

Foreword

Everette E. Dennis
Fordham University

The ink on paper newspaper just passed its 200th birthday when its Internet counterpart was born. Although electronic and digital newspapers were envisioned before the Internet emerged as a viable medium, it has sparked an extraordinary revolution in communication across time and distance truly unimagined in times past. And although early online newspapers were both amateurish and tentative, they quickly scaled their way to the commanding heights of communication. Thus, understanding this phenomenon both as a media enterprise and as an object of study is clearly warranted.

That's what media researcher Xigen Li and his colleagues at several universities have attempted in *Internet Newspapers: The Making of a Mainstream Medium.* In doing so, they have succeeded admirably in producing an innovative, thoughtful, and important volume. That this work was mostly produced by young scholars makes it especially appealing, for who could better observe this new phenomenon than those who have grown up with it through graduate school and into budding academic careers. The work is fresh and filled with insights and will, no doubt, inspire other studies as Internet newspapers survive and succeed. This is more than a collection of research papers, but a gracefully edited and integrated narrative, thanks to Professor Li's seminal role, both as the originator and editor of the work, but also as author of several of the chapters.

Developed in three parts—information delivery and access; the emerging, interactive process of these media; and their impact on the public and on public consciousness—the book cuts a broad swath across the digital landscape, both in function and form. And seamlessly, it also understands and treats the global/international nature of the Internet newspaper along with its domestic presence in the United States.

Here we have a brisk sketch of the history of the medium alongside a look into its content and usage trends. This being a largely visual medium, graphics also get front-row-center treatment. Some of the studies are broad sweeps at the whole field, whereas others focus in on individual newspapers in specific locales. We are treated to the interplay of economics and technology—and policy—in several of the studies while being ever conscious of how the online "paper" plays alongside its conventional old media sibling.

This volume benefits from Xigen Li's intellectual leadership as an early Internet media researcher drawn from his background first as a science writer and subsequently as a communication researcher. From his early career on a leading science and technology daily in China, he has known the practicalities of the newspaper world while looking beyond mundane details to the larger picture, something that systematic research affords. He has assembled a cast of leading characters here as co-authors and contributors, including Jennifer Greer, Donica Mensing, Mark Tremayne, Wilson Lowrey, Jinmyung Choi, Zhanwei Cao, Qian Zeng, Renee duPlessis, Hsiang Iris Chyi, Dominic Lasorsa, Carolyn Lin, Michael Salwen, Erik Bucy, Robert Affe, and Xianyi Ye. Whereas some of these colleagues are already well known, most are not, but I'd hazard a guess they will be—and soon. This volume of 16 original studies—eight of which involve Professor Li—offers insights and inspiration for anyone interested in and concerned about this fascinating new platform for a venerable medium.

Internet Newspapers represents a remarkable joint enterprise of rigorous researchers whose careful observations and search for meaning have resulted in a worthy contribution to the scholarly literature and to immediate public and professional understanding. Readers well beyond the academic community, such as strategic planners and investors, will find benefit here as well as students and teachers with an eye toward monitoring, assessing, and analyzing today's Internet newspapers as a prelude to the next generation of these extraordinary media.

As one who has traced today's digital media products including Internet newspapers from their origins in the theories of convergence, this book is an eye-opening window on the process, dynamics, and ultimate impact of this singular digital enterprise.

Preface

In October 1994, when the first beta version of Netscape was released, few people thought that they would be able to access news through the Web browser. The birth of Netscape installed a milestone in the history of newspaper publishing. Netscape opened an unlimited universe that was previously unimaginable and unreachable for newspaper publishers and audiences. Soon we saw newspapers publishing news on the Internet. Right from the beginning, I was fascinated by the emerging medium; I followed every new development. Benefiting from access to the content of newspapers around the world, I took a closer look at the emerging news medium. Starting from the perspective of a traditional journalist, I looked into the new medium from many different aspects. Several research projects were developed and completed as I observed its growth.

Ten years have elapsed, and the Internet has undergone tremendous changes. Looking at Internet newspapers today, we find them almost a different animal from what we remember of the early ventures of the print newspapers. They are more mature, more sophisticated, and more efficient in delivering information, and they are no longer a newcomer to the family of news media. The more the Internet newspaper grows, the more questions arise about its operation, functions, effects, and interaction with society. Research on Internet newspapers has become a significant area that attracts more and more scholars each year.

While exploring the new medium, I found it challenging to conduct research on it. We did not have much knowledge about the type of medium on which we could build our studies. Very little literature could be found on Internet newspapers. The identification and application of appropriate theories in the studies were also not easy tasks. Whereas it has always been exciting and rewarding for us to conduct research in an underexplored area, it has also required more time and effort to work on any project exploring this new medium with the hope of producing high quality pieces of research. There is no shortcut for any groundbreaking work. Taking the challenge to explore an uncharted area is the starting point for success. After conducting research on the news media and the Internet for a few years, I thought a collection of research works on the topic might help researchers in this area and stimulate more significant contributions to the understanding of the emerging medium.

That thought leads to one of the purposes of this book: to entice more scholars to work in the area by presenting a collection of works on Internet newspapers. Research always lags behind social activities. The earliest Internet newspapers are now 10 years old; however, research in this area is much younger. We have just started to explore some of the basic issues regarding Internet newspapers. The reality is that not much literature on Internet newspapers exists. We still don't know much about the operations, functions, and effects of the new medium. The nature and scope of the current body of research on Internet newspapers are quite limited. In presenting this volume of research work on Internet newspapers, we hope to stimulate further exploration and discussion of the important issues about this emerging medium. Several of the chapter authors make important contributions to the study of Internet newspapers by introducing new concepts and new perspectives on the news media in this networked world. They also attempt to apply a variety of theoretical approaches to study in this area. The research works in this volume provide many intriguing ideas for interested scholars to think through the issues regarding the new medium, generate new ideas and dimensions in their exploration of the medium, and expand their line of research.

The second purpose of this volume is to show how researchers can benefit from the empirical approach in their examination of the Internet newspapers. All studies included in this book took an empirical approach to explore the new medium. A variety of research methods were used, including surveys, content analysis, and experiments. Some of the research designs are rather innovative. The volume shows how different research methods can be used to solve problems in examining this new medium.

This book makes a contribution to the field by providing, in a single place, a comprehensive and systematic look at the state of Internet newspapers based on empirical data. The book explores the theoretical and practical issues associated with Internet newspapers and the process whereby they grew into a mainstream medium. It looks at Internet newspapers from both the academic and the practitioner's perspectives. Compared to other texts on online journalism and news media on the Internet, this book is different in several aspects: (a) It is a systematic examination of the evolution and state of Internet newspapers; (b) it offers empirical data as evidence of its core theses; and (c) it breaks some new ground conceptually, including the cognitive flexibility theory as a way of understanding newspaper readership, particularly online, and the application of network theory to the use of external links on news Web sites. Equally importantly, the volume contains interesting normative, descriptive, and analytical data: the blend of theory and practice.

The intended readers of this book are researchers in journalism and mass communication, advanced undergraduate and graduate students in journalism and mass communication, and those in other academic disciplines offering courses in communication, information technology, and media studies. Journalism practitioners, such as publishers, editors, and journalists, and other people working in designing and publishing newspapers on the Web will also find the book quite relevant to their work.

For researchers and students of journalism and mass communication, the book can be used as a reader on newspapers in the information age and new media technology for several courses. Graduate students may find the book very useful in their classes on contemporary news media, theory and research of media technology, applied research in mass communication, advanced research methods, and other classes with social and behavioral perspectives. Undergraduate students may find the book interesting and helpful with their courses about mass media and society, online journalism, Internet communication, new media technology, and media theory and research.

Journalism practitioners should use this book to understand newspapers on the Internet, their development and changes, the influential forces on the operation and functions of news media on the Internet, and the impact of this emerging medium on other media, audience, and society. The book also offers much insight on how to improve operation and performance of newspapers on the Internet to serve the public better and to achieve a competitive advantage.

ACKNOWLEDGMENTS

I thank all the contributors for their work. Among the list of contributors, you will find seasoned scholars such as Carolyn Lin, Michael Salwen, and Erik Bucy, who devoted their years of academic careers to the study of new media technology and the development of media theories. You will see young scholars who are among the pioneer researchers in the study of news media and the Internet such as Hsiang Iris Chyi, Jennifer Greer, and Wilson Lowrey. They are taking an active leading role in exploring the Internet newspapers, the growing mainstream medium, and their research represents the best work in the field.

During the process of developing the project and editing the book, I received much inspiration and help from colleagues at the institutions with which I have been affiliated, especially several mentors at Michigan State University. Some of the work I did in this book benefited from the advice of more than a few people that I could mention here. I want to thank Steve Lacy, Fred Fico, Bella Mody, Charles Salmon, Lucinda Davenport, Folu Ogundimu, Jim Detjen, Hairong Li, and James Dearing, who taught me how to conduct theory-based research and guided me as I developed my research interest in Internet newspapers. Steve Lacy and Tsan-Kuo Chang offered encouragement and advice on working as a book editor.

My colleagues at Louisiana State University gave me tremendous help while I worked on the book. Renita Coleman helped me initiate the book proposal and offered detailed advice on managing an edited book volume. Ralph Izard, Richard Nelson, David Perlmutter, and Louis Day lent their hands to me any time I needed help. Russell Shain, Joel Gambill, and Gilbert Fowler at Arkansas State University offered valuable support as I continued to work on the book in the fall 2004. I really appreciate that they value high-quality research in this underexplored new area. I also want to thank my students at Louisiana State University who worked with me either as co-authors or assistants in collecting data for several research projects. I am grateful to the following scholars who reviewed the manuscripts and provided helpful suggestions: Jennings Bryant, University of Alabama; Bruce Garrison, University of Miami; Maxwell E. McCombs, University of Texas at Austin; and John V. Pavlik, Rutgers University.

—Xigen Li

Introduction

Xigen Li
Southern Illinois University Carbondale

Each new medium born from technology advancement has great expectations when launched. But not all of them end up with mass adoption and remarkable success. Videotex, a medium with some features similar to the Internet newspapers and once a very promising new communication device, failed repeatedly in the 1980s (Ettema, 1989). The newspapers on the Internet were born with a much lower profile, though not free from the prophecy of media analysts (Bogart, 1994; Calamai, 1995; Kirsner, 1999; Riley & Keough, 1998; Robertson, 1997). Not as many great expectations were placed on them compared to other new media derived from technological innovations (Giles, 2000; Ingle, 1995). Yet in less than 6 years, the Internet newspapers not only survived, but also expanded exponentially. The Internet newspaper is a phenomenon along with the growth of the Internet.

In 2004, almost all U.S. newspapers have an Internet presence. There are over 4,000 U.S. newspapers on the Web alone (NewsLink, 2004). Few would doubt that the Internet newspapers are in a position of a mainstream medium now. But many may find it hard to reach that conclusion before they take a serious look at the Internet newspapers. The Internet newspapers grew into a mainstream medium so fast before many of us had enough opportunities to learn about the medium itself, the technology that supported the medium, and social and institutional factors that shaped the medium. A look back at the timeline of the medium may help us understand its fast growth and increasing power.

A BRIEF TIMELINE OF INTERNET NEWSPAPERS

U.S. newspapers started to publish on the Internet as early as 1992, but not in the format as we see them on the World Wide Web today. Newspaper content was

1

text-based and was delivered through BBS or online services such as Prodigy and America Online. On September 12, 1994, Netscape released the beta version of its Navigator, a graphic Web browser. Newspapers formally established their presence on the World Wide Web soon after that. There were approximately 60 North American newspapers with sites on the Internet or with dial-up services by the end of 1994. However, there were fewer than 10 Internet newspapers accessible through the World Wide Web; among them, *Raleigh News & Observer* (9/94), *San Francisco Examiner/Chronicle* (11/94), and *San Jose Mercury News* (12/94) were the pioneers. In 1996, approximately 500 North American newspapers established sites on the Internet or through dial-up services, but only half of them, 248 daily newspapers, published on the World Wide Web by September 1996. Newspapers on the Internet reached the critical mass scale around 1997. By September 1997, 745 U.S. newspapers, about half of the U.S. dailies, published on the Internet (Meyer, 1997). The growth of newspapers on the Internet accelerated in 1997. There were 1,290 U.S. newspapers online in March 1998. The number reached 2,059 as of September 27, 1998, a growth of 60% in 6 months and 176% in 1 year (Peng, Irene, & Hao, 1999). More than 3,400 U.S. newspapers were online by June 2001. Most of the U.S. newspapers published on the Internet in 2001 (Poynter, 2004).

With the extensive presence of newspapers on the Internet, the content of the newspapers changed, too. Before 1996, a newspaper Web site was merely a place to introduce the newspaper, or just a claim of its Web presence. Now, newspapers on the Internet are serious publications. They are comparable to the daily print newspapers in content and timeliness. They deliver information to a much broader audience than their print counterparts. Newspapers on the Internet are becoming one of the mainstream media that play as important a role as their print counterparts in delivering information and informing the public (Eveland, Marton, & Mihye Seo, 2004). On many occasions, audiences rely more on newspapers on the Internet for information because they are more accessible, updated more often, and richer in content than print newspapers (Chyi & Lasorsa, 1999; Nicholson, 1999). According to a study of the Newspaper Association of America in 2002 (NAA, 2002), newspaper Web sites were rated the number one source of local news and information online, beating out other local media sites and national brands such as Yahoo!.

ISSUES ARISING FROM GROWTH
OF INTERNET NEWSPAPERS

From 1996 to 2002, in about 6 years, more than 4,000 U.S. newspapers were created on the Internet. The magnitude of media proliferation on the Internet has been unprecedented. This new medium is still under development both in its function to serve the public and its use of advanced technology. However, with all the development of the newspapers on the Web, and a new medium playing a more visible role in people's lives, newspapers on the Internet have not been a topic adequately addressed by the academics. There is not much literature on newspapers on the Internet. Of the literature that could be found on newspapers on the Web, most was simple descriptions of the new medium following its trend of development. Although the descriptions of the Internet newspaper development at each stage have their value in documenting the history of news media, they do not offer much insight about the mechanism of the development of the emerging medium. Nor do they provide a better understanding of the interactive relationship between the Internet newspapers, the factors shaping the new medium, and the consequences brought about by its growth. With the rapid development of the newspapers on the Internet, the simple descriptions of the new medium were never able to catch up with the pace of the development.

The growth of the new medium offers great opportunities to examine existing media theory, explore relationships between the old and the new media, and explain and predict what the new medium brings to media industry as well as the whole society. Searching the literature available since the Internet newspapers established their presence, it is rare to find studies about newspapers on the Internet that explore the new medium from a theoretical perspective (Althaus & Tewksbury, 2002; Dimitrova, Connolly-Ahern, Williams, Kaid, & Reid, 2003; Singer, 2001; Tewksbury, 2003). Although the development and practice of the new medium offered wonderful opportunities to test and challenge media theory and the theoretical framework and assumptions that applied to traditional media, not much work has been done to advance our knowledge about the news media using a theoretical approach.

The following are a few questions that should no longer be ignored if we want to understand how the Internet newspapers and other media operate, perform, and affect our society in the Internet-pervasive age. These questions range from an individual level to societal level, from an audience perspective to organization and institution perspectives, and from within the medium itself to between the media: How do newspapers on the Internet differ in their functions from their print counterparts? How do newspapers on the Internet interact with their print counterparts and other aspects in and out of media? Are newspapers on the Internet playing a more powerful role than print newspapers in influencing the audience on certain issues? Are the Internet newspapers an agenda-setter as powerful as print newspapers? What organizational and institutional factors played the most important role in shaping Internet newspapers? How did user experience with the Internet newspapers affect their gratification with the medium? Do readers perceive more control in accessing information from Internet newspapers than they do from print newspapers? There are more questions like these that remain unanswered.

WHAT THIS BOOK ATTEMPTS TO ADDRESS

This book attempts to fill the void in exploring the emerging medium, newspapers on the Internet. The objective of this book is to explore the theoretical and practical issues associated with the Internet newspapers and the process in which they grew into a mainstream medium. It tries to provide answers to some of the compelling questions that are critical in understanding this emergent new medium. This book explores newspapers on the Internet from an academic perspective and with an empirical approach. It attempts to provide thought-provoking discussions on theories relating to new media and the applicable technology used by newspapers on the Internet. It examines different aspects of newspapers on the Internet with regard to theoretical applications in the new media environment, the relationship between traditional and new media, and the role that newspapers on the Internet play in informing the public.

The book is divided into parts covering three aspects of newspapers on the Internet: (a) Information Delivery and Access of Internet Newspapers; (b) Emerging Medium in an Interactive Process; and (c) Internet Newspapers and the Public.

Information Delivery and Access of Internet Newspapers

Part I examines the information delivery and access features of the Internet newspapers and how these features affect the communication process between the communicators and the audience.

Unlike other descriptive studies, Greer and Mensing (chap. 1) explore the Internet newspapers from their earlier age to the present. They tracked U.S. Internet newspapers from 1997, the year the new medium picked up speed in its growth. The longitudinal approach of their study provides a most comprehensive picture of how the Internet newspapers grew from something hardly noticeable to a most conspicuous mainstream medium.

While studying graphic use and interconnectedness of the Internet newspapers in their earlier age, Li (chap. 2) explores a new communication model evolved from the structure and presentation of the Internet newspapers. Li argues that the news links and the multiple communication channels adopted by Internet newspapers in Web page design created a new environment of communication, involving more than host newspaper and initial audience. With interconnected links, the traditional one-to-many newspaper publishing process turned into many-to-many communication centered on and facilitated by the host Internet newspapers.

Tremayne (chap. 3) tested emerging network theory against a subsample of the Web: stories on U.S. national news Web sites. The study found that news Web stories contain links to external sites less frequently than just a few years ago. As each organization builds up its own archive of Web content, this material appears to be favored over content that is off-site when links are added to stories. The findings from three major U.S. newspapers, two news magazines, and five U.S. television networks post a serious question: Will news Web sites become increasingly isolated from other parts of the Web?

Chapter 4 by Li examines the process of obtaining news from newspaper Web sites of different designs. A content analysis found that Web design becomes a critical chain in creating a smooth news flow on the Internet and facilitating news retrieval efficiency. The study provided empirical evidence of the power shift from senders to receivers of information as Internet newspapers offered more freedom and easier access to new information that gave readers control over what to get and how to get it. This study also made a considerable contribution by establishing a measurement instrument of news retrieval efficiency, the main property in evaluating the effectiveness of a newspaper Web site.

Observing how readers actually obtain news from the Internet newspapers offers more insight on how information structure and presentation affect information retrieval. An experimental study (Li, chap. 5) found that the means facilitating users to get information is also important in predicting value associated with the medium. The implication of functional alternative perspective of uses and gratifications theory is demonstrated through obtained gratification, news retrieval efficiency. This study expanded the scope of the functional alternative perspective from across the media to within the medium. The Internet newspapers with different designs are functional alternatives available to audiences in all markets and are likely to compete for the same audience in their selection of communication channels within the medium.

Lowrey and Choi (chap. 6) contribute to the literature on hypermedia news by testing the application of cognitive flexibility theory (CFT), a theory from the field of education, to the production of Internet news stories. The CFT hypermedia format is designed to improve ability to apply knowledge in varied "real world" settings and to reduce oversimplification. An experiment was conducted to see if the CFT format, applied to an Internet news story, would increase ability to apply news knowledge by increasing perceived ability to publicly discuss a complex news issue. Subjects found the CFT-formatted site to be the most enjoyable of the three sites tested. Higher prior knowledge of the issue increased the effect of the CFT format on extremity of opinion and selectivity of reading.

Emerging Medium in an Interactive Process

Part II examines Internet newspapers in an interactive process of development. The Internet newspapers interact with their print counterpart as they grow. They affect other aspects in and outside media industry. The emerging medium was also under the influence of institutional and social forces.

Cao and Li (chap. 7) look at the trend of newspaper circulation and its relationship with the growth of the Internet newspapers. The study found the readership of the Internet newspaper had been growing considerably since 1995. The growth of the Internet newspaper yielded a slightly negative impact on print newspapers' circulation. But about half of the newspaper publishers and online editors did not regard the Internet newspaper as a major factor that reduced readership of print newspapers. The findings of the study suggest that the theory of relative constancy needs further testing in view of the increasing readership of the Internet newspapers.

Interactivity is a key feature of the Internet newspapers. Zeng and Li (chap. 8) explore this topic and the factors influencing interactivity. The findings indicated newspaper size, strength of technical staff, and newspaper's region of coverage had significant effect on interactivity of Internet newspapers. Overall, the online newspapers did better in content interactivity than interpersonal interactivity.

The rising of cross-media partnership also made its way to the Internet newspapers. DuPlessis and Li (chap. 9) examine the new trend of the newspaper sites on the Internet, cross-media partnership, and technology convergence. Through a content analysis of the top 100 newspapers in the United States, the study found cross-media partnership is related to technology convergence of Internet newspapers: Newspapers with cross-media partnership had a higher level of technology convergence.

Chyi and Lasorsa's study (chapter 10) offers discerning observations on the relationship between the Internet and print newspapers. The study was conducted in Austin, Texas, to investigate the public's response to local, regional, and national newspapers' print and online editions. Print readership was strongest among readers of that same newspaper's online edition. The substantial overlap of online and print readerships for the local daily suggests the potential of a complementary product relation. The print format was preferred—even among Internet users—when compared with the online edition, other things being equal.

Chyi expands her observation on relationship between the Internet and print newspapers (chap. 11) by looking at the market in Hong Kong, where more than a dozen newspapers and their online editions compete for readership. Results showed the print editions enjoyed significantly higher penetrations than their online counterparts. The study also identified the overlap of the same newspaper's online and print readerships. Readers of a newspaper's online edition were more likely to read the same newspaper's print edition and vice versa. The results from Hong Kong demonstrated striking similarities with what the U.S.-based study has found—suggesting the existence of a universal pattern characterizing the market relation between online and print newspapers.

Internet Newspapers and the Public

Part III addresses how online news is used by audiences in fulfilling their needs and the impact of Internet newspapers on the public life and social concerns. It looks at the relationship between content and tools concerning public life integrated into the publication of the Internet newspapers, and how the related content and tools interact with and affect public life and democracy advancement.

Uses and gratifications in the environment of the Internet is an area calling for extensive research to advance media theory. Lin and Salwen (chap. 12) take the challenge and examine whether the use of offline newspaper and online news sources involve the same or different perceived utilities for acquiring the news. Online news sources are perceived as providing information-skimming utility more efficiently than offline newspapers. The findings add to the understanding of online news in fulfilling the needs of audiences compared to offline newspapers. What is more important, the findings expand the scope of the explaining power of theoretical propositions of Uses and Gratifications in media use on the Internet.

Bucy and Affe (chap. 13) investigate the extent to which major metropolitan newspaper sites are facilitating civic participation in cyberspace as online media organizations transition into a "third generation" of Internet news. The analysis attempts to deepen our understanding of civic involvement at a moment of digital convergence, when media organizations are providing a burgeoning context for citizenship and civic involvement on the World Wide Web.

Public forum of the Internet newspapers is considered a place to encourage user involvement in public affairs. Ye and Li (chap. 14) examine public forums of the Internet newspapers and user involvement. The results show that there was a relatively low user involvement in the public forums regardless of newspaper size. Although the topics on public affairs dominated public forums of the Internet newspapers, they attracted only a limited number of users. The findings suggest that the forums of the Internet newspapers have yet to be developed as an effective tool to advance public discourse and democracy deliberation.

Media's agenda-setting function has been studied for more than two decades. Few studies using the theoretical framework have probed into the Internet newspapers. Li (chap. 15) explores the potential agenda-setting function of the Internet newspapers through a content analysis of three print newspapers and an experiment involving readers of the print and the Internet newspapers. Findings show news of priority issues identified from the two versions were considerably different. The findings also suggest that readers of the Internet newspapers may notice and read somewhat different stories from what appear in print newspapers. However, it is unlikely that readers will read less news of social significance if they access news information from the Internet newspapers.

Mensing and Greer (chap. 16) looked at the difference in news content of the print and Internet newspapers from a different perspective. They compared the lead stories of the two versions in the three largest national general-news newspapers in the United States. Results show that the lead story in the print version matched the lead story in the online version less than half the time. The findings are consistent with Li's study and have important implications for media's agenda-setting function.

CONCLUSION

The history of Internet newspapers is brief. Research on Internet newspapers is insufficient. Researchers have addressed very limited scopes and issues concerning the new medium. Even less research was conducted from a theoretical perspective and with an empirical approach. The theoretical perspective in conducting research requires proper selection and application of theory in connection with the issues under study, the knowledge of theory building and testing, and the capacity of logic thinking and derivation. The empirical research asks for rigorous design and implementation of a research project and careful interpretation of the results. All these requirements made high quality studies of Internet newspapers difficult to accomplish.

The collection of studies in this volume is an attempt to raise issues concerning growth of the Internet newspapers and probe for the possible answers through academic inquiries. The contributors to this book made all efforts to offer original research reflecting the most up-to-date research on the subject. The studies bring interesting and thought-provoking findings that may spark new thoughts and perspectives about the new medium. They also made contributions to theory building and testing through researchers' conscientious efforts in integrating related theory into the inquiries. The chapters discuss new models of communication brought about by Internet newspapers, different aspects of uses and gratitifications associated with Internet newspapers, theories of organizational and institutional influence on media content of Internet newspapers, and agenda-setting function of Internet newspapers. These are good examples of how a theoretical approach may enhance and raise the quality of research on Internet newspapers. They also show that the Internet newspaper is an area that has great potential for theoretical inquiry. The problems investigated and issues probed may well stimulate researchers to further explore unsolved puzzles concerning the emerging medium. They may ignite thoughts and ideas on intriguing and compelling issues associated with Internet newspapers, and generate more research projects about Internet newspapers to test, challenge, amend, and rebuild media theory.

When looking at the studies in this book critically, we may also find limitations in some chapters, both conceptually and methodologically. The scope of some studies was relatively narrow. Whereas several of the studies tried to examine Internet newspapers from theoretical perspectives, the theory to which the studies related and the extent to which the theory applied were still within a tight range. On the method side, problems such as small sample size, subject selection, and response rate resulted in limitations of external validity and leave much room for improvement in future studies. Further research on Internet newspapers could be refined with expanded theoretical scope, more rigorous conceptualization and craftily designed projects, and rigidly implemented methods. We expect more high-quality research on the Internet newspapers to generate a stronger body of knowledge about the new medium, the social forces that influence the medium, and the aspects affected by the medium, and to elevate the significance of studies with their theoretical and professional implications.

REFERENCES

Althaus, S. L., & Tewksbury, D. (2002). Agenda setting and the "new" news: Patterns of issue importance among readers of the paper and online versions of The New York Times. *Communication Research, 29*(2), 180–207.

Bogart, L. (1994, Winter). Highway to the stars or road to nowhere? *Media Studies Journal, 8,* 1–15.

Calamai, P. (1995). Another link with readers. *Nieman Reports, 49*(1), 39.

Chyi, H. I., & Lasorsa, D. (1999). Access, use and preferences for online newspapers. *Newspaper Research Journal, 20*(4), 14–27.

Dimitrova, D. V., Connolly-Ahern, C., Williams, A. P., Kaid, L. L., & Reid, A. (2003). Hyperlinking as gatekeeping: Online newspaper coverage of the execution of an American terrorist. *Journalism Studies, 4*(3), 401–414.

Ettema, J. S. (1989). Interactive electronic text in the United States: Can videotex ever go home again? In J. L. Salvaggio & J. Bryant (Eds.), *Media use in the information age: Emerging patterns of adoption and consumer use* (pp. 105–123). Hillsdale, NJ: Lawrence Erlbaum Associates.

Eveland, W. P., Jr., Marton, K., & Mihye Seo, K. (2004). Moving beyond "Just the facts": The influence of online news on the content and structure of public affairs knowledge. *Communication Research, 31*(1), 82–108.

Giles, B. (2000). Journalism in the era of the web. *Nieman Report, 54*(4), 3.

Ingle, B. (1995). Newspaper vs. on-line versions: A discussion of the old and new media. *Nieman Reports, 49*(2), 17.

Kirsner, S. (1999, April). Do newspapers have a future on the Net? *Editor & Publisher,* 6–13.

Meyer, E. K. (1997). *An unexpectedly wider Web for the world's newspapers,* American Journalism Review *News Link.* Retrieved December 4, 1997, from http://www.newslink.org/emcol10.html

NAA. (2002). *Online newspapers are the top source for local news on the Web.* Newspaper Association of America. Retrieved May 31, 2004, from http://www.naa.org/utilartpage.cfm?TID=NR&AID=4205

NewsLink. (2004). *Newspapers on the Internet.* Newslink. Retrieved May 31, 2004, from http://newslink.org/news.html

Nicholson, J. (1999, October 30). NAA survey finds many online users read a daily newspaper. *Editor & Publisher, 132,* 34.

Peng, F. Y., Irene, N., & Hao, X. (1999). Trends in online newspapers: A look at the U.S. Web. *Newspaper Research Journal, 20*(2), 52–63.

Poynter. (2004). *New media timeline.* Poynteronline. Retrieved May 31, 2004, from http://www.poynterextra.org/extra/Timeline/nt96.htm

Riley, P., & Keough, C. M. (1998). Community or colony: The case of online newspapers and the Web. *Journal of Computer-Mediated Communication, 4*(1). Retrieved February, 2005, from http://www.ascusc.org/jcmc/vol4/issue1/keough.html

Robertson, L. (1997, November 8). The future of online newspapers. *Editor & Publisher, 130,* 35.

Singer, J. B. (2001). The Metro Wide Web: Changes in newspaper's gatekeeping role online. *Journalism & Mass Communication Quarterly, 78*(1), 65–75.

Tewksbury, D. (2003). What do Americans really want to know? Tracking the behavior of news readers on the Internet. *Journal of Communication, 53*(4), 694–710.

I

INFORMATION DELIVERY
AND ACCESS
OF INTERNET NEWSPAPERS

The Evolution of Online Newspapers: A Longitudinal Content Analysis, 1997–2003

Jennifer D. Greer
Donica Mensing
University of Nevada–Reno

Electronic newspapers have been available in some form since the early 1970s, with the first Web-based newspapers launched in the mid-1990s (Gunter, 2003). In the United States, the Casper, Wyoming, *Star-Tribune* launched an ISP and Web-based newspaper (called the *Electronic Signpost)* in April 1994, just before the first version of Netscape Navigator 1.0 was released. *The Electronic Telegraph,* the online edition of the British *The Daily Telegraph,* produced its first Web edition in late 1994 (Gunter, 2003). Six months later, in May 1995, *Quill* reported that 150 papers worldwide had Web editions (Cochran, 1995), with newspapers in Barcelona; Singapore; Sydney; Chicago; Raleigh, North Carolina; and San Jose, California, all providing Web-based news. *The New York Times* started its Web edition in early 1996, as did *The Times* of London (Gunther, 2003) and *Le Monde,* France's largest daily newspaper (Carlson, 2003). In April 1996, the National Newspaper Association reported that 175 North American dailies were online; 775 publications were online worldwide (Carlson, 2003). One year later, nearly 1,600 newspapers were being published online, including 820 in the United States (Levins, 1997). A review of three online newspaper directories (American Journalism Review, NewsLink, and NewsDirectory.com) placed the population of daily online U.S. newspapers at 1,279 by mid-2003.

Although the newspaper industry has long experimented with a variety of electronic technologies—including proprietary services, videotext, and bulletin boards—publishing on the World Wide Web has proven to be the most successful and enduring form of online newspaper publishing. In the first decade that newspapers have been publishing on the Web, journalists, Web designers, and computer programmers have experimented with a variety of formats and types of content. Whereas early newspapers were criticized as adding up to "little more than static boards displaying weather, tourist and civic information, or telephone numbers of editors at the newspaper" (Noack, 1997, p. 323), the most recent online newspapers are producing sophisticated breaking-news reports, augmented with audio, video, and various interactive elements.

As online newspapers have added more timely, in-depth, and original reporting to their sites, use of the sites has increased significantly. Less than 5% of the U.S. population went online for news in 1995; by 2002 that number had increased to 35% (Pew, 2002). Coverage of the 2003 Iraq war, for example, provided plenty of opportunity for online news to compete with broadcast news for the attention of viewers. More than half of all online users reported using the Web to get news about the war in the first days of the conflict (Rainie, Fox, & Fallows, 2003). Online newspaper analyst Steve Outing (2003) described the online news coverage of the Iraq war as containing "Web-centric, well-planned, compelling multimedia content (with) breaking-news headlines and video delivered at nearly the speed of television (at least for broadband users)" (p. 41).

As online newspapers have evolved, researchers have studied a variety of emerging features, including content (Kamerer & Bressers, 1998), use of technology (Dibean & Garrison, 2001), interactivity (Massey & Levy, 1999; Schultz, 1999), potential revenue sources (Harper, 1996; Thompson & Wassmuth, 2001), and news efficiency (Li, 2002). Most of this research has relied on data collected at a single point in time. A few online newspaper content analyses have focused on a single issue over a few years (Hyde, 2001; Singer, 2002).

This study moves beyond the cross-sectional analyses offered by previous research to examine, longitudinally, how online newspapers have evolved since their inception. Building on an introductory content analysis of 83 online newspapers published by U.S. dailies (Gubman & Greer, 1997), this study presents 7 years of content analyses of those same newspapers, from 1997 to 2003. This longitudinal approach allows for a more comprehensive examination of the changes occurring in online newspapers. It also establishes a baseline of changes in content, technology, and services during the critical early years of Web-based newspapers. Specifically, this study examines trends in news presentation and content, multimedia use, interactivity, and potential revenue sources. Additionally, the study examines how circulation size of newspapers relates to the types of features present in their online versions.

FEATURES AND CONTENT OF ONLINE NEWSPAPERS

Early online newspapers were harshly criticized for simply reproducing the print product online (Katz, 1997; Lasica, 1996; Pogash, 1996; Reason, 1995). One early observer warned publishers: "Simply sticking your content—or shovelware—on a Web site just doesn't cut it any more. With the tsunami of newspapers flooding the Internet, the need to differentiate yourself is crucial" (Regan, 1995, p. 78). Peggie Stark Adam, a Poynter associate in visual journalism, told publishers not to be overwhelmed by technology and simply dump their print versions onto Web sites. Instead, she urged them to think creatively through the development, creation, and delivery of information (Reason, 1995).

The cross-sectional studies mentioned in the introduction provide context for any longitudinal online newspapers analysis. These cross-sectional studies are summarized later, with findings divided into the four primary areas of interest in this study: news, multimedia, interactivity, and potential revenue sources. Most of the past studies focused on one or two of these areas, investigating a few variables in each section.

News Content and Presentation

Online newspapers were created at least in part with the primary purpose of providing frequently updated news and information. However, this was not always the case in the early development of Web papers, particularly in smaller markets. Some early papers used their sites simply to provide contact information for the paper or to promote subscriptions. More than one quarter of online newspaper sites analyzed in 1997 had not updated the site in more than 24 hours (Gubman & Greer, 1997).

Since those early days, however, news has become the dominant feature of online newspapers. The news content of online newspapers has for the most part mirrored the content found in print newspapers, with local news dominating. Two content analyses, of 74 and 166 online dailies, nondailies, and specialty papers, found that 92% of all the sites featured local news by the end of 1997. The percentage of sites with national news present increased from 45% to 53% during the 6-month period between the data collections (Kamerer & Bressers, 1998).

Researchers also have studied presentation of news content, as news sites have experimented with alternative front-page designs, updates, and story formats. A survey sent to 247 online daily U.S. newspapers operating in 1997 found that smaller, local newspapers tended to provide a directory-like listing of stories on their front pages, whereas the majority of national/metropolitan papers followed a more traditional newspaper design. News in larger papers' sites was presented through news headlines, text, and graphics on the front page (Peng, Tham, & Xiaoming, 1999). More than two thirds of the papers surveyed reported providing electronic access to archives. Half said they updated their Web editions only once a day; the other half said they did so more frequently (Peng et al., 1999). In another 1997 survey, 57% of the 135 online newspaper editors surveyed said they updated their sites every 24 hours, whereas 41% said they updated more frequently and 2% less frequently (Tankard, 1998).

Few studies have examined the format and presentation of news stories online. Some have recommended that news sites break up lengthy news stories into short "nuggets" and use graphics to convey complex information (Lowrey, 1999). A content analysis of 230 genetic cloning stories on three broadcast-related news sites (CNN, ABC, and MSNBC) and three national newspapers (*The New York Times, The Washington Post,* and *USA Today*) from 1996 to 1998 found that online news stories were 20% to 70% shorter than print news stories (Hyde, 2001). More than half of the online articles were provided by outside services such as news wires, whereas staff reporters wrote about 90% of the print stories. Online stories also cited fewer sources and used less variety in sources (Hyde, 2001).

Efficiency of news retrieval is an important attribute in online newspapers as readers seek to save time and effort. Minimizing the number of links readers must follow before finding useful content is one measure of efficiency. A 1999 study of the efficiency of five online newspapers found wide variation in site design in terms of the number of links and layers users had to navigate before reaching useable content (Li, 2002).

Multimedia

Another feature of online newspapers that distinguishes them from print papers is the ability to enhance static images and text with audio, video, and animation. However, newspapers have been slow to integrate these technologies into their online news mix. One 1998 survey found that fewer than 10% of responding editors reported using animated graphics, audio clips, or video clips on their sites (Tankard, 1998). In the same year, only two of 44 English-language online newspapers in Asia provided multimedia content (Massey & Levy, 1999). However, at least one later study documented an increase in multimedia use at online newspapers. Dibean and Garrison (2001) reported an increase in the use of audio and video between November 1998 and July 1999. Still, less than one third of the newspaper sites they studied employed these technologies.

Most of these studies examined the use of multimedia features in news stories. However, some anecdotal accounts have suggested that some advertisers on online sites embraced these multimedia elements, even when news editors didn't. As broadband becomes more accessible, use of these sophisticated technologies, as well as of Flash and other graphic-rich programs, is expected to increase in advertising as well as news presentation online.

Interactivity

The ability to engage readers in two-way communication has been one of the distinguishing features of online publishing. Yet early studies of interactivity in online news found few sites taking advantage of the potential that interactivity promises (Schultz, 1999). Kamerer and Bressers' (1998) two content analyses in 1997 found that online newspapers were increasing their use of e-mail to enhance the ability of readers to interact with writers and editors. During the first collection period, the researchers found that 73% of newspapers provided an e-mail address for contacting the paper and 47% provided e-mail for an individual. Six months later, 94% of the papers provided a newspaper e-mail address and 57% had individual e-mail addresses for staff members (Kamerer & Bressers, 1998). All of the online newspapers in a 1997 census study (with one exception) had a general e-mail address, and one third provided interactivity by sponsoring forums and live-chat environments (Peng et al., 1999). Tankard (1998) found similar results in his survey of 135 online newspapers in 1997, with 74% of responding editors reporting that their sites provide staff e-mail links.

A study of six online newspapers in November 1998 and July 1999 found that a majority of newspapers used forums, related information, electronic mail, site searches, and consumer services to encourage interactivity with readers. However, few papers offered chat rooms, polls, or signups for customized news delivery (Dibean & Garrison, 2001). A 1998 study of 44 English-language online newspapers in Asia showed that almost all of the newspapers offered e-mail links for feedback to the newsroom, whereas just over one third allowed readers to contribute site content. One fifth of the newspapers provided real-time chats and forums (Massey & Levy, 1999).

Singer's (2002) study of five online Iowa newspapers during the presidential primaries indicates that sites are capable of employing significant interactive features when responding to specific news events. All five newspapers studied by Singer provided links from their stories to national news, political party, or candidate sites. Interactive features present on at least one site included polls and poll results, real-time chats with major candidates, streaming video, discussion of the debates, online quizzes, and an interactive town hall feature. All newspapers offered e-mail links to the newspaper and to individual reporters.

Revenue Sources

A critical question at the inception of Web-based publishing and one still facing online newspapers today is the development of sustainable revenue streams to support online ventures. When online newspapers were started, publishers expected them to become profitable—or simply self-supporting—in a few years. But even today, few online newspapers report profits. Early revenue models focused on advertising, both classifieds and display. Some papers experimented with subscription fees, but those experiments were generally short-lived. Harper's early survey of 40 online newspapers found 13 charging for subscriptions, seven with no ads at all, and three providing free advertising. Another seven provided direct Internet access for readers (Harper, 1996). Kamerer and Bressers (1998) noted in their 1997 content analysis that 76% of sites carried classified ads, 60% carried display ads, and 6% were trying other forms of revenue-generating activities (such as site hosting, sale of books, serving as an Internet service provider or ISP, and providing Web page design services).

The 1997 survey of 247 U.S. online dailies found that 75% of the papers carried advertisements. Of the national/metropolitan newspapers examined, 87% featured ads, compared with 73% of the local dailies (Peng et al., 1999). Just over 5% of the papers reported charging subscription fees for the online edition, and about 10% charged for access to archives. A 1998 study of 75 online newspapers found that 91% published classified ads online, but many sites did not take advantage of existing technologies to deliver effective, interactive classified ads (Thompson & Wassmuth, 2001).

Circulation Comparisons

Print newspapers with smaller circulations generally have fewer features than their larger counterparts; the same trends are observed online. Although the afore-mentioned findings are presented, for the most part, for all online newspapers, many of these studies reported clear differences based on size of the newspaper. In summary, online sites for smaller circulation newspapers had less content, less frequent updates, fewer multimedia elements, and fewer interactive features than Web sites associated with larger newspapers. Tankard (1998), for example, found that sites with large staffs were more likely than those with small staffs to update content frequently, to add hypertext links to stories, and to provide video or audio clips. Another study found that smaller newspapers were less likely to provide interactivity through discussion forums and chat rooms (Schultz, 1999).

RESEARCH QUESTIONS

The review of the literature indicates that newspapers published on the World Wide Web have undergone changes since their inception in the mid-1990s. This study systematically tracks a panel of online newspapers over 7 years to answer the following questions:

- RQ1: How did *news content and presentation* at online newspapers change between 1997 and 2003?
- RQ2: How did the use of *multimedia elements,* especially in news-related sections, change during the study period?
- RQ3: How did *interactivity* provided by online newspapers change over time?
- RQ4: How did the potential sources of *revenue* apparent on sites change over time?
- RQ5: Is *circulation size* of the print counterpart related to sophistication of news, multimedia, interactivity, and revenue sources present on the sites?

METHOD

To answer the research questions outlined, a longitudinal content analysis of U.S. newspaper sites was conducted between February 1997 and February 2003, with data collection taking place each February. This approach allows for trend analysis over time, unlike the cross-sectional approach used by most online content analysis.

Population and Sample

The population of interest is online newspapers connected with daily print U.S. newspapers. When the study began, in February 1997, a list of all online newspapers then publishing in the United States was obtained from the *Editor & Publisher* site's online newspaper section (then www.mediainfo.com). At that time, the site listed about 880 online newspapers, alternative publications, publishing groups, news magazines, and specialty publications. About 60% of the total publications listed on the site at the time were classified as daily newspapers.

Researchers selected a purposive representative sample of newspapers in 1997 by first selecting one online newspaper under each state listing. Next, sites were selected under the "national" category. Additional newspaper sites were added to the sample to achieve a balance among online sites connected with large newspapers (defined in this study as those with circulation greater than 300,000), midsized newspapers (100,000 to 300,000), and smaller newspapers (circulation less than 100,000). Weekday circulation figures were taken from the 1996 edition of the *Editor & Publisher Yearbook*. Finally, additional papers were selected to achieve a balance between early adopters (sites started in 1994 or 1995) and newer sites (those started in 1996 or 1997). The resulting sample consisted of 83 online news publications connected with U.S. dailies, about 9.4% of the 880 U.S. sites listed by *Editor & Publisher* in 1997, but about 20% of sites meeting the criteria defined by the researchers. The panel of 83 newspapers was followed over seven data collection periods through 2003, when 81 sites were analyzed. Between 1997 and 2003, one site went offline and another merged with a newspaper group site. By 2003, the 81 sites represented 6.3% of the population of online daily U.S. newspapers, which was determined by the researchers to be a total of 1,279.

Procedure

The unit of analysis for this project was the entire online publication. This included looking at news sections, special features, advertising, entertainment, in short, anything hosted on the site. Researchers followed links, but stopped once the link took the visitor outside of the newspaper's site. Although analyzing entire sites was not difficult in the early years of this project, this analysis became more difficult over time as the content on sites grew larger and more complex. How-ever, for most coding categories described in the following, coders simply had to acknowledge the presence or absence of a feature. Once presence was found, the coder moved on to the next category.

First, researchers collected demographic information about the online site and its corresponding printed newspaper, including location, circulation size, and date the site was launched. Next, researchers developed coding categories designed to examine each of the four areas previously discussed.

News Content and Presentation

For news content, coders noted the presence or absence of local news, national news, links to an automated news wire such as *The Associated Press,* and news archives. These were simply coded as 1 for present or 0 for not present. For archives, coders noted how far back archival news was available.

For news presentation, coders examined the following: (a) whether news was updated daily or less frequently; (b) whether news content was first presented on the first level of the site (the homepage), the second level, or the third or lower lev-els; (c) whether the first exposure to the site was dominated by news, site informa-tion, or an even mix of the two; and (d) whether news, when first presented, was in the form of headlines only, headlines and capsules, or headlines and full stories.

To create a score examining sophistication of news content and presentation, sites were given one point for each of the following nine variables, if present: local news, national news, a link to an automated news wire, archival content, long-term archives, daily updates, news on the homepage, mixed information on homepage, and headline and lead on homepage. News content sophistication scores, in theory, could range from 0 to 9.

Multimedia

To examine if online versions of newspapers were going beyond the standard text and static graphics found in their print editions, coders looked for any use of audio, video, or animation on the site, whether in news, entertainment, or advertis-ing content. Coders noted whether any of these multimedia elements were being used in news stories and not just in advertising or entertainment-based content. Sites were given a multimedia sophistication score computed by scoring one point for the presence of audio, video, animation, and the use of multimedia in news stories. This score, theoretically, could range from 0 to 4.

Interactivity

For interactivity, coders noted whether the sites allowed any user feedback. This could be as simple as providing a general e-mail link to the paper for comment.

Next, coders examined whether readers could contact news staff directly, either through an e-mail link to a reporter placed in a story or through a news staff e-mail directory. Coders also examined whether electronic communications sent to the site were posted in a variety of formats (e.g., forums, letters to the editor, or reader comments attached to the story page). Finally, coders noted the presence of customizable news options including the individualization of a homepage or a personal news e-mail highlighting selected topics of interest. One point was given for each of these four items, creating an interactivity score that could range from 0 to 4.

Revenue Sources

Because advertising is the business model of choice for print newspapers, five categories of advertising were investigated: (a) any advertising present, (b) real estate ads present, (c) real estate ads enhanced with images, (d) classified ads present, and (e) classified ads enhanced with searching capability. Beyond advertising, other indicators of potential revenue-producing sources examined were: (a) subscription—defined as a charge to access any sort of news items (beyond archives), (b) registration—defined as visitors having to sign in to use any part of the site, (c) Internet access—meaning the site could be used by readers as an ISP, (d) charges for archives—defined as the site charging for searching or accessing any archival material, and (e) providing in-house online advertising services—determined by a site hosting an advertiser's page (the link on the display ad did not take visitors out of the site).

With the five types of advertising features and the five types of other revenue sources combined, online sites could have a business model sophistication score ranging from 0 to 10.

Intercoder Reliability

Each year, two coders attended a training session and used a nine-page protocol to collect data. In total, eight coders worked on data collection over the 7 years. To test intercoder reliability, two coders both checked about 10% of the sample each year. Using the formula provided by North, Holsti, Zaninovvch, and Zinnes (1963), reliability within years ranged from .74 to .98 with an average intercoder reliability score of .89. Computing intercoder reliability between data collection periods was more problematic because entire sites could not be archived for analysis the following year. Therefore, obvious coding differences emerged in some years, despite the training and standard protocol. Where possible, these variables were eliminated from the study. However, in the following analyses, what appear to be year-to-year coding errors are apparent on a few variables. These were left in because the focus of the chapter is a long-term trend analysis, not a year-to-year comparison.

FINDINGS

The 83 sites were connected with print newspapers ranging in circulation size from 1,435 to 1.89 million. Nearly 40% (33) were classified as small newspapers; 33.7% (28) were midsized papers; 25.3% (21) were large papers.[1] Papers were evenly distributed throughout the country: 22 (26.5%) were in the West; 18 (21.7%) were in the Midwest; 17 (20.4%) were in the South or Southeast; and 22 (26.5%) were in the Northeast. Another four papers (4.8%) were located in Alaska, Hawaii, or the U.S. Virgin Islands. Six papers (7.2%) went online in 1994; 29 (34.9%) in 1995; 33 (39.8%) in 1996; and one (1.2%) in 1997.[2] Over the seven collection periods, 566 codesheets were completed on the sites, ranging from 83 in 1997 to 78 in 2001. In all other years, 80, 81, or 82 of the sites were analyzed.[3]

Research Question 1: News Content and Presentation

The first research question examined news content and presentation style at online newspapers from 1997 to 2003. As Table 1.1 shows, each of the items investigated in this category became significantly more common over the study period. For the news variables, and all other variables analyzed in this study, crosstabulations with chi-square analyses were run examining the presence (1) or absence (0) of the variable over the 7 years. In virtually every case, the differences were significant at $p < .05$. Therefore, these statistics are not reported by variable in this report.

Local news was a staple on the sites from the beginning when 89.2% of papers provided this content; by 2003, 95% featured local news. National news content

TABLE 1.1
Percent of Sites Analyzed With News Content
and Presentation Feature Present

	1997	1998	1999	2000	2001	2002	2003
Local news	89.2%	93.9%	97.5%	93.8%	93.6%	95.1%	95.0%
News on homepage	53.0%	80.5%	88.9%	92.6%	94.9%	88.9%	93.8%
Archives	69.9%	73.2%	86.4%	91.4%	92.3%	92.6%	93.8%
Mixed information on homepage	31.3%	52.4%	81.5%	88.9%	91.0%	91.3%	92.5%
Daily updates	71.1%	68.3%	74.1%	88.9%	92.3%	91.4%	90.0%
Headline, lead on homepage[a]	66.3%	77.2%	76.5%	80.0%	81.6%	86.3%	83.5%
National news	54.2%	72.0%	74.1%	75.3%	83.3%	82.7%	83.8%
Long-term archives	38.6%	48.8%	66.7%	67.9%	73.1%	70.4%	67.5%
Link to wire	39.8%	53.7%	51.9%	43.2%	48.7%	37.0%	55.0%
Average news score	4.80	5.65	6.16	6.32	6.58	6.43	6.61
Total	83	82	81	81	78	81	80

[a]Percentage is based only on sites with news content present.

showed a bigger jump, from being present on 54.2% of the sites in 1997 to 83.8% in 2003. Newswire provision showed fluctuation over the years. Archives were present on 69.9% of the sites in 1997; by 2003, 93.8% of the sites had them. The number of papers with long-term archives jumped from 38.6% to 67.5%. The most dramatic increase came in the number of sites providing news on the first layer of the site: in 1997, only 53.0% did so, in 2003, 93.8% did. Finally, only 71.1% of sites were updating daily or more frequently in 1997; 90% were in 2003. The number of sites providing news on the homepage increased from about half to all but five by the end of the study. The information on the homepage changed as well. In 1997, 31.3% had an even mix of news and site information; by 2003, 92.5% of the sites analyzed had this even mix on the homepage. As for the presentation of news stories on the first screen, in 1997, 66.3% featured a headline and a lead; 7 years later, the vast majority of sites (83.5%) featured a headline and lead. Table 1.1 presents news content and presentation variables in descending order from most frequent to least frequent from 1997 to 2003.

These nine news content and presentation variables, all coded as 1 for present and 0 for not present, were summed in Table 1.1 to create a news sophistication score. Using a one-way Analysis of Variance (ANOVA), it was determined that the average news score increased significantly ($F = 10.42$, $df = 6, 559$, $p < .001$) over the study period from 4.80 to 6.61 (on a score from 0 to 9).

Research Question 2: Multimedia

The second research question examined multimedia elements being used on the sites, whether present in news, advertising, or other content. As Table 1.2 shows, all multimedia features examined in the study increased (with some fluctuation) over the study period. Animation was most common in 1997 and it remained so throughout the study period, even with the fluctuation noted between 1997 and 2000. By 2003, 93.8% featured animation. Audio content was rare in 1997, when only 15.7% of the sites featured it; by 2003, 43.8% of sites had audio present. Video showed an even more dramatic increase from 7.2% in 1997 to 43.8% in 2003. Only 14.5% of the sites were using any of the multimedia features in relation

TABLE 2.2
Percentage of Sites Analyzed With Multimedia Elements Present

	1997	1998	1999	2000	2001	2002	2003
Animation	53.0%	26.8%	81.5%	64.2%	88.5%	95.1%	93.8%
Audio	15.7%	25.6%	13.6%	14.8%	35.9%	25.9%	43.8%
Video	7.2%	23.2%	13.6%	13.6%	24.4%	23.5%	43.8%
Multimedia in news	14.5%	6.1%	9.9%	14.8%	26.9%	24.7%	42.5%
Average multimedia score	0.90	0.82	1.19	1.07	1.76	1.65	2.26
Total sites analyzed	83	82	81	81	78	81	80

to news stories in 1997. That number had increased to 42.5% by 2003, with the biggest jumps between 2000 and 2001 and again between 2002 and 2003.

The average multimedia sophistication score showed a dramatic increase over the study period, from 0.90 to 2.26 on a 0 to 4 scale ($F = 13.67$, $df = 6$, 559, $p < .001$).

Research Question 3: Interactivity

The third research question investigated interactive features present on sites. Unlike the previous two questions, interactivity variables examined did not show as dramatic increases over time. As Table 1.3 shows, allowing readers to connect to the site through the most basic of all interactivity, general e-mail, was present on 95.2% percent of the sites in 1997 and 100% in 2003. Posting reader responses in some form (forums, attached to the story, e-mail letters to the editor) only increased slightly, from 57.8% to 75.0%.[4]

Customizable news started off being rare (offered by 9.6% of sites in 1997), peaked at 26.8% in 1998, and dropped off again until 2002 and 2003, when 23.8% of sites analyzed offered this feature. The peak in 1998 may be due, in part, to coding error that year. However, even without that year, it is clear that customizable news was not common until 2002. The one variable in this group that showed a significant jump over time was the provision of staff e-mail addresses. Between 1997 and 1999, less than 60% of sites provided the addresses. Between 2000 and 2002, staff e-mails were available on 70% to 80% of sites. In 2003, that percentage jumped to 87.5% of sites.

Combining the scores on these four interactive elements to create an interactivity sophistication score showed that the sites used significantly more of these elements over time. Interactivity scores increased from 2.18 to 2.86 (on a scale of 0 to 4) over the study period ($F = 5.07$, $df = 6$, 559, $p < .001$).

Research Question 4: Revenue Sources

The fourth research question examined features that could provide revenue for the site. Five advertising features were investigated. As Table 1.4 shows, general advertising, real estate ads, and classified ads were popular in 1997 (on 88.0%, 72.3%, and 72.3% of sites, respectively) and became significantly more popular over the 7 years. By 2003, all three were present on more than 95% of sites analyzed. The more dramatic growth came in "enhancement" to these ads. Search capabilities for classified advertising were present on only 51.8% of sites in 1997 but on 82.5% of sites in 2003. Real estate ads enhanced with visuals grew from being present on 22.9% of sites in 1997 to 48.8% in 2003.

Next, five other potential revenue sources were examined. Two of these sources, providing Internet access (serving as an ISP) and creating or hosting advertiser sites internally, were preferred business models in 1997. These two potential rev-

TABLE 1.3
Percentage of Sites Analyzed With Interactivity Feature Present

	1997	1998	1999	2000	2001	2002	2003
General e-mail	95.2%	91.5%	93.8%	100.0%	96.2%	95.1%	100.0%
Reporter e-mails	55.4%	51.2%	58.0%	72.8%	69.2%	76.5%	87.5%
Post reader response	57.8%	65.9%	65.4%	74.1%	78.2%	74.1%	75.0%
Customizable news	9.6%	26.8%	13.6%	8.6%	7.7%	22.2%	23.8%
Average interactivity score	2.18	2.35	2.31	2.56	2.51	2.68	2.86
Total	83	82	81	81	78	81	80

TABLE 1.4
Percentage of Sites Analyzed With Potential Revenue Sources Present

	1997	1998	1999	2000	2001	2002	2003
Any advertising	88.0%	95.1%	100%	98.8%	100%	100%	98.8%
Classified ads	72.3%	90.2%	93.8%	95.1%	97.4%	96.3%	96.3%
Real estate ads	72.3%	86.6%	91.4%	95.1%	96.2%	95.1%	95.0%
Classified searching	51.8%	78.0%	76.5%	79.0%	76.9%	72.8%	82.5%
Archive charges	47.0%	59.8%	65.4%	91.4%	88.5%	86.4%	77.5%
Real estate visuals	22.9%	14.6%	19.8%	32.1%	34.6%	46.9%	48.8%
Registration	N/A	N/A	N/A	4.9%	3.8%	11.1%	48.8%
Subscription	6.0%	2.4%	1.2%	1.2%	2.6%	7.4%	15.0%
Internal ad services	71.1%	36.6%	44.4%	23.5%	26.9%	43.2%	11.3%
Internet access	20.5%	24.4%	11.1%	7.4%	2.6%	3.7%	2.5%
Average revenue score	4.52	4.88	5.04	5.28	5.29	5.63	5.76
Total	83	82	81	81	78	81	80

enue sources declined dramatically over the next 6 years. ISP services dropped from being offered by 20.5% of sites in 1997 to 2.5% of sites in 2003. Whereas 71.1% of sites hosted and created internal ad services in 1997, only 11.3% did so in 2003. These percentages made them the two least popular revenue sources in 2003. In contrast, the other three sources showed slight or dramatic increases. Paid online subscriptions, used by 6.0% of sites in 1997, declined through the middle of the study period, with only 1.2% (one site) charging a subscription in 1999 and 2000. However, subscriptions showed an upward trend after that and were charged by 15.0% of sites in 2003. Registration for use of any part of the site, a variable added in 2000 when registration started becoming common, grew from 4.9% of sites that year to 48.8% in 2003. Finally, whereas 47.0% of sites charged for archives in 1997, 77.5% of sites did so by 2003. Table 1.4 presents potential revenue sources variables in descending order from most common to least common as of 2003.

Combining scores for the five advertising features and the five other revenue sources examined produced a revenue source sophistication score, indicating whether online producers were looking toward multiple revenue sources to increase economic viability. As Table 1.4 shows, the average revenue source sophistication score (on a scale from 0 to 10) increased from 4.52 in 1997 to 5.76 in 2003 ($F = 6.24$, $df = 6$, 559, $p < .001$).

Research Question 5: Circulation Size

The final research question investigated whether the size of the print newspaper producing the online site made a difference in news content, multimedia, interactivity, and revenue sources featured. To conduct this analysis, a total site sophistication score was created by summing the sophistication scores for news content, multimedia, interactivity, and revenue sources. Next, means of the total sophistication score were analyzed using a factorial Analysis of Variance (ANOVA) with newspaper size and collection time as the independent variables. The total sophistication score increased significantly over time for all newspapers (from 11.76 to 16.58). The large main effect for time ($F = 16.04$, $df = 6$, 558, $p < .001$) was expected. But an even larger main effect emerged for newspaper size ($F = 116.78$, $df = 2$, 558, $p < .001$) and a significant interaction between time and newspaper size also emerged ($F = 1.91$, $df = 12$, 558, $p < .05$).

As the literature suggested, newspaper size did make a significant difference. Larger- and medium-sized newspapers had significantly higher scores across the board than smaller newspapers, as suggested by earlier studies. A more interesting pattern emerges when examining the means of small, medium, and large newspapers over time (see full reporting of the means in Table 1.5).

Whereas the means for all three circulation categories of newspapers differed significantly in 1997, means for medium- and large-sized newspapers' sophistication scores became more similar over time. In some instances, the medium-sized newspapers had slightly higher scores than their larger counterparts. In contrast, although the small newspapers showed significant increases on the scores throughout the period of study, their scores in all four areas still lag significantly behind the medium and larger papers. As Table 1.5 shows, the total sophistication scores were virtually identical for large and medium newspapers from 2000 to 2003. Despite their gains, small newspapers still lagged significantly behind overall.

DISCUSSION

Two clear trends emerged over the 7 years spanned by the study. First, online newspapers are offering more of everything: news content, multimedia, interactivity, and revenue-generating features. Instead of discontinuing one type of feature when another is added, the sites, on the whole, have added to their offerings. Second, size matters for online newspapers. Although medium- and large-sized newspapers' sites are virtually identical in the total number of features offered, the

TABLE 1.5
Sophistication Scores by Circulation Size/Year

	Small	Medium	Large
1997			
News	3.79	5.18	6.00
Multimedia	0.40	1.00	1.62
Interactivity	1.70	2.25	2.91
Revenue sources	3.49	4.93	5.62
Total	9.36	13.36	16.14
1998			
News	4.09	6.29	7.29
Multimedia	0.03	1.07	1.71
Interactivity	1.72	2.57	3.10
Revenue sources	3.91	5.25	5.91
Total	9.75	15.18	18.00
1999			
News	4.84	6.89	7.24
Multimedia	1.00	1.12	1.62
Interactivity	1.94	2.50	2.67
Revenue sources	4.45	5.11	5.86
Total	12.23	15.61	17.38
2000			
News	5.36	6.89	7.10
Multimedia	0.49	1.21	1.81
Interactivity	2.26	2.71	2.86
Revenue sources	4.65	5.57	5.86
Total	12.74	16.39	17.62
2001			
News	5.63	7.30	7.15
Multimedia	1.10	2.11	2.35
Interactivity	2.17	2.78	2.80
Revenue sources	4.60	5.59	6.00
Total	13.50	17.78	18.30
2002			
News	5.94	6.89	6.48
Multimedia	1.45	2.00	1.52
Interactivity	2.35	2.89	2.95
Revenue sources	5.23	5.50	6.33
Total	14.97	17.29	17.29
2003			
News	5.90	6.96	7.14
Multimedia	1.27	2.82	2.77
Interactivity	2.57	2.89	3.23
Revenue sources	4.93	6.07	6.50
Total	14.67	18.74	19.64

offerings on small papers' sites are significantly less varied. Each of these trends is explored in the following.

More of Everything

Each of the four areas of online content analyzed for this study showed significant increases in the breadth and total number of features offered. For news, the core content for all newspapers, local reports still dominate. But papers have increasingly offered other types of content, including archives, national news, and news wires. Clearly online newspapers are becoming stand-alone news products rather than supplements or mere advertising vehicles for their print parents.

Presentation of news content also has changed dramatically. Online newspapers are more likely to update frequently, providing more timely information to readers. News is now presented on the first layer of the sites. And readers see an even mix of site information and news when they first log on. Most sites have switched to providing headlines and news capsules on the first news layer, allowing readers to scan through this page quickly to select stories they'd like to read. These changes in presentation show that Web designers are constantly experimenting with and perhaps learning about what works well online. Future studies should examine presentation in more sophisticated ways through the very basic measurements used in this study. For example, research could examine standardization in presentation across sites or presentation of news beyond the basic layout.

Multimedia use increased steadily over the study period, and these trend lines have become steeper in just the last few years, suggesting acceleration in the use of these features. Audio and video use show marked increases, but perhaps a more interesting trend is the sharp rise in using multimedia in news stories since 2000, especially since 2002. This rise may mean that true multimedia storytelling is set to become the staple on news sites in this decade, especially as more users switch to broadband connections. Future research should track not just the use of multimedia in news but how these elements are being integrated into online news sections over the next few years. For example, researchers could track the types of multimedia used and what types of stories most often are enhanced with these features.

Although interactive features are significantly more prevalent today than in 1997, the only real growth in interactivity was the addition of reporters' e-mail addresses. The data suggest that newspapers are still working to find interactive elements that function well in an online news environment. Research indicates that hosting successful interactive elements online is challenging for many types of sites. A study of 500 high-traffic Web sites found that only 15.9% of the sites featured links to real-time interactivity (audio, video, chat, or Web cameras) off the homepage (Bucy, Lang, Potter, & Grabe, 1999). Other research points to the difficulty newspapers have had in running successful discussion forums (Imfeld & Scott, 2003). Those studies, as well as the findings presented in this study, suggest an area ripe for additional research. Examining effective use of interactivity might be best accomplished through quasi-experimental studies and focus groups that test audience response to interactive elements online.

For advertising and other revenue sources, newspapers have clearly abandoned two revenue streams that looked promising initially—serving as an ISP and creating or hosting advertisers' pages. This is probably because these sources did not deliver the income that Web developers hoped they would. Instead, newspapers have enhanced their advertising in hopes that this standard business model for print journalism will finally work online. In addition, more papers are charging for archive use and, in some cases, for use of special sections or for use of the entire site. Finally, newspapers are more likely to require registration for use of at least portions of their sites. With registration, newspapers are able to track demographics of users, making their sites more valuable to advertisers. Some papers also might be selling this information or at least using it for their internal marketing efforts. The documented increases in different types of potential revenue generators corroborate what many in the industry already know—no one clear business model has emerged as most online newspapers continue to operate at a financial loss.

Of course, one of the major limitations of this study is that the researchers use only content analyses to draw conclusions about changes taking place in online newspapers. Although this method might work well for news content, multimedia, and interactivity, the method is more problematic for revenue sources. With content analyses, we can only examine features that on the surface have the potential to generate revenue. Future studies could include surveys of online editors about business models. These responses could be invaluable to support any of the conclusions that this study makes based on content.

Size Matters

Beyond the overall analysis of the 83 sites, analyses of the data based on circulation size paint an interesting picture about which sites are becoming more sophisticated over time. When newspapers went on the Web in the mid-1990s, some touted the Web's potential as an "equalizer," meaning smaller entities—or even individuals—with access to the relatively inexpensive technology could enter the world of publishing once controlled only by those with enough money to purchase the presses. But this certainly wasn't the case in 1997, when large newspapers had more sophisticated sites than medium newspapers, which in turn had more sophisticated sites than small newspapers. And, after 7 years, small newspapers still haven't capitalized on the equalizing potential of the Web.

Whereas medium and large newspapers now have equally sophisticated sites, the small newspapers lag behind in every measure analyzed in this study. They clearly have made gains over time, but small newspapers' adoption rates of different forms of news content, multimedia, interactivity, and revenue sources are not growing at a rate that suggests they will ever match their larger counterparts.

What's even more telling is how small newspapers were defined in this study—as papers with circulations of less than 100,000. Many other studies have defined small newspapers as those with circulations of less than 50,000. When these very small papers were broken out for separate analyses, the disparity between the haves and the have-nots becomes even more pronounced. Future research looking specifically at factors influencing the amount of resources devoted to online versions at large, medium, and small newspapers would help shed light on this issue. For example, one newspaper that would be considered small by the definition used in this study, *The Lawrence Journal-World,* employs 20 people on its online staff, more than some of the large papers employ. This type of anecdotal evidence suggests that wide variation exists in sophistication of sites among the papers that fell within the small newspaper category as defined by this study. Examining how resources devoted to online news relates to the content available would allow researchers to examine these issues with factors other than circulation size.

CONCLUSION

The value of a longitudinal study is that it allows for the close observation of both significant and incremental changes over time. Some have contended that after the initial rush of excitement as newspapers created online editions and began daily electronic production, changes in structure and navigation of many online newspaper sites appeared to stagnate. Designers and editors developed a sense of what worked and didn't work online, and changes in the content and look of online newspapers slowed.

This study shows that rather than stagnating, online newspapers have continued to evolve each year as they develop features responsive to the changing needs of news organizations and audiences. No doubt some online journalism professionals are eager to see even more change and experimentation, but the careful evaluation of the panel of online newspapers in this study, using consistent criteria over time, shows that sites are undergoing steady growth and development even as the first decade of Web publishing comes to an end.

The findings in this study suggest that online newspapers continue to search for a successful business plan, while adding new features and discarding those that have failed to deliver significant revenue. The sites are responding to the increased sophistication of online readers, providing more multimedia features, deeper content, and more frequent updates. The first simple, gray background pages of blinking icons and long scrolling pages available in 1994 have given way to tightly packed, content-rich news sources available 24 hours a day to significant numbers of readers around the world.

dy suggests that online newspapers are not only evolving, but that they g—at least in terms of variety of content and features available. News-developers are experimenting, adding new elements, and abandoning features that do not work. As the industry begins its second decade, this experimentation is sure to continue.

ACKNOWLEDGMENTS

An earlier version of this chapter was published in *Newspaper Research Journal,* Spring 2004, *25*(2), pp. 98–112. Reprinted with permission.

ENDNOTES

1. Circulation size was unavailable for one title.
2. Online start date could not be determined for 14 sites, 16.9% of the sample.
3. In some years, sites were undergoing reconstruction or were not accessible on several attempts; two sites ceased publication during the study period.
4. These were two chi-square analyses in the study that were not significant at $p < .05$.

REFERENCES

Bucy, E. P., Lang, A., Potter, R. F., & Grabe, M. E. (1999). Formal features of cyberspace: Relationships between Web page complexity and site traffic. *Journal of American Society For Information Science, 50*(13), 1246–1256.

Carlson, D. (2003). David Carlson's online timetable. *David Carlson's Virtual World.* Retrieved March 25, 2003, from http://iml.jou.ufl.edu/carlson/frames.htm

Cochran, W. (1995). Searching for the right mixture. *Quill, 83*(4), 36.

Dibean, W., & Garrison, B. (2001). How six online newspapers use Web technologies. *Newspaper Research Journal, 22*(2), 79–93.

Gubman, J., & Greer, J. D. (1997, July–August). *An analysis of online sites produced by U.S. newspapers: Are the critics right?* Paper presented at the annual meeting of the Association for Education in Journalism and Mass Communication, Chicago.

Gunter, B. (2003). *News and the Net.* Mahwah, NJ: Lawrence Erlbaum Associates.

Harper, C. (1996). Online newspapers: Going somewhere or going nowhere? *Newspaper Research Journal, 17*(3–4), 2–13.

Hyde, J. E. (2001). Decoding the codes: A content analysis of the news coverage of genetic cloning by three online news sites and three national daily newspapers, 1996 through 1998 (Doctoral dissertation, New York University, 2001). Dissertation Abstracts International-A 61/10, 3814.

Imfeld, C., & Scott, G. (2003). *Under construction: Measures of community building at newspaper Web sites.* Paper presented to the Newspaper Division of the Association of Education in Journalism and Mass Communication, Kansas City, MO.

Kamerer, D., & Bressers, B. (1998, August). *Online newspapers: A trend study of news content and technical features.* Paper presented at the annual meeting of the Association for Education in Journalism and Mass Communication, Baltimore, MD.

Katz, J. (1997, October). Online or not, newspapers suck. *HotWired.* Retrieved March 21, 2003 from http://www.hotwired.com/wired/2.09/departments/electrosphere/news.suck.html

Lasica, J. D. (1996, Nov. 12–18). Goodbye, Guttenberg. *American Journalism Review NewsLink.* Retrieved March 27, 1997, from http://www.newslink.org/arjad4.html

Levins, H. (1997). Time of change and challenge (Online newspapers). *Editor & Publisher, 130*(1), 58.

Li, X. (2002). Web page design affects news retrieval efficiency. *Newspaper Research Journal, 23*(1), 38–49.

Lowrey, W. (1999). From map to machine: Conceptualizing and designing news on the Internet. *Newspaper Research Journal, 20*(4), 14–27.

Massey, B. L., & Levy, M. R. (1999). Interactivity, online journalism, and English-language Web newspapers in Asia. *Journalism and Mass Communication Quarterly, 76*(1), 138–151.

Noack, D. (1997). Off-line newspapers: Too small, too busy, or too unsure, some move slowly into cyberspace. *Editor & Publisher, 130*(6), 321–331.

North, R. C., Holsti, O., Zaninovvch, M. G., & Zinnes, D. A. (1963). *Content analysis: A handbook with applications for the study of international crisis.* Evanston, IL: Northwestern University Press.

Outing, S. (2003). Hold on (line) tight. *Editor & Publisher, 129*(7), 41.

Peng, F. Y., Tham, N. I., & Xiaoming, H. (1999). Trends in online newspapers: A look at the U.S. Web. *Newspaper Research Journal, 20*(2), 52–63.

Pew Research Center for the People and the Press. (2002, June 9). *Public's news habits little changed by September 11.* Retrieved October 30, 2003, from http://people-press.org/reports/display. php3?PageID=612

Pogash, C. (1996, Dec. 10–16). Cyberspace journalism. *American Journalism Review NewsLink.* Retrieved May 21, 2003, from http://www.newslink.org/arjpog.html

Rainie, L., Fox, S., & Fallows, D. (2003, April 1). The Internet and the Iraq war: How online Americans have used the Internet to learn war news, understand events, and promote their views. *Pew Internet & American Life.* Retrieved October 30, 2003, from http://www.pewinternet.org/reports/ toc.asp?Report=87

Reason, R. (1995). A call for new thinking for the new media. *Poynter Online.* Retrieved March 27, 1997, from http://www.reporter.org/poynter/

Regan, T. (1995, Winter). News alone is not enough. *Nieman Reports, 49,* 78.

Schultz, T. (1999). Interactive options in online journalism: A content analysis of 100 U.S. newspapers. *Journal of Computer Mediated Communication, 5*(1). Retrieved March 25, 2003, from http://jcmc .huji.ac.il/vol5/issue1/schultz.html

Singer, J. B. (2002). Information trumps interaction in local papers' online caucus coverage. *Newspaper Research Journal, 23*(4), 91–96.

Tankard, J. (1998, August). *Online newspapers: Living up to their potential?* Paper presented at the annual meeting of the Association for Education in Journalism and Mass Communication, Baltimore, MD.

Thompson, D. R., & Wassmuth, B. L. (2001). Few newspapers use online classified interactive features. *Newspaper Research Journal, 22*(4), 16–27.

2

Graphic Use and Interconnectedness of Internet Newspapers: A Many-to-Many Communication Model

Xigen Li
Southern Illinois University Carbondale

This chapter is an exploration of the Internet versions of three U.S. newspapers that were among the earliest to publish on the World Wide Web. It tries to identify their approaches to Web page design and graphic use, examines how the approaches facilitate delivering news information and change the process of communication, and explores an alternative model of Internet newspapers based on several models relating to Internet communication.

The Internet newspaper is defined as a publication produced by a newspaper publishing company and delivered through the World Wide Web, a colorful platform provided by navigation software. Such news sites use Hypertext Markup Language (HTML) and other computer-assisted graphic devices to present text and graphics containing news information on a computer screen. Graphics refer to news photos and graphs used to illustrate stories or display advertisements.

Newspapers started to deliver information electronically years ago, but their presence in the field had never been popular until they started to publish their electronic version on the World Wide Web, which allows them to deliver information to a broader audience than the earlier version through commercial carriers. The role of the Internet newspaper is more noticeable as more people go to newspaper Web sites for information and the newspapers put more updated information on their Web sites. Electronic content of the 1996 presidential election is one of the earliest examples. Audiences flooded the Web sites of mainstream media for the election result (Tedesco, 1996). *The Dallas Morning News* created a significant stir by publishing a story about Timothy McVeigh on its Web page hours before the newspaper was published. Sending a story to a Web site prior to traditional publishing lent credibility to news on the Web (Rieder, 1997).

A Medium of Innovations

Lapham (1995) argued that the real beauty of Internet technology is its ability to enable newspapers to not only enhance their researching and reporting capabilities but also to deliver a better, more audience-aware product in an immediate and inexpensive way. Using the hypertext capabilities of the Web totally eliminates the proverbial "news hole" and opens up an unlimited amount of "space" for presenting the news product.

In contrast, Katz (1994) blasted the typical user interface of today's Internet newspapers, saying that reading a newspaper online is difficult, cumbersome, and time consuming. Much of what still works about a paper—convenience, visual freedom, a sense of priorities, a personal experience—is gone. Online, papers throw away what makes them special.

When looking at a structure of Web pages, McAdams (1995a) argued, one of the problems that handicaps current hypertext systems is that readers get lost. They make so many jumps away from the article they started reading, they can't find their way back.

The World Wide Web has an advantage over print newspaper because it is excellent for displaying colorful graphics. During the last decade, the most striking change of American newspaper design has been the increased use of graphics (Baird, 1993) because of technological advances (Garcia, 1987). With the more advanced computer technology today, retrieving graphics from databases and updating them as required in an Internet newspaper can be completed in minutes. The trend of increasing newspaper use of graphics can continue in the Internet environment.

Inquiries About the New Medium

Despite the fast growth of the Web newspapers, few studies have been published in this area. Morris and Ogan (1996) noted that, until recently, mass communications researchers have overlooked the Internet, staying instead with the traditional forms of broadcast and print media that fit much more conveniently into models for appropriate research topics and theories of mass communication.

Some studies of Internet news media have focused primarily on the effect of new technology on the dominance of existing media (Glascock, 1993; Wood & O'Hare, 1991). Because the Internet newspapers emerged at such a fast pace, the examination of the new practice fell far behind the reality. For example, when some studies were still talking about the newspapers available only on a commercial online service, such as America Online (Garrison, 1995; Kamerer & Bergen, 1995), hundreds of newspapers appeared on the World Wide Web. Although some contended that access to newspaper content on the Internet was a privilege only belonging to the most technically advanced readers (Mueller & Kamerer, 1995), thousands of people plunged into the Internet because surfing the net required little skills.

Others have examined Internet newspaper use. For example, Mueller and Kamerer's (1995) study of 62 subjects found that Internet newspapers were preferred for more global information and traditional newspapers were preferred for localized information. They argued that the interface of an Internet newspaper should be so transparent that no computer experience is needed to read it.

McAdams (1995b) noted that the importance of a good user metaphor could not be underestimated. A person's expectations and assumptions about how an online system works and what it can (and cannot) do come largely from this metaphor. A designer must choose metaphors that help the users understand the system, such as using the "front page" as the entry point to the system. Middleberg and Ross (1996) found in their annual survey of journalists that photos were the most often cited to make a site useful.

Information Flow and a Model of Internet Newspapers

Few studies have focused on how Web page design and the information flow of Internet newspapers might affect efficiency of information retrieval. Researchers have not sufficiently addressed changes in the communication process in the Internet environment. Although there is no model that specifically addresses the Internet newspaper, several models proposed for Internet communication are useful for building a model of Internet newspapers.

Interactivity Model. Rogers (1986) noted that the most essential capacity of electronic media is that of interactivity. *Interactivity* has been assumed to be a natural attribute of interpersonal communication, but as explicated by Rafaeli (1988), the concept is more recently applied to all new media, from two-way cable to the Internet. Rafaeli's definition of interactivity includes three distinct types, which he identifies as two-way (noninteractive) communication; reactive (or quasi-interactive) communication; and fully interactive communication.

Rheingold (1994) discussed the role of the people in Internet communication as an interactive group, and he argued that this new communication revolution was shifting power to the people. This power shift seriously threatens the dominance of traditional mass media forms, specifically television, radio stations, magazines, and newspapers, which were built from the one-to-many communication model.

However, Neuman (1991) claimed that it is not just interactivity that is significant in recent change. It is also the interconnectedness of new technologies which underlies the "logic" of electronic media growth that is significant. One-way systems become two-way or even multiple network.

New Hybrid Model. Gilder (1994) summarized the marriage of the computer and the newspaper. He observed that the computer complements the newspaper. It allows print media to deliver news products in real time and tremendously expands the amount of information available to the audience. The new medium that will update the news with full screen photos and videos significantly improves the depth and timeliness of the news. The computer creates a new environment for the audience to read the paper as they do today, and turns the control of selecting stories to the audience at their own time and place.

By using computer technology to produce and deliver a new product, newspapers have welded both the old (literacy-print) with the new (computers-digital delivery) and created a hybrid model. However, these models do not address the impact of Web page design or effect of different approaches on the communication process.

The hybrid model only provides a general idea of how the function of a newspaper is enhanced by computer technology. It does not measure the impact of relative levels of interactivity nor does it identify where the old component, the convention of newspaper publishing, and the new component, the technology, stand in the model, and how they work together and react to each other.

Media Transition Model. When discussing the new pattern of information traffic, Bordewijk and van Kaam (1986) developed a model that summarized the given models. They described four basic communication patterns and showed how they were related to each other.

1. *Allocation:* Information is distributed from the center simultaneously to many peripheral receivers, which is typical of the "old media" of mass communication.
2. *Conversation:* Individuals interact directly with each other, bypassing a center or intermediary and choosing their own partners as well as the time.
3. *Consultation:* Refers to a range of different communication situations in which individuals look for information at a central store of information.
4. *Registration:* The consultation pattern in reverse, in that a center "requests" and receives information from a participant at the periphery (usually without their awareness).

Bordewijk and van Kaam concluded the trend is from allocatory to consultative to conversational. This implies a broad shift of balance of communicative power from sender to receiver. However, to what degree does the shift of control take place in Internet newspapers? The model provides no answer. If the shift of control of communicative power is really taking place in Internet communication, as the Internet newspaper is still in its infancy, the shift could be unfolding, but a dramatic shift is yet to be seen.

By exploring the approaches to Web page design and graphic use in three Internet newspapers, this chapter examines how Internet newspapers demonstrated a change from the convention of newspaper publishing to new media age. It also looks at how Web page design and graphic use reflect the interconnectedness and a shift of control from sender to receiver, and how these approaches affect the flow of news information in the Internet environment.

This study observed 10 days of the Web pages of *The New York Times, The Washington Post,* and *USA Today* in October 1996.[1] By looking at the design of the home pages, front pages and the news articles within the front pages, and graphic use on all three levels, this study tested the following hypothesis:

H1: Although the computer screen provides a good platform for displaying graphics, the Internet newspapers will tend to give more priority to providing textual information than graphic information.

In the hybrid model, Internet newspapers combine the old convention of newspaper publishing with new technology. As the old convention remains a dominant part in the early stage of a shift of control, Internet newspapers are likely to maintain the traditional convention of newspaper publishing by providing more text-based information in their liaison with new technology.

H2: Eye-catching graphics are more likely to appear on the home pages and the front pages than on the news article pages.

H2 tests the notion of the hybrid model that Internet newspapers take advantage of new technology in a limited way. The main body of news content bears the feature of conventional newspaper in graphic use. Although technology promoted a shift from convention of newspaper publishing to the format adapted for the new media in Internet newspapers, the shift has occurred in a restrictive manner.

H3: The Internet newspapers are less likely to use large pictures and graphs to illustrate news articles.

H3 assumes that graphic use in Internet newspapers complies with the rules of the interactivity model, which takes into account user expectation, makes Internet newspapers an audience-aware product, and reflects a gradual shift of balance of communicative power in Internet communication.

H4: With the interconnected newslinks, detailed news and related information are more likely to be retrieved with few steps (clicks), and the information retrieved can go beyond the original news content.

H4 tests the assumption that Web pages of Internet newspapers are interconnected logically. With receivers involved in producing information, the original sender Internet newspapers, as suggested by the Media Transition Model, no longer have the exclusive control of news content.

METHOD

This study was conducted through a content analysis. The content examined was drawn from the Web sites of three national newspapers including their home pages, front pages, and the news articles within the front pages. In the case of *USA Today,* its front page was actually the initial page, the home page. The categories under the initial page do not include the front page. The category "Top News," which was similar to the front page, was selected instead. The content observed referred to the page components, which made up the home pages, front pages, and news article pages, rather than news content of the Internet newspapers.

Traditional layout practices assume that the front page each day should be sufficiently similar to those of previous and following days so that they form a recognizable physical personality of the newspaper (Turnbull & Baird, 1980). With an observation of 3 days' publications of three Internet newspapers 1 month before and after the coding period, the author found that the page design of the Internet newspapers tended to be relatively stable after adopting a certain design and layout pattern. During that 2-month period, the page design of the three Internet newspapers basically remained unchanged. The relative stability of page design of the Internet newspapers over a time period provides an opportunity for researchers to study the current features of the Internet newspaper page design with a relatively small sample.

Ten days (September 9 through September 18, 1996) of home pages, front pages, and news article pages of three national newspapers were collected and coded through a coding scheme. A *home page* is defined as an initial site of a newspaper on the World Wide Web, and it provides information both directly and via links to other files of the same publication or to files on other computers located on remote networks (Anonymous, 1996). A *front page* is similar to the concept of the print version; it usually appeared as a section on the home page. A *news article page* is the page carrying the full article, which is directed by the links on the home page and front page.

The unit of analysis is one day's publication. The variables examined include major page components: pictures, graphs, news articles, and news links. A *picture* is defined as a representation of somebody, something, or some event made by photographs; *graph* is defined as visual presentation of data, objects, concepts, or processes; *news article* refers to the complete content of a news item; *news link* is defined as a hyperlinked headline or a combination of words and phrases that directs readers to the content of information represented by the headline through activation.

The sizes of pictures and graphs on the Web pages were predefined in pixels. Graphics remained relatively the same size no matter how large the computer screen was. To make the size of graphics easier to perceive, the pictures and graphs were measured in inches by their size appearing on a 14-inch computer screen. The graphics were divided into three categories—large, medium, and small—based on the whole range of graphic size. The categories were decided by the following procedures: Calculate the square size of each picture and graph, add them up, and divide by the number of pictures and graphs. The number obtained equaled the midpoint (50%) of graphic size. Above 67% was large; between 34% to 66%, medium; and below 33%, small. The square sizes of each category were then standardized to the ratio relatively close to 4:3 and in conformity with the real size of the graphics in the Internet newspapers.

News articles and Web links were measured in their quantities. The home pages and front pages were coded for numbers of pictures, graphs, news items, news links, format of page organization, and textual information presentation. The news articles within the front pages were coded for numbers of pictures, graphs, news items, news links leading to the relating information, and steps (clicks) needed to get the information.

Two coders participated in the coding process. A check of intercoder reliability was conducted with the data collected during the first 3 days. Because the greater part of the coding scheme was to count the numbers of page components, and little coder judgment was needed to place units into categories, a relatively high degree of intercoder reliability was expected. Using the Spearman-Brown Prophecy Formula (S-B),[2] the reliability coefficiency was calculated. Standardized Item α is .92, which was within the expected range.

RESULTS

The analysis of data reveals that although all three newspapers were relatively uniform in restricting the use of large pictures and graphs, each of the newspapers had its own approach to Web page design. *The New York Times* adopted a simple and clear approach in its Web page design. The home page and front page both were short one-page print-outs. *The Washington Post* offered more categories on its home page. Whereas readers may have more options when they open the home page, it also requires more effort to find what they need. *USA Today* appears to have a more graphical front page, but not on the news article level.

The home pages of all three newspapers average 3.4 news items per day. More news stories appeared on the front pages, with an average of 10 news items each day. Among 310 news articles in 10 days, only 41 (13%) articles in *The New York Times* had the accompanying pictures. Neither *The Washington Post* nor *USA Today* had any news story illustrated with pictures except some headlines on

TABLE 2.1
Frequencies of Page Components of Three Internet Newspapers

Newspaper	News on Home Page	News on Front Page	News With Pictures		News With Graphs		News With Full Story		News With Links	
NYT	20	65	41	63%	7	11%	65	100%	62	95%
WP	50	70	0	0%	0	0%	70	100%	0	0%
USA	30	175	0	0%	0	0%	91	52%	73	42%
Total	100	310	41	13%	7	2%	226	73%	135	44%

the home pages. Although all 65 news articles of *The New York Times* had small graphs on the same page, only 7 (11%) small graphs were illustrations of the news articles. Eighty-nine percent of the small graphs on the news article page were advertising links. None of the news articles in *The Washington Post* and *USA Today* had graph illustrations, although small advertising graphs appeared on most of the news article pages.

The front page of *The Washington Post* and the "Top News" of *USA Today* provided abstracts of top news as well as links to full stories of news headlines. The front page of *The New York Times* only displayed headlines with links to full stories. *The New York Times* and *The Washington Post* tended to provide a full story for all of the news displayed in headlines or abstracts on their front pages, whereas *USA Today* only provided full stories for half of the headlines presented in "Top News" (see Table 2.1).

The analyses of the data of Web page design and graphic use of three newspapers reveals the following results:

Use of Graphics

> Hypothesis 1, that the Internet newspapers tend to give more priority to providing textual information than graphic information, is supported.

All three newspapers used pictures in their Internet versions, but newshole was primarily devoted to textual information. Graphic information comprised a very limited portion. There was normally one picture on the home pages, and there was no picture on the front page (*USA Today*'s "Top News") in all three newspapers. On the news article level (within the front page through hyperlinks), only *The New York Times* had some articles illustrated with small pictures. During the 10 days, of 62 articles within the front page of *The New York Times,* 42 (68%) articles had small pictures of 1 × 1 inch, and the space allocated for the pictures within the front page was negligible. Neither *The Washington Post* nor *USA Today* had any pictures illustrating news articles.

Graphs of small size appeared on home pages, front pages, and news article pages. Most of them were graphic advertising links, which took very little space on the news article page when compared to the space given to the news articles.

TABLE 2.2
Pictures Use in Three Newspapers

Paper	Large Pictures 5" × 3.5" or Larger			Medium Pictures 3.5" × 2.5"			Small Pictures 2" × 1" or Smaller			Total
	Home	Front	News	Home	Front	News	Home	Front	News	
NYT	0	0	0	10	0	0	0	0	53	63
WP	0	0	0	10	0	0	0	0	0	10
USA	0	0	0	13	0	0	4	0	1	18
Total			33			4			54	

Hypothesis 2, that eye-catching graphics are more likely to appear on home pages and front pages than on the news article pages, is supported.

Eye-catching graphics refers to the pictures and graphs at least 3.5 × 2.5 inches. No pictures larger than 3.5 × 2.5 inches appeared on the home pages and the front pages of all three newspapers, although there was usually one picture of 3.5 × 2.5 inches each day on the home pages. Neither front pages nor news article pages had any picture equal to or larger than 3.5 × 2.5 inches. Only part of the news articles within the front page of *The New York Times* were illustrated with small pictures, which were about 1 × 1 inch. No news graphs larger than 3.5 × 2.5 inches appeared on the home pages, front pages, and news article pages of all three newspapers. Only *The New York Times* had a few small graphs illustrating the news articles.

More small pictures were used than the larger ones. Although *The New York Times* used some small pictures on news article pages, pictures typically appeared on the home pages in all three newspapers in about 3.5 × 2.5 inches size (see Table 2.2).

Like its printed version, *USA Today* used more striking graphics on its front page (home page) than *The New York Times* and *The Washington Post*. More small graphs were used on all three newspapers than those larger than 3.5 × 2.5 inches. *The New York Times* and *The Washington Post* did not tend to use graphs larger than 3.5 × 2.5 inches on all of the three levels. No graphs were used to illustrate the news stories in the *The Washington Post* and *USA Today*; *The New York Times* did use small icons (see Table 2.3).

Hypothesis 3, that Internet newspapers are less likely to use large pictures and graphs to illustrate news articles, is supported.

Medium size pictures of about 3.5 × 2.5 inches were used only on the home pages in all three newspapers in limited quantity, usually one picture a day. *The Washington Post* and *USA Today* had no intention to illustrate news articles with graphics as there were neither pictures nor graphs on the front pages and on the

TABLE 2.3
Graph Use in Three Newspapers

Paper	Large Graphs 5" x 3.5" or Larger			Medium Graphs 3.5" x 2.5"			Small Graphs 2" x 1" or Smaller			Total
	Home	Front	News	Home	Front	News	Home	Front	News	
NYT	0	0	0	0	0	0	20	30	126	176
WP	0	0	0	0	0	0	38	20	64	122
USA	10	0	0	10	0	0	8	10	133	171
Total	10			10			66	60	323	

news article pages (in *USA Today* within "Top News"). *The New York Times* tended to illustrate news articles with graphics, but implemented their ideas in a subtle way. Whenever a news article within the front page was presented with a related picture or graph, the graphic was always presented in the size about 1 × 1 inch, which could be enlarged into 6 × 4 inches.

Interconnectedness of News Content

Hypothesis 4, that with the interconnected news links, detailed news and related information are more likely to be retrieved with few steps (clicks), and the information retrieved can go beyond the original news content, is supported.

The Web pages of all three newspapers were interconnected, and all news content was interconnected through hyperlinks. On both home pages and front pages, headlines of top news were displayed. To view the full story with headlines displayed on home pages, only one click was needed. To read more top news, the reader had to click the link and go to the front page, where either news abstracts or links to full stories were provided. For the brief stories without a link to the full story, one click from the home page enabled the reader to get them. For stories with more detail, no more than two clicks were needed from home pages to get the full stories.

The New York Times was more likely to provide links to the related stories and information for the news articles on the front page; 95% of the news articles were linked to the related stories and other related information. *USA Today* provided links to related stories for 42% of its news articles, whereas *The Washington Post* provided no links to the related stories for its news articles within the front page. The links were not restrictive in directing to the news content of the host newspaper. Instead, the links often led to the information provided by other Web publications and went far beyond news content.

DISCUSSION

Web page design and graphic use in the Internet newspaper conform in part with proposed models for Internet communication, but also present a new territory undefined by these models. The support for Hypothesis 1 suggests that within the hybrid, the new technology plays an important part in making the Internet newspaper possible. Although a shift from newspaper convention to a new media age is taking place, when looking at the approach of Web page design, the old component, the traditional newspaper concept, still outweighs what new technology can bring. In presenting news content, the Internet newspaper did not go too far from the conventional norm in terms of graphic use. The findings of this study suggest text information is still dominant as newspaper content on the World Wide Web. Internet newspapers do not take full advantage of available technology.

The use of eye-catching graphics on the Web page supports the notion that a shift from newspaper convention is unfolding in the Internet newspaper, although in a relatively limited manner. Being consistent with the hybrid model, graphics were used primarily on the home pages, whereas the inner pages, the front page, and news article pages were dominated by text, instead of more graphics as a technology-dominant hybrid model would expect.

The support for H3 and H4 confirms the usefulness of the Interactivity Model. The practice of graphic use in illustrating news articles presents a typical part of the interactivity model. The Internet newspapers can be read only under the interactive environment. All headlines and links need clicks to activate. When designing a Web page and setting guidelines for graphic use in the Internet newspaper, interactivity is a key element to be considered. Although retrieving text-based information requires a reader's interaction, retrieval of graphics needs more effort from the audience members. Viewing graphics in newspapers and in the Internet environment is entirely different in terms of immediacy, which creates a different level of audience expectation. The compliance with the rules of an interactive medium and taking account of audience's expectation in Web page design makes an evident sign of shift of balance of communicative power from publisher to audience.

However, the findings also show the limitation of the interactivity model for explaining the Internet newspaper. As direct communication links are established between editor and audience in Internet newspapers, feedback becomes immediate and continuous. The publishing cycle is no longer a barrier for editors, who can put up the latest information based on the feedback from the audience. The interactivity model works well up to this point. With the introduction of the news link, a symbol of interconnectedness, part of the news content goes beyond the scope of the content provided by the host newspaper, and interactivity is no longer confined between the host newspaper and its audience.

The findings support the notion advanced by the Media Transition Model, the shift of communicative power from sender to receiver. On the interconnected Web site, the media content is no longer provided solely by the news media. Instead, part of the content may be contributed by other Internet newspapers or sources of information, including sources from the audience, which drastically alter the way of media content control. The content connected to the host newspaper by the links, which could be considered part of the media content, is now produced and controlled by the senders other than the newspaper, and they may just be the receivers of the original news content of the host newspaper.

An Alternative Model of the Internet Newspapers

In this new environment, the product of a newspaper is no longer confined to the original content provided by the host newspaper. With interconnected links that lead to information beyond the news content provided by a host newspaper, receivers now have more power to choose what to read, and acquire a product that may be much different from what the original Internet newspaper provides.

Consequently, the alternative model of the Internet newspaper that was discussed previously, though bearing the features of the general interactivity model, evidently differentiates it from the general interactivity model. It now includes a many-to-many communication process, with newspaper operating at the center, and facilitating the interconnected links for many-to-many communication, as shown in Fig. 2.1.

The hybrid model of the Internet newspapers suggests that although technology offers an opportunity to dramatically change the appearance of a newspaper published on the World Wide Web, the deviation of the Internet newspaper from the conventional newspaper is not substantial, especially in graphic use. All three newspapers preferred small graphics to the larger ones when they used them to illustrate news articles or display them as advertisements. It can be expected that the technology component in the hybrid model will increase its weight as technology advances, but the change will be gradual rather than instantaneous, and is restricted by the other component of the model, the convention of newspaper publishing.

Restrictive use of graphics is more of an approach to take into account audience expectation, and it indicates that a shift of control of communicative power is unfolding in Internet communication. The Internet newspaper confirms what the media transition model predicted. The shift of control is seen firstly from Web page design and graphic use based on audience expectation in an interactive environment. Secondly, Internet newspaper turns into a product in which audience is involved in its production. Thirdly, a newspaper is no longer the sole controller of news content.

This study is not an attempt to build a complete model for the Internet newspaper. Instead it is only a test of how well several models of Internet communication can be applied to an Internet newspaper. The study is limited because it only examined three U.S. newspapers; there are more than 2,000 U.S. newspapers

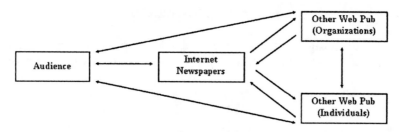

FIG. 2.1.   A many-to-many communication model of the Internet newspapers.

publishing on the World Wide Web. The study also observed a rather short time period, whereas the practice of Internet newspaper publishing can change over time, especially as technology advances.

Although the findings support the notion that the old component, newspaper convention, has relatively more weight in the hybrid model, the reason for such weight in Internet newspapers is unclear. Further research should expand the time span of the study, and include more newspapers to examine the approaches of Web page design and graphic use of a larger group of Internet newspapers. Other questions worth probing include the following: As more institutional and individual publishers participate in the communication centered with a host Internet newspaper, to what degree will Web page design and graphic use and interconnected links define the level of interactivity? How is information flow affected by the newspaper-centered many-to-many communication? How does the shift of balance of communicative power change the process of Internet newspaper publishing? What are the key indicators that predict the shift of balance of communicative power in Internet newspapers?

CONCLUSION

The new computer technology available may change some of the practices of Internet newspaper publishing, but no dramatic changes are likely to occur in the near future for two reasons: First, the conventional newspaper is still among the primary sources for people to get information. It is the people who run newspapers who decide which way Internet newspapers should go. Second, a large number of computer users are connected to the Internet through modem, whose speed increase is restricted by the telephone line. It will have a profound impact on the Web page design and graphic use of Internet newspapers.[3] The current logic of Web page design and relatively restricted use of graphics in the Internet newspapers is likely to remain an accepted practice of the newspaper publishers for at least 2 or 3 years, although a shift of control of balance of communicative power has already taken place.

ACKNOWLEDGMENTS

An earlier version of this chapter was published in *Journalism and Mass Communication Quarterly, 75*(2), Summer 1998, pp. 353–365. Reprinted with permission.

ENDNOTES

1. The websites of the three newspapers studied: www.nytimes.com, www.washingtonpost.com, and www.usatoday.com
2. Spearman-Brown Prophecy Formula (S-B): Reliability coefficiency $= N\,rxx/1 + (N - 1)$ *rxx. rxx* = mean correlation, N = number of coders.
3. When only a modem is used to connect to the Internet, it provides connection speeds up to 56.6 Kbps. Due to FCC rules that restrict power output, however, the download speeds through modem are limited to 53 Kbps. Upload speeds are limited to 33.6 Kbps. Actual speeds may vary depending on line conditions. With the adoption of broadband technology, the limit in connection speeds with the modem could be significantly eliminated.

REFERENCES

Anonymous. (1996). *Glossary of Internet/WWW terms.* Retrieved May 16, 2004, from http://www.lib. grin.edu/resources/glossary.html

Baird, R. N. (1993). *The graphics of communication: Methods, media, and technology* (6th ed.). Fort Worth, TX: Harcourt Brace Jovanovich.

Bordewijk, J. L., & van Kaam, B. (1986). Towards a new classification of tele-information services. *Intermedia, 14,* 16–21.

Garcia, M. R. (1987). *Contemporary newspaper design* (2nd ed.). Englewood Cliffs, NJ: Prentice-Hall.

Garrison, B. (1995). Online services as reporting tools: Daily newspaper use of commercial databases in 1994. *Newspaper Research Journal, 16*(4), 74.

Gilder, G. F. (1994, Jan/Feb). Fidler's Electronic News Panel is a better bet for the future than home shopping. *The Bulletin of the American Society of Newspaper Editors,* 9–11.

Glascock, J. (1993). The effect of cable television on advertiser and consumer spending on mass media, 1978–1990. *Journalism Quarterly, 70,* 509–517.

Kamerer, D., & Bergen, L. (1995). Patterns of use, exposure in paper's audiotext system. *Newspaper Research Journal, 16*(1), 48.

Katz, J. (1994, September). Online or not, newspapers still suck. *Wired,* 50.

Lapham, C. (1995, July 1). The evolution of the newspaper of the future. *Computer-Mediated Communication, 7.*

McAdams, M. (1995a). *Driving a newspaper on the data highway: Home shopping? Movies on demand? What about information?* Retrieved May 16, 2004, from http://www.well.com/user/ mmcadams/online.newspapers.html

McAdams, M. (1995b). *Inventing an online newspaper.* Retrieved May 16, 2004, from http://www .sentex.net/~mmcadams/invent/invent3.html

Middleberg, D., & Ross, S. (1996). *The media in cyberspace.* Retrieved May 16, 2004, from http:// www.mediaresearch.cro.net/text/04_2/02–0004–0143–0173.htm

Morris, M., & Ogan, C. (1996). The Internet as mass medium. *Journal of Communication, 46*(1), 39–50.

Mueller, J., & Kamerer, D. (1995). Reader preference for electronic newspapers. *Newspaper Research Journal, 16*(3), 2–13.

Neuman, W. R. (1991). *The future of the mass audience.* Cambridge, England & New York: Cambridge University Press.

Rafaeli, S. (1988). Interactivity: From new media to communication. In R. P. Hawkins, J. L. Wiemann, & S. Pingree (Eds.), *Advancing communication science: Merging mass and interpersonal process* (pp. 110–134). Newbury Park, CA: Sage.

Rheingold, H. (1994, June). *The electronic landscape: A writer's perspective.* Paper presented at the Writers' Retreat on Interactive Technology & Equipment Conference, University of Vancouver, Vancouver, British Columbia.

Rieder, R. (1997, April). A breakthrough in cyberspace. *American Journalism Review, 19*(3), 6.

Rogers, E. M. (1986). *Communication technology: The new media in society.* New York: Free Press.

Tedesco, R. (1996, November 11). Heavy traffic jams Net. *Broadcasting & Cable, 126*(47), 24.

Turnbull, A. T., & Baird, R. N. (1980). *The graphics of communication: Typography, layout, design, production* (4th ed.). New York: Holt, Rinehart & Winston.

Wood, W. C., & O'Hare, S. L. (1991). Paying for the video revolution: Consumer spending on the mass media. *Journal of Communication, 40*(1), 24–30.

3

Applying Network Theory to the Use of External Links on News Web Sites

Mark Tremayne
University of Texas at Austin

Compared to traditional media, the Web allows journalists greater flexibility in constructing sophisticated stories, stories that can be consumed in different ways by unique subsets of readers. Hypertext is allowing for stories that are less linear and more segmented than was possible before. As a result, news stories on the Web are more heavily linked every year (Tremayne, 2004b). The unique features of the Web were identified a decade ago as potential difference-makers in stimulating public dialogue of important issues (Rheingold, 1994; Rosen, 1995). Web news editors influence the flow of user traffic on the broader Web by providing links to certain sites and avoiding others. And site managers encourage particular patterns of use within their sites. News Web sites such as *The Dallas Morning News* and the *Chicago Sun-Times* and even, at one point, *National Public Radio*, have posted policies on their sites prohibiting so-called "deep linking" to news stories. They want Web traffic to pass through the homepage where the expensive advertising is displayed.

Beyond trying to influence how a reader gets to a site, the Web editor can guide the reader's path through the site. Some sites offer links to related material, both internally and externally, and in this way the collective choices of news editors on the Web help to create its infrastructure of public discourse. This chapter examines the use of external links, those that lead off a news organizations site and out into the larger Web.

Now comprised of billions of individual pages, the Web is one of the largest networks ever. Emerging theory is beginning to explain how networks grow, how information flows along networks, and why some nodes in a network become hubs. In a preliminary study examining the first few years of Web news, the author used network theory to identify trends in the use of external hyperlinks on national news Web sites (Tremayne, 2004a). This chapter reexamines those findings and tests the trends against 2 more years of Web news data. A database of more than 1,700 stories is used to track changes in the use of external links over 6 years. First, though, an explanation of network theory and how it is applied in this chapter.

NETWORK THEORY AND THE GROWTH
OF THE WEB

Swiss mathematician Leonhard Euler introduced the study of graphs, or networks, when studying a problem concerning bridges and land masses (Barabasi, 2002). In this case, the network consisted of four land masses (nodes) connected by seven bridges (links). A network is any distribution of similar objects that are interconnected in some way. Networks occur in nature, such as neural networks, or can be man-made, such as power distribution grids. An explanation for how commonly occurring networks structures form came more than 200 years after Euler's discoveries, in the work of mathematicians Paul Erdos and Alfred Renyi (Barabasi, 2002; Watts, 2003). They proposed random graph theory, the idea that networks are essentially the end result of links being formed between random pairs of nodes. Each link forms independently of all others and clustering of links around some nodes is explained by chance. This explanation went unchallenged as most researchers focused instead on information flow on networks rather than evolution of the network itself.

In the 1960s, Rogers (1983) studied the flow of ideas through social systems. This work explored both the individual adoption process and the large group diffusion process. In the latter area, Granovetter (1973) made the case that ideas are spread most widely not by persons in the middle of a cluster of acquaintances, but by peripheral members who spend time in multiple social circles. Milgram (1967) demonstrated what has come to be known as the "six degrees of separation." Although he never used that phrase, Milgram found that it took almost that many friendship links to connect any two people in the United States.

Granovetter's (1973) work suggested that the independence assumption of random graph theory was violated in the case of social networks. His conceptualization of the "strength" of a social tie included how much time individuals dedicated to its establishment and maintenance. Because an individual's time is limited, establishment of future ties is dependent, in part, on the existence of current ties. Certainly geography and other factors also limit possible social ties. For this type of network, and many others, theories such as random graph theory could not sufffice. An alternative explanation is needed.

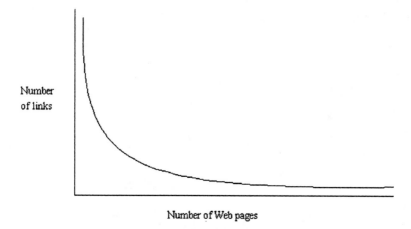

FIG. 3.1.   Power law distribution.

Constructing a Theory of Network Growth

Barabasi and Albert (1999) used the rapid growth of the Web as a testing ground to construct a theory of network development. Each Web page has a number of ties (links) to other Web pages. If random graph theory applied to the World Wide Web, there would be a small number of pages with few or no links, a small number with a huge number of links, and the majority with an average number of links, in other words, a normal distribution. Barabasi and Albert found instead a scale-free power-law distribution, like the one in Fig. 3.1.

The general formula for a distribution of this type is: $N(k) \sim k^{-\gamma}$, where the parameter γ is the degree exponent. This value varies from network to network. For the Web, they found a curve with a degree exponent of 2.1 for incoming links to a page and an exponent of 2.5 for outgoing links from Web pages.

Figure 3.1 shows a small number of pages with hundreds or thousands of links and a large number of pages with few links. The ones with hundreds of links or more are called *hubs*.

Distributions following a power law also conform to Pareto's law, the so-called 80/20 rule. Pareto, a 19th-century engineer, observed that approximately 20% of the population earns 80% of the income. This pattern can be observed in a number of other contexts and in each case a plot of individual cases will look like Fig. 3.1.

Only in the late 1990s did researchers begin understanding why naturally occurring networks follow this pattern (Adamic & Huberman, 2001; Barabasi & Albert, 1999; Watts, 1999). Using computer simulations, Barabasi and Albert (1999) discovered two principles that explain all distributions that follow a power law: *growth* and *preferential attachment*.

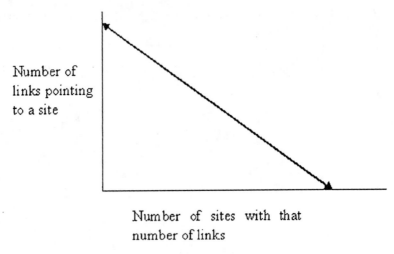

Number of
links pointing
to a site

Number of sites with that
number of links

FIG. 3.2.   Distribution based on growth alone.

Web Growth.   Another example from the Web helps illustrate the theory. If we plot Web pages by links pointing to them we will find that some (yahoo.com or ebay.com) are linked to by thousands or even millions of Web pages. But most Web pages have very few other pages that link to them. A plot of this would look very much like Fig. 3.1. So why do the hubs have so many links pointing to them? One reason is that some sites have been around a long time (for the Web this means since the mid-1990s). As more pages and more links appear the older sites have a disproportionately greater chance of being linked to than those that are young. So the very growth of a network favors the original nodes. But if this were the only way hubs grew, then instead of a power curve we would see a relatively straight line with old nodes having the most links, "middle age" nodes having a mean number of links, and young nodes having few links (see Fig. 3.2). The reason this is not the case has to do with the second principle of network growth: preferential attachment.

Recognition of the benefits of early entry into the Web drove the dot.com rush of the 1990s. But it is the second principle of network theory that causes the line in Fig. 3.2 to curve, and allows the rich to get richer still.

Preferred Attachment.   When a node in a network has more connections than other nodes it becomes even more useful to connect to comparatively. So eBay benefited by being on the Web early, but its edge grew because buyers and sellers would prefer to reach the largest possible market. In this way the straight line of Fig. 3.2 bowed so that just a few sites obtained nearly all the auction traffic. Hundreds of copycat sites exist but each has a relatively small number of other sites that link to it.

Naturally occurring distributions of this type depart from scale-free power curves in one respect; they are not truly scale-free. The tails of true power curves stretch to infinity, whereas real networks are finite (Watts, 2003). One reason for this is the cost associated with adding links. Network theory assumes a low cost. Where the cost of establishing new ties is high, growth of hubs is stunted.

The growth and preferred attachment principles apply to networks of all types. An earlier study analyzing the use of hyperlinks in Web news stories found a similar power law distribution with 31% of stories in the sample accounting for 80% of all the links (Tremayne, 2004b). That study confirmed the growth principle; news stories on the Web have more links in each succeeding year. The study also suggested that preferred attachment in this case stemmed from editor decisions regarding the need for context in stories. Stories about international relations contained significantly more links than spot news stories about crimes and accidents. The contextual possibilities of the former, historical, geographical, social, and political, were offered as an explanation for the increased hyperlinking on those stories.

Context and the Linking Debate

When reporting on events journalists must decide what context is necessary to understand the story. The debate over how much context and interpretation are required is an old one. Lippmann (1922) concluded that *news* should be about events and facts but that *truth* will "set them into relation with each other" (p. 226). Although not his intention, the media's pursuit of truth has led to a greater role for context and interpretation. Schudson (1982) documented a decline of facts and an increase in interpretation in reporting on the presidential State of the Union address from 1790 to 1980. Barnhurst and Mutz (1997) also found an increase in context and interpretation in newspaper reporting over the last century.

As news organizations migrated to the Web one facet of the medium created a new opportunity for putting current events into context: hypertext. On the Web, additional information could be linked off the primary text, either to another Web site altogether or to material within the domain. This development helped address two of the problems journalists routinely face. The first is the question of how much of the previous day's events need to be recapped in today's story. On the Web, the journalist could link to yesterday's news and dispense with a background paragraph. The second benefit concerns alternative points of view, those that are often excluded in favor of more mainstream views (typically two). A Web story might still focus on the two dominant opinions but provide, as well, links to other groups or organizations. Even for dominant viewpoints links to organization sites can provide greater depth for reader understanding.

These lessons have not been completely ignored by commercial news providers in the United States. Take, for example, a campaign story posted to the NYTimes. com on March 3, 2004 at 3:33 P.M. EST. A regular feature of the online *New York*

Times, the "Times on the Trail" is presented in "blog" style, updated frequently by the paper's political reporters. Unlike most of the stories on NYTimes.com, this one uses external links liberally. The most recent update concerned a controversy over campaign ads for President George W. Bush that included images of firefighters in New York in the aftermath of the 9/11 attacks. The updates contains links to the campaign Web sites of Bush and John Kerry, as well as a link to the International Association of Firefighters. Other updates contain links to a dozen other politician Web sites.

Along the side of the news updates are links to other campaign articles, not just those produced by the *Times* but to 30 other publications, including *USA Today, The Washington Post,* and *The Wall Street Journal.* In addition to these established media outlets, the *Times* also links to several blog sites such as Wonkette.com and Bopnews.com.

In total, the "Times on the Trail" story contained 62 external links. It provided interested readers with a wealth of information about the 2004 elections including easy access to stories on other sites. Additionally, it gave readers a gateway to candidate Web sites where, at least potentially, readers could actually get involved in the democratic process.

With so many external links, this Web news story was atypical. But the existence of a few heavily linked stories follows the pattern of the Web as a whole.

Hypothesis and Research Questions

Network theory rests on the premises that networks grow and evolve and that links are added not randomly but attach to nodes by the principle of preferential attachment. For the case of journalism, the decisions of Web editors regarding the proper hyperlinks for a given story has been offered as the mechanism through which preferred attachment operates (Tremayne, 2004b). And a study on the use of external links tested the idea that an editor preference for internal linking rather than external linking would lead to relative decline in external linking (Tremayne, 2004a). Here we test network theory on a sample of more than 1,700 stories with the following hypothesis:

H1: The proportion of external links in Web news stories will decrease over time.

In addition to this hypothesis, four research questions are explored. Because previous research found that overall use of hyperlinks varied by news topic (Tremayne, 2004a), this study investigated the following question:

RQ1: How does the use of hyperlinks vary by news topic?

An earlier study (Tremayne, 2004a) found U.S. government and military sites to be the most common type of external link, followed by commercial sites. External site type was measured again using the expanded data set this question:

RQ2: What types of sites are linked to most frequently by national news stories on the Web?

The earlier study also made note of a decline in the use of external links to Web sites outside the United States. Here we formally explore this trend and see if it continues:

RQ3: Does the downward trend in the use of links to sites outside the United States continue in 2003 and 2004?

Finally, the earlier study found a small but statistically insignificant difference in the use of external links by print-affiliated Web sites versus those affiliated with broadcast companies. To see if this difference has reached significance, this question is posed:

RQ4: Are there any differences in the use of external hyperlinks between Web sites of print and broadcast companies?

METHOD

Answering the research questions required a content analysis of news Web sites. An after-the-fact data collection scheme, such as one that might be conducted for a newspaper content analysis, would not be practical for the ever-changing Web. Instead, a sample of Web news content was created by periodically recording the home pages of 10 national news Web sites.

The Sample

U.S. news organizations with the largest circulations or audiences that had a Web presence in 1999, and that were national in scope, were selected for analysis. Among the selected media, five are the Web counterparts of newspapers or magazines. These are *The New York Times, The Washington Post, USA Today, U.S. News & World Report,* and *Time.* The other five are the Web counterparts of broadcast companies. They are *ABC, CBS, CNN, Fox News,* and *MSNBC.*

Sampling

A systematic sample was recorded using the following scheme. In March of each year, the 10 Web sites were visited every 4 days with a random start for a total of 7 days each year. Main page stories appearing on the screen of a standard-sized monitor were examined. This resulted in 1,758 stories over the 6 years examined, or an average of 293 stories per year.

Key Variables

Over the course of the project a number of variables were measured including topic, hyperlinks per story, node modality (audio, video, text, etc.), internal versus external links, and so on. Five of these are of interest here: hyperlinks, external links, type of external site (commercial, governmental, etc.), location of site, and topic.

Hyperlinks were defined as any clickable text or graphic that leads the user to additional material directly related to the story. Also included were rollover graphics that present new material when the cursor is placed on them (without clicking). What constituted "related" was left to the coders but specifically excluded standard site navigation icons and advertising. Also excluded were next page links and those beyond the first level.

External hyperlinks were those that led to a Web address off the site of the news story. Sites that were co-owned or in cooperation with each other sites (such as *MSNBC* and *The Washington Post*) were not considered external.

Type of external site and *location of site* were determined by the Web address. Sites were categorized by the URL suffix (com, gov, mil, org, etc.) and, if the country of the site was still unclear, by examining the site for a postal address.

Topic was coded after data collection using the headline and subhead. There were 12 categories including miscellaneous. When two or more news categories applied, the coder was instructed to select the one considered primary.

Coding and Reliability

Coding occurred at two points. In the first years of the study, two coders accessed, on computers in separate rooms, two stories on each of the 7 coding days. The 10 Web sites were each represented by one or two stories in the reliability sample. These 14 stories represented 5% of the total sample that year. Reliability on links per story was very high, .99 by Krippendorf's alpha (this statistic adjusts for small reliability samples). By 2001 software made it easier to preserve digital copies of hypermedia stories; another test of reliability was conducted in 2003. For this portion of the data, a simple random sample of 100 stories was selected. Agreement was .94 on links per story, .87 on link type, and .95 on type of external site, .81 on location, and .86 for story topic (by Krippendorf's alpha).

RESULTS

The sampling procedure yielded 1,758 stories over the 6-year period, an average of 293 stories per year. Most stories in the sample had few hyperlinks, including

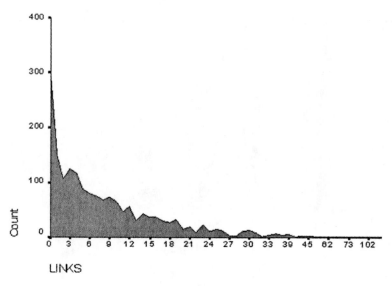

FIG. 3.3.   Hyperlink per story by number of cases (count).

300 with none and 148 with only one. One story had 137 hyperlinks. The mean was 8.50 hyperlinks per story. As predicted by network theory, a graph of stories by number of hyperlinks follows a power curve (see Fig. 3.3).

The 1,758 stories contained 9,166 hyperlinks. Of these, 13% were links to external Web sites (1,934 links). The hypothesis and research questions concern variations in this percentage over time, by news topic, and by medium, as well as an examination of what types of external sites are linked to most often. Because the links variables follow a power curve rather than a normal distribution, non-parametric statistics were employed in the analysis that follows.

The Trend Over Time.   If the hypothesis is correct, the use of external hyperlinks should diminish over time relative to the use of internal links. Figure 3.4 illustrates the trend. The percentage of links that go to sites external to a news organization's site is diminishing over time. This trend was tested statistically by creating a "gap" variable. The gap variable was calculated for each case by subtracting the number of external links for a story from its internal links. For all 1,758 stories, the mean gap between external and internal links is 6.3 links. As hypothesized, the gap grows year to year. A Kruskal-Wallis test confirmed significant differences among years ($H = 134.5, p < .05$ by Bonferroni procedure). Additionally, a test of linear trend using an ANOVA procedure also confirmed the trend ($F = 55.6, p < .001$). ANOVA is not typically used for data that do not follow a normal distribution because of a loss in statistical power, but with larger sample sizes can yield accurate p values (Wilcox, 2001). The analysis confirmed

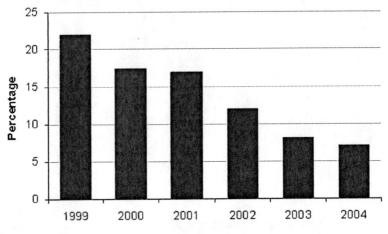

FIG. 3.4.   External hyperlinks by year.

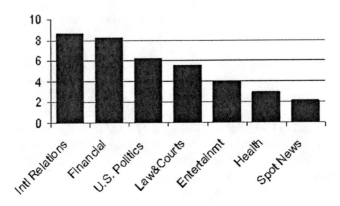

FIG. 3.5.   External–internal link gap by topic.

the hypothesis. The use of external links in stories on national news Web sites is diminishing relative to internal links. Even in absolute terms the number of external links is at its lowest in 2004 (0.7 links per story), compared to a high in 2000 (1.6 links per story).

External Links and News Topic.   The first research questions asks: "How does the use of hyperlinks vary by news topic?" Four of the 12 news topics had less than 50 cases in the sample and are excluded from analysis here, as is the miscellaneous category. The remaining stories had an average of 6.9 fewer external links than internal ones. Figure 3.5 shows the results by topic.

The proportion of external links was particularly low for two news categories: financial and international relations stories. International relations stories had almost nine fewer external links than internal. Possible reasons for this are discussed in the next section. Financial stories were also much more likely to be linked internally rather than externally. Many of the sites in this sample have built up a large business archive, including profiles of most publicly-traded companies. This allows for a significant amount of internal linking.

Two topics, health and spot news, had a relatively small gap, meaning a more equal distribution of internal and external links. The differences in the internal–external gaps among topics are statistically significant (Kruskal-Wallis $H = 122.3$, $p < .001$).

External Site Type.   The second research questions asks: "What types of sites are linked to most frequently by national news stories on the Web?" The external Web site links that appeared in national Web stories during the study period were categorized by domain suffix (.com, .edu, .gov, etc.). Dot-com sites were also categorized as media and nonmedia.

Military and government Web sites, both in and outside the United States, are the most common external link category (40%), followed by commercial non-media sites (23%), nonprofit organizations (21%), media sites (13%), and educational institutions (3%).

Location of External Sites.   Research Question 3 concerns the location of the sites for which external links appear. Most of the external links, 73%, are to U.S.-based Web sites. This figure alone is unsurprising, but the trend over time is revealing. In 1999, when online journalism was still in its infancy, links to Web sites outside the United States constituted 60% of external links. By 2004, that number was down to just 5%. Figure 3.6 shows the results by years.

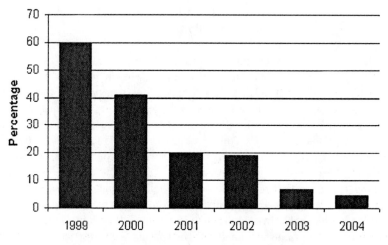

FIG. 3.6.   Percentage of external links to non-U.S. Web sites.

The drop in the use of external links to Web sites outside the United States is due mainly to a decreased use of non-U.S. government or military sites. In 1999, government Web sites outside the United States accounted for 71% of all government links. That percentage subsequently fell every year to reach a low of just 4% in 2004. Increasingly, when U.S. news Web sites include links to external sites, those sites are U.S.-based.

Print Versus Broadcast. Research question 4 asks about differences between U.S. print and broadcast companies in the use of external linking. In overall terms, the broadcast sites used more hyperlinks (10.9 per story) than the print sites (5.8) over the 6 years in question, a statistically significant difference (Mann-Whitney $U = 262979$, $p < .001$). As for external links specifically, national print and broadcast Web sites were closer, but broadcast sites offered more (1.3) than print sites (0.9) at a statistically significant rate (Mann-Whitney $U = 328875$, $p < .001$). As a percentage of all links offered, however, more links on print stories were external (15.9%) than for stories on the broadcast sites (11.7%).

DISCUSSION AND CONCLUSIONS

This study examined a 6-year sample of national news stories on the Web and found the use of external links is continuing to decline in ways predicted by network theory. News Web sites are linking to external sites less frequently than just a few years ago. At the same time, use of internal links has moved sharply higher (Tremayne, 2004b). The conclusion is clear: As each organization builds up its own archive of Web content, this material is being favored over content that is off-site. This is just one example of *preferred attachment,* which is the driving principle of network theory. As predicted by network theory, a plot of external links per story has a distribution that follows a power curve.

Figure 3.7 shows that most stories in the sample (1,272 out of 1,758) have no external links whereas a few have dozens. Although we can only infer the reasons behind this example of preferred attachment, one obvious possibility is that Web managers are trying to keep users from leaving their pages. If this is indeed the case, it's another example of market-driven journalism (McManus, 1995). To more fully explore this possibility, a survey of Web editors or a series of in-depth interviews could be conducted. Among other possible explanations for the trend are fear of association with external sites and/or legal concerns associated with possible libelous statements on those sites.

Although not tested here as a hypothesis, a similar pattern is occurring with links to foreign Web sites. In 1999, 60% of external links went to sites outside the United States. By 2002, that number was just below 20% and this study found it falling even further, to just 5% in 2004. The foreign Web sites seeing the largest decrease are government-run sites. Two possible causes are suggested here. One

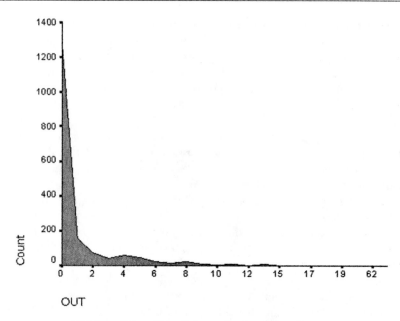

FIG. 3.7.   External hyperlinks per story by number of cases.

is that Web editors track user traffic and have found those links to be little used. Another possibility is a post-9/11 effect; a rallying around the flag by Web editors in the United States.

Some topics are more likely to receive external linking than others. Stories about spot news and health had a more evenly divided source of linked material than other topics. In the case of spot news, this has more to do with the relative lack of links overall than with special attention being paid to external linking. Spot news is the least "linked" news category of the 12. Because of the nature of these stories, Web editors have relatively few options for including linked material. In some cases, links to other Web sites may be the only choice.

Health stories, on the other hand, present a more interesting case. It may be that Web editors recognize the public benefit of directing interested users to important medical information. And because of the delicate nature of medical advice, they may see this as a safer choice.

Financial news and international relations stories had the widest gaps between internal and external linkages. The former is not surprising. Many news Web sites have built extensive business news sections, partly because early Web adopters tended to be more affluent than the population as a whole. This is a classic case of the growth principle combining with preferential attachment (by editors) to generate a fairly huge amount of internal content that editors can choose from on a daily basis. And the more links there are on these stories the longer this highly sought after readership will stay on the site.

The gap for stories about international relations is unfortunate. These types of stories provide for many opportunities to link to external sites. Rather than doing this, Web editors are teaming up with other content providers, such as encyclopedia publishers, to keep users on their sites. The benefit of this is that some contextual material not available through traditional media channels is available online. Of course, the downside is that U.S. users are increasingly isolated from a world of ideas and points of view.

This study found relatively little difference in the using of external links between news sites run by print companies and those of broadcast outlets. Although the broadcast sites used slightly more external links per story, the print sites still have a greater overall percentage of external links.

Are the documented patterns inevitable? Because the linking patterns evident on the news Web sites examined here are predicted by network theory it may seem that way. But there is another possibility. Independent content providers, called *bloggers,* thrive by linking users to a virtual public sphere where current events are debated. The blogosphere is reciprocal in nature; those who link to other sites are linked to in turn. Bloggers often link to traditional media sites, but many, in response to the anti-deeplinking practices of media sites, are no longer providing those links. The impact of this for most media sites is small, at present. If the amount of traffic on nonmedia sites grows, Web editors may want to reconnect with that network of users. Such a move is advocated by many independent journalists (Dube, 2003). If that occurs, a new preferred attachment principle may create a different pattern in the use of external links.

The "Hubs" of External Linking

The existence of hubs in networks was long ago observed. The value of network theory is that it provides a systematic explanation for the distribution common to so many networks and helps us understand how hubs form. Like the use of links overall, this study found that the use of external links in news stories on the Web also follows a power distribution. A fair question, then, is what types of stories are the "hubs" of external linking? The sample in this study contained one story from 2003 that contained more than 40% of the external links for all stories from that year: 84 external links in all. The story was posted to USNews.com on March 3, 2003 and, like *The New York Times* story mentioned earlier, is presented in blog style with the most recent update at the top. This ongoing story is the "War on Terror" and the latest update concerned the arrest of an al Qaeda suspect in Pakistan. The page provides a series of stories related to the war on terror and links to 34 USNews.com stories. Additionally, it provides external links to raw source material, mostly documents on U.S. government Web sites, 49 in all. There are also links to 14 other media sites that have related stories and 12 links to nonprofit sites such as the ACLU.

News pages such as this one are exceedingly rare, but they do exist. Rather than adding external links to daily news stories, editors appear to favor these "repository" pages that can be added to and reposted to the site as events warrant. The result is a small number of pages with dozens of external links and a large number of pages with few or no external links.

The USNews.com story on terrorism and the NYTimes.com story on the campaign trail share some features that might have resulted in them becoming "hubs" for external linking. Each concerned a topic that had been in the news a lot over the preceding 2 years. Each story was ubiquitous, covered by all news organizations, with little advantage in coverage from one outlet to the next. Each story involved government and related to, potentially, hundreds of government or political Web sites. As Web editors appear to favor U.S. government Web sites to all other types, this provided them with ample material for external linking.

If the patterns documented in this study continue, we can expect a growing percentage of stories that have few or no external links and a simultaneous rise in the number of external links on a very small number of news stories. These stories are likely to be on topics that have been in the news for many months or years and ones involving government.

REFERENCES

Adamic, L. A., & Huberman, B. A. (2001). The Web's hidden order. *Communications of the ACM, 44*(9), 55–60.

Barabasi, A.-L. (2002). *Linked: The new science of networks.* Cambridge, MA: Perseus.

Barabasi, A.-L., & Albert, R. (1999). Emergence of scaling in random networks. *Science, 286,* 509–512.

Barnhurst, K. G., & Mutz, D. (1997). American journalism and the decline in event-centered reporting. *Journal of Communication, 47*(4), 27–53.

Dube, J. (2003). *News sites loosen linking policies.* Retrieved October 28, 2003, from http://www.cyberjournalist.net/news000720.php

Granovetter, M. (1973). The strength of weak ties. *American Journal of Sociology, 78,* 1360–1380.

Lippmann, W. (1922). *Public opinion.* New York: Penguin Books.

McManus, J. H. (1995). *Market driven journalism: Let the citizen beware.* Thousand Oaks, CA: Sage.

Milgram, S. (1967). The small world problem. *Psychology Today, 2.*

Rheingold, H. (1994, June). *The electronic landscape: A writer's perspective.* Paper presented at the Writers Retreat On Interactive Technology and Equipment Conference, University of Vancouver, Vancouver, British Columbia.

Rogers, E. M. (1983). *Diffusion of innovations.* New York: Free Press.

Rosen, J. (1995, August 7). Cheap speech. *The New Yorker,* 75–81.

Schudson, M. (1982). The politics of narrative form: The emergence of news conventions in print and television. *Daedalus, 3*(4).

Tremayne, M. (2004a, August). *News websites as gated cybercommunities.* Paper presented at the annual conference of the Association for Education in Journalism and Mass Communication, Toronto, Canada.

Tremayne, M. (2004b). The Web of context: Applying network theory to the use of hyperlinks in journalism stories on the Web. *Journalism & Mass Communication Quarterly, 81*(2), 237–253.

Watts, D. (1999). Networks, dynamics, and the small-world phenomenon. *The American Journal of Sociology, 105*(2), 493–527.

Watts, D. (2003). *Six degrees: The science of a connected age.* New York: Norton.

Wilcox, R. R. (2001). *Fundamentals of modern statistical methods: Substantially improving power and accuracy.* New York: Springer-Verlag.

4

Web Page Design and News Retrieval Efficiency: A Content Analysis of Five U.S. Internet Newspapers

Xigen Li
Southern Illinois University Carbondale

Most U.S. newspapers publish an Internet version, which provides more content than the original printed edition. Although newspapers feel more comfortable distributing information over the Internet after being online for a couple of years, they are still trying to determine the best way to disseminate information in the Internet environment. Periodic changes in the Web design and the structure of the Internet newspapers reflect the publishers' efforts in exploring a more effective way to provide news information to the Internet audience. For example, *The New York Times* changed the home page of its Internet version from a one-page design to multiple page design, while the *Chicago Tribune* changed the home page of its Internet version from multiple-page design to one-page design at the time of this study. By examining the Web design and the news information retrieval process of five major U.S. newspapers, this chapter explores how Web design of an Internet newspaper can affect information retrieval efficiency. It also attempts to shed some light on the shift of power from publishers to readers in the realm of Internet newspapers due to the new pattern of information distribution.

WEB DESIGN OF INTERNET NEWSPAPERS

In the Internet environment, news information is stored in a computer server for readers to access any time. Whereas technical factors such as a low connection

.e information retrieval, the Web page design of an Internet news-
...ii also generate blocks. A poorly designed Web site may fail to deliver
tne intended information (Kirsner, 1997). Besides external attractiveness, an
efficient retrieval process is the ultimate goal of the publishers (Stone, 2000).
Although publishers have experimented with different styles and formats in their
designs since they created news sites, few have developed a clear and effective
approach through which smooth news information retrieval is easily achieved
(Houston, 1999; Lucia, 1999; Small, 1998). In scholarly research, the effect of
Web design on news information retrieval is an area little explored. Few studies
have addressed how Web design will affect information retrieval efficiency in the
Internet (McMillian, 2000).

There are two dimensions concerning Web design approaches: *presentation*
and *navigation*. There are three basic presentation approaches in Web design:
graphic, textual, and *balanced.* A graphic site could be more visually appealing,
but may also take more time to access. After adopting one of these approaches, the
designers have to decide a method of navigation, that is, how to structure a Web
site for readers to navigate and retrieve information (Fleming & Koman, 1998;
Niederst, 1999; Nielsen, 2000).

Earlier studies looked at the characteristics of media Web sites (Katz, 1994;
Mueller & Kamerer, 1995). More recent studies examined the relationship
between Web sites and news organizations behind them. Tremayne's (1999) study
found newspaper Web sites use fewer links than broadcast news station Web sites.
Gubman and Greer (1997) found that sites associated with larger newspapers
were more likely than sites associated with smaller newspapers to put news on the
first screen, and update frequently. Peng, Irene, and Hao (1999) studied presentation styles of U.S. Web newspapers, and found that national/metropolitan papers
tended to follow the traditional newspaper format, but the majority of local dailies
were more likely to list only the directories of the content. These studies, although
valuable in revealing current status of news Web sites, add little to the theoretical
understanding of the news media on the Internet.

Media practitioners address the issues regarding Web design and its impact on
content retrieval since the early years of the Internet newspaper. Immediate access
to information is one of the key concerns. They call for publishers not to dump
their print versions onto Web sites, but to think creatively and holistically through
the development, creation, and delivery of information. They advise editors to
design a shallow structure online by offering news on the first available screen and
argue immediacy is key in capturing users (Reason, 1995).

A smooth news flow is another aspect desired for the news sites. Veen (1997)
observed that a Web site's front door requires the designer to provide clues about
the site's depth and focus to readers. The Web site creator needs to be aware of
balance between navigation, graphic art, and information display. Siegal (1997)
noted that in the information realm, sites must satisfy impatient, directed visitors.
In a survey conducted by P. Zazz Marketing Company, 62% of respondents said

they feel frustrated when a site takes more than a half a minute to load—and 34.3% said they give up and try an alternate site. Sites with fewer, smaller images and gimmicks received high approval ratings (Erbacher, 1999).

RELATIONSHIP BETWEEN CONTENT AND FORMAT

Few scholarly studies looked at the relationship between content and format of news Web sites. Davenport, Ogundimu, and Bourgeois (1999) study measured the efficiency index. The efficiency of content presentation tests Web site users' perception of userfriendliness, graphic interface, advertiser presence, and informativeness. By compiling the mean scores of this index, the study measures relative rankings of the Web news media based on panel members' judgment. Despite the merit of the index in measuring design efficiency, it does not offer any insight into how news information can be retrieved most efficiently.

Li (1998) examined interconnected links and found the traditional publishing process that one newspaper delivers information to a large audience (one-to-many) turned into a new practice, where newspapers and other organizations and individuals on the Internet disseminate information to audience worldwide facilitated by the host Internet newspapers (many-to-many). With this changing pattern of communication in the Internet, the audience is gaining power of control of media content. However, Li's study only looked at the Web page design and the information structure of three Internet newspapers. It did not address how such Web page design could affect news information retrieval from the reader's side, and how the Web design of the Internet newspapers met audience expectation in retrieving news information and rendered audience more control of power in the Internet.

The interactivity approach in studying Internet newspapers proposed by Massey and Levy (1999) based on Heeter's definition looked at how much control readers get in accessing news information. They proposed an added dimension of interactivity: immediacy. They looked at the presence of a publication date or an "update ticker" on a Web site, and examined the updatedness of news information, but neglected the more important aspect of immediacy: immediate access to information on a Web site, which is the key in solving the problem that both publishers and readers face, that is, how to retrieve news information efficiently from an Internet newspaper.

Change in information control as an issue emerged after news information was delivered through the Internet. O'Keefe (1997) noted that the Web provides a two-edged sword. On the one hand, organizations have a robust media environment in which they can tell their own story in their own words. On the other hand, they cannot control exactly what route individuals will take after they arrive at a Web site. Researchers observe that online journalism empowers the audience. Khoo and Gopal (1996) called this "prosumerism." Dennis (1996) observed that content producers ceded to content consumers the power to control, to varying degrees, their interaction with the news.

Two theoretical models might help understand the process of information distribution in the Internet environment. The New Media Information Flow Model describes how data flow within differing media systems, both traditional and new media (Negroponte, 1995). The Media Transition Model illustrates the relationship between information center and the involving participants in the information distribution process (Bordewijk & van Kaam, 1986). Neither model is able to address the specific issues in the process with which both publishers and readers are more concerned: how to retrieve news information most efficiently from a newspaper Web site. This calls for studies addressing key issues in news information retrieval to amend these two models and expand our understanding on information flow on the Internet and how newspaper Web sites may facilitate the information exchange between senders and receivers.

INFORMATION RETRIEVAL EFFICIENCY

This study examines information retrieval efficiency from Internet newspapers with different Web designs. *Efficiency* is a concept in economics measuring the maximum output from effective inputs (Picard, 1989). It refers to the ability to accomplish a job with a minimum expenditure of time and effort (Random House, 1997). *Efficiency* in this study is defined as the level of easiness, speediness, and smoothness (uninterrupted) in locating and accessing the news information from an Internet newspaper, that is, whether a reader can retrieve the requested information on a news Web site with the least effort in identifying the news items, the fewest steps, and the least amount of time.

According to the literature, a site with immediate access to the requested information through simple and direct navigation is more likely to save readers effort and time, and hence offers higher efficiency. The literature and the two theoretical models also indicate that *immediate access to news information, smoothness of news flow,* and *control over information* on the Internet are three key aspects associated with efficiency. By examining the process of news information retrieval, this study explores the effect of Web designs on news retrieval efficiency. The following three theoretical propositions will be tested:

Proposition 1. The more immediate access to news information through Web design, the higher the level of information retrieval efficiency.

This proposition is based on the assumption that immediate access is the primary concern of Internet newspaper publishers. If the publishers consider immediate access a priority in Web design, as immediate access is the key component of information retrieval efficiency, it will have a positive effect on information retrieval efficiency. A high level of immediate access is likely to lead to a high level of information retrieval efficiency.

Proposition 2. The smoother the news flow, the higher the level of information retrieval efficiency.

This proposition suggests that information retrieval efficiency does not depend only on immediate access to information. Other aspects that make information retrieval smooth also need to be considered to boost information retrieval efficiency. The smooth news flow (available news items, directness, navigation options, and loading time) and the amount of information retrievable are also essential aspects associated with efficiency in information retrieval.

Proposition 3. The higher the level of information retrieval efficiency, the easier access to information for readers in the Internet environment.

This proposition reflects readers gaining control over the way that information is accessed in the Internet. It connects the trend of Web page design for Internet newspapers and the shift of power from publisher to readers in the Internet environment. As the publishers try to improve Web design for smooth information dissemination and adopt a user-centered approach in delivering information in the Internet, the Internet newspapers offer readers more control over the information retrievable at the Web site. Whereas the Media Transition Model and previous studies identified the shift of power from publisher to readers in general in the Internet, this proposition specifies how an Internet newspaper demonstrates such gradual shift through an efficient Web design.

By measuring the process to retrieve news information from newspapers with different Web designs, this study also tries to answer the following research questions:

1. What home page design approach achieves the highest efficiency of news retrieval?
2. What story page design approach achieves the highest efficiency of news retrieval?
3. How does news flow produced through different Web designs affect efficiency of news retrieval?
4. Which design approach leads to the highest efficiency of news retrieval?

METHOD

Content analysis was used to analyze the elements of the Web design and news information retrieval process. Two national newspapers, *The Washington Post* and *USA Today,* and three metropolitan newspapers, the *Chicago Tribune,* the

Los Angeles Times, and *The Boston Globe,* were selected for study. A total of 10 days of publication (April 14 through April 23, 1999) of these newspapers on their respective Web sites was studied. These particular newspapers were chosen for several reasons. They disperse across three presentation design approaches: graphic, textual, and balanced. They are among a few scores of the earliest U.S. dailies that published on the Internet and have gone through experiments to improve their Web design; these papers have the resources to hire professional Web designers to create and maintain updated Web sites; they are somewhat geographically representative.

This study was conducted through a computer lab-based content analysis. The researcher examined the process to identify and access two stories from three sections in each newspaper: Top News, National, and World. During the 10 continuous days, a total of 300 news items from five newspaper sites was identified and the process to access these items was coded. Newspaper Web design remains stable over a period of time. A relatively small sample is usually sufficient to catch the essence of Web design (Li, 1998). The unit of study is one day's publication of news content by a newspaper. The recording unit is the Web page component including graphics, news items, hyperlinks, and elements of Web design such as number of screens needed to display a home page, file size and loading time of the home page and a story page, and steps to access news stories.

News retrieval efficiency is measured by recording the options available for readers to select news items, steps to access a news story, time needed to retrieve the content of a story, and the amount of information retrieved through certain steps and during a certain period of time. The efficiency score of home page, first screen, second screen, story page, and news flow was measured by aggregating the standardized score of the related Web design components. News retrieval efficiency score was calculated by adding up efficiency scores of key aspects of Web design (see tables following).

To ensure the objectivity of measurement, Doctor HTML (1999a) was used. Doctor HTML is a Web page analysis tool that retrieves a Web page with a specific URL and reports the properties of that specific page. It standardizes the retrieving process and the measurement. The primary focus of this tool is to provide a clear and comprehensive report of information relating to a Web page for the purpose of improvement.

Doctor HTML measured the text and graphic file sizes (in kilobytes) of a specific page, and the time (in seconds) needed to download the home page and a story page over a standard modem connection that Doctor HTML selected. Doctor HTML selected 28.8k bps (bauds per second) as a standard measure of the amount of information transmitted across the computer network through a modem over a certain period of time. The actual time needed to download a page or a picture under different connection speed is converted to this standard measure. It is considered a better measure of the image's size than other standards because it is directly related to the user's experience (Doctor HTML, 1999b). The content was measured using a 17" monitor, Netscape browser, and 800 by 600 resolution.

Two coders participated in the coding. Ten percent of the coding content was used for intercoder reliability check. The coding of news content was conducted according to the prescribed procedures by Riffe, Lacy, and Fico (1998). Scott's Pi was used to test the intercoder reliability for nominal variables; Pearson's correlation coefficient was selected for ratio variables. The result of the test showed that intercoder reliability ranged from .90 to .99 for nominal variables, and .86 to .99 for ratio variables. The remaining content of Web publication of five newspapers was coded by one of the coders after satisfactory intercoder reliability was established.

FINDINGS

Home Page Efficiency (Table 4.1)

The newspaper with the highest home page efficiency score (62) was the *Chicago Tribune*. The *Chicago Tribune* had a one-page design for its home page, which earned it the highest score for home page screen number. It also had the smallest text file size. These two elements helped reduce the loading time of the home page. Even though the home page of the *Chicago Tribune* was highly graphic, its one-screen design reduced the graphic file size of the home page to that close to the *Los Angeles Times*, the newspaper with the lowest graphic file size for its home page.

The next newspaper was the *Los Angeles Times* with a home page efficiency score of 60. The *Los Angeles Times* earned the second highest home page efficiency score with its three-screen home page and low graphic and text size. These three

TABLE 4.1
Home Page News Retrieval Efficiency of the Five Internet Newspapers

Newspaper	Screen Number	News Item	Load Time	Graph File	Text File	Efficiency Score
The Washington Post	4.5	13	66	67	49	46
USA Today	5.5	10	110	173	52	31
Chicago Tribune	1	6	33	56	2	62
LA Times	3	11	51	55	36	60
The Boston Globe	4.5	10	70	91	33	45
Total average	3.7	10	66	88	34	49

Note. Home Page Efficiency score is a standardized measure of the Web page components containing five items of the average page component properties with a scale raging from 1 to 100. Load time is measured in seconds, graphic file size in kilobytes, and text file size in kilobytes.

elements reduced the loading time. The home page design did not sacrifice the amount of information delivered through the home page. The *Los Angeles Times* provided 10 news items on its home page, the second among all five newspapers.

The newspaper that earned the lowest home page efficiency score (31) is *USA Today*. *USA Today* had a home page with 5.5 screens and a graphic design with a graphic file size of 173 kilobytes. Its home page had a total loading time of 110 seconds. Although its home page text size was also the largest among the five newspapers, it provided only six news items on its home page.

First Screen Efficiency (Table 4.2)

The newspaper that earned the highest first screen efficiency score (70) was *The Washington Post,* having the highest number of news item and section links on the left side on its first screen. Although its image size was relatively large, it provided more navigating images on its first screen. The amount of information and the choice for information on its first screen earned *The Washington Post* the highest first screen efficiency score.

The newspaper that scored the next highest with a score of 53 was *USA Today*. Although *USA Today* was the most graphic newspaper among the five, the image size of its first screen did not run too large with its 27 square inches. Its first screen 20-section links also helped boost efficiency score. The newspaper that earned the lowest first screen efficiency score (40) was *The Boston Globe*. *The Boston Globe* offered fewer choices for its readers on its first screen. It had only 2.5 news items, and 11.6 section links. Its image size was low, and it also had fewer navigating images.

Second Screen Efficiency (Table 4.3)

The newspaper that earned the highest second screen efficiency score of 66 was the *Los Angeles Times*. It provided the highest number of news items and navigating images on its second screen, while keeping the image size the lowest.

The newspaper with the next highest second screen efficiency score (58) was *The Washington Post*. It had the highest number of section links. Even though its second screen image size was high, the relatively large number of news items on the second screen balanced against the graphic elements. The newspaper that earned the lowest second screen efficiency score (54) was *USA Today*. Its second screen was not as graphic as its first screen, but had relatively few news links. This translated into few choices for readers.

Story Page Efficiency (Table 4.4)

The newspaper that earned the highest story page efficiency score (58) was *The Boston Globe*. It offered relatively few steps to access a news story, and its story

TABLE 4.2
First Screen News Retrieval Efficiency of the Five Internet Newspapers

Newspaper	News Item	Section Link	Navigate Image	Image Size	News Link	Efficiency Score
The Washington Post	7	20.7	3.4	31.4	6.7	70
USA Today	3.1	20.3	3.2	27.1	3	53
Chicago Tribune	5.9	9.8	0.3	52	6.1	42
LA Times	3.9	7.7	3.3	29.1	3.8	48
The Boston Globe	2.5	11.6	2.2	27.8	2.4	40
Total average	4.48	14.02	2.48	33.48	4.4	51

Note. Screen Efficiency score is a standardized measure of the Web page components containing five items of the average Web page component properties with a scale raging from 1 to 100. Image size is measured in square inches.

TABLE 4.3
Second Screen Efficiency of News Retrieval of the Five Internet Newspapers

Newspaper	News Item	Section Link	Navigate Image	Image Size	News Link	Efficiency Score
The Washington Post	6.3	20.4	1	6.8	7.2	58
USA Today	6.4	12.5	1.1	3.9	6.1	54
Chicago Tribune	0	0	0	0	0	0
LA Times	7.2	4.2	2.5	2.6	7.3	66
The Boston Globe	7.3	14.8	1	4.7	7.4	57
Total average	5.44	10.4	1.12	3.6	5.6	47

TABLE 4.4
Story Page Efficiency of News Retrieval of the Five Internet Newspapers
(*N* = 300)

Newspaper	Access Steps	News Flow	Load Time	Graph File	Text File	Word Number	Efficiency Score
The Washington Post	1.60	74.17	48.40	57.42	18.47	953.27	57
USA Today	1.12	40.83	42.75	52.05	22.53	334.57	47
Chicago Tribune	1.87	76.25	42.55	37.52	37.28	777.42	53
LA Times	1.55	57.92	37.25	39.25	26.18	621.58	52
The Boston Globe	1.57	67.50	32.95	39.17	18.35	592.95	58
Total average	1.54	63.33	40.78	45.08	24.56	655.96	53

page graphic size was among the lowest. It provided a reasonable amount of information measured by number of words for each story, yet it required the least time to access a news story. Yet, most of the stories with full text could be accessed more directly through fewer steps.

The newspaper that earned the second highest story page efficiency score (57) was *The Washington Post*. Although it had the highest graphic size and the highest loading time, its more direct news flow and the amount of information measured by number of words with very small text size earned it the second place in story page efficiency score. The newspaper that earned the lowest story page efficiency score (47) was *USA Today*. It had the fewest access steps, but the stories were mostly in the abstract format or presented indirectly. Its graphics size on the story page was high, whereas the amount of information was low measured by number of words.

News Flow (Table 4.5)

News flow measures available news items, directness, access steps, and story in full text or abstract. The newspaper that earned the highest news flow score (62) was *The Washington Post*. It had the highest number of first screen news items and headlines on the home page leading to stories. *The Washington Post* had the second highest story flow score, which indicated that most of the stories were presented directly from the first layer of the site, that is, on the home page or on the section page with full text.

The newspaper with the second highest news flow score (58) was *The Boston Globe*. The number of stories available through the second page and the images leading to news stories helped *The Boston Globe* earn a high news flow score. The newspaper with the lowest news flow score (43) was the *Chicago Tribune*. Its one-screen design saved space on the screen, but offered fewer choices for readers to select news information and required more steps to access a news story. It did

TABLE 4.5
News Flow of the Five Internet Newspapers ($N = 300$)

Newspaper	1st Screen News	2nd Screen	Image to Text	Headline to Text	Access Steps	Story Flow	News Flow
The Washington Post	7	6.3	1.1	11	1.60	74.17	62
USA Today	3.1	6.4	1.9	6	1.12	40.83	52
Chicago Tribune	5.9	0	1.0	6	1.87	76.25	43
LA Times	3.9	7.2	1.4	10	1.55	57.92	56
The Boston Globe	2.5	7.3	2.1	9	1.57	67.50	58
Total average	4.48	5.44	1.32	8	1.54	63.33	54

Note. News flow score is a standardized measure of Web page design elements containing six items of the average news flow properties with a scale ranging from 1 to 100.

offer more news items on the first screen, but the absence of news items available through the second screen lowered its total news flow score.

Total Efficiency (Table 4.6)

The newspaper that earned the highest news retrieval efficiency score (59) was *The Washington Post*. Its multiple-screen home page design did not earn it high home page efficiency, but it excelled in first screen efficiency, story efficiency, and news flow.

The newspaper that earned the second highest news retrieval efficiency score (56.4) was the *Los Angeles Times*. It had the highest second page efficiency score, and the second highest home page efficiency score and news flow score. The newspaper that had the lowest news retrieval efficiency score (40) was the *Chicago Tribune*. Its home page efficiency was the highest among the five newspapers with its one-screen design, but it fell short in its first screen efficiency and news flow.

Propositions on News Retrieval Efficiency.   The first proposition that the more immediate access to news information through news site design, the higher level of information retrieval efficiency did not get full support from this study. Whereas some newspapers with higher levels of immediate access also scored high in their total efficiency, immediate access did not necessarily lead to higher levels of efficiency because other aspects of Web design, such as news flow and amount of information available, might affect the total efficiency in information retrieval. The finding suggests that although immediate access is important in measuring information retrieval efficiency, other aspects in the process should also be carefully examined to determine the level of efficiency.

The second proposition that the smoother (news items available, directness, navigation options, and quick-loading) the news flow, the higher level of efficiency in information retrieval is supported by the findings. The consideration of Web

TABLE 4.6
News Information Retrieval Efficiency of the Five Internet Newspapers ($N = 300$)

Newspaper	Home Page	1st Screen	2nd Screen	Story Page	News Flow	News Retrieval
The Washington Post	46	70	58	57	62	58.6
USA Today	31	53	54	47	52	47.4
Chicago Tribune	62	42	0	53	43	40.0
LA Times	60	48	66	52	56	56.4
The Boston Globe	45	40	57	58	58	51.6
Total average	49	51	47	53	54	50.8

Note. News retrieval efficiency score is the average of the efficiency scores of newspaper Web page components containing five items with a scale ranging from 1 to 100.

design that leads to directness in getting a fair amount of news stories, navigation easiness, and quick loading of news content greatly boosts the total efficiency score. Those newspapers that did well in creating a smooth news flow achieved a higher level of total efficiency. The findings suggest that measuring news flow with indicators besides immediate access provides more accurate assessment of information retrieval efficiency in Internet newspapers.

The third proposition that the higher the level of information retrieval efficiency, the easier access to information for readers in the Internet environment is supported by the findings of this study. The newspapers with a higher level of retrieval efficiency were more likely to offer readers more choices and a larger volume of information while demanding less time for information retrieval. The components of information retrieval efficiency covered a variety of aspects of an effective Web site. All of them were connected to the ultimate goal of a newspaper Web site, to facilitate users to access information easily and efficiently. The newspaper that excelled in information retrieval efficiency offered a user-centered environment for readers to access news information with the least effort.

DISCUSSION

The examination of the Web design elements and news information retrieving process of five newspapers reveals that no newspaper was superior in all aspects of retrieval efficiency. Each design approach had its own advantages and disadvantages for news information retrieval. The newspaper that offered more choices for information retrieval or a larger amount of information with least consumption of retrieval time earned the highest news retrieval efficiency score.

The *Chicago Tribune* was the best in home page efficiency (63) comparing to *USA Today* (27). But it had the lowest first screen efficiency score, news flow score, and total news retrieval efficiency score. *The Washington Post* was not visually eye-catching with its Web design. However, because it offered more choices for the reader to retrieve information as well as the largest amount of information with the news stories retrieved, it earned the highest news retrieval efficiency score. *USA Today* looked appealing at first glance for its relatively graphic design. But the longer loading time and less noticeable effort for news retrieval efficiency earned it the second lowest news retrieval efficiency score along with the lowest home page efficiency score and story page efficiency score. The *Los Angeles Times* might be considered a more acceptable model. It did not earn the highest news retrieval score among the five newspapers, but it excelled in several of the aspects that this study examined. It had the second highest news retrieval efficiency as well as the highest second screen efficiency and the second highest home page efficiency.

The findings of the study supplement The New Media Information Flow Model (Bordewijk & van Kaam, 1986) regarding information distribution in the Internet environment. The study shows information flow on newspaper Web sites is not just decided by how much information the publishers distributed, but also decided by how efficient information retrieval is set up with an appropriate Web design. Without an efficient way of information retrieval, the news information that the publishers intend to deliver within the media system on the Internet may actually be blocked, ignored, or staled due to lack of immediate delivery. Web design becomes a critical chain in creating a smooth news flow on the Internet.

This study offered ample data regarding the propositions on news retrieval efficiency. The first proposition regarding the role of immediate access to news information through Web design was clarified with the test result. Immediate access interacted with other factors in influencing news retrieval efficiency. Immediate access means fewer steps to access a news story. It was also measured by how many stories and how much information in a story could be accessed through fewest steps and least amount of time. By providing more stories and more information in a story a Web site boosted its level of immediate access. However, it might also slow down the speed to access the news information and affect news flow of a Web site. Immediate access to information is one of the most important indicators in Web design of the Internet newspapers. It will help boost news retrieval efficiency if it works effectively with other factors in Web design.

Support of the second proposition regarding the effect of a smooth news flow on news retrieval efficiency reveals that a smooth news flow played a decisive role in news retrieval efficiency. Smooth news flow includes directness in getting a fair amount of news items, navigation options, and loading time of news content. The news retrieval efficiency is realized through access to each story. An efficient Web site is composed of news stories that can be retrieved easily and directly. The finding suggests, when constructing a newspaper Web site, making more efforts in creating a smooth news flow is likely to generate high return in news retrieval efficiency and make the site more effective in delivering information.

The support of the third proposition indicates that news retrieval efficiency is the foundation of easy access to news information of the Internet newspapers. News retrieval efficiency is a relatively complex measure. It contains various aspects of how a newspaper Web site delivers information and facilitates users to access information. By examining the components of news retrieval efficiency, this study found that the main consequence that news retrieval efficiency brought to Internet communication is choices and freedom of readers in accessing information from the Internet newspapers. As news retrieval efficiency is a measure based on readers' expectation when they visit a news Web site, the level of news retrieval efficiency provides an adequate indicator of the power growth on the readers' side. As news information retrieval efficiency increases with the improvement of Web design, the user-centered Web sites of newspapers demonstrate a clear trend of power shift from publisher to audience as described in The Media Transition Model (Negroponte, 1995). Although some publishers may not be willing to give up total control of media content on the Internet, the unique environment of the

Internet communication and the requirements for effective delivery of and access to information on the Internet newspapers make the power shift from senders to receivers inevitable.

This study offers some insight on the relationship between Web design and news information retrieval. It makes important contributions to the understanding of the Internet newspapers and provides empirical evidence of the power shift from senders to receivers of information as Internet newspapers offer more freedom and easier access to new information that allows readers to control what to get and how to get it. This study makes a considerable contribution in the way of measuring news retrieval efficiency, the main property in evaluating the effectiveness of a newspaper Web site. First, the study creates a comprehensive measure of news retrieval efficiency and tests the propositions regarding news retrieval efficiency with ample data. The measurement initiated in this study could be used by both practitioners and scholars in their study of newspapers' Web sites. Second, the measurement of news retrieval efficiency went beyond the conventional content analysis. By introducing Doctor HTML, the process of measuring the key components of news retrieval efficiency became dynamic. Instead of looking only at what appeared on a computer screen, Doctor HTML looked at a live URL and provided data on a live Web site as the site was actually run. It measured the properties that could not be measured by just looking at the Web site on a computer screen, such as text and graphic file size and the loading time of a page and a story. The dynamic measurement of the properties of a Web site provided a more accurate and reliable assessment for further analysis of newspaper Web design and effectiveness of information delivery.

However, the significance of the findings is limited by the scope of the study and the limited literature that this study could be based on. Although this study tried to examine the aspects most essential to information retrieval efficiency, we still don't know the critical level of choices judged by readers. More choices to readers may indicate the power on the readers' side and earn a higher efficiency score. It could also exceed the critical level and reduce readers' power and efficiency by overwhelming them. Although a computer-lab-based content analysis is valuable for providing an objective measurement, an experimental study on the information retrieval process with distinctive designs will tell us more about an audience's perspective on Web design and the factors that play a role in the process.

The shift of power from publisher to audience reflected in the information delivery of the Internet newspapers was confirmed by this study through increasingly accessible newspaper Web sites. However, the content analysis only explored one dimension of the issue: to what degree Internet newspapers offered readers more options and easy access to news information. A survey of publishers may reveal to what degree their effort in improving Web design really reflects their intent to accommodate audience expectation and their yield of power to audience. A study of Internet newspaper readers will explain whether such power shift is perceived by the audience and how the audience's behavior in using the media will change accordingly.

CONCLUSION

This study addresses a problem that both publishers and readers of Internet newspapers face: efficiency of news information retrieval affected by Web design of the Internet newspapers. The findings of the study indicate that there is no one set model for Web design of all Internet newspapers. News information retrieval efficiency can be achieved by different design approaches. The newspaper that earned the highest efficiency score provides a high level of immediate access to news information and a smooth news flow. The findings suggest that whereas some of the news sites look more visually appealing, they might not be more efficient for readers to retrieve news information. As the efficiency of news retrieval is measured by several aspects of Web design of a newspaper site, the Internet newspapers need to consider the critical factors in Web design such as immediate access to news information and a smooth news flow to achieve news information retrieval efficiency.

The findings regarding information retrieval efficiency of Internet newspaper add to our understanding of new media information flow and confirm that news readers are gaining more control in the Internet environment as the concern for user-centered efficiency of news retrieval is integrated into the Web design of the Internet newspapers. The shift of power from publishers to audience is proceeding in the Internet as the user-centered efficiency increases with improving Web designs, although this shift is taking place gradually.

ACKNOWLEDGMENTS

An earlier version of this chapter was published in *Newspaper Research Journal, 23*(1), Winter 2002. Reprinted with permission.

REFERENCES

Bordewijk, J. L., & van Kaam, B. (1986). Towards a new classification of tele-information services. *Intermedia, 14,* 16–21.

Davenport, L., Ogundimu, F., & Bourgeois, S. (1999). *Website userfriedliness and graphics don't always correlate with informativeness and credibility.* East Lansing: Michigan State University.

Dennis, E. E. (1996). Values and value-added for the new electronic journalism: Public debate and the democratic dialogue. *Media Asia, 23,* 107–110.

Doctor HTML. (1999a). *Doctor HTML, Quality assessment for the Web.* Retrieved May 16, 2004, from http://www2.imagiware.com/RxHTML

Doctor HTML. (1999b). *Image analysis explanation.* Retrieved May 16, 2004, from http://www .doctor-html.com/RxHTML/cgi-bin/ssi.cgi?l=ImageAnalysis.html#Time

Erbacher, J. (1999). *Waiting for the Web doors to open.* Retrieved May 16, 2004, from http://www .ebookhelper.com/Article10.html

Fleming, J., & Koman, R. (1998). *Web navigation: Designing the user experience.* Beijing, China, & Sebastopol, CA: O'Reilly.

Gubman, J., & Greer, J. (1997, July 30–Aug. 2). *An analysis of online sites produced by U.S. news-papers: Are the critics right?* Paper presented at the Association for Education in Journalism and Mass Communication, Chicago.

Houston, F. (1999, July/Aug). What I saw in the digital sea. *Columbia Journalism Review, 138,* 34–37.

Katz, J. (1994, September). Online or not, newspapers still suck. *Wired,* 50.

Khoo, D., & Gopal, R. (1996, June). Implications of the Internet on print and electronic media. *Journal of Development Communication, 29.*

Kirsner, S. (1997, July). Web of confusion. *American Journalism Review, 19,* 34–39.

Li, X. (1998). Web page design and graphic use of three U.S. newspapers. *Journalism and Mass Communication Quarterly, 75*(2), 353–365.

Lucia, M. (1999, April 10). Papers ponder how to integrate Web sites. *Editor & Publisher, 132,* 28–29.

Massey, B. L., & Levy, M. R. (1999). Interactivity, online journalism and English-language Web newspapers in Asia. *Journalism & Mass Communication Quarterly, 76*(1), 139.

McMillian, S. (2000). The microscope and the moving target: The challenge of applying content analysis to the World Wide Web. *Journalism and Mass Communication Quarterly, 77*(1), 80–98.

Mueller, J., & Kamerer, D. (1995). Reader preference for electronic newspapers. *Newspaper Research Journal, 16*(3), 2–13.

Negroponte, N. (1995). *Being digital* (1st ed.). New York: Knopf.

Niederst, J. (1999). *Web design in a nutshell: A desktop quick reference* (1st ed.). Beijing, China, & Sebastopol, CA: O'Reilly.

Nielsen, J. (2000). *Designing Web usability: The practice of simplicity.* Indianapolis, IN: New Riders.

O'Keefe, S. (1997). *Publicity on the Internet: Creating successful publicity campaigns on the Internet and the commercial online services.* New York: Wiley.

Peng, F. Y., Irene, N., & Hao, X. (1999). Trends in online newspapers: A look at the U.S. Web. *Newspaper Research Journal, 20*(2), 52–63.

Picard, R. G. (1989). *Media economics: Concepts and issues.* Newbury Park, CA: Sage.

Random House. (1997). *Random House Webster's college dictionary* (2nd ed.). New York: Author.

Reason, R. (1995). *A call for new thinking for the new media.* Available from Poynter Online, http:// www. poynter.org

Riffe, D., Lacy, S., & Fico, F. (1998). *Analyzing media messages: Using quantitative content analysis in research.* Mahwah, NJ: Lawrence Erlbaum Associates.

Siegel, D. (1997). *Creating killer Web sites: The art of third-generation site design* (2nd ed.). Indianapolis, IN: Hayden Books.

Small, J. (1998, March). The perfect size for an opening home page: Field reports and the latest survey results. *Editor & Publisher,* 20–21.

Stone, M. L. (2000, June 12). Getting 'real' in redesigns. *Editor & Publisher, 133,* 124–127.

Tremayne, M. (1999, May). *Use of nonlinear storytelling on news Web sites.* Paper presented at the International Communication Association, San Francisco.

Veen, J. (1997). *HotWired style: Principles for building smart Web sites* (1st ed.). San Francisco: Wired, Publishers Group West.

5

Functional Alternatives in Obtaining News Online: An Experimental Study of Three U.S. Internet Newspapers

Xigen Li
Southern Illinois University Carbondale

After being online for 9 years, the publishers of Internet newspapers are more comfortable in constructing a visually appealing Web site and putting news content online according to their perceptions of what a news Web site should be (Lowrey, 1999). The technology developed for presenting information on the Web provides more dynamic ways in distributing news content online. However, whether their efforts in creating a Web site to distribute news information really match audiences' expectation and receive positive response, and whether a specific approach to deliver news information really facilitates news retrieval from a user's perspective remain questions mostly unanswered. A clear understanding of the factors that produce an effective news Web site is indispensable to improve news delivery and accessibility of news content on the Internet.

One key issue in Web creation and information distribution on the Internet is whether the information can be retrieved efficiently, that is, whether a reader of an Internet newspaper can get news content from a Web site with the least effort, shortest path, and least time. This study examines the factors that affect information retrieval efficiency of newspaper sites with different design approaches. Based on a lab experiment in retrieving news items from three newspapers distinctive in their Web design, this study examines to what degree the design approaches the three newspapers adopted in delivering news content affected information access by readers. It also tries to answer whether presentation style, visual appeal, and time a reader spends in retrieving news items affect the information retrieval efficiency of newspaper Web sites.

KEY CONCERNS IN NEWSPAPER WEB DESIGN

Professionals working in newspaper Web design started to explore different approaches in 1994. Lowrey (1999) noted the most acceptable pattern comes from print newspaper design. There are few if any rigid conventions for reading or designing Internet news. Fredin (1997) contended journalists and users are borrowing from schemas used to process linear print news. Immediate access to information, simplicity, and ease of navigation are the key concerns of many Web designers. Richmond (1995) specified that good Web sites design with the concern on "how easy it is to navigate, how long it takes for content to display on the screen and how concise and compelling the content is" (p. 167). Abels, White, and Hahn (1998) suggested a simple graphic design. Reason (1995) advised editors to design a shallow structure online by offering news on the first available screen. Newhagen and Levy (1997) identified the role of editors as pathfinders on the Internet to guide readers through the complex environment.

Few scholarly studies looked at the issues regarding Web design of newspaper sites and how it facilitated readers' access to news information. In a study of user preference of online newspapers, Chyi and Lasorsa (1999) found that 75% of Web users preferred the printed newspaper, but failed to address what users actually prefer from newspaper Web sites. Katz and Aspden (1997) found Internet users cited complicated design and difficult navigation as "the least attractive aspects of the Internet" (p. 180). Several researchers (Ramsay, Barbesi, & Preece, 1998) found that users will not return to sites in which they must wait to download large graphics. Fredin and David (1998) found that users with high self-efficacy will lower their level of achievement when they encounter obstacles in exploring news sites.

Other researchers addressed more specific issues regarding Internet newspapers. Li (1998) examined graphic use in three Internet newspapers and found that the Internet newspapers gave more priority to textual information than to graphic information. Li's (2000) study of news information retrieval from five Internet newspapers suggests Web sites with different presentation styles and navigation structures produce variations in news retrieval efficiency. In a study by User Interface Engineering, the researchers found that the flashier sites with more graphics and animation and less text scored lowest in usability (Spool et al., 1997).

From in-depth interviews with the creative designers of four key news sites and the literature review, Lowrey (1999) compiled a list of recommendations for the designers of news Web sites to consider. Among the recommendations, he noted that newspaper Web sites should be designed with the technological limitation of the users in mind. Most of the recommendations point to one goal: design for efficient retrieval. *Efficiency* is a concept in economics measuring the maximum output from effective inputs (Picard, 1989). Li (2000) defined *efficiency of news retrieval* as the level of easiness, speediness, and smoothness (uninterrupted) in locating and accessing the news information from an Internet newspaper. Li measured efficiency of news retrieval through a combination of content analysis and a standardized Web page analysis tool (Doctor HTML, 1999).

Summarizing all the demanding features of an efficient Web site, news retrieval efficiency contains the following aspects: easiness to navigate, easiness to locate information, immediate access (fewer hierarchies and steps), speediness, smoothness (even, uninterrupted path), and overall control of information-retrieving process. One of the major factors affecting retrieval efficiency is *presentation style*, whether a site is balanced between graphic and textual, that is, graphic elements and textual information are properly weighted to offer easy access to news information. Another factor is *visual appeal*, which integrates page layout and use of type and graphic elements to produce a high level of visible attractiveness. This study examines how these two design factors affect news information retrieval.

USES AND GRATIFICATIONS AND ALTERNATIVE COMMUNICATION CHANNELS

Some researchers tried to use theoretical approaches to study communication process of the Internet newspaper (Singer, 1998). Williams, Strover, and Grant (1994) suggested that perspectives such as uses and gratifications could help us understand relationships among people and technologies. Drawing on the uses and gratifications perspective in mass communication research, Eighmey and McCord (1998) examined the audience experience associated with five commercial Web sites.

Uses and gratifications theory provides an explanation for changes in media use patterns following adoption of a new communication technology (Morris & Ogan, 1996). People select media based on the gratification they expect. Gratifications have been conceptualized as the utilities that explain media choice by consumers (Dimmick, 1993). Media choice depends on people's experience with and perceptions about how well different communication channels can fill various needs (Becker & Shoenbach, 1989). People's perceptions about the utility of different media are influenced by attributes of the media themselves, especially characteristic content and modes of transmission (Adoni, 1985; Salomon, 1984). Communication channels based on new technology, which can fill similar communication needs and may have similar types of content, if with more utility, are most likely to displace the alternatives with fewer utilities (Anderson & Collins, 1988; Perse & Courtright, 1993).

The alternative communication channels that have been explored in previous studies were television versus newspapers (Finn, 1997; Salomon, 1984), cable versus television (Perse & Courtright, 1993; Sparkes & Kang, 1986), more recently, computer and World Wide Web versus television (Coffey & Stipp, 1997; Ferguson & Perse, 2000), and e-mail versus telephone (Dimmick, Kline, & Stafford, 2000). Whereas most of the scholars looked at the issues regarding channels based on different media, few paid attention to the issues within the medium. Uses and gratifications perspective can be applied not only to cross-media studies, but also to intramedium inquiry, if the different formats of the medium offer a variation of utility and make one the alternative of the other. For example, information delivery through e-mail and World Wide Web goes through two channels within the platform of a computer and they have different levels of utility.

The print newspapers published in different markets are rarely alternative communication channels competing against each other unless they are easily accessible to audiences in different markets. Newspapers published on the Internet change the scenario, because they are available to audiences in all markets. The variety of options and easy access to news information through different Web designs creates alternatives for the audience to make a selection in their information-seeking process. The technical attributes of a computer have an impact on how people use the medium (Steinfield, Dutton, & Kovaric, 1989). The Internet newspapers offer readers a different level of utility through their special features and formats. People will select from among the functional alternatives (Palmgreen, Wenner, & Rayburn, 1981; Rayburn, Palmgreen, & Acker, 1984).

Palmgreen and Rayburn (1985) have reformulated uses and gratifications theory as centrally having to do with an increment of valued satisfactions obtained relative to an original expectation, and developed an expectancy-value model of media gratifications sought and obtained. The model expresses the proposition that media use is accounted for by a combination of perception of benefits offered by the medium and the differential value attached to these benefits. The model distinguishes between expectation (gratification sought or GS) and satisfactions (gratification obtained or GO). Where GO has a noticeably higher value than GS, higher audience satisfaction and high ratings of appreciation and attention are anticipated (McQuail, 1984). The theory was applied to medium, program, and content, and had some success in explaining the motives of audience in seeking gratifications from media, such as television news (Palmgreen, 1981).

This study attempts to apply functional alternative perspective in uses and gratifications theory and the expectancy-value model to examine user expectation and evaluation of newspaper Web design and information access. According to functional alternative perspective and expectancy-value model, a newspaper Web site with a user-centered design approach that facilitates information access is more likely to be considered as efficient and receive high ratings from users. Assuming readers have access to the newspaper sites with different design approaches and they maintain a constant level of gratification sought, of the sites with similar news content, the site with the highest obtained value measured in retrieval efficiency will provide higher utilities and reward to meet users' expectation. The site is more likely to become a functional alternative to the similar sites and is likely to draw users' repeated visits to seek news information.

Based on uses and gratifications theory and the expectancy-value model, the effect of three key factors in Web design—presentation style, visual appeal, and time spent on news retrieval efficiency—is examined. The following hypotheses are proposed and will be tested.

H1: *Presentation style* is likely to be associated with retrieval efficiency.

Presentation style can be categorized as graphic, balanced, and textual. According to the literature, a highly graphic Web site is likely to slow down news retrieval and thus lower the information retrieval efficiency. It is expected that presentation style affects retrieval efficiency, and a relatively balanced site is associated with higher news retrieval efficiency.

H2: *Visual appeal* of a news site is likely to be associated with retrieval efficiency.

Because visual appeal integrates page layout, use of type, and graphic elements, a site with high visual appeal usually makes it easy for the readers to process and access news information through its coherent visual elements. As Internet newspapers try to achieve a high level of visual appeal, their efforts are likely to produce higher ratings of information retrieval efficiency.

H3: *Time spent to get news items* is negatively correlated with retrieval efficiency.

A Web site designed with user expectations for efficient retrieval is likely to require less time for the users to retrieve news items. It is expected that users will give a site higher rating if they spend less time to obtain the news information they seek.

H4: The *distinctive Web designs* of the three Internet newspapers are likely to produce significant difference in news retrieval efficiency.

The three newspapers selected are distinctive in structuring the news content, presenting information, and setting the navigation path. Although they present similar news content for the users to access, the distinctive design approaches differentiate the newspapers from each other in news retrieval efficiency composed of the demanding features of an effective Web site.

METHOD

Web Design of Three Internet Newspapers

A computer lab-based experiment was conducted to test effect of Web design approach on news retrieval efficiency. Three major U.S. newspapers, *The Washington Post, USA Today,* and the *Chicago Tribune* were selected for study for several reasons. They were distinctive in their presentation style. *USA Today* was relatively more graphic than other newspapers, the *Chicago Tribune* used the fewest graphics among the three, and *The Washington Post* was somewhere in between on its home page, and more textual on its story pages. Each newspaper structured its news content in a unique way for the users to get information. *USA Today* offered many links on its home page and extended the page to a total of six screens. *The Washington Post* also offered many links but limited its home page to three screens. Without too many graphics but looser text links, the *Chicago Tribune* extended its home pages to more than six screens. The three Internet newspapers met the criteria that construct the levels of the independent variable, newspaper design approach.

Other reasons in selecting these papers were: They were among a few scores of the earliest U.S. dailies that published on the Internet. Through years of publishing on the Internet, they became more established with their special features in Web design. Their Web sites were carefully maintained and updated regularly. All three newspapers went through experiments to improve their Web design. For example, the *Chicago Tribune* changed from its one-screen home page design to a multiple screen home page in mid-1999.

Subjects

A total of 115 students enrolled in a communication course at a southern U.S. university participated in the experiment as an in-class assignment. Fifty-five of the students were enrolled in Fall 1999, and the other 60 students were enrolled in Fall 2000. The students ranged from sophomore to senior. The course was a popular elective for non-communication majors. About one third of the participants were non-communication majors from a variety of academic areas on campus.

Research Design and Procedures

The one-way random-effect analysis of variance for a repeated measure was employed to test the hypotheses (Slater, 1991). The independent variables included newspaper design approach, presentation style, visual appeal, and time spent to get news. Newspaper design approach is the repeated measure with three levels. Each level was represented by the overall design of one Internet newspaper. The researcher exposes the same subjects to three Web design situations. The subjects retrieved news items from three newspapers with distinctive designs. The effects of the different situations appear as variations within the same person's performance rather than as differences between groups of people. Each subject acts as his or her own control, thus the design is considered quite sensitive to detecting treatment differences (Wimmer & Dominick, 2000).

The experiment was conducted in a computer lab with 18 computers. A total of eight sessions were held for the experiment. Each session contained about 15 subjects, with a total of 115 subjects. The computers were connected to the Internet through Local Area Network with T1 connection speed, which could download up to 100MB a second. The newspaper Web sites were displayed using a 17-inch monitor, Netscape browser, and 1024 × 768 resolution.

In each session, the subjects were asked to go to each of the three newspapers' Web sites and spend 15 minutes at each site to complete the following tasks:

1. Retrieve two news items from each of the following sections: (a) Top News (Front Page), (b) National, (c) World. Retrieve six most important news items identified from each newspaper site during the four sessions in 2000.
2. Write down the title of the news items retrieved to make sure that each subject went through news retrieval process.
3. Record the time spent to identify and retrieve six items in minutes.

Before the experiment started, the subjects were reminded that they were surfing the newspaper's Web site to get news as normal readers, and they should retrieve news as they would normally do at any newspaper site. After a subject retrieved a total of six news items, if he or she still had time, he or she was advised to spend the rest of time to continue exploring the site until 15 minutes were over. The subjects then answered several questions regarding that particular newspaper site. The subjects were not allowed to proceed to the second newspaper until they were instructed to do so. All subjects completed three 15-minute news retrieval tasks and filled out the questionnaire regarding their retrieval process and evaluation of the Web sites. A total of 345 observations were obtained. The experiment was completed in 2 consecutive days in November 1999 and November 2000. The design of the three Internet newspapers remained unchanged at the two points of time when the experiment was conducted, whereas the news content was updated.

To avoid carryover effects in repeated-measures designs, the order to access each Web site was set up according to Latin Square Design, that is, the first subject started with *The Washington Post*, the second subject started with *USA Today*, and the third subject started with the *Chicago Tribune* (Wimmer & Dominick, 2000). To ensure subjects followed the procedures properly and recorded the time accurately, two supervisors were present in the lab and monitored all sessions of the experiment.

Measurement

In the expectancy-value model, both gratifications sought and gratifications obtained need to be measured. But for the purpose of testing the effect of Web design approach on retrieval efficiency, obtained gratifications of design approach will be sufficient. Assuming that the lowest level of efficiency associated with a Web design approach is the minimum gratification sought, to compare obtained gratifications associated with the three Internet newspapers, only gratification obtained needs to be measured.

TABLE 5.1
Principle Component Analysis of Six Items
Measuring News Retrieval Efficiency

Items	Factor Loading	Communality
Easiness to navigate	.85	.72
Easiness to locate news items	.88	.77
Quickness in getting news items	.78	.60
Immediate access to news items	.82	.67
Smoothness in getting news items	.83	.69
Perceived power in getting information	.66	.44
Eigenvalue	3.90	
Variance explained	65%	
Cronbach's alpha	.88	

One dependent variable, news retrieval efficiency (gratification obtained), was measured with six items through a self-report questionnaire using Likert scale. The subjects rated each site according to their experience of information retrieval. Retrieval efficiency score was computed using the values obtained on all six items. A reliability test of the six items using Cronbach's alpha yielded a standard item alpha .88. Principal component analysis yielded one factor, eigenvalue 3.9 with 65% variance explained. All items loaded higher than .66 on one factor (see Table 5.1).

Two other independent variables, presentation style and visual appeal, were also measured through the questionnaire after information retrieval was completed at each site. Presentation style was measured with four levels, from *very graphic* to *textual*. Visual appeal was measured with a Likert scale indicating five levels of visual attractiveness.

FINDINGS

Demographics

Of all the subjects, 68.7% considered themselves to have good computer skills and 26.1% medium computer skills. Only 5.2% claimed to have poor computer skills. There is no difference in the means of retrieval efficiency by the level of computer skills ($F = 1.77$, $df = 3, 341$, $p > .05$). Sixty-four percent of the subjects preferred print newspaper, whereas the other 36% preferred to read news online. There is a slight difference in the means of retrieval efficiency between the subjects who preferred print newspaper (21.88) and those who preferred news online (23.10) ($t = 4.87$, $p < .05$).

Effect of Web Design Approach on News Retrieval Efficiency (Table 5.2)

The presentation styles of the three newspapers identified by the participants are distinctive. Seventy-seven percent of the participants considered *The Washington Post* balanced or somewhat graphic, and 12% considered *The Washington Post* very graphic. Sixty-four percent of the participants considered *USA Today* balanced or somewhat graphic, and 21% considered *USA Today* very graphic. In comparison, 66% of the participants considered the *Chicago Tribune* textual, and 33% considered the *Chicago Tribune* balanced or somewhat graphic.

H1, that presentation style is likely to be associated with retrieval efficiency, is supported. Figure 5.1 shows that presentation style was related to retrieval efficiency, $F(3, 341) = 19.17$, $p < .01$. The means of retrieval efficiency by presentation style were: *very graphic* (24.23), *somewhat graphic* (22.41), *balanced* (23.92), *textual* (19.68). Measure of association between presentation style and retrieval efficiency was also significant (Eta = .38, Eta^2 = .14). Whereas there was no difference in retrieval efficiency between very graphic and balanced sites (24.23 vs. 23.92, $t = .42$, $p > .05$), there was a significant difference in retrieval efficiency between textual and all other presentation styles.

H2, that visual appeal of a news site is likely to be associated with retrieval efficiency, is supported. Figure 5.2 shows that visual appeal was related to retrieval efficiency, $F(4, 340) = 27.97$, $p < .01$. *Very appealing* scored the highest mean (26.52), followed by *somewhat appealing* (23.79), *neutral* (20.91), *not very appealing* (19.17), and *no appeal* (17.5). The result of measure of association between level of visual appeal and retrieval efficiency was significant (Eta = .50, Eta^2 = .25). The mean score of retrieval efficiency increased as the level of visual appeal of the newspaper site increased. Rank order correlation showed a relatively

TABLE 5.2
Differences in Presentation Style, Visual Appeal, Time Spent
and News Retrieval Efficiency of the Three Internet Newspapers
($N = 345$)

Newspaper	The Washington Post	USA Today	Chicago Tribune	Analysis of Variance		Measures of Association	
	Mean	Mean	Mean	F	Sig.	Eta	Eta²
Presentation style[a]	2.38	2.57	1.56	40.89	.01	.44	.19
Visual appeal[b]	3.70	3.51	3.04	14.70	.01	.28	.08
Time spent	7.50	7.44	9.24	6.39	.01	.21	.05
Retrieval efficiency	25.62	22.59	18.81	80.83	.01	.57	.32

[a]Presentation style. The larger the number, the more graphic the site. [b]Visual appeal. The larger the number, the higher level of visual appeal.

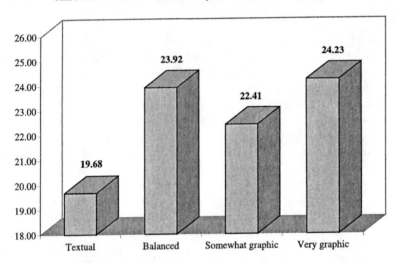

Association of Presentation Style and Retrieval Efficiency

FIG. 5.1.   Association of presentation style and retrieval efficiency of the three Internet newspapers ($N = 345$). ANOVA: $F = 19.17$, $df = 3$, 341, $p < .01$. Measure of Association: Eta = .38, Eta^2 = .14.

strong relationship between the level of visual appeal and retrieval efficiency ($r = .53$, $p < .01$).

H3, that time spent to get news items is negatively correlated with retrieval efficiency, is supported. The correlation between time spent to get the news items and retrieval efficiency was statistically significant ($r = -.28$, $p < .01$); r^2 was .08, which meant 8% of the variance of retrieval efficiency was due to the change in time spent to retrieve news items. The time spent to retrieve six news items ranged from 2 to 15 minutes, with an average of 7.99 minutes. The average retrieval time for *The Washington Post* was 7.51 minutes, followed by *USA Today,* with 7.44 minutes, and the *Chicago Tribune,* with 9.24 minutes. There was no difference between the average retrieval time of *The Washington Post* and *USA Today* ($t = .13$, $p > .05$). There was a significant difference between the average retrieval time of the *Chicago Tribune* and *The Washington Post* ($t = -3.03$, $p < .05$), and the *Chicago Tribune* and *USA Today* ($t = -3.22$, $p < .05$).

H4, that the distinctive Web designs of the three Internet newspapers are likely to produce significant difference in news retrieval efficiency, is supported. Figure 5.3 shows that newspaper design approach was related to retrieval efficiency, $F(2, 342) = 80.83$, $p < .01$. The retrieval efficiency scores ranged from 8 to 30 among all three Internet newspapers, with a mean of 22.34. *The Washington Post* scored the highest (25.62), followed by *USA Today* (22.59), and the *Chicago Tribune* (18.81). Tukey's test of the mean efficiency scores of each two newspapers

Association of Visual Appeal and Retrieval Efficiency

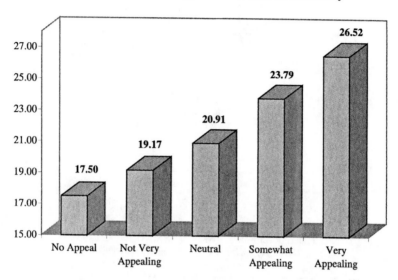

FIG. 5.2. Association of visual appeal and retrieval efficiency of the three Internet newspapers ($N = 345$). ANOVA: $F = 27.97$, $df = 4, 340$, $p < .01$. Measure of Association: Eta $= .56$, Eta$^2 = .31$. Rank Order Correlation: $r = .53$, $p < .01$.

Impact of Web Design Approach on Retrieval Efficiency

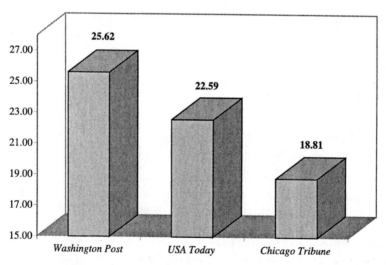

FIG. 5.3. Impact of web design approach on retrieval efficiency of the three Internet newspapers ($N = 345$). ANOVA: $F = 80.83$, $df = 2, 342$, $p < .01$.

91

TABLE 5.3
Multiple Comparison of the Mean Efficiency Scores
of the Three Internet Newspapers

Newspaper (I)	Newspaper (J)	Mean Difference (I–J)	Sig
The Washington Post	USA Today	3.03[a]	.01
	Chicago Tribune	6.81[a]	.01
USA Today	The Washington Post	−3.03[a]	.01
	Chicago Tribune	3.78[a]	.01
Chicago Tribune	The Washington Post	−6.81[a]	.01
	USA Today	−3.78[a]	.01

[a]Tukey's test: The mean difference is significant at the .01 level.

TABLE 5.4
Impact of Design Approach, Presentation Style, and Visual Appeal
on News Retrieval Efficiency of the Three Internet Newspapers
(N = 345)

Source	Sum of Squares	df	Mean Square	F	Sig	Eta^2
Main effects	3595.60	6	599.27	42.70	.01	.43
Newspapers	1415.25	2	707.63	50.42	.01	.17
Presentation style	24.37	2	12.19	.87	.42	.00
Visual appeal	852.26	2	426.13	30.36	.01	.10
Residuals	4743.72	338	14.04	—	—	.57
Total	8339.32	344	24.24	—	—	1.0

indicated that the differences between the means were significant at the .01 level (see Table 5.3).

ANOVA Model of Effect of Design Approach on News Retrieval Efficiency

Using newspaper design approach, presentation style, and visual appeal as independent variables, and news retrieval efficiency as a dependent variable, the researcher tested ANOVA Model of Effect of Design Approach on News Retrieval Efficiency. Table 5.4 shows main effects of design approach, presentation style, and visual appeal on retrieval efficiency, $F(6, 338) = 42.70$, $p < .01$. Eta^2 is .43. Newspaper design approach had the largest effect on news retrieval efficiency, $F(2, 338) = 50.42$, $p < .01$, Eta^2 was .17, followed by visual appeal, $F(2, 338) = 30.36$, $p < .01$, Eta^2 was .10. Presentation style showed no effect on news retrieval efficiency, $F(2, 338) = .87, p > .05$. Interactions among the independent variables were also tested and none of the interaction results was statistically significant.

DISCUSSION

The findings suggest Web design approach had a significant effect on news retrieval efficiency. The Internet newspapers with different design approaches produced different level of gratification obtained. With variation in utility reflected through news retrieval efficiency, the Internet newspapers are likely to become functional alternatives to obtaining news online.

As the result of H1 indicated, presentation style is a factor that affects retrieval efficiency. A balanced site between graphic and textual is more likely to achieve high retrieval efficiency. A balanced site like *The Washington Post* used a moderate number of graphics and fewer scrolling screens on its home page. The restriction in using more graphics is likely to reduce the time to download the page and fewer scrolling screens will also speed up the process to locate and access the news items. A textual site may take less time to load content, yet it may contain more textual information on one or several screens. In the case of the *Chicago Tribune,* with more than six screens for the home page, the information that a user looked for might be buried in the textual screens. It could take more time and require more effort to find it.

There was not much difference in retrieval efficiency between relatively graphic and balanced sites. The reason could be that although it usually takes more time to download a graphic page on a dial-up computer connection measured in a standardized instrument (Li, 2000), the lab setting with a high connection speed could minimize the difference, which may affect overall retrieval efficiency. The result clearly shows that a textual site falls behind in retrieval efficiency. The retrieval efficiency measured six aspects of news retrieval process. A balanced site is more likely to contain the advantages in these aspects that help achieve higher efficiency.

The finding regarding H2 suggests that a Web site with high retrieval efficiency could also be highly visual appealing. Visual appeal is a feature that both publishers and users demand. A site with visual appeal adds to the easiness to process and access news information. It may be hard to measure what is really visually appealing for a news Web site. But the finding that a balanced site like *The Washington Post* received the highest score of visual appeal at least suggests that a visually appealing site needs not to be highly graphic. Too many graphics may increase the time to get the news items, and they may not necessarily add to the level of visual appeal.

Support for H3 indicates that time is an important factor in achieving high retrieval efficiency, but may not be the factor accounting for much of the variance of retrieval efficiency. With r^2 equal to .08, only 8% of the variance of retrieval efficiency was due to the change in time spent to retrieve news items. The findings suggest that less time spent to get news items will not necessarily help a site achieve a higher retrieval efficiency. Other aspects in retrieving news items play more important roles in achieving high retrieval efficiency than time spent to get news items. *USA Today* average retrieval time is close to that of *The Washington Post*. But the average efficiency score of *The Washington Post* is much higher than that of *USA Today*.

Support for H4 suggests that Web design approach does make a difference in news retrieval efficiency. The three Internet newspapers were distinctive measured by presentation style, level of visual appeal, and the time spent to retrieve news items. The effectiveness of design approach was reflected through retrieval efficiency. *The Washington Post* looks like the relatively ideal approach for newspaper Web design. It excelled among the three in retrieval efficiency. The *Chicago Tribune* was rich in information distributed, but the findings suggest that the relatively textual site needs to make an improvement in its presentation style, visual appeal, and other aspects regarding retrieval efficiency.

Design Approach, News Retrieval Efficiency, and Functional Alternatives Within the Medium

The result of ANOVA Model of Effect of Design Approach on News Retrieval Efficiency provides an aggregate picture. The main effects are strong with Eta^2 of .43. Newspaper design approach played the biggest role in the model, followed by visual appeal. Although presentation style was found associated with retrieval efficiency when examined individually, it did not play an evident role in the model. It could be due to the effect pattern of presentation style on retrieval efficiency. Presentation style matters only whether a site is perceived as distinctively textual.

The findings are consistent with that of Li's (2000) study on news retrieval efficiency using content analysis and standardized objective measurement. This study confirms that the Web design approach and information retrieval process can be measured objectively using a standardized instrument such as Doctor HTML (1999), although it has to be combined with content analysis. The standardized objective measurement could be especially useful when an experimental study is not feasible, and if the researchers want to control the factors affected by human behavior. No data generated by such standardized measurement instrument are of much value to scholarly research unless they are theoretically based. This study establishes the theoretical base that the standardized objective measurement could apply in assessing information retrieval efficiency.

The value attached to the more desirable Web design approach demonstrated through retrieval efficiency clearly indicates what users expect from a news Web site when retrieving news information. Whereas previous studies of uses and gratifications suggest that media content has predicting value associated with the medium, this study demonstrates the means that facilitates users to get information is also important in predicting value associated with the functional alternatives of the medium. When communication channels based on the same technology and within the same medium have similar types of content, those with more utilities show higher expectancy value. The functional alternatives within the same medium, such as Internet newspapers with different design approaches now available to audiences in all markets are likely to compete for audiences in their information-seeking process. Putting aside the factors such as locality, political orientation, and publication style of the Internet newspapers, if the audience only needs one channel to access certain information and they are free to select from among the functional alternatives, the Internet newspaper with the most desirable retrieval efficiency is most likely to be their favorable channel.

This study made several contributions in studying the Internet newspapers. It is the first experiment-based study to test the effect of Web design on news retrieval efficiency. It created an effective measure of news retrieval efficiency for experimental studies to test to what degree Internet newspapers facilitate access to news information. The measurement was tested through the experiment and achieved high reliability. The study identified several factors affecting the gratification obtained in retrieving news information from Internet newspapers: presentation style, visual appeal, and time spent to get news information. With the measurement of news retrieval efficiency, this study identified some of the key variables to be used in testing uses and gratifications theory and expectancy-value model in the study of the Internet newspapers. It made a special contribution through demonstrating the applicability of functional alternatives within the medium apart from what is normally considered across the media. Previous studies looked at functional alternatives only among different types of media. This study argues that information channels within a medium could also become functional alternatives with their different level of utility and gratification obtained through use. The findings of the study offer ample support to the notion that Internet newspapers with different design approaches that produce different news retrieval efficiency are likely to serve as functional alternatives in obtaining news online.

CONCLUSION

The Web design approaches of the Internet newspapers reflected through the way the publishers structure the news content, present information, and set the navigation path, made the three newspapers distinctive in their retrieval efficiency. The implication of the functional alternatives perspective of uses and gratifications theory is demonstrated through obtained gratification, news retrieval efficiency. This study expanded the scope of the functional alternatives perspective from across the media to within the medium. When looking at the Internet newspapers now available to audiences in all markets, this expanded perspective becomes especially important. Only the Internet newspapers that excel in perceived utility and hence gratification obtained will win more readers. Although researchers found that content is more important than navigation issues, user interface, or even site speed (Abels et al., 1998; Katz & Aspden, 1997), the findings of this study emphasize that attributes of the functional alternatives within the medium such as Web design are also important in audience selection of a specific Internet newspaper.

Web design should follow some basic rules, and this study makes some of the rules clearer through examining the news retrieval process and hypothesis testing. It created a specific measurement to evaluate news retrieval process by readers. However, Web design is not only a practice governed by the basic rules, it is also an art. Sometimes, the creativity may be a major concern of a publisher to attract certain groups of readers, and it can interact with the effect of basic rules on Web design, as seen in the impact of level of visual appeal on retrieval efficiency. In this regard, it is useful to find the most important factors in Web design for an efficient retrieval of information through a quantitative approach, hence to know the expected gratification sought by users. It is also necessary to know the limitations of these tangible rules or expectations. They may help an Internet newspaper achieve its goal in one way. On the other side, sticking to the rules may sacrifice the value of a Web site from a creative designer's perspective. The publisher of an Internet newspaper needs to make a decision on which way to go before the newspaper site can achieve anticipated high retrieval efficiency.

The nature of the nonrandom sample of the Internet newspapers limits the significance of the findings. Although the three Internet newspapers selected were distinctive in their design approaches, a carefully selected Internet newspaper pool with a larger sampling frame would yield a more representative sample, hence more generalizable results. College students as subjects also limit the scope of the findings. To sample the subjects from a more diversified population will generate more persuasive results, which will be more helpful to the publishers of thousands of Internet newspapers, and add to our understanding of uses and gratifications theory and expectancy-value model applied to the use of Internet newspapers.

REFERENCES

Abels, E., White, M., & Hahn, K. (1998). A user-based design process for Web sites. *Internet Research, 8*(1), 43.

Adoni, H. (1985). Media interchangeability and co-existence: Trends and changes in production, distribution and consumption patterns of the print media in the television era. *Libri, 35,* 202–217.

Anderson, D. R., & Collins, P. A. (1988). The impact on children's education: Television's influence on cognitive development (Working Paper No. 2). Washington, DC: U.S. Department of Educational Research and Improvement, U.S. Department of Education.

Becker, L. B., & Schoenbach, K. (1989). When media content diversifies: Anticipating audience behaviors. In L. B. Becker & K. Schoenbach (Eds.), *Audience responses to media diversification: Coping with plenty* (pp. 1–27). Hillsdale, NJ: Lawrence Erlbaum Associates.

Chyi, H. I., & Lasorsa, D. (1999, Fall). Access, use and preferences for online newspapers. *Newspaper Research Journal, 20*(4), 2–13.

Coffey, S., & Stipp, H. (1997). The interactions between computer and television usage. *Journal of Advertising Research, 37*(2), 61–67.

Dimmick, J. (1993). Ecology, economics and gratification utilities. In A. Alexander, J. Owers, & R. Carveth (Eds.), *Media economics* (pp. 135–136). Hillsdale, NJ: Lawrence Erlbaum Associates.

Dimmick, J., Kline, S., & Stafford, L. (2000, April). The gratification niches of personal email and the telephone: Competition, displacement, and the complementarity. *Communication Research, 27*(2), 227–248.

Doctor HTML. (1999). *Image analysis explanation.* Retrieved May 16, 2004, from http://www.doctor-html.com/RxHTML/cgi-bin/ssi.cgi?l=ImageAnalysis.html#Time

Eighmey, J., & McCord, L. (1998). Adding value in the Information Age: Uses and gratification of sites on the World Wide Web. *Journal of Business Research, 41,* 187–194.

Ferguson, D., & Perse, E. (2000, Spring). The World Wide Web as a functional alternative to television. *Journal of Broadcasting & Electronic Media, 44*(2), 155–174.

Finn, S. (1997, October). Origins of media exposure: Linking personality traits to TV, radio, print, and the film use. *Communication Research, 24*(5), 507–529.

Fredin, E. (1997). Rethinking the news story for the Internet: Hyperstory prototypes and a model of the user. *Journalism and Mass Communication Monographs, 163,* 7–8.

Fredin, E., & David, P. (1998, Spring). Browsing and the hypermedia interaction cycle: A model of self-efficacy and goal dynamics. *Journalism and Mass Communication Quarterly,* 49–50.

Katz, J., & Aspden, P. (1997). Motivations for and barriers to Internet usage: Results of a national public opinion survey. *Internet Research, 7*(3), 180.

Li, X. (1998, Summer). Web page design and graphic use of three U.S. newspapers. *Journalism & Mass Communication Quarterly, 75*(2), 353–365.

Li, X. (2002, Winter). Web design affects news retrieval efficiency. *Newspaper Research Journal, 23*(1), 38–49.

Lowrey, W. (1999, Fall). From map to machine: Conceptualizing and designing news on the Internet. *Newspaper Research Journal, 20*(4), 14–27.

McQuail, D. (1994). *Mass communication theory* (3rd ed.). London: Sage.

Morris, M., & Ogan, C. (1996). The Internet as mass medium. *Journal of Communication, 46*(1), 39–50.

Newhagen, J., & Levy, M. (1997). The future of journalism in a distributed communication architecture. In D. Borden & K. Harvey (Eds.), *The electronic grapevine* (p. 18). Mahwah, NJ: Lawrence Erlbaum Associates.

Palmgreen, P. (1981). Gratifications discrepancies and news program choice. *Communication Research, 8,* 451–478.

Palmgreen, P., & Rayburn, J. D. (1985). An expectancy-value approach to media gratifications. In K. E. Rosengren, L. Wenner, & P. Palmgreen (Eds.), *Media gratification research* (pp. 61–72). Beverly Hills, CA, & London: Sage.

Palmgreen, P., Wenner, L. A., & Rayburn, J. D. (1981). Gratifications discrepancies and news program choice. *Communication Research, 8,* 451–478.

Perse, E. M., & Courtright, J. A. (1993). Normative images of communication media: Mass and interpersonal channels in the new media environment. *Human Communication Research, 19,* 485–503.

Picard, R. (1989). *Media economics, concepts and issues.* Beverly Hills, CA: Sage.

Ramsay, J., Barbesi, A., & Preece, J. (1998). A psychological investigation of long retrieval times on the World Wide Web. *Interacting with Computers, 10*(1), 77–86.

Rayburn, J. D., Palmgreen, P., & Acker, T. (1984). Media gratifications and choosing a morning news program. *Journalism Quarterly, 61,* 149–156.

Reason, R. (1995). Newspapers online: Successes and challenges: Part III. Access Atlanta carries the torch. In *Poynter Online* [On-line]. Retrieved from http://www.reporter.org/poynter/ (The site relocated to current address December 1996; article no longer published.)

Richmond, W. (1995, September). Design on the World Wide Web. *Communication Arts, 37*(5), 167–168.

Salomon, G. (1984). Television is "easy" and print is "tough": The differential investment of mental effort in learning as a function of perceptions and attributions. *Journal of Educational Psychology, 76*(4), 647–658.

Singer, J. B. (1998). Online journalists: Foundations for research into their changing roles. *Journal of Computer-Mediated Communication, 4*(1), Available from http://www.ascusc.org/jcmc/vol4/issue1/singer.html

Slater, M. D. (1991). Use of message stimuli in mass communication experiments: A methodological assessment and discussion. *Journalism Quarterly, 3*, 412–421.

Sparkes, V. M., & Kang, N. (1986). Public reactions to cable television: Time in the diffusion process. *Journal of Broadcasting & Electronic Media, 30*, 213–229.

Spool, J. M., Scanlon, T., Schroeder, W., Snyder, C., & DeAngelo, T. (1997). *Web site usability: A designer's guide*. North Andover, MA: User Interface Engineering.

Steinfield, C. W., Dutton, W. H., & Kovaric, P. (1989). A framework and agenda for research on computing in the home. In J. L. Salvaggio & J. Bryant (Eds.), *Media use in the information age: Emerging patterns of adoption and consumer use* (pp. 61–85). Hillsdale, NJ: Lawrence Erlbaum Associates.

Williams, F., Strover, S., & Grant, A. E. (1994). Social aspects of new media technologies. In J. Bryant & D. Zillmann (Eds.), *Media effects: Advances in theory and research* (pp. 463–482). Hillsdale, NJ: Lawrence Erlbaum Associates.

Wimmer, R. D., & Dominick, J. R. (2000). *Mass media research: An introduction*. Belmont, CA: Wadsworth.

6

The Web News Story
and Cognitive Flexibility

Wilson Lowrey
Jinmyung Choi
The University of Alabama

The news media have been accused of oversimplifying multifaceted news topics, of covering political strategies and polling results while ignoring the intricacies of issues (Cappella & Jamieson, 1997; Fallows, 1997; Valentino, Buhr, & Beckmann, 2001), and of reporting social issues from within single, constraining perspectives (Domke, Shah, & Wackman, 1998; Fishman, 1980). The inability to translate the complexities of the social world to news audiences, and the probability that audiences are unlikely to read such coverage were it produced, threaten the notion of an informed public. It is proposed here that use of the Internet and adoption of theory from the field of education offer a partial solution to this problem.

Cognitive flexibility theory (CFT), a theory from education technology that is grounded in the use of hypermedia, was envisioned as a way to improve instruction of complex knowledge areas such as medicine and engineering (Jacobson & Spiro, 1995; Spiro, Feltovich, Jacobson, & Coulson, 1991; Spiro & Jehng, 1990). According to the theory, instruction that "crisscrosses" different case examples with different theoretical perspectives through the use of hypermedia produces a flexible kind of knowledge that can be applied to changing real-world conditions. This study proposes that CFT and hypermedia story structures may also help audiences develop flexible knowledge of news issues that may be applied to changing real-world conditions. Exploration of the CFT format for news content is consistent with recent calls in the news industry for innovative approaches in online journalism (Anzur, 2001; Chan-Olmsted & Park, 2000; McAdams, 2000; Outing, 2000). It also fits well with a small but growing scholarship on news

99

stories with hypermedia formats that are "nonlinear"—that is, that can be read out of sequence and that are interconnected through hyperlinks (Eveland & Dunwoody, 2001, 2002; Eveland, Marton, & Seo, 2004; Lowrey, 2004; Paul & Fiebich, 2002).

COGNITIVE FLEXIBILITY THEORY

CFT was designed to aid the instruction of complex, or advanced, knowledge areas. A knowledge area is considered "advanced" if it must be learned across different sorts of cases, or situations, and from different conceptual perspectives. For example, an engineer must flexibly apply knowledge of building bridges across a variety of geographical conditions, government regulations, and so on. In such situations, rote memorization of a technique is not enough. Through this crisscrossing of the conceptual landscape, advanced learners can build interconnected and flexible cognitive structures rather than rigidly prepackaged schema (Spiro et al., 1991; Spiro & Jehng, 1990). Computer-based hypermedia typically aid CFT-based instruction because hypermedia are essentially nonlinear. They allow learners to easily and quickly compare different cases from a knowledge area, to assess cases in light of different conceptual perspectives, and to revisit these cases and concepts.

Education researchers have tested CFT a number of times, with mixed results. Spiro and colleagues (1991) tested a computer-based hypermedia learning tool that presented students with a case-based approach to teaching the film *Citizen Kane*. Students could hyperlink among film clips, which served as the "cases," and they could also hyperlink to different themes offered by film scholars and compare cases in light of these themes. Results showed that the cognitive flexibility format did not aid ability to recall information, but it did aid transfer of knowledge to new problem-solving situations (Spiro et al., 1991). Balcytiene (1999) found that the CFT format helped all subjects in an experiment recognize knowledge of architectural history, and that the nonlinear CFT format was slightly more helpful in this regard than a linear paper format. Balcytiene also found that those with less prior knowledge of the topic benefited most from the nonlinear format. This finding stands in contrast to findings from most studies of nonlinear instruction (Charney, 1994; Shyu & Brown, 1995). In testing a linear "electronic book" format against a CFT-based format, Demetriadis and Pombortsis (2000) found no difference in lower level cognitive processing but found that the CFT format was significantly more effective in aiding understanding of complex, case-specific problems. Siegel et al. (2000) used CFT to design a program for teaching education and found that video-based learning cases encouraged reading about the content, but that subjects tended to ignore the hyperlinked conceptual perspectives.

Not all CFT experiments have met with success. Jaffe (1995) found that the CFT format had no effect on self-efficacy for learning first aid and CPR. Results from a study by Rossner-Merrill, Parker, Mamchur, and Chu (1998) suggested students in a CFT-structured online course had some trouble seeing the "larger picture" of the course content for all the individual case examples. Niederhauser, Reynolds, Salmen, and Skolmoski (2000) found that the CFT structure confused users and obstructed learning.

HYPERMEDIA FORMATS AND THE NEWS

Enthusiasts of online news advocate that online news stories should be less linear, more interactive, and more connected with other Web sites (Lanson, 2000; Lasica, 2003; Outing, 2000, 2003; Rich, 1999; South, 1999). Fredin (1997) proposed a prototype for a "hyperstory," which is a network of online news information constructed by readers, and he suggested that this constructivist approach could entice readers to the public space and encourage interest in public issues. Despite such optimism, studies show that, as yet, relatively few news organizations are taking advantage of nonlinear and interactive features on the Internet (Lowrey, 2003; Singer, 2003), and relatively few readers seem anxious to use them (The Pew Research Center, 2000; Singer, 2002).

A handful of studies have assessed whether these features actually benefit audiences, and, generally, their effects have been weak. Nonlinear, hyperlinked formats, of which the CFT format is a type, have received particular attention. Story formats are considered nonlinear if their structure and navigation scheme facilitate and encourage nonsequential reading. It should be noted that a nonlinear structure does not ensure nonlinear reading, and the opposite is true as well—the traditional novel is structured linearly, but a reader may choose to skip around in the text.

Eveland and Dunwoody (2001) compared a print version of a news story with linear and nonlinear Web versions of the same story and found no significant differences between the Web sites in subjects' ability to recall story information. In a separate study the same researchers found that Web-based stories increased the likelihood that readers would scan stories, skipping information they found less interesting; this in turn led to reduced learning (Eveland & Dunwoody, 2002). Results from an experiment by Lowrey (2004) suggested that nonlinear formats for news stories increased the perception that users had control over the reading experience but did not aid recognition or recall. Nonlinear formats actually discouraged opinion feedback from readers. In a study of Internet news browsing, Fredin and David (1998) found that users preferred browsing sequences that were not too complex and confusing, but that were not so simple as to become tedious.

CONCEPTS AND HYPOTHESES

Multifaceted and broad perspectives on news issues are rare (Hendrickson & Tankard, 1997) and, interestingly, this is similar to the problem faced by education scholars. Theorists of CFT have complained that traditional instruction of complex knowledge areas suffers from oversimplification and from a reductive bias. If the problems between education and journalism are similar, could the solution be similar as well?

This study's research question is a general one: Does a CFT hypermedia format, adapted for Internet news stories, benefit news audiences? The study partly adopts a model by Eveland and Dunwoody (2000), which proposes causal relationships between hypermedia news formats and various cognitions and behaviors. Their model incorporated several outcome variables, including *recall, recognition, cognitive load* (i.e., disorientation resulting from overloading working memory), *self-efficacy,* and *reader selectivity.* The present study tests these dependent variables and also introduces the variable *understanding of format,* which is the degree of shared understanding between audiences and media producers about media formats and their use. This variable, labeled "media logic" by Lowrey (2004), was cited as a possible explanation for why nonlinear formats did not improve learning. The variable *reader satisfaction,* which previous studies have also examined (e.g., Van Nimwegen, Pouw, & Van Oostendorp, 1999), is examined here.

Dependent variables for the present study are grouped into three sets. The first set of variables most directly address advanced learning. These include *self-efficacy,* or confidence in ability to apply learning, and *extremity of opinion,* which reflects exposure to the gray areas and multifaceted nature of complex issues. The second set of variables address the immediate reading experience, and these include *satisfaction, perceived credibility, selectivity during reading,* and *understanding of format.* The third set addresses basic cognitive processing of news content, and these include *recognition* and *cognitive load.*

Hypotheses

The first two hypotheses are concerned with advanced learning. According to CFT, readers who crisscross a knowledge area through multiple cases and multiple perspectives should develop more thorough and flexible schema than readers of non-CFT formats. Because of this flexible cognitive development, they should be better prepared to apply knowledge to varied real-world settings. It is proposed here that the most important real-world application of news knowledge is public discussion of news issues, and that readers of the CFT format will be better prepared, and perceive they are better prepared, to engage in public discussion in all its varieties. Therefore readers of the CFT format should demonstrate greater self-efficacy, or confidence in their ability to discuss these issues.

H1: Readers of news stories with a Cognitive Flexibility format will have a higher degree of self-efficacy in regard to their ability to discuss the story's issues than will readers of news stories with other formats.

Exposure to the multiple, varied perspectives and cases of the CFT format should signal to readers that the issue is complex and challenging. The experience should make it more likely readers will perceive the gray areas and uncertainties of the issue and less likely they will engage in reductive, bipolar thinking. This should result in measured, middle-course responses to opinion questions.

H2: Readers of news stories with the Cognitive Flexibility format will be less extreme in their opinions about the issue in the story than will readers of news stories with other formats.

Hypotheses in the second set assess relationships between format and the immediate reading experience. A number of past studies of hypermedia learning have incorporated reader satisfaction variables, and in general, readers find that nonlinear structures provide more control over the reading experience and are more enjoyable to use (Hannafin & Sullivan, 1996; Morrison, Ross, & Baldwin, 1992). Enjoyment, or satisfaction, is particularly relevant to the reading of news because, unlike students in a class, news readers are not required to read and therefore may need to be enticed. It is proposed that readers of the CFT format will be more satisfied with their reading experience because it allows more reader activity and control through the hyperlinking of brief multiple stories and perspectives.

H3: Readers of news stories with the CFT format should feel greater satisfaction with the reading experience than readers of other formats.

Credibility is an important issue in journalism, particularly in the wake of several high-profile scandals in the field. Studies show that as readers have become more accustomed to news information on the Web, online news has fared better in perceived credibility (Flanagin & Metzger, 2000; Johnson & Kaye, 2000, 2002; The Pew Research Center, 2000). However, it is proposed here that the unfamiliar nature of the CFT format may lead readers to question the story's credibility.

H4: Readers of news stories with CFT formats should view these news stories as less credible than readers of news stories with other formats.

Readers of CFT and other nonlinear formats may be more likely to scan or selectively read some content and to ignore other content because they perceive they have greater control over the reading process (Eveland & Dunwoody, 2002; Siegel et al., 2000). Eveland and Dunwoody (2002) found that selectivity was a determinant of ability to recall story information because those who scanned tended to skip information.

H5: Readers of news stories with CFT and other nonlinear formats will read more selectively than readers of stories with linear formats.

Readers may also have difficulty understanding the format's logic, in other words, the norms and rules of the format used by audiences and media producers to make sense of the story content. Audiences rely on these norms and rules to sort information, distinguish relevancy, and make judgments (Altheide & Snow, 1979; McQuail, 2000). For example, both audiences and journalists understand that newspaper stories that run "above the fold" are more important than those below the fold. The shared understanding of Web story formats is less clear.

H6: Readers of news stories with CFT and other nonlinear formats will have less understanding of the nature of the format than readers of stories with linear formats.

Hypotheses in the third set assess relationships between format and cognitive processing. Previous studies have shown that the CFT format and other nonlinear formats are likely to reduce, or not significantly aid, lower level cognitive processing such as the ability to recall and recognize story information from memory. A possible explanation is that the challenges of nonlinear formats add cognitive load, which can overwhelm working memory, disorient readers, and ultimately inhibit learning. Cognitive load is a common variable in studies of hypermedia effects (Baylor, 2001; Eveland & Dunwoody, 2001), and at least one study suggested that the CFT format may have prohibited learning because of cognitive load (Niederhauser et al., 2000).

H7: Readers of news stories with CFT and other nonlinear formats will be less able to recognize story information from memory than will readers of linear formats.

H8: Readers of news stories with CFT and other nonlinear formats will experience greater levels of cognitive load than readers of stories with linear formats.

Finally, much prior research on hypermedia effects has shown a positive relationship between prior knowledge and the benefits of hypermedia (Charney, 1994; Shyu & Brown, 1995), though this finding is not universal (Balcytiene, 1999). It is proposed here that prior knowledge should increase the benefits of CFT because when schema are already somewhat developed, complex knowledge is more easily and thoroughly stored and developed (Charney, 1994). Also, more prior knowledge leads to greater perceived control over the learning experience (Shyu & Brown, 1995).

H9: The CFT format will more strongly aid the recognition ability of readers with more previous knowledge of the news issue area than it will aid the recognition ability of readers with less previous knowledge of the area.

Interaction effects between prior knowledge and story formats will also be assessed on the other dependent variables.

METHOD

Participants

After obtaining IRB approval, 106 college students were recruited from mass communication classes with an incentive of extra credit. Students were mostly undergraduate communication majors. Ages ranged from 18 to 25, but 88% of the participants were 21 or under. Written consent was obtained, and students were randomly assigned to three groups, one for each of three experimental conditions.

Design and Procedure

For the three conditions of *format type,* three versions of a news report on the issue of cloning were created and loaded onto the World Wide Web. The first report was created with a structure informed by CFT, the second was created with a general nonlinear structure, and the third was created with a linear structure. Reports contained identical photos and graphics, and text was close to identical, with some adjustments necessary for format changes. Because prior research on hypermedia has demonstrated the importance of orienting users to navigation (Dee-Lucas & Larkin, 1995; Jacobson, Maouri, Mishra, & Kolar, 1995), the home pages of all three sites contained brief guidance on site use. The researcher provided no spoken guidance, as this would have undermined external validity.

The CFT news report contained five brief news stories, each approximately 200 to 250 words in length, and included brief "perspective" paragraphs (each between 30 to 100 words) that could be linked from the main story. Each of the five stories could be crossed with the perspectives. Readers opening the site first encountered a home page with an overall headline across the top of the page. Running down the left side of the page below the headline were five sentences and accompanying small photos that teased and linked to five brief stories (Fig. 6.1). When readers linked to a story, the full story appeared in a column running down the middle of the page. The stories served as the multiple cases for the learning experience, as recommended by CFT. At the top and bottom of each full story were jump menus allowing readers to link to the four "perspectives" on each story. When linked, a few sentences offering interpretation of the story from a particular perspective appeared in a column running down the right side of the page. Readers could in this way crisscross multiple stories and perspectives on the news issue.

The nonlinear story treatment was designed to mimic nonlinear story formats often seen in in-depth, magazine-style stories on news Web sites (sometimes called "Web specials"). The nonlinear site was segmented into six different story segments and readers were provided links to each segment in a navigation bar across the top of each page. Readers could start the story at any of the six story parts, which were written to stand alone, and could read the story in any order. In addition, links that allowed users to link to other pages within the site were

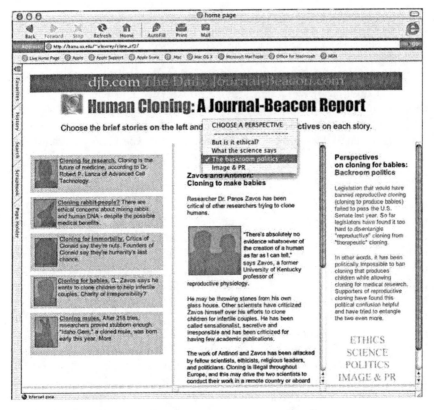

FIG. 6.1.   The CFT news report. Actual photos were used in closed-network experimental Web sites.

embedded within story content. None of the links sent users to other Web sites; this constraint was put in place so that users of the linear and nonlinear sites would have roughly the same amount of content. The site format loosely followed guidelines for Web story production presented in online design seminars and in textbooks on online communication (Garrand, 2001; Rich, 1999). Previous research on nonlinear stories has also adopted this general nonlinear format (Eveland & Dunwoody, 2001; Lowrey, 2004).

In contrast, the linear version of the report consisted of four pages linked to each other so that readers could move forward and backward but could not skip around in the page order. There were no embedded links within the text. The only links appeared in the form of backward and forward arrows at the bottom of each page. The format was intended to reflect the format of a lengthy "repurposed" news story, used routinely by many newspaper Web sites. Photos and graphics were indented into the text at points where graphic content reflected story content.

There are numerous news issues suitable for such an application, but the topic of cloning was chosen because it is a complex issue with a variety of competing frames of reference. The issue has been debated at the political level, the religious and ethical level, and at the scientific level.

The issue of cloning involves a variety of case examples. For the present study, two cases involved cloning for the purpose of medical research, one case involved cloning to produce a racing mule, one case involved cloning attempts to help infertile couples, and one case involved cloning attempts by a religious sect to produce babies as a first step toward human immortality. Readers were able to examine each story in light of four different angles, or perspectives: a science perspective, a politics/legislation perspective, an ethics perspective, and a media portrayal perspective (which pertains to the implications of public perception).

Text for each perspective provided interpretation of implications for each cloning case. For example, for the case involving cloning for infertile couples, the clickable "Politics" perspective offered the observation that it has been awkward to ban cloning that produces children while allowing cloning for research purposes, and that those supporting cloning for babies have used this confusion to their advantage. For the same case, the "Ethics" perspective offered observations from two expert sources: Leon Kass, Chairman of the President's Council on Bioethics, was quoted as saying that parents who try to replicate children who have died are exercising despotism over future generations, whereas Professor of Philosophy Gregory Pence says having children for self-serving reasons is nothing new, as for example, people have always thought of their children as a safety net in old age.

The experiment was administered to students in two department computer labs. After random assignment to the three experimental conditions, each subject was seated at a computer terminal and instructed to fill out a pretest survey containing 22 questions. Questions addressed demographics, use and expertise with the Web, and perceived expertise and interest in the issue of cloning. Subjects were then asked to open the browser windows on their computer screens and read the story. Subjects were given 20 minutes to read the story. Five minutes into the reading, subjects were asked to fill out a brief three-question survey measuring the dependent variable cognitive load. They were then told to resume reading. At the end of the 20-minute reading time subjects were told to close the browser and were given a 32-item posttest questionnaire. The questionnaire measured the dependent variables *self-efficacy, satisfaction, perceived credibility, selectivity of reading, format understanding, memory recognition,* and *cognitive load* (for a second time). Finally, subjects were given a fourth questionnaire, which asked subjects to read two brief cloning cases and to provide opinions on these cases, which served to measure *moderation of opinion.*

Measures of Dependent Variables.   Self-efficacy was measured by four items, each on a 7-point scale: "I feel I could understand a debate by policy makers about human cloning," "I feel I could carry on an intelligent conversation about the topic of human cloning," "I feel I could make an effective argument to defend my opinions about human cloning," and "I feel I could successfully answer questions about the story I just read." Previous research on self-efficacy suggests this focus on measuring "feeling of confidence" (Bong & Hocevar, 2002). These four items were tested for reliability (*Cronbach's alpha* = .78) and were summed, with a range of 4 to 28 (*M* = 18.79, *SD* = 4.67).

Extremity of opinion was measured by asking subjects to respond to two opinion questions about cloning, each on a 7-point scale. For each question responses of 3, 4, or 5 were recoded as a "1" on the extremity scale, responses of 2 or 6 were recoded as "2," and the most extreme responses of 1 and 7 were recoded as "3." The result was a scale of degree of extremity for each question ranging from 1 = *least extreme* to 3 = *most extreme*. Measures for each opinion question were summed (*Cronbach's alpha* = .71) to produce the final "extremity" measure with a range of 2 to 6 (*M* = 3.69, *SD* = 1.51).

Degree of story satisfaction was measured with two items, each on a 7-point scale: "I enjoyed reading the story," and "I would like to see more news stories written this way." These items scaled together with an alpha of .79, and were summed. The range was 2 to 14 (*M* = 8.88, *SD* = 3.20). Credibility was measured using five 7-point items from the Graziano and McGrath (1986) scale: Is the news report fair? Is the report accurate? Is the report biased? Can the report be trusted? Does the report tell the whole story? Items were summed (*alpha* = .80) to produce a measure with a range of 5 to 34, *M* = 22.33 and *SD* = 5.78. A higher score indicates higher credibility. Reported selectivity of reading was measured with two 7-point items: "I skimmed through the news report" (*strongly disagree* = 1, *strongly agree* = 7) and "I only read sections of the news report that looked interesting or important" (*strongly disagree* = 1, *strongly agree* = 7). These measures were used reliably by Eveland and Dunwoody (2002). Results were summed (*Cronbach's alpha* = .78) and the final variable ranged from 2 to 14, *M* = 4.57, *SD* = 3.11, with a higher score indicating more selectivity, or scanning. Perceived understanding of format was measured using the statements "The report seemed like a work of journalism," "I did not understand what the writers of the report were trying to do," and "I was confused about what kind of story this was supposed to be." Results were summed and had a marginal reliability coefficient, at .50. Responses ranged from 4 to 21, *M* = 15.95, *SD* = 3.33. A high score indicated less understanding of format.

The recognition measure was a sum of correct answers (each correct answer = 1) for 14 multiple choice and true–false questions about the cloning story. The final measure ranged from 3 to 14, *M* = 9.36 and *SD* = 2.47. Cognitive load was measured by three 7-point items: "How difficult was it to follow what this news report was about?" (*extremely easy* = 1, *extremely difficult* = 7), "I felt lost reading this news report" (*strongly disagree* = 1, *strongly agree* = 7), and "It was clear how all the information in the news report fit together" (*strongly agree* = 1, *strongly disagree* = 7). The three questions were administered twice: once 5 minutes into the reading period and once immediately after the reading period. Similar measures have been used in previous studies (Eveland & Dunwoody, 2001; Gellevij, van der Meij, de Jong, & Pieters 2002). Results were summed (*Cronbach's alpha* = .77) and ranged from 6 to 33, *M* = 13.89, *SD* = 6.88. A higher score indicated greater cognitive load.

Finally, the independent variable format type had three values, with 1= *linear format*, 2 = *nonlinear format*, and 3 = *CFT format*. Prior knowledge had two values, with 1 = *low prior knowledge* of the cloning issue and 2 = *high prior knowledge*. Prior knowledge questions were asked on the pretest: "How knowledgeable are you about the issue of human cloning?" and "How extensively have you studied the issue of human cloning?" These two 7-point items were summed (*Cronbach's alpha* = .83) and dichotomized at the median.

RESULTS

Multivariate Analysis of Variance was performed in order to test the relationship of story format type and prior knowledge to the dependent variables as a group. According to all four algorithms commonly used in MANOVA (Wilks', Hotelling's, Pillai's, Roy's), format type had no significant main effect on the eight dependent variables when they were tested as a group. There was an overall significant main effect from prior knowledge, $F(8, 93) = 6.14$, $p < .05$. The interaction effect between format type and prior knowledge proved insignificant for three of the four algorithms and tested as significant for Roy's Largest Root, $F(8, 94) = 2.31$, $p < .05$.

Univariate F tests were analyzed to assess individual hypotheses. Hypothesis 1 received no support when self-efficacy was measured by the scaled variable. Readers of the CFT format were no more likely to express high self-efficacy about their ability to publicly discuss cloning than were readers of the other two formats (Table 6.1). However, the individual self-efficacy measure "I feel I could carry on an intelligent conversation about human cloning" tested as significant, $F = 3.45$, $p < .05$, with the mean for the CFT format at 4.65, and the mean for the linear format at 3.74. This item was assessed individually because it seems to be the closest to a direct measure of the perceived ability to engage in public discussion. There was no interaction effect with prior knowledge (Table 6.2).

Hypothesis 2, which proposed that readers of the CFT format would be less extreme in their opinions, received mixed support. Readers of the CFT format tested as slightly less extreme than readers of the other two formats, but the differences were not significant. However, there was a significant interaction effect with prior knowledge. Among those with higher prior knowledge of the cloning issue, opinions were significantly less extreme for readers of the CFT format than of the other two formats, and opinions were most extreme among readers of the linear format. This finding suggests that, in order for the CFT format to enhance ability to see gray areas of an issue, individuals must already have some understanding of the issue. This finding supports CFT, which is targeted at advanced instruction

TABLE 6.1
MANOVA Univariate Results: Impact of Story Format
on Dependent Variables

Dependent variables	CFT Means (n = 37)	SD[a]	Nonlinear Means (n = 35)	SD	Linear Means (n = 34)	SD	F Value	p < .05
Self-efficacy (range 4–28)	19.49	4.67	19.11	4.40	17.65	4.85	1.03	.36
Extremity of opinion (range 2–6)	3.59	1.30	3.83	1.58	3.68	1.66	.074	.79
Satisfaction with site (range 2–14)	9.84	2.94	9.06	3.32	7.62	3.19	3.13	.04
Perceived credibility (range 5–34)	22.70	4.94	22.43	6.56	22.38	5.77	.073	.96
Reader selectivity (range 2–14)	4.81	2.63	4.14	2.80	4.41	3.79	.83	.11
Understanding of format (range 4–21)	16.60	3.17	16.41	3.30	14.74	3.44	3.07	.05
Memory recognition (range 3–14)	9.46	2.64	9.66	2.26	9.24	2.37	.305	.74
Cognitive load (range 6–33)	13.85	6.96	13.00	7.20	15.41	7.10	.29	.59

Note. Measure of dependent variables: high score means higher value of the measurement. For example, the measure of self-efficacy ranges 4 to 28; higher score means more self-efficacy.

[a]*SD* = standard deviation; *F* value = strength of effect. The data meet the criteria for MANOVA. The determinant value of Bartlett's Sphericity test is small, with a significance of .001, which indicates the dependent values are sufficiently correlated. Homogeneity has not been violated, as results of a Box's M test are not significant.

and advanced learners. Among those with lower prior knowledge, opinions were most extreme for readers of the nonlinear format and least extreme among readers of the linear format. For readers who are already challenged by lack of familiarity with the subject matter, perhaps the severely nonlinear structure of the CFT format was more difficult to understand than the somewhat more traditional nonlinear format.

Hypothesis 3 received support, as format type had a significant main effect on satisfaction, $F = 3.13$, $p < .05$. Means comparison shows that on a satisfaction scale of 2 to 14, readers "enjoyed" the CFT site best, scoring it at 9.84, the nonlinear site at 9.06, and the linear site at 7.62. There was no significant interaction effect with prior knowledge.

TABLE 6.2
MANOVA Univariate Results: Impact of Interaction Between Story Format
and Prior Knowledge on Dependent Variables

Dependent Variables	CFT Means (n = 37)		Nonlinear Means (n = 35)		Linear Means (n = 34)		F	
Level Prior Knowledge	Low	High	Low	High	Low	High	Value	p < .05
Self-efficacy (range 4–28)	18.00	20.95	18.29	20.91	16.50	19.75	.038	.96
Extremity of opinion (range 2–6)	3.56	3.63	4.20	3.82	3.37	4.25	3.87	.02
Satisfaction with site (range 2–14)	9.17	10.47	8.54	10.18	6.68	9.33	.43	.65
Perceived credibility (range 5–34)	22.83	22.58	21.54	22.83	23.50	21.77	.53	.59
Reader selectivity (range 2–14)	4.50	5.11	4.20	4.00	5.61	2.25	3.93	.02
Understanding of format (range 4–21)	16.72	16.10	16.54	16.91	14.64	14.91	.23	.80
Memory recognition (range 3–14)	8.67	10.21	9.29	10.45	8.23	11.08	1.21	.31
Cognitive load (range 6–33)	14.61	11.89	12.58	13.90	15.72	14.83	.70	.50

Note. F value = strength of the effect. The data meet the criteria for MANOVA. The determinant value of Bartlett's Sphericity test is small, with a significance of .000, which indicates the dependent values are sufficiently correlated. Homogeneity has not been violated, as results of a Box's M test are not significant.

Hypothesis 4, which posited that the CFT format would be perceived as less credible, was not supported, as the relationship between format type and credibility was not significant. Prior knowledge also had no effect on this relationship. This finding is consistent with at least one prior study, which found no relationship between linearity of format and perceived credibility (Lowrey, 2004), and also supports recent research finding that audiences are increasingly likely to view Internet news as credible (e.g., Johnson & Kaye, 2002; The Pew Research Center, 2000).

Hypothesis 5 received mixed support. Overall, readers were no more likely to scan CFT or nonlinear stories than the linear story, but there was a significant interaction with prior knowledge. Individuals with high prior knowledge were significantly more likely to scan the CFT format and less likely to scan the linear format. Apparently, having higher prior knowledge makes it more likely that format will have an impact on reading pattern. Presumably, when given the CFT format, those who already have some understanding of the cloning issue are more likely to scan across cases and perspectives. They are apparently less interested in reading the story from beginning to end. However, those with higher prior knowledge were also substantially more likely to "fall into the narrative" of the linear story and to read it from beginning to end without skipping or scanning. Among those with lower prior knowledge, format had less of an impact on reading pattern, though they were somewhat more likely to scan the linear story than the nonlinear stories—perhaps reflecting a lack of interest with the longer, less interactive narrative.

Hypothesis 6 received fairly strong support. As predicted, readers were less clear about the format of the CFT story and most clear about the linear story, but there was little difference between the CFT and nonlinear stories on this measure. There was no significant interaction between prior knowledge and understanding of format.

Results offered no support for Hypotheses 7 and 8, which proposed relationships between format type and the cognitive processing variables. There were no significant differences among the three formats for ability to recognize information, and changing the format did not alter degree of cognitive load. It was hypothesized that the CFT and nonlinear sites would lead to more cognitive load and decrease ability to recognize story information, but the null finding suggests nonlinearity is not a stumbling block to rote memorization, despite the finding on Hypothesis 6 that readers said they understood the CFT format less. If this finding does not lend support to optimism about nonlinear formats, neither does it support concern that readers will find nonlinear formats to be disorienting.

Hypothesis 9 predicted that higher prior knowledge would enhance the impact of the CFT format on recognition, but there was no significant interaction effect for recognition (Table 6.2). As mentioned, there were significant interaction effects on extremity of opinion, $F = 3.87$, $p < .05$, and on selectivity of reading $F = 3.93$, $p < .05$.

Prior knowledge had a significant multivariate effect. In univariate tests, direct effects of prior knowledge on self-efficacy, recognition, and satisfaction tested as significant. This means that, regardless of format type, higher prior knowledge of the cloning issue leads to greater confidence in the ability to discuss cloning, $F = 10.39$, $p < .01$, and increased ability to recognize story information, $F = 16.24$, $p < .01$. Individuals with higher prior knowledge also expressed a significantly greater level of satisfaction with the reading experience than those with lower prior knowledge, $F = 9.12$, $p < .01$.

DISCUSSION

Findings suggest the CFT format is moderately beneficial for news audiences, though to some degree this conclusion depends on readers' prior knowledge. Among the three formats, readers viewed the CFT story as most enjoyable, but readers were least likely to understand the CFT story as a journalism story. The significance of the single self-efficacy measure provided some evidence that the CFT format increases confidence in publicly discussing news knowledge. Though the scaled self-efficacy variable, which is more conceptually broad, was not related to story format, the significance of the measure of carrying on "an intelligent conversation" about the issue is worth noting. On its face, this measure lies close to the heart of the concept of public discussion, that is, engaging in a meaningful and open exchange of views. More exploration is needed of the measurement of this important concept.

Readers of the CFT format who had prior knowledge of the cloning issue were less likely to express extreme opinions than were readers of the other formats, and were also more likely to scan for material in which they were interested than to read the whole story. These findings make sense within the constructivist framework of cognitive flexibility theory. The theory says that those with less rigid, more developed schema are better able to incorporate the complexities and gray areas provided by the multiple cases and perspectives of the CFT format. Also, individuals with more prior knowledge have more sophisticated cognitive maps of the knowledge area and therefore find it less necessary to read through the entire story in a linear way. Individuals with less prior knowledge are more likely to read the CFT story by the same method they read the linear story, that is, from "front to back."

Interestingly, readers with more prior knowledge were much more likely to read the linear story in a sequential manner (i.e., front to back) than were readers with less prior knowledge. It may be that the more knowledgeable readers were also more interested in the topic and therefore more likely to "lose themselves" in the linear narrative. Perhaps those with less knowledge, and presumably less interest, were more likely to grow restless while reading the lengthy and passive linear story.

It would seem that readers with more prior knowledge are more able to take control of the reading experience. Those with prior knowledge were presumably less burdened by the need to get a "big picture" of the issue of cloning (what education scholars call "mapping the knowledge domain"), and they were therefore more able to adjust their reading patterns across different formats. They were perhaps more able to use the CFT-formatted story as a sort of scannable reference text, while they were also able to take better advantage of the narrative quality of the linear story. Those with less prior knowledge demonstrated less variability in reading patterns across the three formats. This conclusion partly echoes findings by Curry et al. (1999) that readers with specific search goals tend to create their own reading patterns, whereas readers without specific goals tend to be guided by the structural qualities of the format itself. It is likely that readers with prior knowledge would have specific search goals because of their more developed schema. However, the finding that those with more knowledge tended to read the linear format in a linear way is not consistent with Curry et al. This difference may be attributable in part to the difference in narrative style between linear news stories and linear instructional text, because the news story is more likely to be written in an engaging, storytelling fashion. These findings demonstrate that prior knowledge of a news issue should be taken into account when assessing the impact of format on reading patterns. Advocating a general increase in nonlinearity and interactivity for news content seems ill-advised.

This study's null findings suggest the CFT format neither magically cures oversimplification of news issues nor strongly stimulates public discussion. But a closer look at these findings shows that further study is warranted. It was predicted that the CFT format would lead to less ability to recognize information, be perceived as less credible, and lead to increased cognitive load. Yet the CFT format presented no more problems in these areas than the traditional linear format. This was the case despite the fact that readers said they understood the nature of the CFT format less than the other formats. That readers "enjoyed" using this format more than the traditional formats suggests additional experiments would be worthwhile. That they found this new format to be comparably credible and that the format failed to significantly disorient them lends weight to findings in recent studies that audiences are growing more trustful of, and comfortable with, Internet content.

Limited effects from this experiment may be due partly to the limited nature of the sample, which consisted almost entirely of undergraduate students. Such a sample constrains the impact of a variable like degree of prior knowledge, and it also constrains possible differences by age, degree of news reading experience, and degree of Web use. Also, the experiment would benefit from a test of a second story to help rule out effects deriving from the unique nature of the story content. And, of course, many lab experiments suffer from questionable external validity. Arguably, this experiment suffered less from this limitation because a communication department computer lab is a likely setting for communication students to sit and read news from the Web. The relatively small number of subjects assigned to each format (around 35) may have also contributed to the paucity of statistically significant findings.

In future research it would be helpful to assess impact of formats on actual discussion of news issues rather than only on confidence in one's ability to discuss them. One way to explore this would be to analyze texts of discussions that were based on reading stories. It would also be interesting to assess correlation between self-efficacy and the nature of these discussions. Subsequent research on CFT should also explore relationships among dependent variables. To what degree does cognitive load, understanding of format, and reading selectivity have an impact on recognition? To what degree does recognition have an impact on self-efficacy?

Because education scholars have conducted substantial research on hypermedia effects, it is logical to explore theory from their discipline. However, researchers should consider the applicability of education concepts to the field of journalism. Education and journalism are different occupations with distinct norms and values, and theories from each area reflect these distinctions. For example, journalists may be on shaky ground when proposing specific perspectives for CFT-formatted news stories because the choice of perspectives may be seen as violating the norm of objectivity. Also, the choice of perspectives presents a practical problem. The perspectives on news issues are not as clearly canonized as perspectives in academic subject areas. And it is much easier to define and assess success in an educational environment where students may be formally tested for knowledge transfer.

Cognitive effects from the CFT format may change in the transfer from an educational environment to a journalistic environment. The difference between findings here and the findings by Curry et al. (1999) are an example. Linear news stories may affect readers differently than linear instructional text because the journalist is more likely to emphasize storytelling so as to engage readers. Also, readers are more likely to leisurely scan an online newspaper than an assigned online reading for a class. In education experiments, the expectation is that subjects will read carefully because they will be tested. In the real world, journalism audiences are not tested, and urging subjects to read thoroughly or to anticipate a test would erode external validity.

Though normative and philosophical differences exist between these fields, mass communication and journalism researchers should continue to explore education theory, particularly in the budding area of hypermedia. In doing so, however, researchers should assess findings with these differences in mind, and ultimately they should work to build theory within the mass communication field.

REFERENCES

Altheide, D. L., & Snow, R. P. (1979). *Media logic.* Beverly Hills, CA: Sage.

Anzur, T. (2001, March). Broadcast news: The Web's beached whale. *Online Journalism Review.* Retrieved May 14, 2004, from http://www.ojr.org/ojr/business/1017961488.php

Balcytiene, A. (1999). Exploring individual processes of knowledge construction with hypertext. *Instructional Science, 27,* 303–328.

Baylor, A. L. (2001). Perceived disorientation and incidental learning in a Web-based environment: Internal and external factors. *Journal of Educational Multimedia & Hypermedia, 10,* 227–251.

Bong, M., & Hocevar, D. (2002). Measuring self-efficacy: Multitrait-multimethod comparison of scaling procedures. *Applied Measurement in Education, 15,* 143–171.

Cappella, J. A., & Jamieson, K. H. (1997). *Spiral of cynicism.* New York: Oxford University Press.

Chan-Olmsted, S. M., & Park, J. S. (2000). From on-air to online world: Examining the content and structures of broadcast TV stations' Web sites. *Journalism and Mass Communication Quarterly, 77,* 321–339.

Charney, D. (1994). The impact of hypertext on processes of reading and writing. In S. J. Hilligoss & C. L. Selfe (Eds.), *Literacy and computers: The complications of teaching and learning with technology* (pp. 238–263). New York: Modern Language Association.

Curry, J., Haderlie, S., Ta-Wei, K., Lawless, K. A., Lemon, M., & Wood, R. (1999). Specified learning goals and their effect on learners' representations of a hypertext reading environment. *International Journal of Instructional Media, 26,* 43–51.

Dee-Lucas, D., & Larkin, J. H. (1995). Learning from electronic texts: Effects of interactive overviews for information access. *Cognition and Instruction, 13,* 431–468.

Demetriadis, S., & Pombortsis, A. (2000, June). *Novice student learning in a case-based hypermedia environment: A quantitative study.* Paper presented at the International Conference of the Learning Sciences, Ann Arbor, MI.

Domke, D., Shah, D. V., & Wackman, D. B. (1998). "Moral referendums": Values, news media, and the process of candidate choice. *Political Communication, 15,* 301–321.

Eveland, W. P., Jr., & Dunwoody, S. (2000). Examining information processing on the World Wide Web using think aloud protocols. *Media Psychology, 2,* 219–244.

Eveland, W. P., Jr. & Dunwoody, S. (2001). User control and structural isomorphism or disorientation and cognitive load? Learning from Web versus print. *Communication Research, 28,* 48–78.

Eveland, W. P., Jr., & Dunwoody, S. (2002). An investigation of elaboration and selective scanning as mediators of learning from the Web versus print. *Journal of Broadcasting & Electronic Media, 46,* 34–53.

Eveland, W. P., Jr., Marton, K., & Seo, M. (2004). Moving beyond "just the facts": The influence of online news on the content and structure of public affairs knowledge. *Communication Research, 31,* 82–108.

Fallows, J. (1997). *Breaking the news.* New York: Vintage.

Fishman, M. (1980). *Manufacturing the news.* Austin: University of Texas Press.

Flanagin, A., & Metzger, M. (2000). Perceptions of Internet information credibility. *Journalism and Mass Communication Quarterly, 77,* 515–540.

Fredin, E. (1997). Rethinking the news story for the Internet: Hyperstory prototypes and a model of the user. *Journalism and Mass Communication Monographs, 163.*

Fredin, E., & David, P. (1998) Browsing and the hypermedia interaction cycle: A model of self-efficacy and goal dynamics. *Journalism and Mass Communication Quarterly, 75,* 35–54.

Garrand, T. (2001). *Writing for multimedia and the Web.* Oxford, England: Focal Press.

Gellevij, M., Van der Meij, H., De Jong, T., & Pieters, J. (2002). Multimodal versus unimodal instruction in a complex learning environment. *The Journal of Experimental Education, 70,* 215–239.

Graziano, C., & McGrath, K. (1986). Measuring the concept of credibility. *Journalism Quarterly, 63,* 451–462.

Hannafin, R. D., & Sullivan, H. J. (1996). Preferences and learner control over amount of instruction. *Journal of Educational Psychology, 88,* 162–173.

Hendrickson, L. J., & Tankard, J. W. (1997). Expanding the news frame: The systems theory perspective. *Journalism & Mass Communication Educator, 52,* 39–46.

Jacobson, M. J., Maouri, C., Mishra, P., & Kolar, C. (1995). Learning with hypertext learning environments: Theory, design, and research. *Journal of Educational Multimedia and Hypermedia, 4,* 321–364.

Jacobson, M. J., & Spiro, R. J. (1995). Hypertext learning environments, cognitive flexibility, and the transfer of complex knowledge: An empirical investigation. *Journal of Educational Computing Research, 12,* 301–333.

Jaffe, M. J. (1995). *Media interactivity, cognitive flexibility and self-efficacy.* Unpublished doctoral dissertation. University of Michigan, Ann Arbor.

Johnson, T., & Kaye, B. (2000). Using is believing: The influence of reliance on the credibility of online political information among politically interested Internet users. *Journalism and Mass Communication Quarterly, 77,* 865–879.

Johnson, T., & Kaye, B. (2002). Webelievability: A path model examining how convenience and reliance predict online credibility. *Journalism and Mass Communication Quarterly, 79,* 619–642.

Lanson, J. (2000, August 24). It's time to make Web an equal partner. *Online Journalism Review.* Retrieved May 14, 2004, from http://www.ojr.org/ojr/business/1017963559.php

Lasica, J. D. (2003, August 7). What is participatory journalism? *Online Journalism Review.* Retrieved May 14, 2004, from http://www.ojr.org/ojr/workplace/1060217106.php

Lowrey, W. (2003). Explaining decision-making about online news at small newspapers. *Newspaper Research Journal, 24*, 83–90.

Lowrey, W. (2004). Linear vs. nonlinear Web stories: An assessment of reader perceptions, knowledge acquisition and reader feedback. *Newspaper Research Journal, 25*, 83–97.

McAdams, M. (2000, December). Lesson 2: Why news is old news. *NewsLink.* Retrieved Nov. 15, 2003, from http://newslink.org/mmcol2.html

McQuail, D. (2000). *Mass communication theory.* London: Sage.

Morrison, G. R., Ross, S. M., & Baldwin, W. (1992). Learner control of context and instructional support in learning elementary school mathematics. *Educational Technology Research and Development, 40*, 5–13.

Niederhauser, D. S., Reynolds, R. E., Salmen, D. J., & Skolmoski, P. (2000). The influence of cognitive load on learning hypertext. *Journal of Educational Computing Research, 23*, 237–255.

Outing, S. (2000, October). Are days of innovation waning for online news? *Editor and Publisher, 11.*

Outing, S. (2003, July 31). Blogs have a place on news Web sites: Reporters and readers can contribute. *Editor & Publisher.* Retrieved May 14, 2004, from http://www.editorandpublisher.com

Paul, N., & Fiebich, C. (2000). *The elements of digital storytelling.* Retrieved May 14, 2004, from http://www.inms.umn.edu/Elements/index.php

The Pew Research Center for the People and the Press. (2000, December 3). *Internet election news audience seeks convenience, familiar names.* Retrieved May 14, 2004 from http://people-press.org/reports/display.php3?ReportID=21.

Rich, C. (1999). *Creating online media: A guide to researching, writing and design on the Internet.* New York: McGraw-Hill.

Rossner-Merrill, V., Parker, D., Mamchur, C., & Chu, S. (1998). Using constructivist instructional design featured in two online courses: Notes from the field. *Journal of Educational Media International, 35*, 282–288.

Shyu, H., & Brown, S. (1995). Learner-control: The effects of learning a procedural task during computer based videodisk instruction. *International Journal of Instructional Media, 22*, 217–231

Siegel, M., Derry, S., Kim, J. B., Steinkuehler, C., Street, J., Canty, N., Faasnacht, C., Hawson, K., Hmelo, C., & Spiro, R. (2000, June). *Promoting teachers' flexible use of the learning sciences through case-based problem solving on the WWW: A theoretical design approach.* Paper presented at the International Conference of the Learning Sciences, Ann Arbor, MI.

Singer, J. (2002). Information trumps interaction in local papers' online caucus coverage. *Newspaper Research Journal, 23*, 91–96.

Singer, J. (2003). Campaign contributions: Online newspaper coverage of Election 2000. *Journalism and Mass Communication Quarterly, 80*, 39–56.

South, J. (1999, June 11). Web staffs urge the print side to think ahead. *Online Journalism Review.* Retrieved May 14, 2004, from http://www.ojr.org/ojr/business/1017968570.php

Spiro, R. J., Feltovich, P. J., Jacobson, M. J., & Coulson, R. L. (1991). Cognitive flexibility, constructivism, and hypertext: Random access instruction for advanced knowledge acquisition in ill-structured domains. *Educational Technology, 31*, 24–33.

Spiro, R., & Jehng, J. (1990). Cognitive flexibility and hypertext: Theory and technology for the nonlinear and multidimensional traversal of complex subject matter. In D. Nix and R. Spiro (Eds.), *Cognition, education and multimedia: Exploring ideas in high technology* (pp. 163–205). Hillsdale, NJ: Lawrence Erlbaum Associates.

Valentino, N. A., Buhr, T. A., & Beckmann, M. N. (2001). When the frame is the game: Revisiting the impact of "strategic" campaign coverage of citizens' information retention. *Journalism and Mass Communication Quarterly, 78*, 93–112.

Van Nimwegen, C., Pouw, M., & Van Oostendorp, H. (1999). The influence of structure and reading-manipulation on usability of hypertexts. *Interacting with Computers, 12*, 7–21.

II

EMERGING MEDIUM IN AN INTERACTIVE PROCESS

7

Effect of Growing Internet Newspapers on Circulation of U.S. Print Newspapers

Zhanwei Cao
University of Texas, Dallas

Xigen Li
Southern Illinois University Carbondale

Early in 1986, when new interactive technologies had been available only for several years in the United States, Rogers (1986) pointed out that these technologies produced a profound effect. He argued that the new media were shaking the foundations of how communication could occur. The potential uses were intriguing and the scale of effects hard to believe. As the Internet newspaper developed in the early 1990s, enthusiasm for online newspapers led some media analysts to predict that "printed newspapers would disappear in the near future" (McCulloch, 1995, p. 56). As the Internet grew, print newspaper users appeared to be shrinking (Stempel, 2000). Considering the advantages of the Internet newspaper over print newspapers, a question arises: Has the Internet newspaper already derived readers from print newspapers?

The purpose of this study is to examine the effect of Internet newspapers on circulation of print newspapers in the United States since 1995. This study aims to find changes of print newspaper circulation and the Internet newspaper readership from 1995 to 2000 and the relationship between growth of the Internet newspapers and circulation of print newspapers.

EFFECT OF NEW MEDIA TECHNOLOGY
ON OLD MEDIA

New technologies bring new opportunities as well as threats to existing media (Peng, Irene, & Hao, 1999). Rogers (1986) discussed the effects of television on film and radio in the 1950s in the United States and noted that leisure time use was affected, as television grabbed huge gobs of time away from radio-listening, reading, and other activities.

In a study of the effect of new technology on existing mass media advertising revenues and consumer spending between 1929 and 1968, McCombs (1972) proposed the hypothesis of relative constancy. He found that media spending by consumers roughly paralleled the growth of consumers' income. Consumer spending on mass media was constant over time. The implication of this proposition for traditional media was clear: If new mass communication technology survived and thrived, it would be at the expense of traditional mass communication media (Bromley & Bowles, 1995; McCombs & Byal, 1980).

However, more recent studies about new media technology suggest that the spending on new communication technology did not follow the trend of relative constancy. These studies showed that total consumer spending on mass media during the diffusion of cable television and videocassette recorder increased rather than remained relatively constant (Dupagne, 1994; Glascock, 1993; Son & McCombs, 1993). Wood (1986) also argued that constancy would fail as consumers devoted a greater share of income to buy new media technology. Wood and O'Hare (1991) found that new video technology, such as VCR, was established without displacing the older mass media. The results of these studies suggest that new media growth may not be at the expense of older media.

As a new media technology, the Internet occurred in the early 1970s, and is becoming a mass medium with unprecedented speed (Morris & Ogan, 1996). The new medium is not simply "a linear extension of the old (Dizard, 1997, p. 11). Compared to print newspapers, the Internet newspapers clearly enjoy some advantages. For example, this medium can deliver the news immediately; Internet sites can be updated whenever a reporter discovers more information (Harper, 1996). The rapid growth of the Internet even changed the ritual of reading a daily newspaper. Once newspaper reading was limited to the one serving people's home city or town plus a national daily like *The Wall Street Journal* or *USA Today*. Now, however, local papers and any one of numerous newspapers from across the country are "only a few clicks away" (Chyi & Lasorsa, 1999, pp. 16–17). With all the advantages, the "virtual newspapers will become a competitive displacement for printed newspapers" (Fitzgerald, 1996, p. 72).

Studies found some support for relative constancy with growth of the Internet newspapers. A survey by *Editor & Publisher* found that more than one third of the users of Web sites run by newspapers said they reduced their reading of print newspapers since going online. A survey conducted in Texas reported that among

PointCast Users who are predominately business people, nearly half of them spend less time reading newspapers (Outing, 1998).

EFFECT OF THE INTERNET NEWSPAPER
ON PRINT NEWSPAPERS

Researchers proposed that print newspapers and their online counterparts were characterized by head-on competition, and readers shifted from print to online (Chyi & Sylvie, 1998). A survey released in September 2000 pointed out that when users surfed online for local information, the first place they were likely to go was their local newspaper's Web site (Phipps, 2000). Across the country, about 66% of the online readers in a representative sample knew about their local newspaper's web sites. Another survey conducted by Barrett (1997) found that 67% of online readers frequently read newspapers on the Internet.

Early in 1996, Bittner predicted that the rapid growth of Internet newspapers would create the most provoking situation that newspaper publishing has to deal with. Nearly half of American newspaper executives felt their papers could be harmed by Internet-based competition. Some news executives said that readers would continue to adopt Internet newspapers for news consumption with enthusiasm (Gleick & Blackman, 1996). They predicted that digital news would soon be as important as or more important than the printed page.

However, other studies revealed that the effect of the Internet on print newspapers was still slight at present (Peng et al., 1999). An Internet usage study of adults 18 and over in the top 50 U.S. markets suggested that time spent on the Internet was not necessarily time taken away from newspapers; just 15% of respondents said they were reading less, another 8% said they were reading more, and 74% said their reading habits had stayed the same since going on the Web (Fitzgerald, 1999).

A survey by research consortium VIPer of AB graded 25- to 54-year-olds in economically active households and also claimed that online newspapers were not reducing traditional readerships (Anonymous, 2000). Of those questioned, 91% said that their readership of newspapers had remained the same despite the presence of a corresponding online version. The survey found that only 3% of those questioned had reduced their readership of national newspapers, and 86% rejected the idea that within 10 years they would be mainly reading their newspaper online.

Changes in readership of print newspapers also varied by newspaper size. An *Editor & Publisher* survey found that about 30% of the users of Web sites run by newspapers with 250,000 circulation or higher said they reduced their reading of print newspapers since going online. At papers with circulation under 250,000, only 20% of online readers said they were reading the print edition less (Fitzgerald, 1999).

During the start-up period for Internet use, use of traditional media remained the same (Bromley & Bowles, 1995). Later studies showed that there was a shift of readers from print to Internet newspapers. But more predictions were heard than hard evidence was found that Internet newspapers were replacing print newspapers. Was the growth of the Internet newspapers associated with the decline of newspaper circulation during the past 6 to 7 years? To what degree did the growth of the Internet newspapers affect newspaper circulation? No previous studies addressed these questions that are critical to newspaper industries. Previous studies looked at the trend of newspaper circulation and readership changes, yet few of them examined the print newspaper circulation changes by taking into account the growth of the Internet newspapers.

Newspaper circulation, which tallies the number of newspapers sold or distributed, has been the "prime gauge of market effectiveness" and "indicator of newspaper industry's health" (Schwirtz & Dori, 1998, pp. 8–10). Unlike previous studies, this study analyzes newspaper circulation, page impressions, and unique users of online newspapers during the 1995 to 2000 period. It also incorporates newspaper publishers' perception when examining the changes of trends of print and Internet newspapers. Based on the previous studies of media transition and replacement and expansion of new media technology, this study aims to test two hypotheses and provide the answer to one research question.

H1: The growth of Internet newspaper readership is negatively related to the circulation of print newspapers.

According to Maxwell McCombs's hypothesis of relative constancy and previous studies of effect of new media technology on existing media, it is expected that as the Internet newspaper readership grows, and fewer people buy and read print newspapers, the circulation of print newspaper declines. Although more recent studies suggested emergence of new media technology may not be at the expense of older media, evidence has to be found from the Internet news media.

H2: The effect of Internet newspapers on circulation of print newspapers varies among newspapers of different sizes.

According to the circulation reports by the Audit Bureau of Circulations (ABC), circulation changes for newspapers of different size were not the same. Also, the literature indicated that the percentages of different-sized Internet newspaper users who said they reduced their reading of print newspapers since going online were different. Therefore, effect of Internet newspapers on circulation of print newspapers may vary among newspapers of different size.

RQ: From publishers' perspective, to what extent was the growth of the Internet newspapers associated with the circulation decline of print newspapers?

Considering the advantages of Internet newspapers over print newspapers, we expect that the Internet newspapers were changing traditional newspaper readers' habit from reading a print newspaper to getting news from the Internet. The publishers monitored closely the circulation as the Internet newspapers grew. Their perception of effect of Internet newspapers on circulation of print newspapers provides supporting evidence to what circulation data will show.

METHOD

This study used an Internet survey to collect data of the U.S. Internet newspapers and publishers' perception of effect of Internet newspapers on print newspapers. This study focused on U.S. daily newspapers for three reasons. First, the U.S. newspaper industry is leading the world in Web publishing with 61% of all the existing Internet newspapers. Second, the United States also leads in communication technologies and Internet accessibility. Third, the Internet is largely an English-speaking medium (Peng et al., 1999).

Although Internet newspapers started publishing in 1994, this study set the year of 1995 as the starting point. According to *Newslink,* at the beginning of 1994, only 28 U.S. newspapers were online (Meyer, 1998), whereas 1995 was "the right busy year in the burgeoning interactive newspaper industries" (Outing, 1996, p. 41). Conducting the study after 1995 would be sufficient to examine the overall effect of Internet newspapers on print newspapers.

Sampling

This study used stratified random sampling. A list of online newspapers from the Web site of *American Journalism Review* (http://newslink.org/daynews.html) was used as the sampling frame. It was considered one of the most reliable and up-to-date lists of online newspapers (Schultz, 1999). There were 1,265 daily newspapers offering full online service in United States at the time of sampling. An e-mail survey of online U.S. daily newspapers by Peng et al. (1999) achieved a 27% response rate. Taking the low response rate of Internet survey into account, the sample size of daily online newspapers should be large enough to ensure that there will be enough cases for data analysis. Fifty percent of the online newspapers were to be selected from each state by stratified random sampling to produce a representative sample. However, according to *American Journalism Review* (http://newslink.org/daynews.html, accessed Jan. 2001), development of Internet newspapers in different states was not balanced. States like California and Pennsylvania had a large number of online newspapers, whereas other states such as Nevada, Montana, and Vermont had relatively few. Due to the imbalance of the number of online newspapers in different states, those states with fewer than five online newspapers were oversampled and at least five online newspapers were selected from each state. A sample of 629 online newspapers was selected.

Key Concepts and Operational Definitions

Page Impressions.   A page impression is defined as the combination of one or more files presented to a user as a single document as a result of a single request received by the server (International Federation of Audit Bureau of Circulations, 2001). It is the exact number of times a specific Web site has been accessed or viewed by a user (Webopedia, 2004), also called page views. It is one of the industry standards to measure Internet newspaper readership. Page impressions are used to measure the number of actual pages of content displayed.

Unique Users.   This is another industry standard to measure Internet newspaper readership. Unique users are used to measure the number of different people who visit the site over a given period of time. A unique user is identified through an IP address plus a further identifier such as User Agent, Cookie, and/or Registration ID (International Federation of Audit Bureau of Circulations, 2001).

Circulation.   The number of print newspapers sold or distributed over a certain period of time is its circulation. In the *Editor & Publisher International Yearbook,* the period is 3 months. The circulation of print newspapers was divided into three categories: small (below 10,000), medium (10,000 to 50,000), and large (above 50,000).

Publishers' Perception of Effect of the Internet Newspapers on Print Newspapers' Circulation.   This indicates whether publishers of the Internet newspapers consider the growth of the Internet newspapers affects print newspapers' circulation. Publishers' perception was measured with three items using the Likert scale: (a) Internet newspapers have shifted traditional readers away from your print newspaper; (b) Internet newspaper users reduced their reading of your print newspaper since the start of the Internet newspaper; (c) as your Internet newspaper grows, the print newspaper circulation declines.

Data Collection

A questionnaire was constructed to collect the data about the Internet newspapers. It contained questions on three aspects: (a) readership change of the Internet newspapers since the startup, including changes of page impression and unique users from 1995 to 2000; (b) number of staff change of the Internet newspapers since the startup; and (c) publishers' perceptions of effect of the Internet newspapers on print newspapers' circulation. Twenty newspapers were first randomly selected from the sample for a pretest. A questionnaire was electronically mailed to their publishers or online editors. The questionnaire was revised according to the six responses received. The questionnaire was then sent to the publishers and online editors of 629 newspapers via e-mail. A follow-up reminder and another copy of the questionnaire was sent to nonrespondents one week after the initial mailing. Among the 629 newspapers, 37 e-mail addresses were not valid. They were thus excluded from the sample. By the deadline, 118 usable survey questionnaires were received from the Internet newspaper publishers and online editors in 48 states, which comprised a 20% response rate. Although the relatively low response rate was consistent with other Internet surveys, the majority of the states where Internet newspapers published were present, which gave nearly a full coverage of the geographic areas of the United States.

The circulation data of the corresponding print newspapers 5 years before and after 1995 were collected from *Editor & Publisher International Yearbook.*

FINDINGS

Circulation

To examine circulation trend within the past 11 years, box plots were used.[1] The 118 newspapers were divided into three categories: small (below 10,000), medium (10,001 to 50,000) and large (above 50,000) according to the size of the average circulation of each newspaper from 1990 to 2000. The results showed the trend of circulation change of the small, medium, and large newspapers during the 11-year period.

Comparing the box ranges of the circulation across the years, small-sized newspapers did not show an evident growing or declining trend. By examining the medium lines within the box of small-sized newspapers, it was found that the circulation had been declining from 1990 to 2000 (–11.7%), and declined more after 1995, especially during 1995 to 1996 (–4.5%). This finding supports the proposition that the levels of circulation decline were different for the two periods: 1990 to 1995 (–3%) and 1995 to 2000 (–9%) (see Fig. 7.1).

The results showed the circulation of the medium-sized newspapers grew slightly from 1990 to 1991, and then showed a 14% decline through 2000 from its peak in 1991. For the medium-sized newspapers, there was no obvious circulation difference between the periods before and after 1995. For the large-sized newspapers, there was no declining trend in their circulation; instead, large newspaper circulation grew 7.3% from 1995 to 2000.

Page Impressions and Unique Users

The data of page impression and unique user of the Internet newspapers were examined at three levels—small, medium, and large. Box plots outlined both the

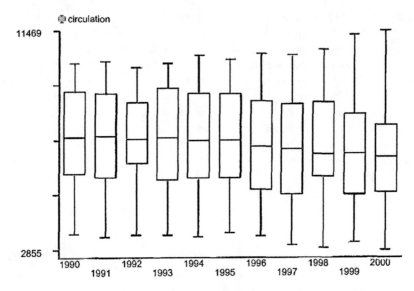

FIG. 7.1.   Box Plot 1: small-sized newspapers.

growing trends of page impressions and unique users. Whether looking from the point of medium line, the box range, or the whole range, all Internet newspapers' (small, medium, and large) page impressions increased substantially from 1995 to 2000. The page impressions of the Internet newspapers grew exponentially in 1997, as high as 1,000% for medium-sized newspapers and 1,900% for large-sized newspapers. The growing trend slowed down after 1999, but still at a rate of more than 50% each year (see Fig. 7.2).

Box plots also revealed that Internet newspaper unique users had been increasing in a similar pattern as page impressions for newspapers of all sizes since 1995, although the growing magnitude was not as substantial as page impressions (see Table 7.1).

Relationship Between Page Impressions/Unique Users and Circulation

Log Linear Model was employed to examine the relationship between growth of Internet newspapers readership and the circulation of print newspapers. Because the data were not normally distributed, the data were transformed to logarithms and a statistical model was built to test the association between the two variables. In addition, Log Linear Model was used for the special purpose of testing the relationships between the variables among time series data. Three Log Linear Models were built for the three newspaper groups—small, medium, and large—assuming that the marginal distribution of circulation for each newspaper since 1995 was

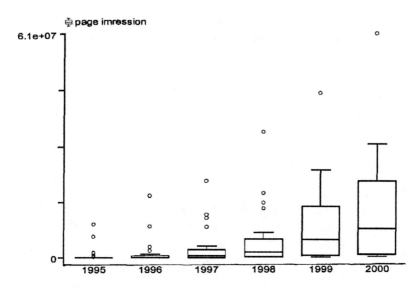

FIG. 7.2.   Box Plot 2: Page impressions of large-sized newspapers.

TABLE 7.1
Changes in Average Circulation of Print Newspapers and Page Impression
of the Internet Newspapers

	Small		Medium		Large	
Year	Circulation	Page Impression	Circulation	Page Impression	Circulation	Page Impression
1990	7,377	N.A.	21,253	N.A.	84,033	N.A.
1991	7,485	N.A.	23,841	N.A.	84,033	N.A.
1992	7,270	N.A.	22,978	N.A.	90,700	N.A.
1993	7,302	N.A.	21,253	N.A.	90,700	N.A.
1994	7,162	N.A.	21,253	N.A.	97,368	N.A.
1995	7,162	500	21,253	1,000	90,700	1,525
1996	6,839	1,000	20,649	6,000	90,700	15,250
1997	6,731	1,500	20,908	70,000	90,700	305,000
1998	6,624	3,500	21,253	405,000	84,033	2,287,500
1999	6,656	5,250	21,253	1,350,000	90,700	5,337,500
2000	6,516	8,750	20,390	2,025,000	97,368	8,387,500

different; circulation changed over time; and the circulation was influenced by the growing readership of Internet newspapers—page impressions and unique users.

Negative Relationship Between Growth of Internet Newspaper and Circulation

Hypothesis 1, that the growth of Internet newspaper readership is negatively related to the circulation of print newspapers, was weakly supported. The findings indicated that there was a slightly negative effect of the growth of Internet newspaper readership on circulation of print newspapers.

Small-Sized Newspapers. The average page impression and unique user increases of the small-sized newspapers were 59,829 and 16,860. The results indicated that the relationship between circulation and page impressions or unique users was present. Small-sized newspapers' circulation decreased 1.19% every year. Adjusting for time trend, every 100,000 increase in page impression corresponded to 1.43% decrease in circulation, and every 100,000 increase in unique users corresponded to 1.50% decrease in circulation. The findings of small-sized newspapers weakly support Hypothesis 1 that the growth of Internet newspaper readership is negatively related to the circulation of print newspapers (see Table 7.2).

Medium-Sized Newspapers. The average page impression and unique user increases of the medium-sized newspaper circulation were 1,559,396 and

TABLE 7.2.
Relationship Between Page Impression/Unique User and Circulation

	Coefficient	Std Error	P value	95% Confidence Interval	
Small					
Time	−.0119177	.0002688	0.001	−.0124445	−.0113908
Page impression	−1.43e−07	8.35e−09	0.001	−1.59e−07	−1.27e−07
Unique user	−1.50e−07	2.62e−08	0.001	9.89e−08	2.02e−07
Constant	32.64	0.54	0.001	31.58	33.69
Medium					
Time	−.000206	.0000982	0.036	−.0003985	−.0000136
Page impression	−3.92e−09	8.92e−11	0.001	−4.10e−09	−3.75e−09
Unique user	−2.86e−09	1.14e−10	0.001	2.63c−09	3.08e−09
Constant	10.61	0.21	0.001	10.21	11.02
Large					
Time	.0103729	.0000603	0.001	.0102546	.0104911
Page impression	−1.70e−09	252e−11	0.001	−1.75e−09	−1.65e−09
Unique user	−1.26e−09	1.94e−11	0.001	−1.30e−09	−1.22e−09
Constant	−8.72	0.18	0.001	−9.06	−8.17

585,855. For medium-sized newspapers, there was also a relationship between page impressions/unique users and circulation. Medium-sized newspapers' circulation decreased 0.02% every year. Adjusting for time trend, every 10,000,000 increase in page impression was associated with 3.92% decrease in circulation, and every 10,000,000 increase in unique users correlated to 2.86% decrease in circulation. The findings of medium-sized newspapers also support Hypothesis 1 that growth of Internet newspapers readership is negatively related to circulation.

Large-Sized Newspapers. The average page impression and unique user increases of the large-sized newspapers were 2,882,068 and 1,391,861. The large-sized newspaper circulation was also influenced by page impressions/unique users. Unlike small and medium newspapers, the overall large newspaper circulation increased 1.0% every year. Adjusting for time trend, every 10,000,000 increase in page impression was associated with 1.70% decrease in circulation, and every 10,000,000 increase in unique users was associated with 1.26% decrease in circulation. Therefore, for large newspapers, the findings also support Hypothesis 1.

Newspaper Size and the Effect

Because the coefficients between page impressions of Internet newspapers and print newspaper circulation showed clear differences among small, medium, and large newspapers, findings support Hypothesis 2 that effect of Internet newspaper growth on circulation of print newspapers varies among newspapers of different sizes. In order to see how the effect of the growth of the Internet newspaper was different for different-sized newspapers, the decrease percentages of circulation corresponding to average page impression increase in the years from 1995 to 2000 were calculated. The average page impressions for the small, medium, and large newspapers during 1995 to 2000 were, respectively, 59,829, 1,559,396, and 2,882,068. Results showed that every 59,829 increase in small online newspaper page impression corresponded to 0.85% decrease in circulation; every 1,559,396 increase in medium online newspaper page impression corresponded to 0.61% decrease in circulation; and every 2,882,068 increase in larger newspaper page impression led to 0.49% decrease in circulation. Therefore, the larger the newspaper, the smaller the effect of Internet newspapers on print newspapers' circulation.

Publishers' Perceptions of the Effect of the Internet Newspaper

The data of the survey provided the answer to the research questions: From a publishers' perspective, to what extent was the growth of the Internet newspapers associated with the circulation decline of print newspapers? Forty-one percent of newspaper publishers agreed that their Internet newspapers had shifted some traditional readers away from the print newspapers, and 43% of newspaper publishers agreed that their current Internet newspaper users had reduced their reading of print newspapers. The findings indicated that the Internet newspaper was associated with the circulation decline of print newspapers to a certain degree. However, more than half of the publishers did not agree Internet newspapers had shifted traditional readers away from the print papers.

The results of the survey indicated that the Internet newspapers had been growing steadily. Fifty-six percent of the publishers said that their Internet newspaper staff had been increasing; 97% of publishers believed that Internet newspaper readership had been increasing since their newspapers went online. Such results were consistent with the findings about growing page impressions and unique users.

Twenty-six percent of the publishers agreed that as Internet newspapers grew, the circulation of print newspapers declined, whereas 44% disagreed. This indicated that about one fourth of online newspaper publishers regarded the growth of the Internet newspaper as a factor accounting for the declining print newspaper circulation.

DISCUSSION

This study analyzed the print newspaper circulation and readership of the Internet newspapers using page impressions and unique users of 118 U.S. newspapers. It explored the relationship between the growth of the Internet newspaper readership and the print newspaper circulation. Moreover, this study employed newspaper publishers' perception as a supporting argument. The results showed growth of the Internet newspapers had a slight effect on print newspapers.

The findings indicated that Internet newspaper readership was growing dramatically since 1995 while the overall print newspaper circulation was declining. An increase in page impression was associated with a decrease of circulation for newspapers of all sizes. But such negative effect on circulation of print newspapers since 1995 was not as significant as analysts predicted. In addition, more than half of the newspaper publishers disagreed that the Internet newspaper was reducing print newspapers' circulation. The findings were consistent with Peng et al.'s (1999) argument that the online newspapers were not greatly eroding traditional readerships.

The findings have important implications for the principle of relative constancy. More recent studies about new media technology suggest that new media growth may not be at the expense of older media. This study explored a new type of media technology, the Internet newspaper. The findings support the arguments on relative constancy in the age of new media technology with new evidence. During 1995 to 2000, the readership of the Internet newspapers grew exponentially; while the newspaper circulation showed a decline trend, the degree of decline was far from remarkable. In the case of small- and medium-size newspapers, there was some decline, but not in a scale that showed evident replacing effect of the Internet newspapers. In the case of large newspapers, instead of a decline, there was an increase of circulation. Overall, as the Internet newspapers grew significantly during 1995 to 2000, the newspaper circulation incurred little changes. When embracing new media technology such as the Internet newspapers, consumers did not abandon print newspapers. It could be true that consumers are willing to spend an increased share of income on mass media in the age of new media technology (Wood & O'Hare, 1991). The findings of the study suggest that the theory of relative constancy needs further test with the increasing readership of the Internet newspapers.

The findings of this study showed limited effect of the growth of the Internet newspaper readership on newspaper circulation. Four reasons may account for this situation.

First, and the most important, Internet newspaper users were more likely to be those who read print newspapers quite often as well. The readership of online newspapers is composed of a special group of newspaper readers, those who read the same newspaper in its hard copy (Peng et al., 1999). Pew Research Center surveys found that online audiences turned to news Web sites mostly to get information of specific interest to them rather than to browse the news and find out what's happening (Kohut, 2000).

Second, the Internet newspapers have not become as popular as print newspapers due to required access to the Internet. When people were unable to have frequent access to the Internet, or had to spend more money on the Internet than buying a newspaper, a print newspaper remained a better option. Moreover, some people still preferred the feel of reading a print newspaper.

The third reason is related to the nature of the Internet newspaper. Although the Internet newspaper was viewed as a new medium, most online newspapers remained complements to traditional print newspapers, despite the fact that online services were expanding rapidly (Keizer, 1995). The Internet newspapers reproduced the substance of their print editions in a way that relates similarly to readers (Barnhurst, 2002). An information-seeking model helps explain the greater newspaper use by Internet users, and this information-seeking behavior may run two ways. Internet users may turn to their newspapers or newspaper readers may go to the Internet for more information on a given topic. Either is possible sequentially as a supplemental information-seeking behavior.

Fourth, the Internet newspaper is not the only news source on the Internet. Readers often turn to other news sources such as MSNBC, CNN Interactive, Wired News, CNET, and Yahoo! News if they cannot find breaking news from their online newspapers. That may explain why the negative effect of the Internet on print newspaper has not reached a significant level.

The findings suggest that the smaller the newspaper, the larger effect the Internet newspapers had on the print newspapers. Three factors may account for this phenomenon.

First, larger print newspapers are more accessible than smaller ones. They are more likely to be sold in neighboring places besides the one of origin. Thus larger newspapers own a more diverse readership group. Small newspapers do not possess many readers outside of its place of origin. Therefore, once a small portion of their readers turns to the online version, their circulation could go down more obviously than larger newspapers facing the same situation.

Second, people are more likely to buy a larger print newspaper than a smaller one assuming that both are accessible. Due to the different characters of the Internet and print newspapers, people may buy a print newspaper even if they read Internet newspapers. It is rational that people buy a larger print newspaper because of the higher quality and wider scope of content while they access the smaller newspapers online.

Third, the circulation decrease of larger newspapers was not as serious as smaller ones in the past 6 years. Therefore, the effect on circulation looked smaller for larger newspapers. Stein (1998) pointed out that larger dailies were focusing more attention on improving editorial content and increasing circulation. Increasing competition and new technologies are forcing all newspapers to revamp their goals, but small papers may be less able to adapt as they are facing more economic pressures. Larger newspapers have a competitive advantage because they benefit from economies of scale and can produce a newspaper for a much lower cost.

Because the effect of the Internet newspaper was not remarkable according to the findings, other factors should also be taken into account when looking at declining newspaper circulation. First, many newspapers raised circulation prices aggressively, which depressed circulation, first to counter sluggish advertising performance during the recession in the early 1990s, then to offset rising newsprint costs in 1994 and 1995. Second, some newspapers eliminated circulation in areas distant from a newspaper's home market, in the belief that such remote circulation was of little interest to local advertisers and therefore unprofitable. Both strategies had economically rational underpinnings, and both contributed greatly to the circulation declines (Morton, 1997). Other news sources such as network TV news, cable news, radio, and weekly publications could also have contributed to the decline. In addition, factors such as population changes and general penetration trends in newspapers may also account for the circulation decline.

On the whole, newspaper publishers and editors considered the Internet little threat to the industry. Only one third of publishers in this study agreed that their online operations had cut into circulation. Peng et al. (1999) argued that the print newspaper would not be replaced by the Internet newspaper for at least the next 10 years. Instead, both print and online newspapers would flourish together. Chyi and Lasorsa (1999) also found that users did not view print and online versions of the same newspaper as competitive, an assumption from which many newspaper owners and editor appear to be operating. One of the most important characteristics of an innovation in terms of its rate of adoption is its relative advantage. Users appear not to view online newspapers as superseding print newspapers, but instead they tend to view the two newspaper versions as complementing each other. Although obviously the use of Internet newspapers is growing at unbelievably rapid rates, the effect on print papers needs further observation. The Internet newspapers as a public news source still mostly co-exist with print newspapers in the lives of online Americans. People's news habits have not been affected much by the growth of the Internet newspapers.

CONCLUSION

This study defied the skeptics who have been proclaiming the demise of print newspapers since the dawn of the Internet age (Case, 2000). It also added some evidence about the argument of relative constancy in the age of new media technology. The growth of new media may not be at the expense of the older media. The Internet newspapers were considered by many newspaper publishers an opportunity to help reverse the trend in declining readership rather than a threat to the print newspaper. With little chance of being replaced by the online version, the print newspapers could grow with the Internet newspapers, which are opening up broader prospects for the newspaper industry.

The findings offered three tentative conclusions. First, the study found circulation of print newspapers has been declining since 1990. There was no difference in circulation changes between the two periods 1990 to 1994 and 1995 to 2000. The later period was marked by the popularity of Internet newspapers. Although the declining trend was not evident for large newspapers, the majority of print newspapers showed obvious decreasing circulation. Second, the study revealed that the readership of Internet newspapers was considerably growing since the Internet newspapers established their Web presence. Third, there was a slightly negative effect of Internet newspapers on circulation of print newspaper. The Internet newspapers weren't eroding traditional readerships significantly. Although 43% of the publishers agreed that Internet newspapers had reduced readership of print newspapers, 44% of the publishers did not consider the growth of the Internet newspapers a factor for the decreasing circulation.

This study offered some evidence on the effect of the Internet newspaper on circulation of the print newspaper. The Internet newspaper as a new medium is still developing as more technological innovations are implemented. It could be simply another vehicle for accessing the same information, or it may become a completely different medium for delivering information from all existing media. The consequences of such innovations and the effect of growth of the Internet newspapers on print newspapers are still largely unknown. From this viewpoint, the knowledge of the effect of the Internet newspaper on the print newspaper will be key to understanding the future dynamics of the media.

Due to the relatively low response rate of the Internet survey, the f the study have limitations in explaining the effect of Internet newspape newspapers' circulation. Only publishers and online editors were surveyed on their perception of the relationship between print and the Internet newspapers. It was possible that publishers were uncertain as there was too much unknown with the development of new media technologies. It was also possible that some publishers were unwilling to admit the negative effect of Internet newspaper on print newspaper circulation. Further studies could aim at a higher response rate using alternative methods, and expand exploring scope from publishers to readers to add up to the understanding of the relationships between the growth of the Internet newspapers and changes in print newspapers.

ENDNOTE

1. A box plot extends from the 25th percentile ($X[25]$) to the 75th percentile, the so-called interquartile range (IQR). The line in the middle of the box represents the median or 50th percentile of the data. The lines emerging from the box are called the whiskers and they extend to the upper and lower adjacent values. The upper adjacent value is defined as the largest data point less than or equal to $X[75]+1.5*IQR$. The lower adjacent value is defined as the largest data point greater than or equal to $X[25]-1.5*IQR$. Observed points more extreme than the adjacent values, if any, are referred to as outside values and are individually plotted.

REFERENCES

American Journalism Review. (2001). Retrieved January 2001 from http://newslink.org/daynews .html

Anonymous. (2000, October). Online newspapers aren't replacing print. *New Media Age, 56.*

Barnhurst, K. G. (2002). News geography & monopoly: The form of reports on U.S. newspaper Internet sites. *Journalism Studies, 3*(4), 477–489.

Barrett, L. (1997, April 21). Status report: U.S. newspapers online. *The Business Journal.*

Bittner, J. R. (1996). *Mass communication* (6th ed.). Boston: Allyn & Bacon.

Bromley, R. V., & Bowles, D. (1995). Effect of Internet on use of traditional news media. *Newspaper Research Journal, 16*(2), 14–27.

Case, T. (2000, September). Fit to print. *MediaWeek, 10,* 38.

Chyi, H. I., & Lasorsa, D. (1999). Access, use and preferences for online newspapers. *Newspaper Research Journal, 20*(4), 14–27.

Chyi, H. I., & Sylvie, G. (1998). Competing with whom? Where? And how? A structural analysis of the electronic newspaper market. *Journal of Media Economics, 11*(2), 1–18.

Dizard, W. P. (1997). *Old media, new media: Mass communications in the information age* (2nd ed.). New York: Longman.

Dupagne, M. (1994). Testing the relative constancy of mass media expenditures in the United Kingdom. *Journal of Media Economics, 7*(3), 1–14.

Fitzgerald, M. (1996, April). The effect of the Internet on print journalism. *Editor & Publisher, 129,* 72.

Fitzgerald, M. (1999, November). Readership measure grows in importance. *Editor & Publisher, 132,* 33.

Glascock, J. (1993). Effect of cable television on advertiser and consumer spending on mass media. *Journalism Quarterly, 70*(3), 509–517.

Gleick, E., & Blackman, A. (1996, October 21). Read all about it. *Time, 148*(19), 66–69.

Harper, C. (1996). Online newspapers: Going somewhere or going nowhere? *Newspaper Research Journal, 17*(1/2), 2–13.

International Federation of Audit Bureau of Circulation. (2001). *Web measurement standards.* Author. Retrieved May 24, 2004, from http://www.ifabc.org/standards.htm

Keizer, G. (1995, June). Read all about it online. *Computer Life, 2,* 50.

Kohut, A. (2000, January). Internet users are on the rise; but public affairs interest isn't. *Columbia Journalism Review, 38,* 68.

McCombs, M. (1972). Mass media in the marketplace. *Journalism Monographs* (24).

McCombs, M., & Byal, C. (1980). Spending on mass media. *Journal of Communication, 30*(1), 153–158.

McCulloch, F. (1995). The real competition: Old-fashioned newspapers, *Nieman Reports, 49*(2), 56.

Meyer, E. K. (1998). An unexpectedly wider Web for the world's newspapers. *NewsLink.* Retrieved May 24, 2004, from http://newslink.org/emcol10.html

Morris, M., & Ogan, C. (1996). The Internet as mass medium. *Journal of Communication, 46*(1), 39–50.

Morton, J. (1997). Saving money, but at a price. *American Journalism Review, 19*(1), 52.

Outing, S. (1996, February 17). Hold on (line) fight. *Editor & Publisher, 129,* 41.

Outing, S. (1998, January 3). New media cutting into old media. *Editor & Publisher, 131,* 43.

Peng, F. Y., Irene, N., & Hao, X. (1999). Trends in online newspapers: A look at the U.S. Web. *Newspaper Research Journal, 20*(2), 52–63.

Phipps, J. L. (2000, October). Can newspapers stay strong online? *Editor & Publisher, 133.*

Rogers, E. M. (1986). *Communication technology: The new media in society.* New York and London: The Free Press; Collier Macmillan.

Schultz, T. (1999). Interactive options in online journalism: A content analysis of 100 U.S. newspapers. *Journal of Computer-Mediated Communication, 5*(1).

Schwirtz, M., & Dori, P. (1998, May). Deconstructing circulation. *Mediaweek, 8,* 8–10.

Son, J., & McCombs, M. (1993). A look at the constancy principle under changing market conditions. *Journal of Media Economics, 6*(2), 24–36.

Stein, M. L. (1998). Goals shift. *Editor & Publisher, 131,* 16.

Stempel, G. H. (2000). Relation of growth of use of the Internet to changes in media use from 1995 to 1999. *Journalism and Mass Communication Quarterly, 77*(1), 71–79.

Webopedia. (2004). *Page impression.* Webopedia. Retrieved May 24, 2004, from http://www.webopedia.com/TERM/P/page_impression.html

Wood, W. C. (1986). Consumer spending on the mass media: The principles of relative constancy reconsidered. *Journal of Communication, 36*(2), 39–51.

Wood, W. C., & O'Hare, S. L. (1991). Paying for the video revolution: Consumer spending on the mass media. *Journal of Communication, 40*(1), 24–30.

8

Factors Influencing Interactivity of Internet Newspapers: A Content Analysis of 106 U.S. Newspapers' Web Sites

Qian Zeng
Louisiana State University

Xigen Li
Southern Illinois University Carbondale

Online journalism disseminating through the interactive medium is fundamentally different from traditional mass media (Neuman, 1994). Compared to traditional journalism, interactivity is a characteristic of online journalism (Millison, 1999). Newspapers need interactivity as an enhancement to their print product, not simply because it reduces reliance on paper and ink, but primarily because it makes newspapers "more interesting, more compelling, more useful, more diverse and vibrant" (Higgins, 1994, p. 10). Although newspapers will remain viable for decades, interactive Internet newspapers will add value to them by providing more gratifying content and personalized services. The future media survival will depend on how to take advantage of the opportunities offered by the Internet (Quinlan, 1994).

Newspapers now extend competition among themselves and with TV stations to the Web (Holliday, 2001). The Internet offers the newspapers a competitive advantage with its interactive features. With the FCC's new rules on media ownership, the media conglomerates will get bigger (Neil, 2003). The only field for relatively small media groups to survive and compete against the media giants is the Internet. Interactive Web sites are the answer for newspapers that face the harsh competition in the converging world.

Various factors in and outside media influence media content (Shoemaker & Reese, 1996). While attempting to describe what is interactivity, few studies have explored the factors that influence interactivity of Internet newspapers. In the new converging world, the factors shaping interactivity become extremely important in understanding and foreseeing the competitiveness of the Internet newspapers. Based on the conceptualizations of some pioneer researchers in studying interactivity and some of the more recent work in defining and measuring interactivity, this study tries to provide a conceptual basis for understanding interactivity of Internet newspapers. This study also looks into some of the factors that are shaping interactivity of Internet newspapers.

WHAT CONSTITUTES INTERACTIVITY?

Mass media scholars have found that the interactive nature of the Internet leads to mass communication models that are extremely different from traditional models. When readers correspond with online journalists, a model combining mass communications and interpersonal communications emerges (Balcytiene, 2001). Interactivity is the central component of Web sites (Lasica, 1996). Being such a critical feature of the Internet media, interactivity of Internet newspapers is, surprisingly, little known. Although efforts have been made to define interactivity, views on interactivity are often found contradictory in scholarly works, and what constitutes interactivity is still unclear (Charney & Greenberg, 2002; Rogers, 2002). Much of the research attempts to describe interactivity of Internet newspapers from generally disparate conceptions of interactivity. The lack of consistent understanding of interactivity can block effective use of Internet newspapers as a powerful medium in two-way communication and prevents Internet newspapers from taking advantages of the latest technology in building their future.

Concept of Interactivity

Interactivity is a critical concept in computer-mediated communications, because it is seen as the key advantage of this medium (Morris & Ogan, 1996; Pavlik, 1996; Rafaeli & Sudweeks, 1997). Rafaeli (1988) made an early effort to define interactivity as a formal communication concept to bridge mass communication and interpersonal communication. He described interactivity as a term that specifies the level of relationship among successive communication exchanges, in which any third (or later) transmission is contingent upon how previous exchanges were related to even earlier transmissions.

However, interactivity is a hybrid construct (Rafaeli & Sudweeks, 1997). Rafaeli's conceptualization of interactivity is viewed from an interpersonal communication perspective (Ha & James, 1998). Similarly from an interpersonal perspective, Blattberg and Deighton (1991) defined interactivity as the facility of direct communication for individuals and organizations. From this perspective, interactivity is a "process-related" communication (Rafaeli & Sudweeks, 1997) and is not a characteristic of the medium (Schultz, 1999). Another conceptualization of interactivity comes from a mechanical perspective that considers interactivity a property of the medium (Ha & James, 1998). For example, Steuer's (1992) computer-mediated communication model defines interactivity as "the extent to which users can participate in modifying the form and content of a mediated environment in real time" (p. 84). In a business setting, interactivity tends to be seen as the "combination of rich content, active intelligence, collaborative communications to create a compelling consumer experience" (Robb, McCarthy, & Sheridan, 1997). Heeter (1989, 2000) posited that interactivity was associated with both the structure of the medium such as available choices, and the processes of communication such as responsiveness to the user and facilitating of interpersonal communication.

As the World Wide Web grows and more interactive information exchanges occur on the Web, examination of interactivity included more aspects of the Web. Ha and James (1998) proposed five dimensions of interactivity: playfulness, choice, connectedness, information collection, and reciprocal communication. Liu (2003) developed a scale to measure the interactivity of Web sites with three dimensions: active control, two-way communication, and synchronicity. Both definitions are helpful in measuring interactive features of certain Web sites, but neither of the definitions covers news interactivity of newspaper Web sites well. Playfulness in Ha and James' definition does not apply to news Web sites for serious news readers. Liu's measurement only includes two-way communication between the visitors and the site, but not among the visitors involved in the Internet forums of newspaper sites. When defining interactivity of online news sites, some researchers base their conception of interactivity on the definition by Heeter (Massey & Levy, 1999; McMillan, 1998), whereas others follow the interpretation of interactivity by Rafaeli and Sudweeks (Coyle & Thorson, 2001; Morris & Ogan, 1996; Schultz, 1999). None of these definitions take into account the dynamic information exchange that occurs in the Internet newspapers. To access Internet newspapers is clearly a combination of mass communications and interpersonal communications. By incorporating the interpretation of interactivity of Heeter from the perspective of content interactivity, Rafaeli and Sudweeks' contribution to interpersonal interactivity, and Liu's measure of interactivity, this study created a more adequate measure of interactivity of Internet newspapers. Two dimensions of interactivity emerged in the dynamic information exchange on the Internet newspapers. One is interpersonal interactivity; the other is content interactivity.

Interpersonal Interactivity

Pavlik (1996) defined interactivity as two-way communication between source and receiver, or, more broadly, multidirectional communication between any number of sources and receivers. Liu's (2003) scale to measure interactivity used effectiveness of two-way communication as one of the key items. Both of them associated interactivity with how the medium facilitates communication between human beings, which asserts that interpersonal interactivity is one of the key components of interactivity. The devices used by Internet newspapers that contribute to interpersonal interactivity include e-mail and discussion forums. E-mail serves as a fast, asynchronous means of interpersonal communication between users and communicators (Schultz, 1999). The e-mail link gives newspapers new ways to solicit reader feedback, to expand information gathering by reporters, and to create a new category of news (Calamai, 1995).

The online forum is a powerful interactive tool that brings people together. Online forums provide a place where users can share their opinions with others, ask questions, and discuss some topics. The user groups, according to Berthon, Pitt, Ewing, Ramaseshan, and Jayaratna (2001), may build a kind of community atmosphere in the site, which in turn may make this site a satisfying option. Lasica (1996) pointed out that such facility strengthens readers' bond to a media source, allowing readers to interact with each other, not just the journalists. An open forum extends two-way communication beyond journalists and readers. Newspaper online forums widen the interaction between readers to readers (Schultz, 1999) and give readers an opportunity to contribute rather than just consume (Lasica, 1996).

Content Interactivity

Internet newspapers are content-rich media compared to business Web sites. Interactive journalism offers the opportunity to address the diverse needs and preferences of readers for content through an interactive process. Some of the indicators of interactivity researchers proposed point to content interactivity. For example, the availability of choice and unrestrained navigation in the cyberspace were considered key components (Ha & James, 1998). McMillan (1998) used the number of links from the home page of newspaper Web sites to test the complexity of choice dimension of interactivity. He argued that a greater number of section links is "an indication of higher complexity of choice."

Hypertext is a key technological innovation of the Internet. The hypertexts in news stories lead readers to deeper context, illustrations, background information, related stories, and so on. Hypertexts "represent the primary mechanism" for an interactive Web news site (Millison, 1999). Interactivity is commonly associated with hypertext, and the hypertext idea is becoming the dominant data structure that Rafaeli declared as deserving "a focus of communication research" (Rafaeli & Newhagen, 1996, p. 4).

Interactivity is a kind of personalization (Lieb, 1998). To get personalized content from Internet newspapers requires interaction between readers and content available on the Web sites. Personalization of content assigns a bigger role to user interests in shaping the model of news and the related information flow (Balcytiene, 2001). Instead of reading what other people think is news, the reader can select his or her own news—judging the news worthiness and setting up their own news collections. A strength of the Web is its ability to provide individual readers with a selection of tailored contents (Bogart, 2000). Fattah (2001) argued that all newspaper sites "must add useful search engines and personalization features" (pp. 14–15). Ghose and Dou (1998) considered it crucial that a Web site is equipped with search engine function. They argued that search engines provide users with personalized information while at the same time the Web sites still "contain a full spectrum of information to meet the potentially diversified information needs" (pp. 40–41) of users.

Factors Influencing Interactivity

News content is influenced by a variety of factors. These factors range from the individual media worker to the media organization (Shoemaker & Reese, 1996). News is also shaped by technological, economic, and cultural forces (Gans, 1957). Although Internet newspapers have grown into a mainstream medium, they are mostly affiliated with traditional print media. Factors inside and outside media are playing important roles in influencing their operation. Internet newspapers vary in their capacity to meet challenges when establishing interactive Web sites. Researchers noticed several factors that affect media content and operation of Internet newspapers. But few studies of the Internet addressed the issue of what factors affect interactivity of Internet newspapers.

Newspaper size is considered an important factor in influencing newspaper operation (Lacy & Simon, 1993; Majid & Boudreau, 1995; Picard & Rimmer, 1999). When setting up a dot-com Web domain, it is hard for those with insufficient capital or marginal journalistic capabilities (Giles, 2000). Among the survivors are the mainstream news organizations that have the resources to build powerful Web sites. Schultz (1999) found newspaper size is a clearer predictor of interactive options of Internet newspapers. But his study of interactivity ignored content interactivity. His interactivity index considers only static e-mail links, without looking into responses to readers' e-mails. Garneau (1996) also reported that the cost of developing new media product made it highly unlikely to compete as small, independent newspapers. However, Chan-Olmsted and Park (2000) examined 300 broadcast TV stations' Web sites and found that market size is the least relevant to the content and structure of a Web site. Lin and Jeffres (2001) also noted that market size is not a significant factor in determining the content on Web sites. Based on more prevailing findings of effect of newspaper size on newspaper operation, the following hypothesis is proposed:

H1: The larger the newspaper size, the higher the interactivity of the Internet newspapers.

The effects of *media ownership* on newspaper content have been the focus of many scholarly studies (Bagdikian, 2000; Beam, 1993; Fradgley & Niebauer, 1995; Lacy, Shaver, & St. Cyr, 1996). Industrial economists have long believed that elements of "market structure" make up the economic environment of firms and induce these firms to behave in a certain way (Caves, 1992). One of the significant elements to surface in the discussion of market structure is "ownership concentration." It is assumed that economic benefits such as scale economies, better bargaining power, and shared group know-how are more likely to be available to firms under chained ownership. In the online setting, Chan-Olmsted and Park (2000) found ownership is related to the content of TV stations' Web site. Schultz (1999) argued that chain newspapers possibly benefit from their media group's experience with Internet sites. Schultz also found that ownership structure was not a good predictor of interactive options of Internet newspapers.

Newspaper content varies according to their *regional scope of coverage.* Conventional wisdom suggests that big national news sites with more money, broader coverage scope, and higher reputation would be in the best position to set up a highly interactive news Web site than local newspapers. According to "The Media Audit," a syndicated survey of both online and traditional media in more than 80 U.S. markets, *The Washington Post* Web site leads the way in attracting an Internet audience. Peng, Irene, and Hao's (1999) findings also indicated the difference in content between national and local media. They found national papers have more interactive facilities than local papers. On the contrary, Dibean and Garrison (2001) found that local newspapers used more Web technologies than national newspapers.

The study will try to answer the following two research questions:

RQ1: Does newspaper's region of coverage affect the interactivity of the Internet newspapers?

RQ2: Does newspaper ownership affect the interactivity of Internet newspapers?

Length of Web presence allows Internet newspapers to gain experience of operation and build interactivity. The Internet is a relatively new medium. Since newspapers went online in the mid-1990s, Web sites have gone through great changes, both in structure and content. Length of Web presence may be another factor influencing the interactivity of Internet newspapers. Deborah (1993) argued that the critical mass for interactive services should be reached in a number of larger cities in 5 years. At the beginning of the Internet boom, a lot of traditional mass media jumped onto the online world and produced Web sites of doubtful value (Schultz, 2000). As the Internet grew, newspapers became more comfortable and experienced with the new medium and operated Web sites that increased interactive features.

Strength of technical staff is a key factor influencing interactivity of Internet newspapers. The growth in the nature of online journalism mirrors the history of the development of Web technology (Sundar, 2000). In the early days, the potential for interactivity was quite narrow, in part a reflection of the available technology (Conhaim, 1992). Despite its blessings, the widespread acceptance of the web and HTML in particular has limited the ability to make web site more interactive (Klein, 2000). More software tools are available now to facilitate interactive devices such as online chat and search engines. Newspaper sites vary in their technical capability to utilize various technical features of the Internet. What makes a difference in the process of creating interactive newspaper Web sites is the technical staff mastering the advanced tools.

With more experience in operation and growing technical capacity, the Internet newspapers are likely to produce Web sites with superior interactivity. The following hypotheses were proposed:

H2: The longer the Web presence, the higher the interactivity of the Internet newspapers.

H3: The more technical staff devoted to the Web sites, the higher the interactivity of the Internet newspapers.

METHOD

This study used content analysis to examine interactivity of Internet newspapers. In addition to content analysis, an e-mail survey and telephone inquiries were employed to collect the data concerning length of Web presence and strength of technical staff of Internet newspapers.

Sampling

Internet newspapers listed on the web site of *NewsLink* (NewsLink, 2004) served as the sampling frame of the study. The site is considered to have the most up-to-date lists of Internet newspapers (Schultz, 1999) and lists over 1,400 daily newspapers in the United States. Systematic stratified sampling was applied. For each of the 50 states in the United States, two of the newspapers were randomly selected. Six newspapers with national coverage scope were selected separately. A total of 106 U.S. online newspapers were included for the study.

Independent Variables

Newspaper Size. This variable was measured by weekday circulation of the corresponding print newspapers according to *Editor and Publisher International Yearbook 2001*. The raw data were also coded into circulation categories using Schultz's (1999) categorization: less than 25,000; 25,001 to 50,000; 50,001 to 100,000; and more than 100,000.

Length of Web Presence.   Using information from a newspaper's Web site, how long since the newspaper has established its Web existence was identified. If the information is not available at the Web site, the e-mail and telephone inquiries were employed to collect the data.

Strength of Technical Staff.   This variable was measured by the number of online technical staff in a newspaper organization. The data were collected through e-mail and telephone inquiries to the newspapers.

Newspaper Region of Coverage: National Versus Local.   Seymour-Ure (1996) listed three general criteria: national reputation, geographical scope, and content breadth. According to Newslink (NewsLink, 2004), *The Christian Science Monitor,* the *Los Angeles Times, The New York Times, USA Today, The Washington Post,* and *The Washington Times* were categorized as national newspapers. The rest of the newspapers were listed as local newspapers.

Newspaper Ownership.   Compaine (1982) defined chain as " the owner-ship of two or more daily newspapers in different cities by a single firm or indi-vidual" (p. 34). Using the data from *Editor & Publisher Yearbook 2001,* each newspaper sampled was identified as owned by media groups or chains, or by entrepreneurs.

Measure of Interactivity

Taking the dynamic features of interactivity into account, the dependent vari-able, interactivity level, was measured using an index created based on several studies: Gubman and Greer's (1997) analysis of online sites produced by U.S. newspapers, McMillan's (1998) analysis of 395 sites on the World Wide Web for models of funding for content in computer-mediated communication, Massey and Levy's (1999) content analysis of English-language online newspapers in Asia, and Schultz's (1999) content analysis of user interactive options in 100 U.S. online newspapers. The index had two dimensions: interpersonal and content inter-activity.

The components of interpersonal interactivity include: (a) *e-mail,* which mea-sures availability of e-mail and responsiveness of the newspapers, and (b) *online forum,* which is the number of forums and topic diversity. The components of content interactivity include: (a) *section links,* the number of section links on the home page; (b) *hypertext,* the underlined or highlighted text that contains links to other documents; and (c) *search engine,* the tool allowing readers to input key words to search for relevant information contained on the site. The index was composed in accordance with the significance that each component con-tributes to interpersonal and content interactivity of Internet newspapers (see Table 8.1).

TABLE 8.1
Measurement of Interactivity

Component of Interactivity	Point
Interpersonal Interactivity	
General e-mail addresses to contact newsroom	1 pt
At least some personal e-mail addresses to editors/reporters	1 pt
E-mail links to at least some authors attached to articles	1 pt
E-mail links to newsroom attached to articles	1 pt
E-mail response	2 pts
Discussion forum	2 pts
Diversified topics	1 pt
Content Interactivity	
Section links (10 to 20)	1 pt
Section links (more than 20)	2 pts
Hypertext in story	2 pts
Hypertext in headline	1 pt
Links to other news Web sites	1 pt
Search engine	2 pts
Total	18 pts

Note. The index measures the level of interactivity of newspaper sites. The maximum score is 18 points and minimum is 0 point. The higher the score, the higher level of interactivity.

Content Analysis

The unit of analysis was one-day's content of an Internet newspaper. According to Schultz (1999), the interactive features of newspaper Web sites are fairly constant. One day's content of an Internet newspaper should be sufficient to catch interactivity level of the site. The items that constitute the capacity of interactivity on the homepage and on all subsequent pages were coded, including availability of e-mail, hypertext in stories, search engines, number of section links, number of online discussion forums, and topic diversity. Two coders participated in the coding. Twelve newspapers were randomly selected to test intercoder reliability. Scott's Pi was used to test the intercoder reliability for nominal variables; Pearson's correlation coefficient was selected for ratio variables. The result of the test showed that intercoder reliability ranged from .81 to 1.00 for nominal variables, and .91 to 1.00 for ratio variables.

Survey

A two-part survey was conducted to collect the data on the Internet newspapers. A list of all editors of the 106 Internet newspapers was compiled through the links of Contact us or About us on the home pages of the newspapers. In case the editor of an Internet newspaper was not listed, the Web technical staff or managing editor was used. An e-mail survey was sent to the 106 editors of the Internet newspapers asking about the length of Web presence and number of technical staff. Two other questions were included in the survey about how to find a specific story from the Web site and how to get a past issue of the newspaper to measure responsiveness of the Internet newspapers. Telephone inquiries followed the e-mail survey to collect the data on the length of Web presence and strength of technical staff from the Internet newspapers that did not respond to the e-mail survey.

Two outside sources were used to collect data on the Internet newspapers. The data regarding newspaper size and ownership of the Internet newspapers were collected from *Editor & Publisher Yearbook 2001*. Newspaper regions of coverage were identified through the Web site of NewsLink.

FINDINGS

The index of interactivity had a total of 18 points with the sum of the components contributing to interactivity, with interpersonal and content interactivity contributing to the index equally. The mean score of interactivity was 8.3 with a standard deviation of 3.05. The highest score was 17 points, which was achieved by the *Los Angeles Times* and the lowest score was 1 point, which was assigned to *The Miles City Star* in Montana. Overall, the online newspapers did better in content interactivity ($M = 3.89$, $SD = 1.53$) than interpersonal interactivity ($M = 2.84$, $SD = 1.16$) ($t = 7.34$, $p < .01$).

Hypothesis 1, that the larger the newspaper size, the higher the interactivity of the Internet newspapers, is supported. Large newspapers scored higher in overall interactivity. The correlation between newspaper size and overall interactivity was statistically significant ($r = .31$, $p < .01$).

Analysis of variance and comparison of means were employed using categorical data of circulation. ANOVA also revealed newspaper size had an effect on interactivity ($F = 7.70$, $df = 3, 102$, $p < .01$). Mean comparison using Tukey's test offered more insight about the difference in mean scores of interactivity among newspapers of different circulation categories. There was no difference in mean scores of interactivity between the newspapers with circulation over 100,000 (10.58) and newspapers with circulation from 50,001 to 100,000 (10.50), $t = -.08$, $p > .05$. But there was significant difference in mean scores of interactivity between the newspapers with circulation below 25,000 (7.43) and those with circulation over 50,000 (10.50). Tukey's test showed a difference of 3.07 (25,000 vs. 50,000 to 100,000) and a difference of 3.15 (25,000 vs. over 100,000). Both were statistically significant ($p < .01$) (see Fig. 8.1).

When looking at interpersonal and content interactivity separately, newspaper size was found to be related to content interactivity, but not to interpersonal interactivity. The correlation between newspaper size and content interactivity

Effect of Newspaper Size on Interactivity

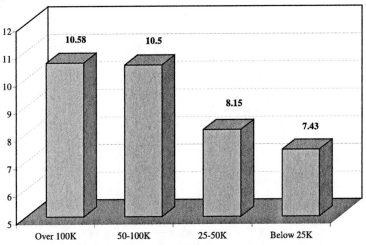

FIG. 8.1. Effect of newspaper size on Interactivity. ANOVA: $F = 7.70$, $df = 3$, 102, $p < .01$. Measure of Association: Eta = .43, Eta^2 = .19.

was statistically significant ($r = .36$, $p < .01$) whereas the correlation between newspaper size and interpersonal interactivity was not ($r = .11$, $p > .05$).

Hypothesis 2, that the longer the Web presence, the higher the interactivity of the Internet newspapers, is supported. The data regarding length of Web presence of 73% of the newspapers were collected. The earliest Internet newspaper site was established in 1994. About 45% of the newspapers established their Web sites around 1997 to 1998. The average length of Web presence was 4.5 years. The correlation between length of Web presence and overall interactivity was statistically significant ($r = .24$, $p < .05$). When looking at interpersonal and content interactivity separately, length of Web presence was found to be associated with content interactivity, but not with interpersonal interactivity. The correlation between length of Web presence and content interactivity was statistically significant ($r = .30$, $p < .01$) whereas the correlation between length of Web presence and interpersonal interactivity was not ($r = .12$, $p > .05$).

Hypothesis 3, that the more technical staff devoted to the Web sites, the higher the interactivity of the Internet newspapers, is supported. The data regarding strength of technical staff of 53% of the newspapers were collected. The correlation between strength of technical staff and overall interactivity was statistically significant ($r = .39$, $p < .05$). The correlation between strength of technical staff and content interactivity ($r = .29$, $p < .05$), and between strength of technical staff and interpersonal interactivity ($r = .35$, $p < .01$) were both statistically significant.

TABLE 8.2
Comparison of Mean Interactivity Scores
by Newspaper's Region of Coverage and Ownership
of Internet Newspapers

Independent Variable	N	Interpersonal Interactivity		Content Interactivity	
		M	SD	M	SD
Region of Coverage[a]					
National	6	3.83	1.94	5.50	.84
Local	100	2.78	1.51	3.79	1.10
Ownership[b]					
Chain	86	2.80	1.47	3.80	1.11
Independent	20	2.85	1.57	3.90	1.17

[a]t-test: Mean difference of interpersonal interactivity = 1.05, $t = 1.31$, $p > .05$; Mean difference of content interactivity = 1.71, $t = 4.76$, $p < .01$. [b]t-test: Mean difference of interpersonal interactivity =.05, $t = .13$, $p > .05$; Mean difference of content interactivity = .11, $t = .39$, $p > .05$.

The data analysis also provided answers to the research questions regarding the relationship between newspaper's region of coverage and ownership, and interactivity.

RQ1: Does newspaper's region of coverage affect the interactivity of the Internet newspapers?

There was significant difference in the means of interactivity between national and local newspapers. National newspapers ($M = 12.33$) lead over local newspapers ($M = 8.04$) ($t = 4.04$, $p < .01$; see Table 8.2). However, national newspapers only led local newspapers in content interactivity with a mean difference of 1.71 ($t = 4.76$, $p < .01$), but not in interpersonal interactivity (mean difference = 1.05, $t = 1.31$, $p > .05$). Further comparison of mean interactivity scores between national and regional newspapers offered more insight about the effect of newspaper's region of coverage on interactivity. There was significant difference in mean interactivity scores between national newspapers and newspapers in the Northeast (mean difference = 4.23, $p < .05$), the Southwest (mean difference = 4.26, $p < .05$), and the Midwest (mean difference = 5.54, $p < .05$). There was no significant difference in mean interactivity scores between national newspapers and newspapers in the Southeast (mean difference = 3.17, $p > .05$) and the Northwest (mean difference = 3.98, $p > .05$) (see Table 8.3).

RQ2: Does newspaper ownership affect the interactivity of Internet newspapers?

TABLE 8.3
Comparison of Mean Interactivity Scores
of National Versus Regional Newspapers

Newspaper (I)	Newspaper (J)	Mean Difference (I–J)	Sig
National (6)	Northeast (28)	4.23[a]	.02
	Southeast (18)	3.17	.23
	Northwest (14)	3.98	.08
	Southwest (14)	4.26[a]	.04
	Midwest (24)	5.54[a]	.00

Note. ANOVA: $F = 3.48$, $df = 6$, 99, $p < .01$. [a]Tukey's test: The mean difference is significant at .05 level.

Comparison of means indicated that chain Internet newspapers ($M = 8.31$) and independent Internet newspapers ($M = 8.15$) did not differ in mean interactivity scores ($t = .24$, $p > .05$). There was no difference in means of interpersonal and content interactivity between chain and independent Internet newspapers either (see Table 8.2). The results suggest that media ownership had no effect on interactivity of the Internet newspapers. The results also showed that independent newspapers had a slightly bigger standard error than chain newspapers, which indicated that the independent newspapers had slightly bigger variation in interactivity of their Web sites.

A hierarchical multiple regression analysis was conducted with five independent variables entered in the equation in the following order to predict interpersonal and content interactivity: ownership, length of Web presence, region of coverage, strength of technical staff and newspaper size. For interpersonal interactivity, only Model 4 (newspaper size not entered) and the full model were statistically significant. The full model with all five predictors was responsible for moderate variance in interpersonal interactivity ($R^2 = .21$, $F = 2.48$, $p < .05$), with strength of technical staff (R^2 change = .11) adding notable variance. Strength of technical staff was a strong predictor ($\beta = .55$, $p < .05$) of interpersonal interactivity in the full model. All other four variables were not statistically significant predictors of interpersonal interactivity.

For content interactivity, except for Model 1 (only ownership entered), all 4 other models were statistically significant. The full model with all five predictors was responsible for considerable variance in content interactivity ($R^2 = .32$, $F = 4.42$, $p < .01$), with length of Web presence (R^2 change = .12), region of coverage (R^2 change = .06), and newspaper size (R^2 change = .11) adding notable variance. Newspaper size ($\beta = 1.52$, $p < .01$), regional of coverage ($\beta = 1.57$, $p < .05$), and strength of technical staff ($\beta = .57$, $p < .05$) were statistically significant predictors of content interactivity. Length of Web presence ($\beta = .22$, $p > .05$.) and ownership ($\beta = .13$, $p > .05$) were not statistically significant predictors of content interactivity (see Table 8.4).

TABLE 8.4
Regression Analysis Predicting Level of Interactivity ($N = 106$)

Predictors	B	Standard β	Sig	Partial r
Overall Interactivity				
Newspaper size	1.55	1.24	.03	.31
Region of coverage	24.61	1.40	.04	.30
Newspaper ownership	1.90	.19	.13	.22
Length of Web presence	.27	.17	.20	.19
Strength of technical staff	.17	.69	.01	.40
$R = .56, R^2 = .31, F = 4.18, p < .01$				
Interpersonal Interactivity				
Newspaper size	2.00	.34	.60	.09
Region of coverage	4.67	.58	.41	.12
Newspaper ownership	1.13	.25	.07	.26
Length of Web presence	.08	.10	.46	.11
Strength of technical staff	.06	.55	.03	.31
$R = .46, R^2 = .21, F = 2.48, p < .05$				
Content Interactivity				
Newspaper size	7.44	1.52	.01	.38
Region of coverage	10.75	1.57	.02	.34
Newspaper ownership	.51	.13	.29	.16
Length of Web presence	.14	.22	.10	.24
Strength of technical staff	.06	.57	.02	.35
$R = .57, R^2 = .32, F = 4.42, p < .01$				

DISCUSSION

This study measured interactivity by taking its dynamic features into account. By looking at both interpersonal interactivity and content interactivity, this study provided a better understanding of the hybrid construct interactivity. The results of this study suggest three of the factors examined—newspaper size, strength of technical staff, and region of coverage—were predictors of content interactivity, but only strength of technical staff was a predictor of interpersonal interactivity. The findings indicate that these organizational factors tend to affect content interactivity more than interpersonal activity. Content interactivity is primarily associated with technology and is easier to be improved as more advanced technologies become available. Interpersonal interactivity requires more efforts from people, both journalists and audience. The expense of processing information from and interacting with audience may constitute a barrier to improvement in interpersonal interactivity of Internet newspapers. Finding more effective ways to motivate and get audience involved in the interactive process is another challenge for Internet newspapers to advance interactivity.

Results on the effects of newspaper size on interactivity from H1 are consistent with the findings of Gubman and Greer in 1997 and those of Schultz in 1999.

Newspapers of larger sizes most likely could afford the high fixed first copy costs in setting up interactive Web sites. The costs of the first interactive copy online are higher than the print papers. The greater financial resources and advertising revenues for larger papers enabled them not only to invest more in staff and in-depth coverage (Lacy & Bernstein, 1988), but also to establish more interactive Web sites. However, larger newspapers with higher content interactivity did not necessarily excel in interpersonal interactivity. Larger newspapers and smaller newspapers alike have to invest more human power to boost interpersonal interactivity.

The result of H2 regarding length of Web presence and interactivity showed a relationship between the two variables. But further examination revealed that length of Web presence was only related to content interactivity. The length of Web presence offered the newspapers a gradual process to build interactivity and gain experience in utilizing the ever-changing new technology. However, length of Web presence helped more with content interactivity than interpersonal interactivity. Interpersonal interactivity requires more human power to facilitate interpersonal communication. Length of Web presence is not necessarily an advantage to boost interpersonal interactivity. Even with content interactivity, length of Web presence may not be a strong factor. Content interactivity is easy to catch up with because the technology that enabled content interactivity does not need years of experience to implement. A newspaper establishing its Web site later could adopt new technology available and soon set itself on a footing equal to others with content interactivity.

The adoption of new technology in newspaper production in the last decade resulted in more technicians needed to operate and service new equipment (Picard, 1998). These technicians were critical for the smooth production and distribution of the print newspapers. When newspapers started developing the Internet version as a tool to generate new readers and possibly new revenue streams, it was expected that the number of online technicians would have positive effect on interactivity of Internet newspapers. The result of H3 demonstrated a relationship between strength of technical staff and both interpersonal and content interactivity of Internet newspapers. The regression model predicting interactivity showed that strength of technical staff was the only predictor of both interpersonal interactivity and content interactivity. Among the five independent variables, strength of technical staff was the only human factor in the model. The finding reconfirms the notion that human power is important for interpersonal interactivity. Responses from the Internet newspapers revealed that a few newspapers in a chain media group were served by technical staff of the parent group, which resulted in few numbers of technical staff needed to operate the Internet newspapers on the technical side. With easy access to a Web site from anywhere, some newspapers outsourced their sites to Web design companies, and only a few technicians were needed to maintain the sites. To let experts take care of newspapers' Web sites in the case of chain papers reduced the cost of operation and resulted in scale of economy. However, Internet newspapers aiming for high interpersonal interactivity will need to enhance human resources in order to facilitate interpersonal communication.

The finding of RQ1 suggested that there was a difference between national and local media in interactivity of Internet newspapers. The finding of this study was consistent with Peng et al.'s (1999) finding that national newspapers had more interactive Web sites than local newspapers. Dibean and Garrison (2001) found that local newspapers used more Web technologies than national newspapers. Using a larger sample, the finding of this study suggests national newspapers did not fall behind local newspapers in using technology for building interactive Web sites. Further examination revealed that national newspapers led local newspapers in content interactivity, but did not do better in interpersonal interactivity. Content interactivity is more technology intensive whereas interpersonal activity is more labor intensive. National newspapers tend to be larger and have more resources devoted to Internet newspapers. Although content interactivity is highly desirable, to maintain competitive advantages, national newspapers have to advance interpersonal interactivity.

The results also revealed that there were some imbalances in interactivity among the local newspapers of different regions. Although overall national newspapers had higher interactivity, they were not necessarily more interactive than local newspapers in all regions. The local Internet newspapers of larger size tended to have higher interactivity. But compared to national newspapers, the local newspapers in a region with higher average size may not be more interactive than local newspapers in a region with lower average size. The findings suggest that when controlling for region of local newspapers, national newspapers, usually larger in size, do not necessarily have higher interactivity than local newspapers in all regions. Further exploration is needed to explain the finding.

The answer to RQ2 confirms Schultz's finding in 1999 that ownership structure was not a good predictor of interactive Internet newspapers. Chan-Olmsted and Park (2000) found ownership had an effect on content of broadcast station Web site. By looking at the effect of ownership on interpersonal and content interactivity, this study revealed that media of different ownership may produce different content on their Web sites, but they were not necessarily different in interactivity. Independent newspapers may have fewer resources to produce higher interactive Web sites compared to chain newspapers. But the technical staff of a chain group serving several newspapers may need more effort to work efficiently to maintain a competitive level of interactivity.

Ownership unrelated to interactivity of Internet newspapers may also be attributed to media routine factors. Although newspaper owners are strategically placed in the flow of information, they rarely exercise their power on a day-to-day basis. Rather, they set the overall policy and exercise their power principally through the selection of editors who in turn select reporters and writers (Seiden, 1975). Editors have the final say over what content will appear on the newspaper, such as what to include in a newspaper Web site and whether to insert links in a story.

CONCLUSION

The regression model predicting interpersonal and content interactivity found that newspaper size, strength of technical staff, and newspaper's region of coverage were strong predictors of content interactivity of Internet newspapers. The only statistically significant predictor of interpersonal interactivity is strength of technical staff. For all Internet newspapers, interpersonal interactivity is still a lagging aspect compared to content interactivity. Internet newspapers are more likely to produce highly interactive Web sites when devoting more resources to facilitating interpersonal communication between journalists and readers and among readers.

All factors examined here were internal, determined by the newspapers themselves. External factors may play an important role as do the internal factors in shaping interactivity of Internet newspapers. For example, interactive features need support of high-speed Internet access, which is more likely available in big markets. Although technology is developing fast, many aspects of life and society have remained fairly constant. For most households, interactivity is still provided by standard telephone lines through dial-up service. Audiences of a big market may have easier and faster access to the Internet. Do means to access interactive Web sites such as availability of high-speed Internet access in a market affect interactivity of Internet newspapers?

Technology itself is changing at breakneck speed. Users must also change their concepts of what can be done with it. Web sites will be getting more sophisticated in terms of interactivity, but can older, less technology savvy readers keep pace? Is different target group of readers a factor influencing the interactivity of Internet newspapers?

Generally higher interactivity is more desirable. But exactly how much interactivity do the readers want? In this study, more section links were measured as more interactive choices available to readers. However, without a good design, more sections may be more confusing to readers. When facing a complex set of choices, readers may feel lost and don't know what to select. Future studies could take into account the Web design of the newspaper sites when measuring interactivity.

Because of the ongoing evolution of Internet technologies, future Web sites will bear little resemblance to most of today's offerings (Gillespie, 1999). Although broadband access to Internet is still a luxury for most of the households today, it may be a universal service in the near future. The changing nature of the Web argues for employing a comparative and longitudinal perspective to study the factors that influence the evolution of Internet newspaper interactivity.

REFERENCES

Bagdikian, B. H. (2000). *The media monopoly* (6th ed.). Boston: Beacon Press.

Balcytiene, A. (2001). Journalism on the net: A few ideas while waiting for a virtual flow of news. *Baltic IT Review* (4).

Beam, R. (1993). The impact of group ownership variables on organizational professionalism at daily newspapers. *Journalism Quarterly, 70*(4), 907–918.

Berthon, P., Pitt, L., Ewing, M., Ramaseshan, B., & Jayaratna, N. (2001, January–March). Positioning in cyberspace: Evaluating telecom Web sites using correspondence analysis. *Information Resources Management Journal, 14,* 13–21.

Blattberg, R. C., & Deighton, J. (1991). Interactive marketing: Exploring the age of addressability. *Sloan Management Review, 33*(1), 5–14.

Bogart, L. (2000, November 27). The death of print. *Editor & Publisher, 133,* 38.

Calamai, P. (1995). Another link with readers. *Nieman Reports, 49*(1), 39.

Caves, R. E. (1992). *American industry: Structure, conduct, performance* (7th ed.). Englewood Cliffs, NJ: Prentice-Hall.

Chan-Olmstead, S., & Park, J. S. (2000). From on-air to online world: Examining the content and structures of broadcast TV stations' Web sites. *Journalism and Mass Communication Quarterly, 77*(2), 321–339.

Charney, T., & Greenberg, B. S. (2002). Uses and gratifications of the Internet. In C. Lin & D. Atkin (Eds.), *Communication technology and society: Audience adoption and uses* (p. 382). Cresskill, NJ: Hampton Press.

Compaine, B. M. (1982). *Who owns the media?: Concentration of ownership in the mass communications industry* (2nd rev. ed.). White Plains, NY: Knowledge Industry Publications.

Conhaim, W. (1992, November). Magazines online. *Information Today, 9.*

Coyle, J. R., & Thorson, E. (2001). The effects of progressive levels of interactive and vividness in Web marketing sites. *Journal of Advertising, 30*(3), 65–77.

Deborah, E. (1993, December 15). Citizens Sikes. *Telephone Engineer & Management, 97*(24), 40–42.

Dibean, W., & Garrison, B. (2001). How six online newspapers use web technologies. *Newspaper Research Journal, 22*(2), 79–93.

Fattah, H. (2001). The cyber newscast. *American Demographics, 23*(2), 14–15.

Fradgley, K. E., & Niebauer, W. E. (1995). London's "quality" newspapers: Newspaper ownership and reporting patterns. *Journalism & Mass Communication Quarterly, 72*(4), 902–912.

Gans, H. J. (1957). The creator-audience relationship in the mass media: An analysis of moviemaking. In B. Rosenberg & D. M. White (Eds.), *Mass culture: The popular arts in America* (pp. 315–324). New York: The Free Press.

Garneau, G. (1996, April 27). Selling family jewels. *Editor & Publisher, 129,* 20.

Ghose, S., & Dou, W. (1998, March/April). Interactive functions and their impacts on the appeal of Internet presence sites. *Journal of Advertising Research, 38,* 29–43.

Giles, B. (2000). Journalism in the era of the Web. *Nieman Report, 54*(4), 3.

Gillespie, G. (1999). Today's interactivity offers glimpse of tomorrow's Web sites. *Health Data Management, 7*(12), 50.

Gubman, J., & Greer, J. (1997, July 30–Aug. 2). *An analysis of online sites produced by U.S. newspapers: Are the critics right?* Paper presented at the Association for Education in Journalism and Mass Communication, Chicago, IL.

Ha, L., & James, E. L. (1998). Interactivity reexamined: A baseline analysis of early business Web sites. *Journal of Broadcasting & Electronic Media, 42*(4), 457–474.

Heeter, C. (1989). Implications of new interactive technologies for conceptualizing communication. In J. L. Salvaggio & J. Bryant (Eds.), *Media use in the information age: Emerging patterns of adoption and consumer use* (pp. 217–236). Hillsdale, NJ: Lawrence Erlbaum Associates.

Heeter, C. (2000). Interactivity in the context of designed experiences. *Journal of Interactive Advertising, 1*(1).

Higgins, S. (1994). Interactive newspapers: A milepost on the road to electronic publishing. *Newspaper Financial Executive Journal, 48*(1), 10.

Holliday, H. (2001, April 30). Papers, TV station extend war to Web. *Advertising Age, 72,* 8.

Klein, L. (2000). The joys of interactivity. *Library Journal, 125*(1), S20.

Lacy, S., & Bernstein, J. M. (1988). Daily newspaper content's relationship to publication cycle and circulation size. *Newspaper Research Journal, 9*(3), 49–57.

Lacy, S., Shaver, M. A., & St. Cyr, C. (1996). The effects of public ownership and newspaper competition on the financial performance of newspaper corporations: A replication and extension. *Journalism and Mass Communication Quarterly, 73*(2), 332–341.

Lacy, S., & Simon, T. F. (1993). *The economics and regulation of United States newspapers.* Norwood, NJ: Ablex.

Lasica, J. D. (1996, November). Net gains. *American Journalism Review, 18*(9), 20–33.

Lieb, T. (1998). Inactivity on interactivity. *Journal of Electronic Publishing, 3*(3).

Lin, C. A., & Jeffres, L. W. (2001). Comparing distinctions and similarities across Websites of newspapers, radio stations, and television stations. *Journalism and Mass Communication Quarterly, 78*(3), 555–574.

Liu, Y. (2003, June). Developing a scale to measure the interactivity of Websites. *Journal of Advertising Research, 43,* 207–216.

Majid, R. A., & Boudreau, T. (1995). Chain ownership, organizational size, and editorial role perception. *Journalism and Mass Communication Quarterly, 72*(4), 863–872.

Massey, B. L., & Levy, M. R. (1999). Interactivity, online journalism and English-language Web newspapers in Asia. *Journalism & Mass Communication Quarterly, 76*(1), 139.

McMillan, S. J. (1998). Who pays for content? Funding in interactive media. *Journal of Computer-Mediated Communication, 4*(1).

Millison, D. (1999). *Online journalism FAQ.* Retrieved June 1, 2004, from http://home.comcast.net/ ~dougmillison//faq.html

Morris, M., & Ogan, C. (1996). The Internet as mass medium. *Journal of Communication, 46*(1), 39–50.

Neil, H. (2003, July/August). The new rules are awful, but the fight is far from over. *Columbia Journalism Review, 42,* 5.

Neuman, R. (1994). A democratization of news and the future of democracy. *Nieman Reports, 48,* 33.

NewsLink. (2004). *Newspapers on the Internet.* Retrieved May 31, 2004, from http://newslink.org/ news.html

Pavlik, J. V. (1996). *New media technology: Cultural and commercial perspectives.* Boston and London: Allyn & Bacon.

Peng, F. Y., Irene, N., & Hao, X. (1999). Trends in online newspapers: A look at the U.S. Web. *Newspaper Research Journal, 20*(2), 52–63.

Picard, R. G. (1998). The economics of the daily newspaper industry. In A. Alexander, J. Owers, & R. Carveth (Eds.), *Media economics: Theory and practice* (2nd ed., pp. 111–129). Mahwah, NJ: Lawrence Erlbaum Associates.

Picard, R. G., & Rimmer, T. (1999). Weathering a recession: Effects of size and diversification on newspaper companies. *Journal of Media Economics, 12*(1), 1–18.

Quinlan, J. (1994, Winter). Confessions of a fallen newspaperman. *Media Studies Journal, 8,* 65–71.

Rafaeli, S. (1988). Interactivity: From new media to communication. In R. P. Hawkins, J. L. Wiemann, & S. Pingree (Eds.), *Advancing communication science: Merging mass and interpersonal process* (pp. 110–134). Newbury Park, CA: Sage.

Rafaeli, S., & Newhagen, J. E. (1996). Why communication researchers should study the Internet: A dialogue. *Journal of Communication, 46*(1), 4–13.

Rafaeli, S., & Sudweeks, F. (1997). Networked interactivity. *Journal of Computer Mediated Communication, 2*(4).

Robb, J. M., McCarthy, J. C., & Sheridan, H. D. (1997). Intelligent interactivity. *The Forrester Report, 1*(12). Retrieved June 15, 1997, from http://204.179.229/fish/reports/fish9702it.asp?Uname=LHA

Rogers, E. (2002). The information society in the new millennium: Captain's log, 2001. In C. Lin & D. Atkin (Eds.), *Communication technology and society: Audience adoption and uses* (p. 50). Cresskill, NJ: Hampton Press.

Schultz, T. (1999). Interactive options in online journalism: A content analysis of 100 U.S. newspapers. *Journal of Computer-Mediated Communication, 5*(1).

Schultz, T. (2000). Mass media and the concept of interactivity: An exploratory study of online forums and reader email. *Media, Culture & Society, 22*(2), 205–221.

Seiden, M. H. (1975). *Who controls the mass media?: Popular myths and economic realities.* New York: Basic Books.

Seymour-Ure, C. (1996). *The British press and broadcasting since 1945* (2nd ed.). Oxford, England, and Cambridge, MA: Blackwell.

Shoemaker, P. J., & Reese, S. D. (1996). *Mediating the message: Theories of influences on mass media content* (2nd ed.). White Plains, NY: Longman.

Steuer, J. (1992). Defining virtual reality, dimensions determining telepresence. *Journal of Communication, 42*(4), 73–79.

Sundar, S. (2000). Multimedia effects on processing and perception of online news: A study of picture, audio, and video downloads. *Journalism and Mass Communication Quarterly, 77*(3), 480–499.

9

Cross-Media Partnership and Its Effect on Technological Convergence of Online News Content: A Content Analysis of 100 Internet Newspapers

Renee duPlessis
Louisiana State University

Xigen Li
Southern Illionis University Carbondale

Online news sources are constantly changing in an attempt to reach their maximum capabilities. What was once the norm, to find only the day's news regurgitated onto the newspaper's Web site, is now becoming obsolete. The newspaper Web sites are no longer like their print counterparts (Dibean & Garrison, 2001). "Newspapers' online versions, no longer bound by static sheets of processed pulp and ink, are now enriching stories not only with more photos and graphics, but also with movement and sound. Television has come to newspapers, as links between online papers and TV stations are formed" (Williams, 2000, p. 133). Numerous media organizations are teaming up together, newspapers, local TV, and online news organizations are operating in the name of convergence, creating a new model of newsroom, with broadcast, online, and print all sharing the same newsdesk (Moses, 2001). With the growth of the Internet, cross-media partnership is growing at fast pace. Cross-media partnership is producing a new type of medium on the Internet as well as media content of news Web sites.

The purpose of this study is to explore the current status of technological convergence of online newspaper sites. This study also examines how the organizational factors such as cross-media partnership and circulation size affect the level of convergence on online newspaper Web sites.

NEWSPAPERS IN THE AGE OF CONVERGENCE

Newspapers, with their rich news-gathering resources and the space to tell in-depth stories, and TV, with its mass-audience reach and visuals, seem to be a match made in heaven for convergence. How publishers and users define the relation between online and print newspapers illustrates the process in which a new medium evolves from an extension of an earlier format into a distinct medium by itself (Fidler, 1997). The genre of the traditional print and broadcast media have been extended by the advent of the Internet. Both content and delivery are affected by the ability to generate multimedia content and immediate, customized delivery regardless of physical location. The digital environment represents a significant change for the news industry. The availability of multimedia, including audio, video, photographs, images, and text has allowed the development of new content for digital news producers and providers (Palmer & Eriksen, 2000).

New Media on the Internet

News media grew remarkably on the Internet since they established their presence in the mid-1990s. Studies looked at how content and delivery of media on the Internet have been affected by technological advancement. Palmer and Eriksen (2000) did a content analysis of 50 news Web sites (newspaper, newsmagazine, and broadcast TV). Results of the analysis revealed that the digital news product's content reflects the producer's original medium (e.g., print version or broadcast) although often augmented with a greater number of articles or additional media. Delivery is immediate and many digital news products are customizing content and delivery through search and retrieval mechanisms.

Studies on delivery show that digital news products can publish "extras" and can be continually updated (Eriksen, 1997). There is an immediacy and inter-activity available through the digital version that cannot be replicated in the paper version (Shaw, 1997) and an interactivity that is hard to replicate in the broadcast version (McMillan, 1999).

Watters, Shepherd, and Burkowski (1998) showed how new communication technologies would enable the integration of news from a wide variety of sources and provide access to supplemental material from enormous archives of electronic news data in digital libraries as well as the continual streams of newly created data. These digital libraries could hold multimedia from all sorts of different types of media, including streaming audio, streaming video, and Flash photo technology.

Studies showed that the Internet newspapers reproduced the substance of their print editions in a way that relates similarly to readers (Barnhurst, 2002). What has been termed "shovelware" is what researchers are calling content-sharing. Several studies have shown in the past that "extensive content sharing characterizes the relation between many online newspapers and their print counterparts" (Chyi & Lasorsa, 2002, p. 93). Zingarelli (2000) examined Internet news to identify factors that affect its state of flux. She noted that at the time of her research in 2000, a large number of Web sites were successful copies of their newspaper or broadcast form. She also stated that there were more sites trying to move away from being a simple carbon copy.

Previous research on newspaper Web sites included studies on content presentation, information delivery, and access. A content analysis on Web design and graphics use of three U.S. Internet newspapers found that the online versions of the papers gave more priority to providing textual information than graphic information, and large graphics were more likely to appear on home pages than on front pages and news article pages (Li, 1998). In addition, several studies on interactivity (Ha & James, 1998; Massey & Levy, 1999; Newhagen, Cordes, & Levy, 1995) all showed that interactivity was a key component to online news. Although these studies showed different aspects of online newspapers that were affected by various technological factors, they either failed or did not have the opportunity to look at the newspaper Web sites at a more technological advantageous level, the convergence that appears quite frequently on the newspaper Web sites today.

Convergence on the Internet

Many researchers have attempted to define the term *convergence*. Stipp (1999) referred to it as the combination of television and computers, which creates a variety of multimedia products and companies from different industry sectors. Others believed convergence focused on the integration of online services into existing multimedia industries (Thielmann & Dowling, 1999). Picard (2000) believed that convergence itself does not produce any revolutionary change in content but simply creates new economies of scope that permit the existing communication and distribution of content to be faster, more flexible, and more responsive to consumer demand.

Some questions were raised here. One such question is: Does convergence produce change in content? With media convergence, not only the newspaper itself, but also other media participate in providing news information. Changes in news content is expected not only in formats, but also in a variety of other aspects. As more sources of information are involved in the information delivery, the Internet newspapers expand their capacity in gathering news. Any time news information is available, whether in text and graph, audio or video, it could be delivered through the newspaper Web sites immediately. One noticeable change would be information updatedness.

With the advancement of technology, more newspaper Web sites are showing the signs of convergence. Although media technology advances so fast, very little has been done to empirically examine the technological convergence of newspaper Web sites, and the factors that brought about such convergence. Those studies that examined the technical features of the Internet newspapers tended to look at their specific features from an isolated perspective. These studies failed to reflect the current status of the Internet newspaper, and ignored such issues as the growing convergence on newspaper Web sites. Quite a few studies have been focusing on text, graphics, and interactivity features. However, few studies examined the remarkable convergence phenomenon on the Internet newspapers from a perspective that connects the media organizational factors and technological advancement with content reform and the changing media nature on the Internet.

Cross-Media Partnership

Cross-media partnership is a form of media alliance in which two or more types of media such as a newspaper and a television station establish a cooperative relationship in order to benefit from a larger pool of resources and achieve a higher goal in media operation. The goal typically is market dominance and increased revenue (Shoemaker & Reese, 1996).

Cross-media partnership could be implemented under the same ownership or different ownership. Cross-media partnership under the same ownership through purchase of a company has rapidly created huge conglomerates that control a number of different types of media in a number of different markets. Small family-owned businesses are bought up quickly by these giant companies. A liaison between a newspaper and a television station could also be established through partnership under different ownership. Cross-media partnership between different types of media under different ownership bears the similar features of cross-media partnership under the same ownership in news content delivery and presentation through newspaper Web sites.

As FCC regulations regarding media ownership change, one company is now allowed to own multiple TV stations in a local market. Newspaper companies may now buy TV stations. This may play a very important role in how technology convergence and cross-media partnership affect operation and content of the Internet newspaper during the next few years. As media organizations get larger and more diverse, parent companies are beginning to merge their subsidiary companies onto one Web site. The media partnerships formed are reflected in a number of different ways. Logos, promotional content, and news information delivered through one media type may appear on a newspaper site containing several partners. No longer are these newspaper Web sites dedicated to the news content produced only by the Internet newspapers.

Examples of cross-pollination abound in markets big and small. *The Wall Street Journal* contributes news programming to CNBC through a partnership with NBC. News-gathering relationships are blossoming in New York, Los Angeles, and Hartford, Connecticut, where the Tribune Company has three new newspaper–TV combinations (Moses, 2000). *USA Today* is on the air. *USA Today* launched *USA Today Live,* a Web and TV news program that will develop the newspaper's stories for all of Gannett Broadcasting's TV stations. *USA Today Live* will feature interviews by the paper's editors and reporters, and, in turn, Gannett TV stations will provide links to news stories for USAToday.com (Anonymous, 2000). According to the Newspaper Association of America, 2002 is a big year for convergence on the Web. Many newspapers allied with local partners in 2002, including *The Bakersfield Californian,* Belo Interactive with *The Dallas Morning News;* the *Chicago Tribune* Interactive; *The New York Times* Digital and *The Washington Post–Newsweek* Interactive (Runett, 2002).

Phoenix-based NBC affiliate, KPNX, and the dominant local paper, *The Arizona Republic,* is another example. Both media outlets are owned by Gannett. The television station's Web site and the newspaper's Web site are the same. *USA Today,* also owned by Gannett, is featured on the site as well, with a link to its own newspaper site. A number of these situations have grown all over the country. Although each faces its own challenges and issues, more and more of such arrangements were started in recent years (Project for Excellence in Journalism, 2003).

Organizational Influence on Media Content on the Web

The organizational approach argues that media content is influenced by the ways in which communications workers and their companies organize work. Organizational influence on news content stems from a number of different factors including the corporate owner or parent company's policies, corporate ownership patterns, and the advertisers and sponsors (Shoemaker & Reese, 1996).

Lin and Jeffres (2001) studied similarities and distinctions of 422 Web sites associated with local newspapers, radio stations, and television stations in 25 of the largest metro markets in the United States. Their results showed that each medium has a relatively distinctive content emphasis, while each attempts to utilize its Web site to maximize institutional goals.

Newspaper size has been studied as a factor influencing news content on the Web. It was found that newspaper size was a clear predictor of interactive options, and use of technological advancements on Internet newspapers (Schultz, 1999). However, Lin and Jeffres' (2001) study found that market size was relatively unimportant, but that the specific type of media helped explain how the websites were differentiated.

Studies have found effect of ownership type on content diversity in television news (Besen & Johnson, 1986; Busterna, 1988), editorials in newspapers (Lacy, Atwater, & Powers, 1988; Picard, Winter, McCombs, & Lacy, 1989), and radio news (Lacy & Riffe, 1994). These studies showed that the parent owner could and did have an effect on news content.

Chan-Olmstead and Park (2000) found ownership is related to content of TV stations' Web sites. They reported that stations with different network affiliations may opt for different Web structures and content. They concluded that, to a certain degree, a TV station that has acquired a competitive audience share and/or is owned by a larger station group is well positioned to take advantage of the strategic value of the Internet.

Dibean and Garisson (2001) studied how market type affected use of Web technology in online newspapers. Market type in their study referred to national, regional, and local newspaper publications. The study found a mixed pattern of Web technology use. Regional newspapers led in many aspects of Web technology use. But national newspapers, usually larger in size, did not necessarily lead in use of Web technology.

Cross-media ownership was also found to affect news content. Project for Excellence in Journalism (2003) conducted a study to examine the tendencies of ownership structures. The results of an analysis of 172 distinct news programs, some 23,000 stories over 5 years, suggested that ownership type did make a difference in content. The study found cross media ownership and the parent company's power over news content did affect the content. Pritchard (2001) studied the news reports of three different newspaper/broadcast duopolies on the same issues and found cross media were likely to produce different content, or influence the content in a different way.

No studies have been done on technological convergence reflected through the latest content development of the Internet newspapers. There was a lack of empirical research on how cross-media partnership affects news content of the Internet newspapers that embraced technological convergence. Technology is changing the delivery and presentation of media content. The Internet newspapers reflect such changes immediately and in an extensive way. The study of change in media content due to technological convergence and the factors that bring about such changes are imminent tasks of researchers of news media on the Internet. In light of the previous discussion, this study attempts to answer the following research questions:

RQ1: What is the current status of cross-media partnerships of online newspapers?

This question explores the situation of different media outlets partnering up on one newspaper Web site under the same or different ownership based on the content presented on the newspaper Web sites.

RQ2: Is there a difference in the level of technological convergence among the newspapers of different sizes?

Technological convergence of the Internet newspapers is reflected through the use of advanced technological devices to deliver and present the content. Researchers were at odds with their findings on whether newspaper size is related to the variation of news content. It is likely that large newspapers with more resources may have advantages over the small newspapers in many aspects. This question examines whether newspaper size matters in level of technical convergence.

H1: The Internet newspapers with cross-media partnership have a higher level of convergence than those that do not engage in cross-media partnership.

Cross-media partnership offer both technical and content resources to achieve higher level of technical convergence. Cross-media partnership is expected to play a positive role in technical convergence of the Internet newspapers.

H2: The more advanced in technological convergence that an Internet newspaper is, the higher the level of content updatedness of the newspaper.

More sources of news information fed into Internet newspapers are likely to provide latest information that requires more frequent updates. Content updatedness is an important indicator of quality of a news Web site. The technological convergence not only brings content diversity and information richness, but also updatedness with latest information, which is one of the critical criteria for an Internet newspaper to be a reliable and credible news source.

METHOD

To answer the research questions and test hypotheses, a content analysis of 100 U.S. online newspapers was conducted in April 2003. The population for this study was the top 100 newspapers in the United States according to circulation. They ranged in circulation size from a little over 100,000 to over 2 million, the smallest being *The Washington Times* with a circulation of 103,505, the largest being *USA Today* with a circulation of 2,149,933. The list of the Internet newspapers was obtained from *Editor & Publisher Yearbook.* The reason that the top 100 newspapers in the United States were selected is that the developments of Internet newspapers in different states are not actually balanced (Barrett, 1997). Larger markets tend to have more media conglomeration than smaller markets and are more likely to have cross-media partnership and higher level of technological convergence in content (Chambers, 2003). NewsLink Web site was used to identify each newspaper under study. NewsLink was chosen because it is the most reliable and has the most up-to-date links of online newspapers (Schultz, 1999).

This study focused on daily Internet newspapers. According to *American Journalism Review,* online daily newspapers with full services is defined as general circulation, mass-market newspapers that publish a full range of regularly updated general news content online and are in print at least 4 days a week. The top 100 circulated newspapers in the United States that this study examines all meet the criteria of the Internet newspapers.

Operational Definitions

Cross-media partnership is defined as a form of media alliance in which a company that owns one type of media such as a newspaper forms the alliance by purchasing or teaming up with a company of a different type of media such as television. Cross-media partnership was measured in two aspects: partnership origination and partnership type. *Partnership origination* was measured with three categories: local, national, or unknown partnership. *Partnership type* was measured with three categories: television, radio, or print news content partner, whether the content displayed an affiliation with any other media format through a logo or other signs of affiliation.

Technical convergence is defined as the level to which an online newspaper utilizes advanced technology that combines the features of different media formats to distribute and present media content on the Web, including streaming audio, streaming video, and Flash photos. Technological convergence is measured by examining the three parts of a newspaper: front page; local/metro page, and "special sections" page to see if the key feature of technological devices are present apart from the general text and graphs. The use of advanced technological devices in presenting the content of all three parts of an Internet newspaper was measured using a weighted measurement. The Front Page was assigned a 1.0 for its use of technological devices. The "Special Features" section was assigned a weight of .75, and The Local/Metro section, a weight of .5. A composite score was calculated to reflect the level of technology convergence of the newspapers.

Content updatedness refers to the degree to which the content of a site is refreshed with the latest information. This is typically exemplified by a note at the top of the front page of the Web site that states, "Site last updated at" with a specific date and time, or when a note is made at the top of a specific article with the time of updating. Five levels were used to measure updatedness of a Web site: hourly, 5 hour, 12 hour, 24, hour and more than 24 hour. If it was not at first evident from the first story, however, at least five stories were examined to find the information.

Newspaper size is measured using the circulation of a newspaper. It is the number of traditional newspapers sold or distributed over a specific period of time. Newspaper size was measured using the average weekly circulation numbers from the *Editor and Publisher's Yearbook*. It was then converted to four circulation groups including: less than 200,000; 200,000 to 499,999; 500,000 to 999,999; and more than 1,000,000.

Content Coding

The Unit of Analysis is one day's publication of an Internet newspaper. According to Schultz, the technical features of newspaper Web sites are fairly constant (Schultz, 1999). One day's content of an Internet newspaper should be sufficient to catch the level of technological convergence of the sites. The front page of each site, the local or metro news section, as well as the "special section" of each site was examined. The content variables coded included *updatedness, symbols of cross-media partnership,* and *use of technical devices* such as Flash, streaming audio, and streaming video.

Two people performed the coding procedure. An intercoder reliability test was conducted with 10% of the total number of newspapers. Ten Internet newspapers out of 100 were randomly selected. Hosti's *R* was used to test intercoder reliability of all nominal variables. The intercoder reliability of all variables ranged from .9 to 1.0 with an average of .97 (see Appendix). The content of the 100 Internet newspapers was coded by one coder after intercoder reliability was established. The Internet newspapers' content was displayed on a 17" monitor using Internet Explorer browser.

FINDINGS

RQ1: What is the current status of cross-media partnerships of online newspapers?

Frequency and Crosstab reports were utilized to answer Research Question 1 and show partnership origination and partnership type. Out of the 100 online newspaper sites, 86% had a cross-media partnership. Of the newspaper Web sites that did have a partnership, 67% of those had a local partner of some type. National partnerships were found in 53% of the cross-media partnership Web sites. A large number of newspaper Web sites had a partnership with both local and national partners.

Within the newspaper Web sites that had a cross-media partnership, 49% of them had a partnership with a television organization, network, or affiliate, and 20% of the cross-media partnering newspaper Web sites had a partnership with a radio network or local radio station. Cross-media partnership newspaper Web sites with a print medium partnership was found to be the highest at 79%. This included a parent print organization such as Gannett or Knight Ridder, or a partnering Web site or national Web network. Nearly half of the Internet newspapers (43%) teamed up with more than one media type. Their Web sites showed a partnership with a combination of television, radio, and other print medium partners.

RQ2: Is there a difference in the level of technological convergence among the newspapers of different sizes?

The level of technological convergence ranged from zero to 6.75. The *Hartford Courant* and *The Columbus Dispatch* earned the maximum score 6.75. Twenty-eight percent of the newspapers scored zero in technological convergence. To explore Research Question 2, a One Way Analysis of Variance (ANOVA) was

TABLE 9.1
Technological Convergence of the Internet Newspapers ($N = 100$)

Variable	Percentage	Mean of Convergence
Newspaper Size		
Less than 200,000	50	1.42
200,000–499,999	39	2.75
500,000–999,999	8	2.59
Greater than 1,000,000	3	1.86
$F = 1.40, df = 3, 96, p > .05$		
Partnership Presence		
Partner	86	2.40
No partner	14	.91
Mean difference $= 1.49, t = 2.72, p < .05$		
Partnership Location		
National	53	2.33
Local	67	2.40
Mean difference $= .29, t = .73, p > .05$		
Partnership Type		
Print	79	2.27
TV	49	2.78
Radio	20	3.42
Combined	43	2.74

used to find relationship between newspaper size and level of technological convergence. The result showed there is no relationship between newspaper size and level of technological convergence ($F = 1.40, df = 3, 99, p > .05$). Tukey's test of mean differences of convergence level showed no difference of means among the newspapers of four sizes (see Table 9.1).

Hypothesis 1, that the Internet newspapers with cross-media partnership have a higher level of convergence than those that do not engage in cross-media partnership, is supported. Eighty-six percent of the newspapers had cross-media partnership whereas only 14% of the newspapers did not engage in cross-media partnership. An independent sample t test was used to compare the means of the level of technological convergence of the two groups, those with cross-media partnership and those without cross-media partnership. The mean of technological convergence of newspapers Web sites with a partnership was 2.40, and the mean of technological convergence of newspaper Web sites without partnerships was .91. The mean difference was 1.49 ($t = 2.72, p < .05$), which was statistically significant at the 95% level.

Hypothesis 2, that the more advanced in technological convergence that an Internet newspaper is, the higher the level of content updatedness of the newspaper, is not supported. Spearman's rank order correlation was used to test the relationship between the independent variable level of technological convergence and the dependent variable updatedness. The correlation coefficient between technological convergence and updatedness was .13, $p > .05$, which was not statistically significant.

The means of convergence by level of updatedness were examined to see if different level of updatedness was related to level of convergence. Three levels of updatedness were identified. The majority of newspapers (92%) updated their Web site hourly and had a mean of convergence of 2.27. Whereas it may take up to 24 hours for other newspapers (8%) to update their Web sites with a mean of convergence (1.54), the difference in means of convergence was not statistically significant ($t = .79$, $p > .05$).

The results also showed there was no difference in means of updatedness among the newspapers of four sizes. ANOVA revealed that there is no relationship between newspaper size and updatedness ($F = .10$, $df = 3, 96$, $p > .05$). Newspapers with and without a partnership did not show a difference in means of updatedness also ($t = .03$, $p > .05$).

DISCUSSION

This study examined the current status of cross-media partnership of the newspaper Web sites and the level of technological convergence of the top 100 circulated newspapers in the United States. Clearly we see that no longer is the news content simply verbatim from the print version. Technology convergence has taken its place in the industry, and has shown a large presence with newspapers that have cross-media partnerships. Out of the 100 newspapers examined, 86% of them had cross-media partnerships. This figure demonstrated remarkable changes compared to what were found in the earlier studies, which stated that the electronic version was simply an identical version of its print counterparts (Barnhurst, 2002; Zingarelli, 2000). The changes in content delivery and presentation in association with the growing cross-media partnership will have important implications on news content consumption and the role that the Internet newspapers play in the society.

The results showed that of the Web sites that had partnerships, 79% of those were partnered with another print organization, whether it be a parent company such as Gannett or Knight Ridder, a partnering local Web site, or a national Web network. With newspaper organizations owning so many other newspapers around the country (like Gannett and Knight Ridder), it is not a surprise that the print partnerships would be at a higher level than the other two forms of media, radio or television. Newspaper Web sites with partners from Television (49%) were also notable. With the relaxed regulations brought down by the FCC earlier in June 2003, this may lead to an even greater percentage of cross-media partnership among the Internet newspapers, as well as seeing the entire media landscape change.

Overall the findings showed a high level of technological convergence among the Internet newspaper Web sites. Newspaper organizations were taking advantage of the technological capabilities to bring a more enriched multimedia product to the online audience. With technological advancement, the trend of technological convergence is likely to grow on the Internet newspapers. Cross-media partnership was found to be a significant factor in determining the level of technological convergence. There was a significant difference in level of technological convergence between the Internet newspapers with and without cross-media partnership. Technological convergence was measured with the use of advanced technical devices in delivering and presenting the news content in different formats on the Web sites. With media of different formats participating in the creation of the news content on the Web, technological convergence is likely to change the scenario of how news content on the Internet newspapers is presented and accessed. Technological convergence is becoming a mainstream in the Internet newspapers, and the news content on the Web will bear fewer and fewer features that distinguish one traditional medium from the other.

The significant changes brought by technological convergence on the Internet newspapers and cross-media partnership have important implications for the media industry. Those who were more prominent on the Internet were those who took advantage of the latest technology and who lead in technological convergence in presenting the news content. Cross-media partnership is one way to achieve that goal. Critics of media conglomeration worried about the single voice and lack of diversity of the media in fewer hands. However, with the FCC ruling of relaxed media ownership regulations and more advanced technology, this could mean significant mergers and/or partnerships, resulting in further convergence and partnerships on the Internet among different media. The technological convergence of the Internet newspapers looks irreversible with increasing cross-media partnership.

The findings of this study confirm the effect of organizational factors on news content. Numerous studies showed that organizational factors influence media operation and news content from a variety of aspects. This study expanded the scope of media content from traditional media to the newspapers on the Internet. The findings add to our understanding of how organizational factors influence media content on the Internet. One of the key findings of the study, that cross-media partnership is a strong predictor of technological convergence of Internet newspapers, has clear implication for news media in the age of convergence. The Internet newspapers are forming all kinds of partnership. The growing cross-media partnership is likely to bring a much higher level of technological convergence. The findings offer a clear picture of the direction in which newspapers on the Internet will develop. To compete on the Internet with news product, newspapers have to make changes in their organization structure and policy, information delivery, and presentation patterns, and adapt to the trend of technological convergence.

Schultz (1999) found newspaper size is a clear predictor of interactive options and use of technological advancements on Internet newspapers. But this study found newspaper size was not related to level of technological convergence. The finding raised some questions on effect of newspaper size on media content. One possible reason for the finding could be the population of the study. This study looked at the top 100 newspapers in the United States. It is expected that the more resources a newspaper has, the higher level of technological convergence could be realized in the Internet newspaper. However, with the top 100 circulated newspapers under study, the variation of the size is limited. The results of the study reflected the status of large newspapers in the United States. A sample of the Internet newspapers with a more diversified size rage may yield a different result about the effect of size on level of technological convergence. The finding should not be taken as strong evidence against Schultz's finding because of the population of this study. Further study is needed to clarify the effect of newspaper size on news content on the Internet.

It is also interesting to know that partnership origination and partnership type did not have an effect on technological convergence. The findings offered some insight on some specific characteristics of media on the Internet. First, national newspapers usually have more resources and are likely to achieve a higher level of technological convergence. But on the Internet, the availability to everyone of the new media technology and the relatively low cost of using new technology compared to purchasing new printing equipment put the national and local newspapers on relatively equal footing. Second, the new technology used to advance the news content on the Web blurred the distinction between the different forms of traditional media. With the Internet space and the new media technology available to all forms of traditional media, all forms of traditional media could achieve the same goal in technological convergence with their news content on the Internet.

The result about H2 that technological convergence of Internet newspapers is not related to content updatedness offered some useful explanation about the nature of updatedness. Content updatedness is an important indicator of quality of a news Web site. It is expected that a higher level of technological convergence may help boost other aspects of Web site quality. The finding indicated that updatedness is more an issue of how publishers define the nature of Internet newspapers than an aspect closely related to technological advances. Updatedness is a demanding feature of high-quality Internet newspapers. The findings showed that the majority of newspapers (92%) updated their Web site hourly. Although the Internet newspapers with cross-media partnership did achieve a higher level of technological convergence, updatedness seemed to be an issue either already solved due to its simple implementation or an issue not so critical in technical advance.

The findings on updatedness also raised an issue about the changes in media content on the Web brought by convergence. Picard (2000) noted that convergence itself does not produce any revolutionary change in content but simply creates new economies of scope that permit the existing communication and distribution of content to be faster, more flexible, and more responsive to consumer demand. The findings about updatedness of news content of the Internet newspapers offered something beyond Picard's argument. With 92% of the newspapers updating their Web site hourly, new content in converged formats was constantly fed into newspaper Web sites. Although this study did not look at the actual content that each update brought to the Web sites, and the changes in content delivery did not seem to be dramatic due to the familiar formats such as audio and video that audience normally get from radio and television, it is clear that information updatedness with convergence enriched news content. The news content of Internet newspapers changed more often than any other media format that audiences had experience with. The latest news information delivered in a combination of media formats offered more multidimensional knowledge about the news events than the audience could ever get from one medium. Whether this could be considered a revolutionary change in content may be debatable due to the different standards and expectations.

Limitations of this study included a population of the top 100 circulated dailies in the United States, whereas examining a sample of newspapers with a more extended range of size may have yielded different results. The larger the paper, the more likely they are to have the technology available and affordable to implement on their Web site. If a sample including the smaller circulated newspaper Web sites were examined, the effect of newspaper size on level of technological convergence would probably be significant.

The measure of technological convergence was limited to the technical devices used by the Internet newspapers. This study tried to cover the range that technological devices used by including three major parts of Internet newspapers, but it did not look at the media operation associated with technological convergence. As the concept of *convergence* is still in the stage of forming with better understanding gained through examination of news media on the Internet, a better measurement of convergence of news media on the Internet may incorporate more aspects concerning media operation, content delivery, and presentation.

CONCLUSION

This study examined 100 top circulated U.S. daily Internet newspapers and found that 86% had a cross-media partnership. Cross-media partnership was developed through acquisition and teaming up with all formats of traditional media, including newspaper, television, and radio. The study confirms the effect of cross-media partnership, the newly emerged organization factor due to regulation changes and technology advances, on news content on the Internet. The results showed that the newspapers with cross-media partnership had a much higher level of convergence than those that did not engage in cross-media partnership. However, no relationship was found between newspaper size and level of technological convergence. The effect of newspaper size on news content on the Internet needs to be further examined. Although the findings showed no relationship between technological convergence and news updatedness, the latest information in a combination of media formats through constant updates is likely to bring changes in content from what audience could normally obtain from traditional media.

Further research could explore the structure of cross-media partnerships and their effects. The study of effect of cross-media partnership on news content could also be expanded in scope, such as effect on diversity of the news content compared to the traditional media, and the way that the content is presented with technological convergence. Future studies could also look at the effect of news content derived from technological convergence on audience. The Internet newspapers with technological convergence are producing dramatically different content from the traditional media. Audiences that access the news content on the Web sites are likely to have a different experience in processing, perceiving, and understanding the news information from the Internet newspapers. How these changes take place and affect news consumption of the Internet newspapers could be an interesting and important area to explore.

APPENDIX: INTERCODER RELIABILITY OF THE VARIABLES CODED

Variables	Reliability Coefficients
Updatedness	1.0
Partner's message on site	1.0
Partner's content on site	1.0
Partnership local	1.0
Partnership national	.90
Partnership unknown	1.0
Partner television	1.0
Partner radio	1.0
Partner print	1.0
Front page radio	1.0
Front page television	1.0
Front page Flash photo	.95
Local page radio	.95
Local page television	.95
Local page Flash photo	.95
Special sections radio	.90
Special sections television	.95
Special sections Flash photo	.95

REFERENCES

Anonymous. (2000, February 21). Gannett plan a model of media convergence. *Editor & Publisher, 133,* 41.

Barnhurst, K. G. (2002). News geography & monopoly: The form of reports on U.S. newspaper Internet sites. *Journalism Studies, 3*(4), 477–489.

Barrett, L. (1997, April 21). Status report: U.S. newspapers online. *The Business Journal* [Online]. Formerly located at http://www.umi.com/pqdweb?Did=000000011498363&deli=I&Mtd=1&1dx =7Sid=45/16/97ype=309

Besen, S. M., & Johnson, L. L. (1986). *Compatibility standards, competition, and innovation in the broadcasting industry.* Santa Monica, CA: Rand.

Busterna, J. C. (1988). Trends in daily newspaper ownership. *Journalism and Mass Communication Quarterly, 65*(4), 831.

Chambers, T. (2003). Structural changes in small media markets. *Journal of Media Economics, 16*(1), 41–59.

Chan-Olmstead, S., & Park, J. S. (2000). From on-air to online world: Examining the content and structures of broadcast TV stations' Web sites. *Journalism and Mass Communication Quarterly, 77*(2), 321–339.

Chyi, H. I., & Lasorsa, D. L. (2002). An explorative study on the market relation between online and print newspapers. *Journal of Media Economics, 15*(2), 91–106.

Dibean, W., & Garrison, B. (2001). How six online newspapers use Web technologies. *Newspaper Research Journal, 22*(2), 79–93.

Eriksen, L. (1997, January). *Digital documents, work and technology: Three cases of Internet news publishing.* Paper presented at the 30th International Conference on System Sciences, Maui, HI.

Fidler, R. F. (1997). *Mediamorphosis: Understanding new media.* Thousand Oaks, CA: Pine Forge Press.

Ha, L., & James, E. L. (1998). Interactivity reexamined: A baseline analysis of early business Web sites. *Journal of Broadcasting & Electronic Media, 42*(4), 457–474.

Lacy, S., Atwater, T., & Powers, A. (1988). Use of satellite technology in local television news. *Journalism Quarterly, 65*(4), 925–929.

Lacy, S., & Riffe, D. (1994). The impact of content of competition and group ownership on radio news. *Journalism Quarterly, 71*(3), 583–593.

Li, X. (1998). Web page design and graphic use of three U.S. newspapers. *Journalism and Mass Communication Quarterly, 75*(2), 353–365.

Lin, C. A., & Jeffres, L. W. (2001). Comparing distinctions and similarities across Websites of newspapers, radio stations, and television stations. *Journalism and Mass Communication Quarterly, 78*(3), 555–574.

Massey, B. L., & Levy, M. R. (1999). Interactivity, online journalism and English-language Web newspapers in Asia. *Journalism & Mass Communication Quarterly, 76*(1), 139.

McMillan, S. J. (1999). Health communication and the Internet: Relations between interactive characteristics of the medium and site creators, content, and purpose. *Health Communication, 11*(4[B]), 375–390.

Moses, L. (2000, August 21). TV or not TV? Few newspapers are camera-shy. *Editor & Publisher, 133,* 22–23.

Moses, L. (2001, November 5). Convergence hits the heartland. *Editor & Publisher, 134,* 7.

Newhagen, J. E., Cordes, J. W., & Levy, M. R. (1995). Nightly@nbc.com: Audience scope and the perception of interactivity in viewer mail on the Internet. *Journal of Communication, 45*(3), 164–176.

Palmer, J., & Eriksen, L. (2000). Digital news: Content, delivery, and value propositions for an intangible product. *Journal of End User Computing, 12*(2), 11–19.

Picard, R. G. (2000). Changing business models of online content services: Their implications for multimedia and other content producers. *International Journal on Media Management, 2*(2).

Picard, R. G., Winter, J. P., McCombs, M., & Lacy, S. (1989). *Press concentration and monopoly: New perspectives on newspaper ownership and operation.* Norwood, NJ: Ablex.

Pritchard, D. (2001). A tale of three cities: "Diverse and antagonistic" information in situations of local newspaper/broadcast cross-ownership. *Federal Communications Law Journal, 54*(1), 31–52.

Project for Excellence in Journalism. (2003, April 29). Does ownership matter in local television news? *Journalism.org.* Retrieved June 1, 2004, from http://www.journalism.org/resources/research/reports/ownership/

Runett, R. (2002, December). *2002 Rewound: Web publishers describe the year's top achievements.* Newspaper Association of America. Retrieved June 4, 2004, from http://www.naa.org/artpage. cfm?AID=4786&SID=104

Schultz, T. (1999). Interactive options in online journalism: A content analysis of 100 U.S. newspapers. *Journal of Computer-Mediated Communication, 5*(1).

Shaw, R. (1997, September 22). News directors are starting to buy into digital. *Electronic Media, 16,* 3–4.

Shoemaker, P. J., & Reese, S. D. (1996). *Mediating the message: Theories of influences on mass media content* (2nd ed.). White Plains, NY: Longman.

Stipp, H. (1999). Convergence now. *International Journal on Media Management, 1*(1), 10–13.

Thielmann, B., & Dowling, M. (1999). Converge and innovation strategy for service provision in emerging Web-TV markets. *International Journal of Media Management, 1*(1), 4–9.

Watters, C. R., Shepherd, M. A., & Burkowski, F. J. (1998). Electronic news delivery project. *Journal of the American Society for Information Science, 49*(2), 134–150.

Williams, J. (2000, February 7). Sites go straight to video. *Editor & Publisher, 133,* 133.

Zingarelli, M. (2000). *Surfing the wave of flux: A journey into how conventional media are adapting to meet the demands of the new online medium.* Unpublished master's thesis, School of Journalism and Communication, Carleton University, Ottawa, Ontario, Canada.

10

The Market Relation Between Online and Print Newspapers: The Case of Austin, Texas

Hsiang Iris Chyi
University of Arizona

Dominic L. Lasorsa
University of Texas at Austin

Since the Internet started gaining in popularity in the mid-1990s, the newspaper industry has been experimenting with this new medium by publishing electronic editions online. As of 2003, nearly 1,500 North American daily newspapers had launched Web sites (Newspaper Association of America, 2003). Unlike pure-play Internet content providers who devote everything to the online venture, newspaper publishers have to worry about the market relation between their online offerings and their core product—the print newspaper.

From an editorial standpoint, online newspapers rarely exist in a vacuum. Because the print paper almost always serves as the content provider for the online edition, extensive content sharing is expected. This raised questions about "shovelware" production—what content makes the most use of this interactive medium.

From an economic perspective, attention has primarily been given to the negative impact of launching a free Web edition on print circulation—the "cannibalization effect." Such a concern dates back to the early stages of the online experiment. Fearing that offering free content online may erode the print edition's subscription base, many sites initially charged users a subscription fee for online news access, but most failed. The advertising model followed, but only with limited success. Confusion still exists with regard to the way users determine the value of online content.

From a theoretical viewpoint, how publishers and users define the relation between online and print newspapers illustrates the process in which a new medium evolves from an extension of an earlier format into a distinct medium by itself (Fidler, 1997). In addition, media economists are curious about whether online and print products compete or complement each other and what factors define that relation. Therefore, understanding the user's response to the online format as opposed to the print—in terms of usage, perceptions, and preferences—may provide theoretical insights.

After years of experimenting, expectations of the Internet as a publishing medium may have changed. But, what have we learned? It seems newspaper publishers as well as media scholars still have not fully understood users' response to online and print content. What is the demand for the online edition as opposed to that for the print edition? Which format serves what readers' needs? What factors influence users' preferences? The relation between online and print products remains unclear, and little empirical evidence was revealed.

Although the Internet as a news medium still is evolving, knowledge of the market relation between online and offline products should be more, not less, important. This study is a scholarly endeavor that explores the market relation between online and print newspapers. Empirical data were colleted in a one-newspaper city (Austin, Texas) to examine the public's response to local, regional, and national newspapers' print and online editions.

INTERNET AND TRADITIONAL MEDIA USE

Every time a new medium emerges, its relation with the traditional media has to be defined. As Perse (2001) suggested, the adoption of each new mass communication technology has simulated research on two major areas: (a) displacement effects and (b) content delivered by new media technologies. Much displacement effects research has focused on displacement in terms of lowering the time devoted to the original medium (McLeod & Reeves, 1980).

Along the line, some media researchers have examined whether Internet use is associated with a decline in traditional media use. One survey conducted in mid-1994—before the Web became a popular interface—found that use of traditional media remained the same during the start-up period for Internet use. Respondents did not spend significantly less time with newspapers as hypothesized (Bromley & Bowles, 1995). A 1995 study found that Internet users were more likely to be newspaper readers, but nonusers used radio and TV news more (Stempel & Hargrove, 1996). A 1998 survey the Pew Research Center for the People and the Press conducted also found that the online population was more likely to read a newspaper than the offline public. But when the media habits of Internet users and nonusers were compared taking their interest in politics and other demographic differences into account, the survey reported heavy Internet news consumers watching relatively less television news than nonusers but reading newspapers and listening to radio news just as often (Pew Research Center, 1999). A 1999 survey examined the impact of Internet use on television, radio, newspaper, and magazine use and found Internet users more likely to be newspaper readers and radio news listeners (Stempel, Hargrove, & Bernt, 2000).

These studies investigated the relation between Internet and newspaper use. Methodologically, they defined media in general terms (e.g., referring to *newspapers* without specifying which newspapers, or to *the Internet* as opposed to specific online news services). As a result, a wide range of media products were lumped together, making any microanalysis impossible. This study attempts to provide a closer examination of the use of print and online newspapers (i.e., whether people read one newspaper's print edition as opposed to that same newspaper's online edition). Online and offline readerships are compared across local, regional, and national newspapers.

CONTENT SHARING AND SHOVELWARE

Extensive content sharing characterized the relation between many online newspapers and their print counterparts. Editorially, online newspapers rarely operate as independent entities. The print edition often serves as the primary content provider for the online edition, and similar information is published in two formats. As Peterson (cited in Martin & Hansen, 1998) suggested:

> The best asset [newspapers' managers] have for recommending their online services is the quality of the newspapers they publish each day. The Wall Street Journal's online news service's success in attracting subscribers may very well be because of the reputation the newspaper has across the country. As more newspapers provide online news services, there may be an assumption by those using the services that the material found online is exactly what would have been found on the same day in that news organization's newspaper. (pp. 106–107)

However, critics have been accusing online newspapers of producing shovelware (i.e., publishing whatever is in the print edition online without repackaging the information). Previous studies produced consistent results on the lack of original content in online newspapers. One survey showed that more than two thirds of news Web sites reported that less than 20% of their content came from outside sources (Fitzgerald, 1997). Another study of 131 online newspapers found that about half the sites surveyed reported that online staff members wrote none of the material in their online news sites. The average percentage of original content was 13%—suggesting a rather heavy recycling of material from the print edition (Tankard & Ban, 1998). A survey conducted by a public relations firm also found

22% of newspapers had less than 5% original content (Ross & Middleberg, 1999). A 1999 survey of online newspapers found national newspapers tended to produce more unique content than their local counterparts, but, overall, the reported percentage of unique online content was low: the mean was 22%, the median was 10%, and the mode was 0% (Chyi & Sylvie, 2001).

The fact that similar or identical information is published in two formats fostered the industry's concern about the negative impact of offering free content online on the print edition's subscription base (i.e., the cannibalization effect).

CANNIBALIZATION AND PRODUCT SUBSTITUTABILITY

As a result, some online newspapers, such as *The Wall Street Journal Interactive Edition,* the *San Jose Mercury News,* and the *San Antonio Express-News,* to name just a few, started as fee-based sites for fear that offering free content online might take away print readers. Later, most abandoned the subscription model to attain a larger audience base. A series of in-depth interviews of 14 online newspaper managers conducted between 1998 and 1999 reported no significant cannibalization effects. With regard to why cannibalization was negligible, participants argued that online and print products had different readerships and constituted different reading experiences (Chyi & Sylvie, 2000). However, in most cases, online and print readerships had substantial overlap (Chyi & Lasorsa, 1999; Chyi & Sylvie, 2000). The market relation between online and print products seemed confusing.

The cannibalization effect can be understood in economic terms as the *substitution effect,* which is the tendency of people to purchase less expensive goods that serve the same purpose (Boyes & Melvin, 1996). For the substitution effect to occur, product substitutability between a newspaper's print and online editions must be high—meaning they have to be substitute goods (i.e., goods that can be used in place of each other). So, when the price of one drops (free online content), the demand for the other (print) will drop, everything else held constant.

Disagreement exists whether online and print newspapers are substitute goods. One study found that the electronic newspaper was not a satisfactory substitute for the traditional format because the new medium was uncomfortable to travel through, unappealing to browse leisurely, and more difficult to read than the print newspaper (Mueller & Kamerer, 1995). But given shovelware production, some argued that product substitutability between print and online products would be high and the demand for a newspaper's print edition may be affected by the demand for its online counterpart in a geographic market where both editions are available (Chyi & Sylvie, 1998). Newspaper publishers, not surprisingly, hoped that the online edition would complement its print counterpart.

Theoretically, the *degree of product substitutability* is defined by cross-price elasticity of demand, the percentage change in the demand for one good divided by the percentage change in the price of a related good, other things being equal (Boyes & Melvin, 1996). According to Picard (1989), cross-price elasticity of demand can determine the extent to which different media compete for different portions of media product and service markets. However, *cross-price elasticity of demand* is more of a concept rather than a measure because even if detailed market data are available, the other-things-being equal condition can hardly be fulfilled in the complex media environment in the real world.

But this does not mean that the market relation between online and offline products cannot be studied. From a practical perspective, an average reader in a typical one-newspaper city in the United States has access to a multitude of print newspapers, including a local newspaper and a few regional and national newspapers, the degree of accessibility and price varying. Online users also have access to these newspapers' online editions—all are equally accessible on the Web and most are free. This study examines how people use one newspaper's online and print editions—exclusively or simultaneously—to explore the nature of the product relation between the two. The existence of a substantial overlap between online and print readerships—if any—would serve as a strong indicator of the potential of a complementary relation between the two related goods.

In addition to usage, this study attempts to tap into readers' preferences for a particular format (online vs. print), regardless of brands, price, accessibility, and content. This inquiry has to be conducted on a hypothetical basis, but, by doing so, the results may more truthfully reflect how users perceive their reading experiences associated with media formats without the interference from the confounding variables such as brands, price, and so forth.

Therefore, this study attempts to answer the following questions:

1. What is the penetration rate for local, regional, and national newspapers' online and print editions in a geographic market?
2. Do online and print editions reach mutually exclusive readers, or do online and print readerships overlap?
3. Does the print penetration increase or decrease among Web users? Does the print penetration increase or decrease among that newspaper's online readers?
4. What is the general public's preference for a particular format (online vs. print)? What factors influence that preference?

METHOD

A random-sample telephone survey of residents in Austin, Texas, was conducted in 1998 to investigate the general public's response to local, regional, and national newspapers in print and online formats. This survey served as a follow-up study and expanded the scope of a 1997 survey (Chyi & Lasorsa, 1999) by increasing the sample size and including two more newspapers available in the area to examine further the use of online and print newspapers of different localities.

Sampling

The survey was conducted in the metropolitan area of Austin, Texas, a city where people had access to one local daily (the *Austin American-Statesman*) and several national newspapers (*The Wall Street Journal, USA TODAY,* and *The New York Times*). It was also within the circulation areas of two other daily newspapers from adjacent cities (the *Houston Chronicle* and *The Dallas Morning News*).

A systematic random sample was drawn from the Austin area telephone book combining the "plus one" method, adding one to the last digit of each number sampled, thereby ensuring every residential telephone (including unlisted and new numbers) an approximately equal chance of being included (Landon & Banks, 1977). The sampled area included Austin and several smaller neighboring communities, yielding a combined population of around 900,000.

Data Collection

Data were collected between February 23 and March 9, 1998. Graduate and upper-level undergraduate students studying communication research completed the interviews after in-class training. The sample size of 818 completed interviews yielded a standard sampling error of ±3.4 percentage points.

Of the original sampling pool of 1,300 numbers, only about 1,000 proved to be actual working numbers. Thus, the gross efficiency of the sampling pool, a measure of how well the survey reached those numbers selected to participate, was estimated to be .77, calculated by dividing the total number of working numbers by all the numbers in the pool. Some of these working numbers, however, proved to be ineligible for the purposes of the survey because they were businesses (345), respondents did not speak English (43), or the line was not used for voice communications, such as a connection to a facsimile machine (182). The efficiency of the pool in reaching eligible households, calculated by dividing possible households by all pool numbers, was estimated to be .65. Once a household was identified as eligible for the survey, up to three callbacks were made to reach respondents. The overall completion rate of .61 was calculated by dividing completions by eligible numbers.

Survey Instrument

The survey, which took an average of 20 min to complete, focused on knowledge, opinions, and behaviors about traditional and online media use. Variables of interest included *computer use; Web access; Web use; use of national, regional, and local newspapers' print and online editions;* and *preferences for the print and online formats. Newspaper penetration* usually is defined as the percentage of households within that geographic area buying or receiving a newspaper (Lacy & Simon, 1993; Picard & Brody, 1997). As this survey involved both print and online newspapers, to afford comparison, penetration was measured by the percentage of respondents who said they read a print/online newspaper at least once a week.

The preference for the print and online formats was measured by a hypothetical question (i.e., "Imagine that you are provided with both print newspapers and online newspapers with the same news content and at the same price. Which would you prefer?") without specifying the name of a particular newspaper. The demographic variables of *gender, age, education, income,* and *ethnicity* also were included.

RESULTS

The sample of 818 Austin residents was reasonably representative of the local population. Respondents tended to be slightly younger, better educated, and wealthier than the population as a whole but not different enough to make the sample unrepresentative.

The sample had slightly more females (52%), as most telephone surveys do. It had more people in the higher education and income categories. In terms of ethnicity, the sample overrepresented White individuals. Table 10.1 summarizes the differences between the survey sample and the Census 2000 statistics of Travis County in several demographic variables.

Online and Traditional Media Use

Results showed that 75% of the 818 respondents used a personal computer at home or work weekly, and 65% had access to the Web—showing a significant growth in Web accessibility from the previous year—52% in 1997 ($\chi^2 = 21.81$, $df = 1$, $p < .001$). Among those who used the Web weekly, the percentage of heavy users (those spending 11 or more hours online per week) also increased, going from 16% to 26% between 1997 and 1998 ($\chi^2 = 8.73$, $df = 1$, $p < .01$). These findings documented the size and the growth of the online population in Austin, one of the most wired cities in the country, during a 1-year period.

In terms of traditional media use, 82% of respondents watched local evening television news and 72% watched network evening news at least 1 day per week, whereas 81% read a daily newspaper, also at least 1 day per week; 81% had cable.

Penetrations of Six Newspapers' Print and Online Editions

The six newspapers' print penetrations (the *Austin American-Statesman, USA Today, The New York Times, The Wall Street Journal, The Dallas Morning News,*

Table 10.1
A Comparison of the 1998 Austin, Texas, Sample
and the 2000 Census of Travis County

	Census 2000 (%)	Austin, Texas, 1998 (%)
Gender		
Male	51	48
Female	49	52
Ethnicity		
Caucasian/White	68	74
African-American/Black	9	7
Hispanic/Latino	(28)[a]	12
Asian or Pacific Islander	5	4
Native American	1	1
Age		
18–24	19	23
25–29	14	15
30–39	23	26
40–49	20	19
50–59	12	8
60–64	3	3
65+	9	6

Note. Information reported in this table is taken from the U.S. Census Bureau (2001).

[a]The Hispanic/Latino (of any race) category and the other racial categories were not mutually exclusive in Census 2000.

and the *Houston Chronicle*) were measured by asking the respondents if they read these newspapers at least once per week. Some 74% of the respondents read the local daily the *Austin American-Statesman* at least once a week, 13% said they read *The Wall Street Journal,* 12% read *USA Today,* 11% read *The New York Times* and *The Dallas Morning News,* respectively, and 9% read the *Houston Chronicle* (Table 10.2). Compared with the 1997 data (Chyi & Lasorsa, 1999, p. 7), these newspapers' print penetrations remained stable.

These newspapers' online penetrations were measured by asking Web users ($n = 484$) whether they read these online newspapers at least once per week. About 30% of Web users visited the *Austin American-Statesman* site (Austin360.com), 14% read the online edition of *USA Today,* 11% read *The Wall Street Journal Interactive Edition,*[1] 10% read *The New York Times on the Web,* and 6% visited *The Dallas Morning News* and the *Houston Chronicle* sites, respectively. Table 10.2 also converts these figures into the percentage among all respondents to afford comparisons.

Results showed that the local daily attained the highest penetration in both print and online formats with the print edition reaching far more readers than its online counterpart. In contrast, national newspapers' online penetration rates

TABLE 10.2
Print and Online Penetrations of Six Newspapers
Circulated in Austin, Texas

Newspaper		Print Penetration (%) Among All Respondents (N = 818)	Online Penetration (%) Among Web Users (n = 484)	Online Penetration (%) Among All Respondents (N = 818)
National	The Wall Street Journal	13	11	6
	USA Today	12	14	8
	The New York Times	11	10	6
Regional	The Dallas Morning News	11	6	3
	Houston Chronicle	9	6	3
Local	Austin American-Statesman	74	30	18

among Web users (10% to 14%) were comparable as their print penetrations among the general public (11% to 13%).

To examine whether the online edition reached nonprint readers or just duplicated the print readership, Figure 10.1 visualizes the overlap of the print and online readerships across all the six newspapers. All six newspapers' online readerships consisted of readers and nonreaders of the print edition. For the national and regional newspapers, about one half of their online users also read the print edition (55% for *The Wall Street Journal Interactive Edition,* 42% for *USA Today* site, 41% for *The New York Times on the Web,* 64% for *The Dallas Morning News* site, and 46% for the *Houston Chronicle* site), but for the local daily, 83% did (i.e., a vast majority of the online users of the local news site also read the print edition of the newspaper). Although national newspapers' online ventures were more likely to reach nonprint users, the local newspaper's Web site tended to duplicate the print readership. The fact that as many as 15% of all respondents simultaneously read the local daily's print and online editions seemed to indicate the potential of a complementary market relation between the two editions.

Print Penetrations Among the General Public, Web Users, and Online Readers

Table 10.3 compares the six newspapers' print penetrations among the public, Web users, and readers of that newspaper's online edition. Print penetration remained the same or slightly higher among Web users. Print penetration also was significantly higher among readers of the same newspaper's online edition across all six newspapers. In other words, online readers were much more likely to read that same newspaper's print edition.

Further analysis compared a newspaper's online and print penetrations among Web users (column 2 in Tables 10.2 and 10.3, respectively). Because Web users

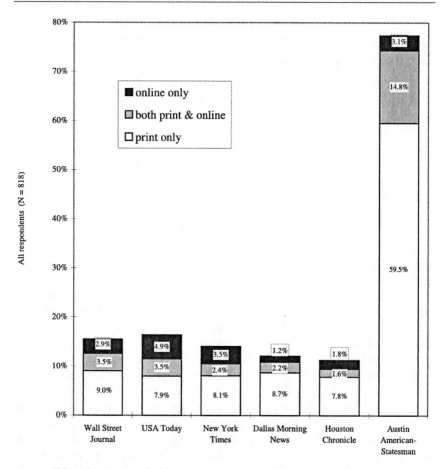

FIG. 10.1.   Overlap of print and online readerships of six newspapers circulated in
Austin, Texas.

have no accessibility problems, the displacement effect (if any) should be the
most salient among this group because they can easily access the free online edition instead of paying for the print edition. However, none of the six newspapers'
online penetrations were significantly higher than their print penetrations, not
even for the national newspapers, which, compared with the local daily, were not
as readily accessible and were more expensive.

Correlation analyses were conducted to examine the relation between the
six newspapers' online and print readerships among Web users, who had access
to both formats. The phi coefficient—a statistic appropriate for measuring the
strength of association of two nominal variables—was calculated. For national
and regional newspapers, phi ranges from .289 to .382 ($p < .001$): .361 for *The
Wall Street Journal*, .356 for *USA Today*, .289 for *The New York Times*, .382 for

TABLE 10.3
Print Penetrations Among All, Web Users, and Online Readers

| Newspaper | Print Penetration (%) | | | |
	Among General Public[a]	Among Web Users[b]	Among Users of its Online Edition	Base[c]
The Wall Street Journal	13	17*	55**	53
USA Today	12	13	42**	69
The New York Times	11	12	41**	49
The Dallas Morning News	11	13	64**	28
Houston Chronicle	9	9	46**	28
Austin American-Statesman	74	74	83*	146

[a]$N = 818.$ [b]$n = 484.$ [c]Number of users of its online edition.
*$p < .05.$ **$p < .001.$

The Dallas Morning News, and .322 for the *Houston Chronicle*—indicating modest correlations between these newspapers' online and print readerships. For the local daily, phi is .118 ($p < .01$). Consequently, print readers were more likely to read the same newspaper's online edition and vice versa.

Preference for Print and Online Editions

This study examined the use of the six newspapers circulated in Austin. But, generally, which format—regardless of brands, accessibility, price, and content—do readers prefer? All respondents were asked this hypothetical question: "Imagine that you are provided with both print newspapers and online newspapers with the same news content and at the same price. Which would you prefer?" Almost 80% said they would prefer the print format, whereas only 20% would prefer the online edition.

With regard to what factors account for the variations in format preferences, cross-tab analysis showed that age and Web use made a difference, whereas gender and education did not. Younger people were more likely to prefer the online format than older people; 27% of those aged 18 to 29 preferred the online format, compared to 20% of those aged 30 to 44, and 15% of those aged 45 or older ($\chi^2 = 9.699$, $df = 2$, $p < .01$). Heavy Web users also were more likely to prefer the online format: 21% of those spending 1 to 5 hr online per week preferred the online format, 26% of those spending 6 to 10 hr online and 45% of those spending 11 hr or more online said so ($\chi^2 = 23.613$, $df = 2$, $p < .001$). Overall, 72% of Web users preferred the print format. The result was comparable with that of the 1997 study, which found that 76% of Web users would prefer the print format (Chyi & Lasorsa, 1999).

Because the overlap of print and online readerships indicated some people simultaneously read both editions, these people's general format preference may somewhat reveal how they perceive their reading experiences associated with different formats. Among those who read both print and online editions of *The Wall Street Journal,* 68% said they would prefer the print format when asked the hypothetical format preference question. Similarly, 61% of *USA Today* readers (who read both online and print editions), 78% of *The New York Times* readers, 75% of *The Dallas Morning News* readers, 77% of the *Houston Chronicle* readers, and 68% of the *Austin American-Statesman* readers would prefer the print format. Across almost all of the subgroups in the cross-tab analysis concerning general format preferences, more respondents would prefer the print format to the online medium, regardless of brands, accessibility, price, and content.

DISCUSSION

The survey was conducted in Austin and it was recognized that the Austin area was not typical of most other areas of the nation. Austinites tend to be slightly younger, better educated, and wealthier than their national counterparts. These differences probably were because of the fact that Austin was a major center for computer technology development, the site of the largest university in the country (the University of Texas with more than 50,000 students), the capital of Texas, and one of the fastest-growing U.S. communities. In addition, Austin was identified as one of the four most-wired cities in the United States with higher online penetrations compared with other metropolitan areas (Progressive Policy Institute, 2001; Survey of Internet Use, 1998). Although these characteristics also may make Austin a good indicator of coming trends elsewhere, especially in terms of Internet usage, one should exert caution when generalizing the results.

Implications of Readership Overlap

This study examined the public's use of six newspapers of different localities (local, regional, national) and in different formats (online, print), one by one, to explore the market relation between online and print newspapers. The analysis focused on the overlap between online and print readerships. The simultaneous use of the print and online editions suggested that to some extent print and online products complemented each other. Therefore, serving as an extension of their print counterparts could be a practical strategy for online newspapers, especially if one considers users' preferences for the print format.

The local daily has seen a substantial overlap between online and print readerships—83% of its online readers also read the print edition. The fact that the online edition attained only a small number of nonprint readers carries a negative economic implication. From the local advertiser's perspective, the online product largely delivered a less-than-unique audience (i.e., a subset of the one currently delivered by the print edition).

Compared with the local daily, national and regional newspapers' online and print penetrations were not so high. But national newspapers' online penetrations were not insignificant if one considers that they operate in a national market consisting of numerous local markets such as Austin. National news sites also benefit the most from the economies of scale in distribution. The challenge is how to transform those readers into revenue streams.

Print Editions in Good Shape

Across all six newspapers, print penetrations were not reduced among Web users, and readers of a particular newspaper's online edition were more, not less, likely to read that same newspaper's print edition. Whereas most online newspapers provided free content, their print counterparts seemed to remain competitive, unthreatened in the marketplace. This could be good news for newspaper publishers because the print newspaper still is their core product. On the other hand, however, this could also suggest that the online venture might not be able to survive intermedia competition.

Perceived Value of Shovelware

Given the same content, price, and accessibility, most respondents indicated their preference for the print format. Because the hypothetical question about format preference actually presumes shovelware ("given the same content"), this carries an implication for evaluating the potential of fee-based online news services: Online newspapers may find charging for online content difficult if the product delivers only shovelware. Online publishers should not expect users to pay for an inferior reading experience as long as a better alternative—the print edition—was as readily available at a comparable price.

Shovelware can be alleviated by content repackaging, which differentiates an online newspaper from its print counterpart. As Chyi and Sylvie (1998) suggested, online newspapers should provide what traditional media fail to serve by developing Internet-specific features such as two-way communication, searchable databases, real-time data transmission, hyperlinking, and multimedia presentation to overcome intermedia competition. More specific suggestions for news repackaging also existed (Pryor, 1999).

From a historical perspective, the Internet as a news medium still is evolving, and crossing the "bridge of familiarity" to achieve creative uses takes time and effort (Fidler, 1997, p. 16). As they transition from print (the familiar) to online (the distinct), online newspapers are following the same course.

FURTHER RESEARCH

This survey examined market penetrations of six newspapers' online and print editions from the demand side. From the supply side, follow-up research also was conducted to investigate the degree of shovelware production among these newspapers by personal interviews and questionnaires (Chyi & Sylvie, 2000, 2001).

This study identified the overlap between online and print readerships across six newspapers. Further research should focus on why and how these readers would use both products. Perhaps users read the online edition at work and the print edition at home, or that some sought breaking news or interactive content (e.g., local restaurant databases or movie listings) online, while still keeping the habit of reading the print edition. Further investigation is essential to understand this seemingly complementary relationship.

This survey did not directly measure the substitution effect. The fact that print penetrations are higher among online readers does not guarantee the absence of the cannibalization effect. First, one cannot rule out the possibility that Internet and online newspaper readers may be more interested in news and thus may consume more news in general as other researchers have speculated (Pew Research Center, 1999; Stempel et al., 2000). Simply because online readers were more likely to read the print edition does not mean that no reader switched from the print to the free online edition. Second, among the six newspapers studied, *The Wall Street Journal Interactive Edition* was the only fee-based site, and its print edition thus should be least subject to cannibalization. Interestingly, this newspaper was characterized by two significant relations unseen in the other newspapers under study: (a) its print penetration among Web users was significantly higher than its print penetration among the general public, and (b) its print penetration among Web users was significantly higher than its online penetration among Web users ($\chi^2 = 6.36$, $df = 1$, $p < .05$). In other words, this newspaper's print penetration among Web users was relatively strong. The fact that this newspaper charged for online news access might account for the print edition's superior performance among Web users. One may wonder whether the other newspapers' print penetrations among Web users would have been even higher if their content had not been offered online for free. Therefore, concluding that cannibalization was absent might oversimplify the underlying phenomenon. Future research should examine online readers' media-switching behavior over time or analyze longitudinal market data to understand better the cannibalization effect.

ACKNOWLEDGMENTS

An earlier version of this chapter was published in *Journal of Media Economics,* *15*(2), 2002, and reprinted with permission. We thank Paula Poindexter, Steve Reese, George Sylvie, and all the telephone interviewers for their contributions to this study.

ENDNOTE

1. At the time of the study, *The Wall Street Journal Interactive Edition* charged users a subscription fee for access to online content. The rate was $29 a year for print subscribers and $49 for others.

REFERENCES

Boyes, W., & Melvin, M. (1996). *Economics* (3rd ed.). Boston: Houghton Mifflin.

Bromley, R. V., & Bowles, D. (1995). Impact of Internet on use of traditional news media. *Newspaper Research Journal, 16*(2), 14–27.

Chyi, H. I., & Lasorsa, D. (1999). Access, use and preferences for online newspapers. *Newspaper Research Journal, 20*(4), 2–13.

Chyi, H. I., & Sylvie, G. (1998). Competing with whom? Where? And how? A structural analysis of the electronic newspaper market. *Journal of Media Economics, 11*(2), 1–18.

Chyi, H. I., & Sylvie, G. (2000). Online newspapers in the U.S.: Perceptions of markets, products, revenue, and competition. *The International Journal on Media Management, 2*(2), 13–21.

Chyi, H. I., & Sylvie, G. (2001). The medium is global; the content is not: The role of geography in online newspaper markets. *Journal of Media Economics, 14*(4), 231–248.

Fidler, R. (1997). *Mediamorphosis: Understanding new media.* Thousand Oaks, CA: Pine Forge Press.

Fitzgerald, M. (1997, February 16). 68% of news Web sites generate own content: Results of new survey announced at conference. *Editor & Publisher Interaction Conference Daily News.* Retrieved from http://www.editorandpublisher.com/

Lacy, S., & Simon, T. F. (1993). *The economics & regulation of United States newspapers.* Norwood, NJ: Ablex.

Landon, E. L., Jr., & Banks, S. K. (1977). Relative efficiency and bias in plus-one telephone sampling. *Journal of Market Research, 14,* 294–299.

Martin, S. E., & Hansen, K. A. (1998). *Newspapers of record in a digital age.* Westport, CT: Praeger.

McLeod, J. M., & Reeves, B. (1980). On the nature of mass media effects. In S. B. Withey & R. P. Abeles (Eds.), *Television and social behavior: Beyond violence and children* (pp. 17–54). Hillsdale, NJ: Lawrence Erlbaum Associates.

Mueller, J., & Kamerer, D. (1995). Reader preference for electronic newspapers. *Newspaper Research Journal, 16*(3), 2–13.

Newspaper Association of America. (2003). *Newspaper interactive services.* Retrieved from http://www.naa.org/info/facts03/20_facts2003.html

Perse, E. M. (2001). *Media effects and society.* Mahwah, NJ: Lawrence Erlbaum Associates.

Pew Research Center for the People & the Press. (1999, January 14). *The Internet news audience goes ordinary.* Retrieved from http://people-press.org/

Picard, R. G. (1989). *Media economics: Concepts and issues.* Newbury Park, CA: Sage.

Picard, R. G., & Brody, J. H. (1997). *The newspaper publishing industry.* Boston: Allyn & Bacon.

Progressive Policy Institute. (2001, April 19). *The Metropolitan New Economy Index: Austin.* Retrieved from http://neweconomyindex.org/metro/austin.html

Pryor, L. (1999, April 9). Old media dig a grave with shovelware. *Online Journalism Review.* Retrieved from http://www.ojr.org/ojr/technology/1017969861.php

Ross, S. S., & Middleberg, D. (1999). *The 1998 Middleberg/Ross media in cyberspace study: Fifth annual national survey.* Retrieved from http://www.middleberg.com/toolsforsuccess/cyberstudy98.pdf

Stempel, G. H., III, & Hargrove, T. (1996). Mass media audiences in a changing media environment. *Journalism & Mass Communication Quarterly, 73*(3), 549–558.

Stempel, G. H., III, Hargrove, T., & Bernt, J. P. (2000). Relation of growth of use of the Internet to changes in media use from 1995 to 1999. *Journalism & Mass Communication Quarterly, 77*(1), 71–79.

Survey of Internet use. (1998, March). *Yahoo Internet Life.*

Tankard, J. W., Jr., & Ban, H. (1998, February 21). *Online newspapers: Living up to their potential?* Paper presented at the mid-winter conference of the Association for Education in Journalism and Mass Communication, Dallas, TX.

U.S. Census Bureau. (2001). *Census 2000, Travis County, Texas.* Retrieved from http://www.census .gov/

11

Re-Examining the Market Relation Between Online and Print Newspapers: The Case of Hong Kong

Hsiang Iris Chyi
University of Arizona

The Web as a new platform for news delivery has created opportunities as well as challenges for the newspaper industry. One of the major concerns surrounds the market relation between online and print newspapers. From the perspective of media economics, whether online and print newspapers compete with or complement each other carries important implications regarding the Internet's impact on the newspaper industry.

A recent survey of some 700 members of the International Newspaper Marketing Association called for more research on competition posed by other media, especially the Internet, from the academic community (Wilkinson, 2003). Further investigation on intermedia competition issues such as the displacement effect (i.e., whether Internet use lowers time for newspaper reading) and the cannibalization effect (i.e., whether offering news online for free would erode the print edition's subscription base) is essential.

As a replication and further extension of previous U.S.-based studies (Chyi & Lasorsa, 1999, 2002), this study re-examines the market relation between online and print newspapers in one of the most media-rich cities in the world—Hong Kong—where more than a dozen newspapers and their online editions compete for readerships. A random-sample telephone survey examined users' response to diverse online and offline media offerings in this new context.

This study attempts to expand knowledge of the market relation between online and print newspapers across national borders. Methodologically, based on a similar quantitative model, this follow-up study compares online and print penetrations of various newspapers in Hong Kong. In the meantime, this study also explores qualitatively users' motives behind their choices of online and print media.

MARKET RELATION BETWEEN ONLINE
AND PRINT NEWSPAPERS

The newspaper industry has seen a decline in readership for years, which, according to Picard (1993), is at least indirectly related to the use of other media. Along this line, many researchers examined the displacement effect but several U.S.-based national surveys found the negative impact of Internet use on newspaper reading insignificant; online users were more likely to be newspapers readers compared with the offline public (Pew Research Center, 1999; Stempel & Hargrove, 1996; Stempel, Hargrove, & Bernt, 2000). This raised interesting questions regarding the impact of the Internet on newspaper readerships. Given extensive content-sharing between online and print newspapers (Chyi & Sylvie, 2001; Fitzgerald, 1997; Tankard & Ban, 1998), why does the displacement effect seem negligible? Why do Internet users still read print newspapers as much, if not more?

As most displacement-effect studies defined media in general terms (e.g., referring to *newspapers* without specifying which newspapers, or to *the Internet* as opposed to specific online news services), Chyi and Lasorsa (1999, 2002) took an alternative approach to examine closely whether people in a well-defined geographic market read one newspaper's print edition as opposed to that same newspaper's online edition. Because of this methodological approach, their study was able to document the penetration rates of the online and print editions as well as the overlap of online and print readerships of six newspapers circulated in Austin, Texas (Chyi & Lasorsa, 2002).[1] As this approach allows for a more accurate analysis of market activities, the current study uses the same measures to evaluate the highly competitive media market in Hong Kong.

Theoretically, this study also serves as the extension of the Austin study (Chyi & Lasorsa, 2002). One of the major findings in that study was the simultaneous use of the print and online editions across all the newspapers under study, which arguably indicated the potential of a complementary product relationship. For the national and regional newspapers, about one half of their online readers also read the print edition. For the local daily (i.e., the *Austin American-Statesman*), as many as 83% of its online readers also read the print edition. Chyi and Lasorsa (2002) suggested that further research reveal why and how so many readers would use both the online and print editions within the same period of time to better understand this seemingly complementary relationship. Therefore, this study attempts to address the following research questions:

- What is the penetration rate for various online news services in Hong Kong? What is the penetration rate for various print newspapers in Hong Kong?
- To what extent do online and print readerships overlap? Why would users read both online and print editions during the same period of time?

In addition, as print newspapers almost always serve as the content provider for their online counterparts, extensive content sharing raised the question regarding the *cannibalization effect*—that is, the negative impact of launching a free online edition on the print edition's subscription base. The Austin study found such an impact trivial, for print penetrations were not reduced among Web users across the six newspapers, and readers of a particular newspaper's online edition were more, not less, likely to read that same newspaper's print edition. To examine whether such patterns also exist in Hong Kong, where more than a dozen newspapers offer online news services, this study also addresses the following research questions:

- Does the print penetration increase or decrease among Web users? Does the print penetration increase or decrease among that newspaper's online readers?
- Among Web users, which edition—online or print—would attain a higher penetration rate?
- How do online and print readerships relate to each other?

THE NEWSPAPER MARKET IN HONG KONG

Hong Kong, with more than a dozen newspapers actively serving the city's 6.8 million residents, is a highly competitive newspaper market in the region. As many as 15 local dailies (two in English and the rest in Chinese) compete for readerships. Overall, the popular press, known for its tabloid-style, sensational coverage, dominates the market, but papers with elite or partisan orientations also exist. As the newspaper industry relies on a street hawker system to deliver its products, subscriptions constitute a relatively small percentage of newspaper sales, and most readers may choose different newspapers every day. (For a detailed account of Hong Kong's newspaper market, see So, Chan, & Lee, 2000.)

In addition to offline competition, most newspapers in Hong Kong also publish an online edition of their paper on the Web. At the end of 2002, 18 local media Web sites provided online news services, of which 12 were operated by newspapers and six by TV or radio stations. An online-only news aggregator (www .now.com.hk) as well as several portals also provided online news services. Six online news sites charged (local and/or overseas) users a fee for access to certain content at the time of the study,[2] but most online content offered to local users was free. Overall, Hong Kong is one of the most wired cities in Asia. As of 2002, 54% of people aged 10 or over had used a personal computer and 48% had used Internet services during the previous 12 months (Hong Kong Census and Statistics Department, 2003). With so many online news services readily available to a large Internet population, the impact of free online news offerings on newspaper penetrations is of particular interest.

As most U.S. cities have only one local newspaper serving the market, the intense competition between multiple online and offline newspapers in Hong Kong provides a unique context for the re-examination of the market relation between online and print newspapers.

METHOD

A random-sample telephone survey of 853 Hong Kong residents was conducted between November 13 and 17, 2002, to examine the general public's response to online and print newspapers. This survey served as a replication and extension of an earlier study conducted in Austin, Texas, by Chyi and Lasorsa (2002).

Sampling

A systematic random sample was drawn from the Hong Kong phone directory combining the "plus one" method, adding one to the last digit of each number sampled, to ensure every residential telephone (including unlisted and new numbers) an approximately equal chance of being included (Landon & Banks, 1977). The sampled area included Hong Kong Island, Kowloon, and the New Territories, yielding a combined population of 6,815,000 (Hong Kong Census and Statistics Department, 2003).

Data Collection

Graduate and undergraduate students in communication completed 853 interviews after undergoing a training session. Interviews were conducted during 6 to 9 P.M. on weekdays and during 10 A.M. to 9 P.M. on the weekend. Up to three callbacks were made to reach the respondents. The sample size of 853 yielded a standard sampling error of ±3.4 percentage points at the 95% confidence level. The response rate was 44%.

Survey Instrument

The survey, which took an average of 15 minutes to complete, focused on usage of and attitudes toward traditional and online media. The questionnaire was developed according to the results of a focus group of 10 students registered in a university in Hong Kong. Revisions were made based on the results of a pretest. The survey instrument measured online and traditional media use including *Internet usage, newspaper usage,* and *penetration rates* of individual newspapers and online news services.

Internet usage was measured by asking this question: On average, how much time do you spend online per day? ____ hours ____ minutes.

Newspaper usage was measure by asking respondents: On average, how much time do you spend on reading newspapers per day? ____ hours ____ minutes.

Penetrations of print newspapers were measured by asking respondents to name the newspaper(s) they read during the past week. Similarly, penetrations of online news services were measured by asking Web users to name the news Web site(s) they visited during the past week. As more than a dozen online news services/ newspapers were available, no pre-set response items were provided during the interview to avoid the ordering effect. Data analysis using SPSS later identified online-only, print-only, and online-and-print (overlap) readerships, respectively, for all the newspapers circulated in Hong Kong.

Demographic information such as *gender, age, education,* and *income* also was collected.

RESULTS

The sample of 853 Hong Kong residents had slightly more females, as most telephone surveys do. The sample overrepresented people aged 15 to 24 and underrepresented those in the lowest education category. Table 11.1 summarizes the differences between the survey sample and the 2001 Hong Kong Census statistics in several demographic variables. Overall, the sample was reasonably representative of the population.

Print and Online Media Use in Hong Kong: An Overview

With more than a dozen local newspapers circulated in Hong Kong, overall newspaper penetration was high: 89% of all respondents read newspapers regularly, spending on average 57 minutes per day reading newspapers.[3] About 42% of all respondents read one newspaper during the 1-week period before the survey, 28% read two papers, 12% read three, and 5% read four or more papers.

Among all respondents, 58% used the Internet, and 55% were active Web users, who used the Web regularly. Active Web users ($n = 469$) had an average of 3 years' online experience. Forty-eight percent spent up to 1 hour online per day, 21% spent between 1 and 2 hours, 18% spent between 2 and 4 hours, and 12% spent more than 4 hours online per day.

Among the 469 Web users, 64% visited one or more local news Web sites during the past week. Thirty-four percent visited one local news site, 18% visited two

TABLE 11.1
A Comparison of the Sample and the
2001 Hong Kong Census Data

	Census (%)	Sample (%)
Gender		
Male	48.6	45.9
Female	51.4	54.1
Age[a]		
15–24	16.4	28.1
25–34	19.8	18.0
35–44	24.3	21.2
45–54	17.2	16.6
55–64	9.0	7.5
65+	13.3	8.6
Education		
Elementary or less	28.9	16.1
Form 1–3	18.9	17.1
Form 4–5	26.3	31.8
Form 6–7	9.4	10.0
Tertiary	16.4	24.9
Monthly Income[b]		
1–6,000	17.9	16.6
6,001–10,000	24.8	24.3
10,001–20,000	34.8	33.6
20,001–30,000	11.3	13.7
30,001–40,000	4.6	6.0
40,001 or above	6.6	5.7

Note. Information reported in this table is taken from the Hong Kong Census and Statistics Department (2003).
[a]Base = people aged 15 or above. [b]Base = people aged 15 or above with income.

sites, and 11% visited three or more sites. About 17% of Web users also visited some nonlocal news sites during the past week, of which more than half said they visited U.S.-based news sites.

Penetrations of Online News Services and Print Newspapers

Regarding the first research question (i.e., What is the penetration rate for various online news services in Hong Kong?), Table 11.2 reports the results. The first column lists 19 news Web sites' penetrations among Web users ($n = 469$). It is clear that the most visited news sites were those operated by the leading newspapers: *Apple Daily* (28%), the *Oriental Daily* (17%), *Ming Pao* (17%), the *Singtao Daily*

TABLE 11.2
Penetrations of Online News Services and Print Newspapers in Hong Kong

	Media Name and URL	Online Penetration Among Web Users (n = 469) (%)	Online Penetration Among All Respondents (N = 853) (%)	Print Penetration Among All Respondents (N = 853) (%)
Newspaper sites	*Oriental Daily* www.orientaldaily.com.hk	17.0	9.4	47.8
	Apple Daily www.appledaily.com	27.9	15.4	40.4
	Ming Pao www.mingpaonews.com	17.0	9.4	17.8
	Sun www.the-sun.com.hk	4.4	2.5	14.5
	Singtao Daily www.singtao.com	7.7	4.2	9.0
	Sing Pao www.singpao.com	1.9	1.1	7.2
	Hong Kong Economic Daily (no website)	NA	NA	6.2
	South China Morning Post (SCMP) www.scmp.com	3.2	1.8	5.9
	Seung Pao (no website)	NA	NA	2.6
	Hong Kong Daily www.hkdailynews.net	0.0	0.0	2.8
	Hong Kong Commercial Daily www.hkcd.com.hk	0.0	0.0	0.2
	Ta Kung Pao www.takungpao.com	0.8	0.5	0.5
	Wen Wei Pao www.wenweipo.com	0.4	0.2	0.5
	Hong Kong Standard www.thestandard.com.hk	0.2	0.1	0.4
Television sites	TVB www.tvb.com.hk	2.8	1.5	NA
	Asia Television (ATV) www.hkatv.com	0.4	0.2	NA
	i-Cable www.i-cable.com	0.6	0.4	NA
	RTHK www.rthk.org.hk	0.9	0.5	NA
Radio sites	Commercial Radio www.881903.com	0.6	0.4	NA
	Metro Radio www.metroradio.com.hk	0.2	0.1	NA
News aggregator	Now www.now.com.hk	1.1	0.6	NA

(8%), and the *Sun* (4%). In contrast, news sites affiliated with television or radio stations failed to attract substantial traffic.

Regarding the penetration rate for various print newspapers in Hong Kong, the third column in Table 11.2 shows the results. The *Oriental Daily* was the leading newspaper in the market, attaining a penetration of 48% among the general public ($N = 853$), followed by *Apple Daily* (40%), *Ming Pao* (18%), the *Sun* (15%), and the *Singtao Daily* (9%).

Results showed that newspapers with higher print penetrations also enjoyed higher online penetrations. Despite their often-free online counterparts, print newspapers remained robust in the market. A comparison of the second and the third columns shows that most newspapers' print editions attained higher penetration rates than their online counterparts.

To take a closer look, the following analysis focuses on the relation between the print and online editions of the top seven newspapers in town (determined by print penetration), they are the *Oriental Daily, Apple Daily, Ming Pao,* the *Sun,* the *Sintao Daily, Sing Pao,* and the English-language *South China Morning Post.* The *Hong Kong Economic Daily* is not included because it offers no online news services.

Overlap of Seven Newspapers' Online and Print Readerships

The second set of research questions address the overlap of a newspaper's online and print readerships—whether the online edition served nonprint readers or just duplicated the print readership. Figure 11.1 illustrates the overlap of the print and online readerships for the seven newspapers.

All seven newspapers' online readerships consisted of readers and nonreaders of their print counterparts. A great number of online readers also read the same newspaper's print edition during the same week (70% for the *Oriental Daily,* 62% for *Apple Daily,* 56% for *Ming Pao,* 53% for the *Sun,* 44% for *Sing Pao,* 40% for *SCMP,* and 36% for the *Singtao Daily*). The overlap is especially significant for the top four newspapers, for which the overlapped readership (those who read both online and print editions) was larger than the online-only readership.

As a number of respondents read both the print and online editions of the same newspapers during the same week, the reason behind such usage patterns may shed light into the product relation between online and print newspapers. A follow-up, open-ended question investigated the overlap of print and online readerships by asking these respondents ($n = 185$) the reasons why they read both editions within the same week. Answers to the question were then content analyzed. The most commonly cited reasons fell into the following categories: "I read the online edition when I don't buy the print edition" (18%); "I read different editions in different places" (12%); "I read different editions for different purposes" (11%); "When I have time, I read both editions; when I'm busy, I read one edition only"

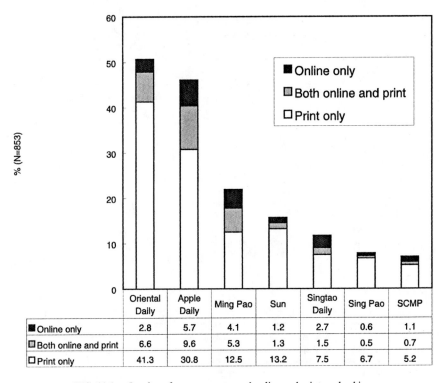

	Oriental Daily	Apple Daily	Ming Pao	Sun	Singtao Daily	Sing Pao	SCMP
■ Online only	2.8	5.7	4.1	1.2	2.7	0.6	1.1
☐ Both online and print	6.6	9.6	5.3	1.3	1.5	0.5	0.7
☐ Print only	41.3	30.8	12.5	13.2	7.5	6.7	5.2

FIG. 11.1. Overlap of seven newspapers' online and print readerships.

(9%); "I check online news when I'm online" (7%); "Because online and print editions provide different content" (7%).

These qualitative data revealed how readers utilize two products differently. Theoretical implications regarding the economic nature of online newspapers are discussed.

Print Penetrations Among the Public, Web Users, and Online Readers

The third set of research questions ask: Does the print penetration increase or decrease among Web users? Does the print penetration increase or decrease among that newspaper's online readers? Table 11.3 compares the seven newspapers' print penetrations among the public, Web users, and readers of that newspapers' online edition. Print penetration remained the same or became higher among Web users. Print penetration also was significantly higher among readers of the same newspaper's online edition across all seven newspapers ($p < .001$). Therefore, online readers were more, not less, likely to read the same newspaper's print edition.

TABLE 11.3
Print Penetration Among All, Web Users, and Readers
of the Online Edition

	Print penetration (%)		
Newspaper	Among General Public (N = 853)	Among Web Users (n = 469)	Among Users of its Online Edition (Base[a])
Oriental Daily	48	48	70*** (80)
Apple Daily	40	47*	63*** (131)
Ming Pao	18	24**	56*** (80)
Sun	15	14	52*** (21)
Singtao Daily	9	11	36*** (36)
Sing Pao	7	8	44*** (9)
SCMP	6	10**	40*** (15)

[a]Number of users of its online edition.
*$p < .05$. **$p < .01$. ***$p < .001$.

TABLE 11.4
Online and Print Penetrations Among Web Users

Newspaper	Penetration of the Online Edition Among Web Users (%)	Penetration of the Print Edition Among Web Users (%)
Oriental Daily	17	48**
Apple Daily	28	47**
Ming Pao	17	24*
Sun	4	14**
Singtao Daily	8	11
Sing Pao	2	8**
SCMP	3	10**
(n = 469)		

*$p < .01$. **$p < .001$.

To address the next research question regarding the competition between a newspaper's online and print editions, Table 11.4 compares a newspaper's online and print penetrations among Web users. Because Web users have easy access to free online content, the displacement effect (if any) of the online edition on the print product should be the most salient among this group. However, none of the seven newspapers' online penetrations were higher than their print penetrations. In fact, the print penetration was higher than the online penetration across all seven newspapers.

To address the last research question (i.e., How do online and print readerships relate to each other?), correlation analyses examined the relation between seven newspapers' online and print readerships among Web users (who had access to both formats). The phi coefficient (a statistic appropriate for measuring the strength of association of two nominal variables) ranges from .338 to .183: .204 for the *Oriental Daily*, .196 for *Apple Daily*, .338 for *Ming Pao*, .225 for the *Sun*, .238 for the *Singtao Daily*, .183 for *Sing Pao*, and .185 for the *South China Morning Post* ($p < .001$). In other words, print readers were more likely to read the same newspaper's online edition and vice versa.

DISCUSSION

As a replication of the Austin-based study (Chyi & Lasorsa, 2002), this survey successfully documented the market relation between online and print newspapers in a new context, Hong Kong. Most results reported in this study share striking similarities with what the Austin study has found: Print newspapers attained higher penetrations compared with their online counterparts. Substantial overlap between online and print readerships existed, that is, a great number of online readers also read the same newspaper's print edition during the same period of time. Print penetrations were not reduced among Web users at all and became even higher among readers of the same newspaper's online edition. Correlation analysis also showed that print readers were more likely to read the same newspaper's online edition and vice versa.

As the research site switched from Austin to Hong Kong, no fundamental differences in people's response to online and print newspapers were found. The similarities between the two studies seem to suggest the existence of a universal pattern characterizing the market relation between online and print newspapers. This study reconfirmed what previous displacement-effect research has revealed: online users are more likely to be newspaper readers (Pew Research Center, 1999; Stempel & Hargrove, 1996; Stempel, Hargrove, & Bernt, 2000)—in a more accurate way.

The methodological approach employed by this study was able to identify individual newspapers' online and print penetrations, and, most importantly, the overlap of online and print readerships. The coexistence of the old media and the new seems to suggest a complementary product relation. As Chyi and Lasorsa suggested (2002), this study went beyond quantitative analysis to explore the rationale behind the simultaneous use of online and print products by asking respondents open-ended, follow-up questions during the interview. This qualitative investigation provides more information regarding the seemingly complementary product relation between online and print newspapers.

Results are somewhat mixed. Reading the online edition in certain locations, for different purposes, or for different content, seems to confirm a complementary relation. However, reading the online edition while not buying the print newspaper seems to suggest the contrary. In any case, context seems to play an important role in readers' decision-making process regarding which medium to use under what circumstances. Future research on the economic nature of online news should examine context-dependent media selection to better understand intermedia competition issues.

In Hong Kong, despite so many news Web sites serving local readers, only a few managed to attain substantial penetration rates. This highly concentrated market resembles a "bi-modal market structure," with an oligopoly (three to four large firms) on one tier that controls 70% to 90% of the market, and a large set of small firms that are fighting for the remaining share on the other tier (Albarran, 1998). This particular market structure has economic implications for online news providers.

Worldwide, Internet advertising still is the major revenue source for online newspapers, and the Internet advertising market also is highly concentrated. According to the Interactive Advertising Bureau (2004), the top 10 advertisement-selling companies accounted for 71% of total online advertising revenue, and the top 50 commanded 96%. As a result, smaller sites may find it difficult to compete with major players for advertising dollars in this winner-takes-it-all market. It is recognized that many online newspapers in Asia attract substantial traffic from overseas and this study measured only domestic usage. But, as previous research suggested (Chyi & Sylvie, 2001), how to transform long-distance usage into reliable revenue streams remains a challenge.

Overall, the Austin study (Chyi & Lasorsa, 2002) concluded that the print edition, compared with its online counterpart, remained competitive, unthreatened in the marketplace. So far, no evidence suggests that the cannibalization effect (if any) has caused any dramatic damage on print readerships. This also is true in the Hong Kong context. The public's commitment to the print format seems stronger than expected, which, on the other hand, indicates online newspapers' lack of competitive advantage in intermedia competition. Future research should examine how users perceive this new medium and the implications of such perceptions to better understand the market relation between online and print newspapers.

ACKNOWLEDGMENTS

The author would like to thank Hao-Chieh Chang and the School of Journalism and Communication at the Chinese University of Hong Kong for their support and contribution to this study. This research project was funded by Direct Grant, Faculty of Social Science, The Chinese University of Hong Kong.

ENDNOTES

1. The six newspapers are: the *Austin American-Statesman, USA Today, The New York Times, The Wall Street Journal, The Dallas Morning News,* and the *Houston Chronicle.*

2. They were the online editions of the *Oriental Daily* (overseas users), *Apple Daily* (overseas users), the *Sun* (overseas users), the *South China Morning Post* (premium content), Commercial Radio (archive), and an online-only news service www.now.com.hk.
3. The median was 45 minutes.

REFERENCES

Albarran, A. B. (1998, February). *Convergence in the mass media industries: Implications for the marketplace and the university curriculum.* Paper presented at the mid-winter conference of the Association for Education in Journalism and Mass Communication, Dallas, TX.

Chyi, H. I., & Lasorsa, D. (1999). Access, use and preferences for online newspapers. *Newspaper Research Journal, 20*(4), 2–13.

Chyi, H. I., & Lasorsa, D. L. (2002). An explorative study on the market relation between online and print newspapers. *The Journal of Media Economics, 15*(2), 91–106.

Chyi, H. I., & Sylvie, G. (2001). The medium is global; the content is not: The role of geography in online newspaper markets. *Journal of Media Economics, 14*(4), 231–248.

Fitzgerald, M. (1997, February 16). 68% of news Web sites generate own content: Results of new survey announced at conference. *Editor & Publisher Interaction Conference Daily News.* Retrieved from http://archives.editorandpublisher.com/

Hong Kong Census and Statistics Department. (2003). Retrieved February 20, 2004, from http://www.info.gov.hk/censtatd/eng/hkstat/index.html

Interactive Advertising Bureau. (2004, April). *IAB Internet advertising revenue report.* Retrieved May 3, 2004, from http://www.iab.net/resources/adrevenue/pdf/IAB_PwC_2003.pdf

Landon, E. L., Jr., & Banks, S. K. (1977). Relative efficiency and bias in plus-one telephone sampling. *Journal of Market Research, 14*, 294–299.

Pew Research Center for the People & the Press. (1999, January 14). *The Internet news audience goes ordinary.* Retrieved from http://people-press.org/

Picard, R. (1993). Economics of the print industry. In A. Alexander, J. Owers, & R. Carveth (Eds.), *Media economics: A reader* (pp. 181–203). Hillsdale, NJ: Lawrence Erlbaum Associates.

So, C., Chan, J. M., & Lee, C-C. (2000). Hong Kong SAR (China). In S. A. Gunaratne (Ed.), *Handbook of the media in Asia* (pp. 527–551). New Delhi, India: Sage.

Stempel, G. H., III, & Hargrove, T. (1996). Mass media audiences in a changing media environment. *Journalism & Mass Communication Quarterly, 73*(3), 549–558.

Stempel, G. H., III, Hargrove, T., & Bernt, J. P. (2000). Relation of growth of use of the Internet to changes in media use from 1995 to 1999. *Journalism & Mass Communication Quarterly, 77*(1), 71–79.

Tankard, J. W., Jr., & Ban, H. (1998, February 21). *Online newspapers: Living up to their potential?* Paper presented at the mid-winter conference of the Association for Education in Journalism and Mass Communication, Dallas, TX.

Wilkinson, E. J. (2003). *Newspaper executives' hopes for academic research: Based on research by the International Newspaper Marketing Association.* Retrieved February 15, 2004, from http://www.inma.org/pdf/newspapers-academia.doc

III

INTERNET NEWSPAPERS
AND THE PUBLIC

12

Utilities of Online and Offline News Use

Carolyn A. Lin
University of Connecticut

Michael B. Salwen
University of Miami

Newspaper reading represents perhaps the most traditional means of acquiring news and public affairs information. Now online news threatens the venerable newspaper medium. But what cognitive and affective differences, if any, do members of the public have as they shift their news medium preference from one modality to another? This chapter, grounded in a uses and gratifications framework, seeks to understand whether the use of offline newspaper and online news sources involve the same or different perceived utilities for acquiring the news.

USES AND GRATIFICATIONS OF NEWS

Uses and gratifications researchers are interested in investigating why and how audiences seek and consume media content, including news content. The theoretical paradigm also subsumes the concept of *audience activity*—occurring in either instrumental or ritualized forms. Audience activity associated with an instrumental tendency reflects a media-use process that is motivated by more specific cognitive needs and goals. By contrast, audience activity related to a ritualized orientation implies a media-use process that is motivated by more diffusive affective needs and goals (Rubin & Perse, 1987). This perspective conceives of audiences comprised of motivated individuals who actively seek media content to fulfill cognitive and affective needs (e.g., Blumler, 1979; Blumler & Katz, 1974; Katz, Blumler, & Gurevitch, 1974; Rayburn, 1996). Researchers have identified gratifications related with news use. Katz, Gurevitch, and Hass (1973) found that individuals assessed newspapers as a source for learning about the environment. Newspapers were seen as satisfying broad informational needs rather than specific personal affective needs. Along a similar line, Elliot and Quattlebaum (1979) found that newspapers offer surveillance of the environment needs but not entertainment needs.

Similarly, Kippax and Murray (1980) tested the perceived importance of 30 media-related needs. They found that newspapers were perceived as providing specific needs associated with information acquisition instead of emotional needs. The needs included understanding, knowledge, and credibility. Lichtenstein and Rosenfeld (1983) reported that radio, television, magazines, and newspapers were viewed as sources of entertainment and information about life. Their other findings suggest that magazines and newspapers were judged by their readers as useful sources of information about the government, but not as outlets for resolving loneliness (or emotional needs).

Weaver (1980) identified yet another news gratification—interpersonal discussion. Weaver's findings established that when interest and uncertainty in political information was high, newspaper use was more strongly related with interpersonal discussion of public affairs than was television viewing. Questions arise about whether gratifications will be similar with different media, but with the same essential content. Interestingly, television news gratifications generally appear to be similar to those of print news. Palmgreen, Wenner, and Rayburn (1980), for example, advanced four gratifications dimensions sought in relation to television news viewing: (a) interpersonal utility, (b) surveillance, (c) entertainment, and (d) parasocial interaction.

Levy and Windahl (1984) clustered three gratification factors—entertainment/parasocial interaction, surveillance, and interpersonal utility—that were nearly identical to Palmgreen et al.'s (1980) four dimensions. Rubin and Perse (1987) generated three slightly different news-viewing motives—entertainment, passing time, and information—emphasizing the diversion aspect of news consumption. Alternatively, McDonald (1990) reported that respondents who sought hard news in newspapers also sought hard news on television.

ONLINE NEWS USAGE

The use of online news has been regularly tracked by a number of online population polls since the mid-1990s. Most notably, reports produced by the Pew Research Center have been widely cited. According to the most recent Pew Research study (2004), the proportion of online users that also accessed news was at 70%. Industry fear of an imminent displacement of offline newspapers by online news operations has yet to materialize. Comparing these findings with a study of audience preferences across the Internet, television, newspaper, radio, and magazine news outlets, the audience still prefers traditional media for information such as weather, entertainment, sports, and general news. Specifically, respondents cited newspapers as their most preferred source for entertainment news (New Media Federation, 2002).

Recent academic studies also confirm the noncompetitive or symbiotic relations between online news penetration and offline news circulation. Stempel, Hargrove, and Bernt (2000) found a symbiotic relationship between Internet news use and traditional news consumption. This suggests that an online news user may also be an avid information seeker with offline news media. Stempel et al. thus argued that online news use was not responsible for the decline in news consumption in television (both network and local), newspapers, and magazines.

Cao and Li (2004) found that the newspaper industry did not identify the growth of online-news popularity as the culprit for offline newspaper circulation decline. Similarly, Chyi's (2004) study suggests that there is an overlap between online and offline news consumers and that the readership of the same offline newspaper edition is thus not reduced as a result. Based on these findings, a complementary relationship seems to exist between offline newspapers and their online news counterparts.

Examining online news access from the aspect of cognitive processing, Eveland, Seo, and Marton's (2002) experimental study found that subjects fared better in news recall with offline news sources (including television and newspapers), but they were able to better process the structure of the news content with online news stories. These results seem to imply that the more structured menu-like layout style of online news pages may influence the users' information processing style differently from offline newspaper stories that are laid out to be read on separate pages continuously (Eveland & Dunwoody, 2002).

This more "structured" layout of online news pages also could afford the users better control of the way they process the news content. For instance, Tewksbury (2003) reported that due to the increased ease over selecting the news content of interest via the presentation style of online news pages, the users tended to access stories that appealed to their unique interests instead of following the news flow "cued" by the news editors and producers. The results also indicated that, with this enhanced user control, online news audiences accessed fewer public affairs stories. This suggests that given the greater degree of "freedom" of choice, online news users who opt for special interest stories may become less informed of important news events.

ONLINE NEWS GRATIFICATIONS

Into the mix of traditional media uses and gratifications comes Internet uses and gratifications. Computer-mediated communications has added new life to the uses and gratifications approach (Ruggiero, 2000). Currently, few online news gratifications studies exist. One is a small-scale pilot study that used a college student convenience sample. Mings (1997) pooled eight dimensions of news and media gratifications from past studies and correlated them with offline and online newspaper use. Her results show that some students' gratifications sought and obtained associated with offline newspapers were related to particular online newspaper usage patterns. However, these relationships must be read with caution because results based on 15 respondents may not be reliable. Nonetheless, the contention that there could be a correlation between offline and online media use gratifications has generally been supported by other online use gratifications studies, either conceptually or empirically.

Althaus and Tewksbury (2000) surveyed 520 undergraduate students and reported that use of the Web as a source of news is associated with newspaper reading, but not with television viewing. These students primarily used the Web as a source of entertainment. The authors predicted that, even if the Web becomes a popular source of news acquisition, it is unlikely to contribute to diminished use of traditional news media.

Dimmick, Chen, and Li (2004) surveyed 211 respondents in the Columbus metropolitan area of Ohio. Their results indicated that the Internet has a competitive displacement effect on traditional media in the daily news domain, with the largest displacements occurring for television and newspapers. The findings also show that there is a moderately high degree of overlap or similarity between the niches of the Internet and the traditional media on the gratification opportunities dimension. In addition, the results suggest that the Internet offers the broadest niche on the gratification opportunities dimension, providing users satisfaction with more needs than any of the traditional media on this dimension.

Choi, Watt, Dekkers, and Park (2004), working within a uses and gratifications framework, sought to understand the motives for Internet use in a cross-cultural context. They studied users in the United States, the Netherlands, and South Korea. Factor analysis revealed that information seeking and self-improvement were common across cultures. Strong correlations across countries were reported between all the motives and satisfaction with the Internet. Expectation and positive evaluation of the Internet were also important attitudes associated with Internet use motives.

Lin (1999) identified three gratification dimensions of Internet use—entertainment, surveillance, and escape/companionship/identity. Although television viewing and online use motives were generally correlated with each other, television-viewing motives were not significant predictors of likely online use. Ferguson and Perse (2000) also examined the association between Internet use and television viewing motives. They reported that more similarities than differences exist between these media. These findings were further confirmed by additional theoretical explications that indicate a lack of displacement between online service adoption and offline media use (e.g., Lin, 2001). Taken together, these two bodies of literature affirm Stempel, Hargrove, and Bernt's (2000) assessment that

online news use is not relevant to the readership or viewership decline in traditional news media outlets.

The limited research does not provide a clear picture whether users of online
news perceive the news delivery modality as sharing the same gratifications or
functional utilities associated with offline newspaper use. There are reasons to
expect similarities as well as differences. As a result, a series of research questions
were proposed:

RQ1: Do newspaper readers and nonreaders perceive online news utilities
differently?

RQ2: Do online news users and nonusers perceive newspaper utilities
differently?

RQ3: Are perceived online news utilities a function of online and offline
news use?

RQ4: Are perceived newspaper utilities a function of online and offline news
use?

RQ5: Are perceived newspaper utilities predictive of online news utilities?

RQ6: Are perceived online news utilities predictive of newspaper utilities?

METHODS

Using the sampling frame obtained from the residential telephone number database, published by the national Select Phone telephone software (Select Phone,
2001), a national random sample was selected via the use of random numbers.
This national sample was proportionately representative of the population from all
50 states and the District of Columbia, based on the 2000 U.S. Census. Telephone
interviews were conducted by trained interviewers during a 5-day period. The
final sample yielded 619 valid responses, representing a 56% response rate. Data
analysis for the present study involved 389 Internet users, reflecting 63% of the
619 original valid responses. This 63% Internet user sample ratio matches the
online population estimate provided by the most recent Pew research (2004).

All the variables measured, including demographic indicators, are defined conceptually and operationally as follows.

Online-News Use.   Respondents were asked whether they accessed news
through an Internet service provider, Internet portal, and news media Web sites. If
they accessed online news at least 1 day per week from any of these sources, their
frequency of access per week—assessed on a 7-point scale—for each source was
combined and averaged to form the "online news use" indicator.

Newspaper Use.   Respondents were asked how many days per week, if
any, they read an off-line newspaper. Their responses were measured on a 7-point
scale.

Perceived Online News Utilities. Fifteen online news utility measures were used to gauge this construct. The factor analysis procedure, executed via principal component extraction and Varimax rotation, generated four different utility dimensions. One measurement item "getting quickly to important news," had a high factor loading on two factors; it was eliminated and a second factor analysis procedure was run. This again resulted in four utility factors.

Four items loaded on the first factor—"finding stories that are fun to read," "coming across amusing news," "finding entertaining news," and "finding stories that are enjoyable." These items were combined to construct the "entertainment" scale ($\alpha = .85$).

Another three items loaded on the second factor—"finding topics to use in conversations with other people," "getting stories to share with other people," and "learning about things to discuss with other people." They were used to construct the "interpersonal communication" scale ($\alpha = .75$).

Four items loaded on the third factor—"keeping up with what is going on in the news," "getting a good overall picture of events in the world," "learning what are the major news events of the day," and "following the major news stories of the day." These four items were collapsed into the "information scanning" scale ($\alpha = .75$).

The three items that loaded on the fourth factor—"going directly to important news stories," "skipping the unimportant news," and "seeking out important news"—were used to compose the "information skimming" scale ($\alpha = .69$). The interitem reliability for this scale is rather low, given the exploratory nature of the scale.

Perceived Newspaper Utilities. Fifteen identical items and measurement scale used to assess perceived online news utilities were adopted to measure the perceived functions of newspaper reading. Although the factor analysis procedure produced an identical set of four factor solutions resulting for the "perceived online news utilities" construct described earlier, the same double-loaded item was eliminated from one factor. The resulting identical four factors were constructed into four identical scales described for the "perceived online news utilities" construct. These four perceived newspaper reading utility scales include: "entertainment" ($\alpha = .81$), "interpersonal communication" ($\alpha = .81$), "information scanning" ($\alpha = .74$), and "information skimming" ($\alpha = .72$).

Demographic information was gathered for the following indicators—*gender, age in years, race/ethnicity, annual income level* (ranging from "under \$25,000" to "more than \$100,000") and *education level* (ranging from "8th grades or less" to "doctoral degree").

Sample Profile

The sample was comprised of 48% males and 52% females. The average age for the respondents was 42 and 54.4% of them had at least some college education. This sample of Internet users had an average annual income of approximately $52,000 per year. In terms of race/ethnicity, 87% of the respondents identified themselves as Caucasians and 9% of the sample considered themselves Hispanic.

In terms of news consumption patterns, 89.6% of the respondents read a newspaper at least 1 day per week; the average number of days these respondents read a paper per week was 4.8. With regard to online news use, 60.4% of the sample accessed an online-news outlet at least once a week. Among online news users, 57.8% visited a news media Web site and 65.3% patronized a news service provided by an ISP or portal in a given week. The average number of days that online news users utilized news media Web sites and ISP/portal news sites was 3.9 and 3.8 per week, respectively.

RESULTS

Addressing RQ1, Table 12.1 assesses whether there is a significant difference between newspaper and non-newspaper readers' perceptions of online news utility. The only online news utility dimension that was significantly differentiated between newspaper readers and nonreaders was "information skimming" ($t = -.26$, $p \leq .01$). This suggests that the offline newspaper readers perceive a greater level of utility in skimming for the "important news" online than do the nonreaders.

Findings associated with RQ2, which queries whether there is a difference in the perception of offline newspaper utilities between online news users and nonusers, are presented in Table 12.2. Online news users perceived a higher level of offline newspaper entertainment utility than nonusers ($t = -2.28$, $p \leq .023$). But these online news users also perceived a lower level of information-skimming utility associated with offline newspaper reading than nonusers ($t = 1.20$, $p \leq .047$).

RQ3 queries whether the level of online news and offline newspaper use influenced audience perception of online news utilities. The univariate general linear

TABLE 12.1
Online News Utilities: Newspaper Readers Versus Nonreaders

Perceived Online-News Utility	Newspaper Reading	N	M	T	Sig
Entertainment	Nonreader	26	4.02	.90	.368
	Reader	189	3.85		
Interpersonal communication	Nonreader	26	4.26	1.24	.215
	Reader	195	4.05		
Information skimming	Nonreader	26	4.14	-2.59	.010
	Reader	195	4.48		
Information scanning	Nonreader	26	4.27	-.44	.663
	Reader	195	4.33		

TABLE 12.2
Offline Newspaper Utilities: Online News Users Versus Non-Users

Perceived Online-News Utility	Online Use	N	M	T	Sig
Entertainment	Non-user	133	3.64	−2.28	.023
	Users	202	3.87		
Interpersonal communication	Non-users	136	4.21	1.52	.130
	Users	202	4.08		
Information skimming	Non-users	133	4.14	1.37	.172
	Users	203	4.00		
Information scanning	Non-users	133	4.34	2.00	.047
	Users	203	4.18		

TABLE 12.3
Online News Utility Model: Entertainment

Source	Mean Square	F	Sig
Corrected model	1.02	1.73	.015
Intercept	917.23	1561.98	.000
Online news use	1.77	3.01	.002
Offline news use	2.37	4.03	.002
Online news use × offline news use	.69	1.19	.273
Error	.59		

$R^2 = .56$ (Adjusted $R^2 = .24$).

model test produced one significant online news utility model—entertainment ($F = 1.73$, $p \leq .015$; see Table 12.3). Individually, the level of online news use ($F = 3.01$, $p \leq .002$) and offline newspaper use ($F = 4.03$, $p \leq .002$) were able to each generate a significant main effect to explain online news entertainment utility. The total variance explained in the model was 56% ($R^2 = .56$; adjusted $R^2 = .24$).

Table 12.4 presents the findings related to RQ4, which speculates on the effect of online news and offline newspaper use levels on the audiences' perception of offline newspaper utilities. Two offline newspaper utility models—entertainment ($F = 1.80, p \leq .008$) and interpersonal communication ($F = 2.34, p \leq .001$)—were statistically significant.

Specifically, the level of online news use generated a significant main effect ($F = 3.39$, $p \leq .008$) on offline newspaper entertainment utility, but the level of offline newspaper use did not ($F = 1.21$, $p \leq .308$). This mixed result is further complicated by the significant interaction effect between the level of online news and offline newspaper use ($F = 1.64$, $p \leq .034$). The total variance explained in perceived newspaper entertainment utility was 55% ($R^2 = .55$; adjusted $R^2 = .25$).

TABLE 12.4
Offline Newspaper Utility Models:
Entertainment and Interpersonal Communication

Source	Entertainment[a]			Interpersonal Communication[b]		
	Mean Square	F	Sig	Mean Square	F	Sig
Corrected model	.96	1.80	.008	.99	2.34	.000
Intercept	881.73	1647.85	.000	987.96	2315.93	.000
Online news use	1.81	3.39	.000	1.07	2.50	.008
Offline news use	.65	1.21	.308	.85	1.99	.077
Online news use × offline news use	.88	1.64	.034	1.18	2.77	.000
Error	.54			.43		

[a]$R^2 = .55$ (Adjusted $R^2 = .25$); [b]$R^2 = .61$ (Adjusted $R^2 = .35$).

Similarly, the level of online-news use generated a significant main effect on the perceived interpersonal-communication utility of offline newspaper reading ($F = 2.50$, $p \le .008$), but the level of newspaper use did not ($F = 1.99$, $p \le .077$). Even as the interaction effect between the level of online news and offline newspaper use was significant ($F = 2.77$, $p \le .001$), a strong level of the total variance was still explained in the model ($R^2 = .61$; adjusted $R^2 = .35$).

RQ5 raises the question of whether the audiences' perception of offline newspaper utilities will be predictive of their perception of online-news utilities. As shown in Table 12.5, all four perceived online news utility models—entertainment ($F = 5.74$, $p \le .001$), interpersonal communication ($F = 13.53$, $p \le .001$), information skimming ($F = 3.91$, $p \le .005$), and information scanning ($F = 2.71$, $p \le .032$)—were statistically significant.

Separately, the online news entertainment utility model ($F = 14.15$, $p \le .001$) was significantly predicted by only its matching offline counterpart—newspaper entertainment utility. Similarly, the significant predictor for the online news interpersonal-communication model ($F = 46.70$, $p \le .001$) was offline newspaper interpersonal-communication utility. The online news information-skimming model ($F = 6.78$, $p \le .01$), likewise, was only significantly predicted by its offline counterpart—newspaper information-skimming utility. By comparison, the online news information-scanning model ($F = 4.67$, $p \le .032$) was significantly predicted by a nonmatching offline utility—newspaper information-scanning utility.

Overall, the total variance explained by the four offline newspaper utility predictors in each of the four online news utility models was as follows: entertainment ($R^2 = .12$; adjusted $R^2 = .10$), interpersonal communication ($R^2 = .23$; adjusted $R^2 = .32$), information skimming ($R^2 = .09$; adjusted $R^2 = .06$), and information scanning ($R^2 = .06$; adjusted $R^2 = .04$).

TABLE 12.5
Online News Utility Models as Predicted by
Offline Newspaper Utility Dimensions

Source	Dependent Variable: Perceived Online News Utility	F	$p \leq$	Partial η^2
Correct model	Entertainment	5.74	.000	.120
	Interpersonal communication	13.53	.000	.244
	Information skimming	3.91	.005	.085
	Information scanning	2.71	.032	.060
Perceived newspaper utility				
Entertainment	Entertainment	14.15	.000	.078
	Interpersonal communication	2.76	.099	.016
	Information skimming	3.57	.061	.021
	Information scanning	.02	.890	.000
Interpersonal communication	Entertainment	1.48	.226	.009
	Interpersonal communication	46.70	.000	.218
	Information skimming	.64	.427	.004
	Information scanning	.15	.698	.001
Information skimming	Entertainment	.09	.767	.001
	Interpersonal communication	2.93	.086	.017
	Information skimming	6.78	.010	.039
	Information scanning	2.40	.123	.014
Information scanning	Entertainment	3.45	.065	.020
	Interpersonal communication	.76	.386	.004
	Information skimming	4.67	.032	.027
	Information scanning	1.85	.176	.011

The test results for RQ6, which questions whether perceived online news utilities will be predictive of offline newspaper utilities, are presented in Table 12.6. Once again, each of the offline newspaper utility models—entertainment ($F = 5.36$, $p \leq .001$), interpersonal communication ($F = 13.15$, $p \leq .001$), information skimming ($F = 3.50$, $p \leq .009$), and information scanning ($F = 3.76$, $p \leq .006$)—was statistically significant.

In particular, online news entertainment utility was a significant predictor for two offline newspaper utility models—entertainment ($F = 13.42$, $p \leq .001$) and information scanning ($F = 5.39$, $p \leq .022$). Although online-news interpersonal-communication utility was a significant predictor for offline newspaper interpersonal-communication utility model ($F = 43.07$, $p \leq .001$), online news information-skimming utility was not a significant predictor for any of the four offline newspaper utility models. By contrast, online news information-scanning utility was predictive of three offline newspaper utility models: interpersonal communication ($F = 4.47$, $p \leq .036$), information skimming ($F = 12.59$, $p \leq .001$), and information scanning ($F = 6.16$, $p \leq .014$).

The total variance explained in each of the four offline newspaper utility models by the four online news utility predictors combined was as follows: entertainment

TABLE 12.6
Offline Newspaper Utility Models as Predicted
by Online News Utility Dimensions

Source	Dependent Variable: Perceived Newspaper Utility	F	Sig	Partial η^2
Corrected model	Entertainment	5.36	.000	.113
	Interpersonal communication	13.15	.000	.238
	Information skimming	3.50	.009	.077
	Information scanning	3.76	.006	.082
Perceived online news utility				
Entertainment	Entertainment	13.42	.000	.074
	Interpersonal communication	.02	.899	.000
	Information skimming	.20	.656	.001
	Information scanning	5.39	.022	.031
Interpersonal communication	Entertainment	.26	.614	.002
	Interpersonal communication	43.07	.000	.204
	Information skimming	.06	.815	.000
	Information scanning	1.91	.169	.011
Information skimming	Entertainment	2.48	.117	.015
	Interpersonal communication	.04	.852	.000
	Information skimming	3.48	.064	.020
	Information scanning	1.00	.318	.006
Information scanning	Entertainment	1.29	.257	.008
	Interpersonal communication	4.47	.036	.026
	Information skimming	12.59	.001	.070
	Information scanning	6.16	.014	.035

($R^2 = .11$; adjusted $R^2 = .09$), interpersonal communication ($R^2 = .24$; adjusted $R^2 = .22$), information skimming ($R^2 = .08$; adjusted $R^2 = .06$), and information scanning ($R^2 = .08$; adjusted $R^2 = .06$).

DISCUSSION

The exploratory theorizing effort put forth in this study via the introduction of two concepts—information scanning and information skimming—was by and large validated, even though the reliability associated with the "online news skimming" scale was less than satisfactory. In particular, the information scanning concept reflects the utility of scrutinizing news content either online or offline to learn about the major events of the day and in the world. The information skimming concept indicates the utility of grazing the news landscape—both online and offline—to search for only the "important" news for consumption.

Conceptually, information scanning may represent the cognitive process that aims to accumulate knowledge about news and world events, whereas information skimming may illustrate the cognitive process that targets glancing over news items that are of special interest to an audience (e.g., sports updates or stock quotes). Applying conventional uses and gratification conceptual terms, information scanning can be likened to the "information learning" gratification that is associated with a more instrumental orientation. Information skimming can be seen as the "surveillance" gratification that is affiliated with a more ritualized orientation (Rubin & Perse, 1987).

It is interesting to find that newspaper readers perceive a greater level of online-news skimming utility than nonreaders (see Table 12.1). The logical explanation for this outcome is that the non-newspaper readers did not have the experience of comparing the process of "skimming" for news headlines between online news outlets and a regular newspaper. Newspaper readers, on the other hand, were able to appreciate the differences that existed in the functional utility between an online news site and an offline newspaper.

Comparing the layout of an online news site and an offline newspaper, it is much easier to skim for news headlines via an online news source than an offline newspaper. As the home page of an online news site can be thought of as the front page of an offline newspaper, an online news home page—like an annotated table of contents—is typically compartmentalized and contains all of the major headlines. An offline newspaper, by contrast, normally does not provide a list of headlines and major news items associated with different departments on the front page. *The Wall Street Journal* may be an unusual close exception to this rule. Even so, skimming over online news headlines for stories of selective interest and clicking on links to access those stories is relatively effortless, compared to finding the news headlines of interest in the right section, page number, and column placement in an offline newspaper.

By the same token, although online news users who accessed offline newspapers could experience the differences in scanning for stories between an online news source and an offline newspaper, non-online news users could not. Hence, it is not surprising that online-news users perceived a lower level of scanning utility associated with online-news than with offline newspaper reading (see Table 12.2). This is because an online news source may not provide the type of extensive news coverage that is generally the domain of major offline newspapers. The qualitative difference that exists in the presentation of news coverage between online news sites and offline newspapers is understandable, as reading an extensive amount of text online is a lot more difficult than reading such text in a newspaper offline.

Offline newspapers were perceived to be more entertaining by online news users (see Table 12.2); this finding was consistent with past research that indicated offline newspapers were deemed the best source for entertainment news across all media types (New Media Federation, 2002). Perhaps when it comes to providing reading pleasure in a substantive manner, offline newspapers still outshine online news outlets from the online news users' perspective. The reason for this perception may also have something to do with the practical logistics related to the more "permanent" physical presence of an offline newspaper. As the online news content is updated daily (or even hourly), the audience who missed any particular day's news will have to dig into the news archive to find the neglected news content. Most news sites don't keep an archive, unless the operator of the news site is a major metropolitan newspaper. And if the archive is dated beyond 1 week or more, most of these online newspaper sites charge the users a fee. By comparison, the audience can read any current or dated issues of an offline newspaper anywhere, anytime, due to their longer shelf life.

With regard to the relations between perceived utilities of news and the level of news access either online or offline, the findings were mixed. The level of online news and offline newspaper use was found to be individually predictive of only one perceived online news utility—entertainment (see Table 12.3). Hence, those audiences who accessed news through an online source and/or an offline newspaper were most enthused about the entertainment utility of their online news use experience. These findings seem to echo Tewksbury's (2003) observation that, given the enhanced technical ease of and increased user control over navigating the news content online, users may opt for accessing stories that appeal to their special interest instead of seeking out the major news events of the day.

By all accounts, online news sources, not unlike any other commercial web pages, usually strive to design their page layout and content in such a way that they will visually "please" the eyes and make reading online text "fun" for their users. They also make an effort to provide a photo gallery, a news video archive, or even a live video webcast to "entice" user attention in a way that a static offline newspaper cannot. All of these pleasing devices that have been strategically embedded within the news web pages may then help compensate for the rather "temporal" nature of online news content, as compared to the more "fixed" nature of their offline counterpart.

According to Table 12.4, there is a significant interaction effect between online news and offline newspaper use levels present in the two statistically significant perceived newspaper utility models—entertainment and interpersonal communication. This indicates that the combined experience of online news and offline newspaper use was instrumental in the audiences' perception of both the enjoyment gratification and communication utility of their newspaper reading experience. The significant main effect produced by online news use level on each of these two models further highlights the fact that online news use might also have engendered newspaper readers to appreciate the value of newspaper reading in providing both a pleasurable experience as well as topics for conversation with others. These findings, then, point to the significance of the much-overlooked leisure and social functions of news consumption.

Turning to the relations between perceived online news and offline newspaper utilities, the findings here are the most theoretically intriguing (see Table 12.5). Three perceived newspaper utility indicators were each a significant predictor for each of the three "matching" perceived online news utility models. In essence, the following offline newspaper utility dimensions—entertainment, interpersonal communication, and information skimming—were each the sole significant predictor for the following three online news utility models, respectively: entertainment, interpersonal communication, and information skimming. These results demonstrate a strong complementary relationship between online and offline news consumption, one where the perceived gratifications associated with offline newspaper use appear to have been directly transferable to the gratifications of online news access.

The only exception in this perfect matching phenomenon involves the finding of perceived information-scanning utility of newspapers as the single significant predictor for the perceived information-skimming (instead of information-scanning) utility of online news outlets. This particular finding further supported the theoretical distinction between information skimming and scanning presented earlier, which explains how online news pages are well equipped for news headline skimming but less desirable for extensive news text scanning. It should be pointed out that, of the four perceived online news utilities, the information-skimming utility had the highest mean value. That mean value was statistically greater than the mean values of information scanning utility ($t = 2.209$, $p \leq .028$), interpersonal communication utility ($t = 5.911$, $p \leq .001$), and entertainment utility ($t = 9.386$ $p \leq .001$).[1]

When using perceived online news utilities as predictors for perceived offline newspaper utilities, the most striking finding is that online news information skimming was an insignificant predictor to all offline perceived newspaper utility models (see Table 12.6). This particular evidence further supports the notion that the information skimming utility received by online news users was unique and not relevant to any potential utilities associated with the experience of reading an offline newspaper. Nonetheless, other types of perceived online news utilities received—entertainment, interpersonal communication, and information scanning—were favorable contributors to the enjoyment of perceived offline newspaper utilities.

Based on these findings, it is reasonable to presume that online news access helped enhance the different perceived utilities of offline newspaper use. In particular, information scanning stood out as the unique utility most "recognized" by the audience. This is further substantiated by the fact that, of the four offline newspaper utility dimensions, the mean value of information scanning utility was the highest. This mean value was also significantly greater than the mean values of the other three utility dimensions—information skimming ($t = -4.755$; $p \leq .001$), interpersonal communication ($t = 2.531$, $p \leq .012$), and entertainment ($t = 8.458$, $p \leq .001$).[2]

To sum up, consistent with past research, perceived entertainment utility of news was lower than other types of utilities experienced by the audience (Lichtenstein & Rosenfeld, 1983). Even so, this utility was an integral part of the news consumption experience, just as using the news topics learned was a conversation starter with others (e.g., Weaver, 1980). Skimming the news headlines was an important function (Elliot & Quattlebaum, 1979), next to scanning the news stories to learn about what is going on in the world (Kippax & Murray, 1980). Lastly, online news outlets were distinct due to their unique content layout style and technical advantage that enabled their users to easily skim the news headlines and go to those stories of special interest. Offline newspapers, on the other hand, were noted for their rich content substance and time-shifting capability that allow their readers to leisurely scan the news content and gain in-depth knowledge about current events.

CONCLUSIONS

This exploratory study made an effort to discover the relations between online news and offline newspaper utilities as perceived by their audiences. Even though online news was much valued for its agility when it comes to providing a convenient headline news service and richer visual content that is unmatched by an offline newspaper, the printed words affixed in a copy remain cherished for their substantive continuity. Online news outlets, at this stage of their evolution, appear to be largely complementary and ancillary to their offline counterparts, when it comes to audience uses and gratifications of the audiences' news consumption experience.

Due to its exploratory nature, the present study contains certain limitations. First, the construct reliability of the measurement items associated with "information scanning" and "information skimming" was lower than expected. Second, the range of news utility measurement items adopted in the study could have been more comprehensive to enhance the construct validity. These limitations are conceptual issues that deserve further attention in future studies.

Future research may also wish to examine how the audience perceives the affective utilities associated with the placement and presentation of visual elements (e.g., photos, graphics) in online news sites and offline newspapers. Furthermore, audience uses and gratifications related to accessing breaking news reported by online news outlets and offline 24-hour cable news networks could be another worthy research topic to explore. In particular, the similarities and dissimilarities between these two modalities of news presentation will represent an interesting venue for later work.

ENDNOTES

1. The mean values for the four perceived online-news utilities are: information skimming ($M = 4.43$; $SD = .65$), information scanning ($M = 4.32$; $SD = .69$), interpersonal communication ($M = 4.08$; $SD = .78$), and entertainment ($M = 3.83$; $SD = .89$).
2. The mean values for the four perceived newspaper utilities are: informatic ($M = 4.25$; $SD = .72$), interpersonal communication ($M = 4.13$; $SD = .79$), skimming ($M = 4.04$; $SD = .88$), and entertainment ($M = 3.78$; $SD = .87$).

REFERENCES

Althaus, S. L., & Tewksbury, D. (2000, January–March). Patterns of Internet and traditional news media use in a networked community. *Political Communication, 17*(1), 21–45.

Blumler, J. G. (1979). The role of theory in uses and gratifications studies. *Communication Research, 6,* 9–36.

Blumler, J. G., & Katz, E. (Eds.). (1974). *The uses of mass communications.* Beverly Hills, CA: Sage.

Cao, Z., & Li, X. (2004, May). *Effect of growing Internet newspapers on circulation of print newspapers in the U.S.* Paper presented at the annual meeting of the International Communication Association, New Orleans, LA.

Choi, J. H, Watt, J. H., Dekkers, A. C., & Park, S. H. (2004, May). *Motives of Internet uses: Crosscultural perspective—The United States, the Netherlands, and South Korea.* Paper presented at the annual meeting of the International Communication Association, New Orleans, LA.

Chyi, H. I. (2004, May). *Re-examining the market relation between online and print newspapers: The case of Hong Kong.* Paper presented at the annual meeting of the International Communication Association, New Orleans, LA.

Dimmick, J., Chen, Y., & Li, Z. (2004). Competition between the Internet and traditional news media: The gratification-opportunities niche dimension. *Journal of Media Economics, 17*(1), 19–33.

Elliot, W., & Quattlebaum, C. P. (1979). Similarities in patterns of media use: A cluster analysis of media gratifications. *The Western Journal of Speech Communication, 43,* 61–72.

Eveland, W. P., & Dunwoody, S. (2002). An investigation of elaboration and selective scanning as methods of learning from the web versus print. *Journal of Broadcasting & Electronic Media, 46,* 34–44.

Eveland, W. P., Jr., Seo, M., & Marton, K. (2002). Learning from the news in campaign 2000: An experimental comparison of TV news, newspapers, and online news. *Media Psychology, 4*(4), 353–378.

Ferguson, D. A., & Perse, E. M. (2000). The World Wide Web as a functional alternative to television. *Journal of Broadcasting & Electronic Media, 44,* 155–174.

Katz, E., Blumler, J. G., & Gurevitch, M. (1974). Utilization of mass communication by the individual. In J. G. Blumler & E. Katz (Eds.), *The uses of mass communications: Current perspectives on gratifications research* (pp. 19–32). Beverly Hills, CA: Sage.

Katz, E., M., Gurevitch, M., & Hass, H. (1973). On the uses of mass media for important things. *American Sociology Review, 38*(2), 164–181.

Kippax, S., & Murray, J. P. (1980). Using the mass media: Need gratification and "perceived utility." *Communication Research, 7,* 335–360.

Levy, M. R., & Windahl, S. (1984). Audience activity and gratifications: A conceptual clarification and exploration. *Communication Research, 11,* 51–78.

Lichtenstein, A., & Rosenfeld, L. B. (1983). Uses and misuses of gratifications research: An explication of media functions. *Communication Research, 10,* 97–109.

Lin, C. A. (1999). Online service adoption likelihood. *Journal of Advertising Research, 39*(2), 79–89.

Lin, C. A. (2001). Audience attributes, media supplementation, and likely online service adoption. *Mass Communication & Society, 4*(1), 19–38.

McDonald, D. G. (1990). Media orientation and television news viewing. *Journalism and Mass Communication Quarterly, 67,* 11–20.

Mings, S. M. (1997). Uses and gratifications of online newspapers: A preliminary study. *Electronic Journal of communication, 7*(3). Retrieved from http://www.cios.org/getfile/MINGS_V7N397

New Media Federation. (2002). The digital age. *Newspaper Association of America.* http://www.naa .org

Palmgreen, P., Wenner, L. A., & Rayburn, J. D., II. (1980). Relations between gratifications sought and obtained: A study of TV news. *Communication Research, 7,* 161–192.

Pew Internet and American Life Project. (2004, April 23). Internet activitie *(March 2000–present).* Retrieved June 20, 2004 from http://www.pewinternet Activities_4.23.04.htm

Rayburn, J. D., II. (1996). Uses and gratifications. In M. B. Salwen & D. W. Sta *grated approach to communication theory and research* (pp. 145–163). Mahwah, NJ: Lawrence Erlbaum Associates.

Rubin, A. M., & Perse, E. M. (1987). Audience activity and television news gratifications. *Communication Research, 14,* 58–84.

Ruggiero, T. E. (2000, Winter). Uses and gratifications theory in the 21st century. *Mass Communication and Society, 3*(1), 3–37.

Select phone pro CD database. (2001). (Version 2.1, Fall ed.). Omaha, NE: InfoUSA.

Stempel, G. H., III, Hargrove, T., & Bernt, J. P. (2000). Relation of growth of use of the Internet to changes in media use from 1995 to 1999. *Journalism & Mass Communication Quarterly, 77,* 71–79.

Tewksbury, D. (2003, December). What do Americans really want to know? Tracking the behavior of news readers on the Internet. *Journal of Communication, 53*(4), 694–710.

Weaver, D. H. (1980). Audience need for orientation and media effects. *Communication Research, 7,* 361–376.

13

The Contributions of Net News to Cyber Democracy: Civic Affordances of Major Metropolitan Newspaper Sites

Erik P. Bucy
Robert B. Affe
Indiana University, Bloomington

With each passing election cycle the Internet is becoming a more decisive factor in political campaigns for candidates and Web users alike. Newspapers, initially slow to realize the World Wide Web's potential (Lasica, 1996; Schultz, 1999), have now embraced the possibilities of the online medium. Effective cyberjournalism requires more than repurposing the offline product, however. The interconnected, continuously accessible character of cyberspace demands that media organizations engage users in interactive processes that keep them involved in the news while keeping pace with a news cycle that never ends. This chapter investigates the extent to which major metropolitan newspaper sites are facilitating civic participation in cyberspace as online media organizations transition into a "third generation" of Net news, characterized by an environment of increased immediacy, information richness, and user control (see Brown, 2000; Bucy, 2004a; Pavlik, 1997).

To deepen our understanding of civic involvement at a moment of digital convergence, when online news organizations have the potential to provide a burgeoning context for public debate and citizenship, the analysis borrows from the human–computer interaction literature to explain the set of actions that major metropolitan newspaper sites make available to users. Understanding the structural aspects of Net news from the standpoint of human–computer interaction may yield important insights about the functions and affordances of online news that neither content-oriented studies of the Web (e.g. Barnhurst, 2002; Kiernan & Levy, 1999) nor small-scale examinations of Web page design (e.g. Li, 1998, 2002) have revealed thus far.

AFFORDANCES OF MASS MEDIA INTERFACES

As information interfaces, the Web sites of local news providers may be profitably studied from the perspective of human–computer interaction (HCI), a branch of computer science concerned with the ways in which users interact directly with computer systems. Central to much HCI research on the effectiveness of different layouts and design features that enhance information retrieval and navigation is the concept of *affordances,* or possible actions that the properties of the medium make available to users (Bradner, 2000; Monkhern, 1997; Norman, 1988, 1999). As a technologically complex medium, the Internet tasks news organizations with the need to make content readily accessible to the broadest range of users at differing skill levels, balancing the novice's need for simplicity and structure with the expert's need for flexibility and depth (Shneiderman, 1998).

Beyond compelling news content, which waxes and wanes with story developments of local and national consequence, attention to the news may depend on skillful information packaging. From the standpoint of perceptual psychology, the structural or design features of online news can be understood in terms of their calls to action, or invitational character. Gibson (1979) introduced the concept of *object affordances* to describe the visual properties of ecological artifacts that determined how they could be recognized and used. By its very appearance a chair affords sitting, a stairway climbing. Applying this concept to technology, Norman (1988) argued that interface design could benefit by emphasizing direct correspondence between functions and appearances, similar to the practice of direct manipulation discussed in the human–computer interaction literature (see Shneiderman, 1982). In an effective direct manipulation system, Norman (1988) asserted, the user should readily see and be able to perform the allowable actions; the effect of each action should be visible and easy to interpret; and, actions should be readily reversible (pp. 183–184).

Here, a distinction needs to be made between *real* and *perceived* affordances. Perceived affordances inform the user what actions can be performed and, to some extent, how to perform them. If a technology's actual properties or real affordances are not detected and understood, they will have little value. Not recognizing real affordances because they are hidden or obscured, or wrongly perceiving a false affordance as real, may lead to mistakes. Perceived affordances, then, distinguish usable interfaces from those that are mysterious and unfathomable (Norman, 1999). Overall, "what makes a system successful is how well the design model is communicated to the user" (Monkern, 1997).

Conceptually, the term *affordances* refers to attributes of both the medium and the user; in order to be utilized, a particular function must be perceived. This dual quality makes the concept a powerful one for thinking about new technologies because it focuses on the *interaction* between technology and users (Gaver, 1991). In this view, online features that support *user-to-user* interactivity, such as e-mail, chat rooms, and message boards, afford a certain level of social interaction; clickable graphics, audio and video downloads, online polls, and searchable databases, on the other hand, afford a type of *user-to-documents/system,* or media interaction (McMillan, 2002; Stromer-Galley, 2000). Electronic media have their own unique properties that enhance and constrain different patterns of usage and thus can be characterized by the affordances they make available to users (Bradner, 2000; Gaver, 1991; Norman, 1999).

A particular danger to interface designers are false affordances that, like the painting of a door in a sealed room, imply activities they cannot support. Some early criticism of online newspapers, which accused the industry of being more concerned with offering the *illusion* of interactivity and democratic discussion than the reality, was evidently inspired by e-mail links to editorial staff that gave readers no more voice or input than that granted during the print era. "The real power," Katz (1994) wrote, "lies not in online exchanges but in daily story conferences among a few editors who don't read e-mail" (p. 54). In this study, only the real (observable) affordances of newspaper Web sites are examined; whether they are perceived and utilized depends on varying degrees of individual expertise and technical literacy within users, which are important factors for future research.

GLIMPSES OF THE BROADBAND FUTURE

As the media industry transitions into a "third generation" of Net news, marked by new methods of storytelling and ways of engaging audiences in public affairs, questions arise as to how online newspapers are engaging users in the news and structuring interactive experiences. Results of a previous content analysis conducted in the weeks before the general elections of 1998 and 2000 indicated that both newspaper and local TV news sites in the top 40 media markets nationally offered a broad range of user options relevant to civic participation (Bucy, 2004a). Consistent with the continuous development and sophistication of online news, news organizations are expected to incorporate a growing amount of interactivity into their sites in 2004. At a time when traditional media outlets are routinely criticized for questionable news judgment and see a decline in circulation and audience share, the imperative to rebuild confidence and credibility in all forms of news and attract new audiences in cyberspace is high. Features of Net news that contribute to user involvement and promote interactivity have consequently become a priority for media organizations' online operations (Bucy, 2004a).

Glimpses of the interactive broadband news future can be had with growing frequency through various Web specials offered on news sites featuring content tailored specifically for the online medium. During the 2003 Iraq invasion, for example, both newspaper and network television news sites presented a package of original coverage, showcasing the Web's capacity to compel, engage, and inform. In addition to news reports, *The New York Times* Web site featured zoomable maps of Iraq and the surrounding area, audio dispatches from the front lines, video coverage of protests in New York, a Web forum for reader postings, e-mail links to *Times'* staff, including the paper's bureau chief in Kuwait City, a slide show of images from the battlefield, and other interactive features in its special section titled "A Nation at War."[1] Beyond just reporting the news, the online coverage invited visitors to *experience* the story by calling up a combination of interactive features, audiovisual feeds, and print coverage from *Times'* staff and wire service reports.

Consistent with this discussion, the present analysis assumes that Web users are attracted to Net news on account of its informational appeal as well as participatory depth. In this analysis, information elements of news sites are presumed to be prevalent and thus are not measured in detail. The analysis instead focuses on the interactive features that facilitate civic engagement online. The next section overviews the changing nature of the newspaper–reader relationship in light of theories about civic journalism and media participation—the process of civically engaging audiences through new media use (see Bucy & Gregson, 2001).

CIVIC JOURNALISM AND ONLINE NEWS

In a broader professional context, new technology is not the only force behind the changing relationship between media organizations and the news audience. The civic or public journalism movement has also been influential in involving news consumers in coverage decisions (see Kurpius, 2000; Rosen, 1999). Civic journalism projects emphasize community-oriented coverage that attempts to create connections between diverse communities, strengthen and encourage democratic processes, and involve citizens in a discussion about important civic issues. Indeed, in the civic journalism model members of the news audience are regarded first and foremost as citizens rather than consumers, or members of a target demographic. "Underlying the broad goals of public journalism is the desire to improve the marketplace of ideas through dialog among citizens, government, and media" (Kurpius, 2000, p. 340). Instead of trickling down from traditional beats and sources, story ideas may bubble up from members of the attentive audience and thereby alter the traditional agenda-setting function of the news.

Citizen concerns are also addressed through special projects launched, sometimes in partnerships with sister media companies, in conjunction with local elections, legislative sessions, or other civic processes. A case in point was

WTHR-TV's joint effort with the *Indianapolis Star* during the 2001 Indiana legislative session to communicate "The People's Agenda" to state lawmakers. Using ballots printed in the newspaper and posted online on each news operation's Web site, the project solicited public opinion on which issues should receive top priority. Approximately 3,400 people responded. Property tax relief finished at the top of the list, followed by restrictions on telemarketing calls. Once a list of priorities was assembled, the news partners conducted a systematic survey to establish where the broader public actually stood on the issues. On the question of telemarketing, 95% of those interviewed supported a measure that would allow residents to place their names on a "do not call" list. The measure, defeated the previous year after heavy lobbying from telemarketers, passed, and now there is a number for citizens to call. Although there was no action taken on property taxes that year, 6 of the 10 issues identified by The People's Agenda were addressed by the legislature (*Civic Catalyst,* 2001).

Civic journalism further places a priority on soliciting citizen feedback in the form of ideas, opinions, and criticisms as a way of improving the news (Kurpius, 2000). Small- to mid-sized newspapers are among the most receptive to this mode of reporting. Of 651 civic journalism projects published between 1994 and 2002 identified by the Pew Center for Civic Journalism, 75% were undertaken by regional dailies with circulations of 250,000 or less (Friedland & Nichols, 2002). Altogether, at least one fifth of all U.S. daily newspapers, 322 of the nation's 1,500 dailies, practiced some form of civic journalism during this period. And most of these projects, 85%, provided space for citizen perspectives (Friedland & Nichols, 2002). The Internet has assumed an important and growing role in both civic journalism and standard news reporting practices. From a mail survey of 54 print journalists at a range of different-sized newspapers, Davis (1999) found that the vast majority, 86%, use the Internet to find sources and 43% said they browse through newsgroups to communicate with potential sources.

Though laudable, such outreach efforts are resisted by many editors and news directors, especially in larger markets, and are only sporadically adopted even when they are practiced by stations and newspapers in small- and mid-sized markets (Friedland & Nichols, 2002; Kurpius, 2000). Moreover, civic journalism efforts, which are both time and labor intensive (and upsetting to journalistic norms of autonomy and editorial independence), do not begin to rival the long-term potential of new media to actively involve much larger numbers of news consumers in the world of public affairs in a less prescriptive manner.

In addition to providing access to news and information, frequently faster and more in-depth than traditional media, the Internet and World Wide Web provide a public space for citizens to debate civic issues and express their support for, or discontent with, policies or office holders. Beyond discussion, the Internet provides citizens with a ready avenue of access to decision makers (even if they choose not to reply) and can serve as a barometer of public opinion by presenting public reaction to events in real time. Despite the tendency to dismiss such activity as marginal, interactive civic experiences that occur in cyberspace, via cable channels, and over the airwaves are considered by audiences to be as useful and important as more recognized forms of conventional, in-person involvement (Bucy, D'Angelo, & Newhagen, 1999). New media use can thus be conceptualized as a mode of civic participation in its own right.

With every new election the number and forms of media participation multiply and the amount of news consumers who engage in civic activity and political information seeking through the Web increases (Pew Research Center, 2000). In the era of mass media, compelling visuals and narrative content delivered distant events to audiences in a daily package—the morning newspaper or nightly newscast. The World Wide Web, and the distributed computing network on which it resides, embraces a wider range of functions than simple information delivery (December, 1997) and promotes user involvement and reciprocal activity by its very design.[2] Through Net news interfaces, users continue to enjoy visual and temporal proximity to important events that mass media have always delivered. Interwoven with news content, however, are interactive features that allow users to experience the story to a greater extent than ever before—informationally, socially, and emotionally (see Bucy, 2004a, 2004b).

In summary, digital developments are giving news organizations increased opportunities for interactivity at the same time that the civic journalism movement is creating renewed awareness of the public obligations of news that extend beyond the traditional function of information dissemination. The potential of new media to redefine civic participation (see Bucy, D'Angelo, & Newhagen, 1999; Bucy & Gregson, 2001) and the growing awareness of the civic potential of online news (Kurpius, 2003; Singer & Gonzalez-Velez, 2003) suggest a two-part research question that this chapter investigates:

RQ1: In the context of cyber democracy, what are the opportunities for interactivity and citizenship that exist on the Web sites of leading U.S. newspapers? More specifically, to what extent do the political sections of major metropolitan newspaper sites provide election-related content, information accessibility features, and mechanisms enabling both media and human interaction?

RQ2: Can the range of user options relevant to political participation during the 2004 presidential campaign be conceptualized as *civic affordances* that recast media consumers into a more active role as engaged citizens?

DATA AND METHOD

To investigate the nature and extent of civic experiences afforded by the digital editions of online newspapers, a content analysis of the Web sites of the 50 highest circulation U.S. dailies was performed. The analysis was first conducted quantitatively using a coding sheet with relevant categories (described later) to determine the presence or absence of certain site features. Then, a follow-up qualitative analysis was performed to provide a more textured description of the type of interactive features available on the sites sampled. Quantitative analysis was used to answer the first research question, and qualitative analysis was relied on to address the second question.

The sample for the study was drawn from a list of the top 50 newspapers listed by AdAge.com as of March 31, 2004. To narrow the analysis to pages with the most civic relevance, the Politics or Election 2004 sections were selected for coding. When a particular news site did not have a politics or election section, the main news section was analyzed instead. Because two of the sites in the sample were business oriented (*The Wall Street Journal* and *Investor's Business Daily*), they were removed from consideration, leaving 48 sites for the analysis. The average daily (offline) circulation of newspapers in the sample was 428,938. *USA Today* was on the high end with 2,192,098 daily subscribers and *The Louisville Courier-Journal* was on the low end with 216,934 daily subscribers.

Coding Instrument

The coding instrument measured *election-related content, interactive features,* and *information accessibility* items of Net news home pages. Following Stromer-Galley (2000), interactive features were divided into two general types. The first, more common type has been termed *media interaction*. This form of interactivity involves the control that news consumers exercise over the selection and presentation of editorial content, whether story text, sound files, audiovisuals, multimedia, or some combination thereof. Unlike traditional media platforms, the online environment allows users to more fully interact with the medium itself by clicking on hyperlinks, taking part in viewer polls and surveys, downloading information, calling up streaming media, searching archives, customizing information delivery, and making electronic purchases, all "without ever directly communicating with another person" (Stromer-Galley, 2000, p. 118).

The second, less common type of interactivity that may occur online, termed *human interaction,* involves person-to-person conversations mediated by the online network (Stromer-Galley, 2000). Such computer-mediated communication includes both synchronous (real-time) and asynchronous (delayed) exchanges, whether in the form of e-mail or its various permutations such as Instant Messenger, chat room discussions, message boards, user forums, and the like. In a political context, site features that serve as mechanisms for volunteering and engaging in community activism can also be considered forms of (eventual) human interaction. Importantly, both types of interactivity may be facilitated by the same Web site, depending on the features offered.

Election-related content was defined as candidate or issue advertising, candidate issue positions, candidate biographies, links to candidate or issue sites, and

TABLE 13.1
Coding Categories

Category	Specific Features
Election-related content	Candidate/issue ads; candidate/issue positions; candidate bios; links to candidate/issue sites; links to party/interest group sites
Human interaction items	Mechanisms for volunteering and community activism; place for visitor comments; links to join a listserv; online chat rooms/forums, bulletin boards, and other discussions
Media interaction items	Instant polls or surveys; information-oriented interactives; quizzes; audio/video downloads; slide shows; interactive Web cams; letter to the editor; links to voter registration forms; downloadable graphics/wallpapers
Information access items	Ability to customize information display/delivery; ability to receive information specific to the user's geographic location; searchable databases

Note. All features were coded as being either *present* or *absent* (not for the total number of times they appeared throughout the section).

links to political party or interest group sites. Lastly, *information accessibility* was operationalized as site mechanisms that enhanced usability, including the capacity to customize the information display or news delivery, the ability to receive information specific to the user's geographic location, and the presence of searchable databases that allowed users to mine for their own information (e.g., for candidate financial contributions). Table 13.1 presents a list of each page feature measured in this study, grouped by category.

Coding Procedure

The unit of analysis was the Politics or Election 2004 section of each newspaper in the sample. Two coders with media industry experience participated in the analysis, which was conducted the first week of July 2004, before the national political conventions were held. Before collecting the data, a pretest was conducted to verify the appropriateness of the coding categories and to add new items that were not captured by the draft version of the instrument.

All features on the coding instrument were coded in nominal terms, as being either present (1) or absent (0), rather than for the total number of times they appeared throughout the section. The rationale for using this approach was to allow a general picture of online news functions to emerge rather than descriptively report the exact content and features of Net news home pages, which change daily. To provide a rich sense of the range of features offered, the analysis was first performed quantitatively, checking for categories on the coding instrument; this numerical picture was then supplemented by a qualitative description of representative sites and features encountered in the sample.

For the quantitative analysis, the entire section was searched for the presence or absence of a particular site feature. Questionable cases were double-checked by a second coder. For reliability purposes, 10% of the sample (five sites) was double coded and the scores were compared using Holsti's reliability formula. Across variables, agreement exceeded .80.

RESULTS

The first research question asked about the opportunities for interactivity and citizenship that exist on the Web sites of leading newspapers, specifically, the extent to which the political sections of major metropolitan newspaper sites provided election-related content, information accessibility features, and mechanisms enabling both media and human interaction. The analysis found that most of the Politics or Election 2004 sections coded (81.3%, $n = 39$) did carry direct election-related content, whether candidate ads or biographies, issue positions, or links to candidate, political party, or interest group sites, in addition to news coverage of the campaign (see Fig. 13.1). The most common form of campaign content

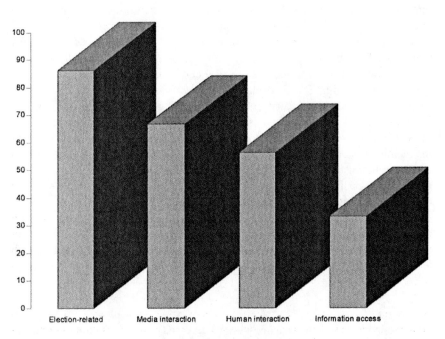

FIG. 13.1.   Percentage of sites with civic affordances.

was candidate biographies, which appeared on 62.5% of sections in the sample, followed by links to candidate or issue sites, which were present on 52.1% of sections sampled.

The next most common set of user options were media interaction items, including online polls and quizzes, audio and video downloads, informational interactive features relating to the campaign, slide shows, and downloadable graphics. At least one of these features was present on two thirds (66.7%, $n = 32$) of the sections sampled. The most common forms of media interaction were video downloads, present in 41.7% of the sections, and informational interactive features, present in 35.4% of sections.

Opportunities for human interaction appeared slightly less frequently but were still present in a majority of the sections sampled (56.3%, $n = 27$). The most common forms of human interaction were links to voter registration forms,[3] appearing in 33.3% of sections, and online chat rooms, appearing in 16.7% of sections. Human interaction mechanisms were spread somewhat thinly over the sites sampled, with individual sections not likely to have more than one or two of these features.

The least common set of features found within the sections were information accessibility items, including the ability to customize news and information delivery, the option of receiving news specific to the user's geographic location, and the presence of searchable databases. One of these features was present in one third of the sections sampled (33.3%, $n = 16$), with the option of receiving news by location present in 25% of the sections.

To assess whether opportunities for interactivity were associated with newspaper size, Tau b correlations were run for the daily circulation variable and summative indices for each of the four general coding categories. The indices were constructed by adding together related elements for each content and interactive category.[4] The analysis revealed a small but positive correlation for circulation and the human interaction index ($b = .33, p < .05$), suggesting that interactive options increased with circulation size. Another significant correlation was found between the media interaction and election content indices ($b = .25, p < .05$), indicating a positive relationship between interactive mechanisms and political information.

In summary, there was more election-related content in the sections sampled than interactive mechanisms, but two thirds of the sections did feature some form of media interaction and over half the sections made possible at least one form of human interaction. The potential for such person-to-person communication or involvement also seemed to increase with newspaper circulation size, although the relationship was only modest.

Civic Affordances

To address the second research question, whether the range of user options relevant to political participation can be conceptualized as civic affordances that recast media consumers into a more active role as engaged citizens, the analysis next highlights the type of interactive features found on the sites sampled. Interactive features were clustered fairly heavily on certain newspaper sites and appeared infrequently or not at all on others. In the sections sampled, 43.8% ($n = 21$) featured no human interaction, and 33.3% ($n = 16$) presented no media interaction.

However, among the sections that did make interactive options available to users, eight (16.7%) offered at least two types of human interaction, and eight more offered at least three forms of media interaction. The most common types of human interaction were represented by links to voter registration forms and online chatrooms, and the most common forms of media interaction included video downloads, dynamic informational graphics (or "interactives"), and online polls.[5]

Typically, the various forms of interactivity evident online were not neatly categorized and displayed in one location (although on occasion they did appear in a framed index to the left or right of the screen) but were spread around the page or section and sometimes embedded in story descriptions or stories themselves. To provide a richer sense of the opportunities available at the time of the study, short descriptions of the interactive features available on five representative sites follow:

• On *The Cleveland Plain Dealer* site, the Politics section encouraged visitors to "speak up!" and offered them the opportunity to take part in either a politics or "chatterbox" forum discussion around a pressing question of the day, and a newsletter link enabled visitors to sign up for daily news updates. In a multimedia area, visitors could download a video recording of the mayor's state of the city speech and browse any number of slide shows about political and election-related events.[6]

• In the Politics section of *The Washington Post*, visitors had the option of comparing the presidential candidates side by side on a range of issues through an interactive feature, posting on message boards about the campaign, and signing up for weekly campaign news briefings. A multimedia section called Camera•Works archived a range of video essays and photo galleries, and a feature called "Charting the Campaign" offered a plethora of election-related poll results and campaign-tracking information.[7]

• The *New York Post*'s Politics section carried a package of interactive features from the Associated Press, including biographical, fundraising, and issues information about the presidential candidates as well as video clips of President Bush's 2004 State of the Union speech and an information graphic, titled "Elections Made Easy," discussing the functions of different branches of government. Another promotion invited visitors to sign up for the paper's interactive newsletters.

• *The St. Petersburg Times,* in its Decision 2004 section, published a "Poll Tracker" feature that presented a range of public opinion about the candidates, political parties, and current issues. Archived video reports allowed visitors to view campaign coverage and candidate profiles online, and a link to the Florida State

Division of Elections gave users the opportunity to download the official voter registration form. A political townhall discussion forum also encouraged visitors to engage in "a free and open exchange of ideas on these message boards."

• The Politics section of the *Los Angeles Times* hosted a variety of interactive features, including an electoral vote tracker that presented historical information and invited users to test their own scenarios for the 2004 election. A polling area presented statewide and national survey results plus a "Stat Sheets Archive" enabled visitors to download statistical reports of most *Times'* polls since 1996. In addition, an ad watch section critiqued televised political ads, and a "Find Your Candidates" service enabled users to locate their particular state and federal elections by legislative district.

To the extent that the interface features described here did make it possible for users to experience the campaign and engage in forms of direct involvement through the newspaper site itself, they probably can be conceptualized as civic affordances that call site visitors to action. Not only did these features provide visual proximity to political developments through photo and videographic essays, they also promoted civic learning, critical examination of campaign messages, and—through discussion forums, chat rooms, and bulletin boards—democratic deliberation with fellow visitors. Beyond information exchange, the Politics and Election 2004 sections of some newspaper sites also encouraged voter registration and helped visitors identify their local races. Taken together, such citizen involvement in interactive environments presents users of new information technologies "with a ready avenue of participation across a variety of communication modalities—and on a continuous, everyday basis, not just during election campaigns" (Bucy & D'Angelo, 2004, p. 23).

DISCUSSION

The civic role of news organizations implies that journalism, including Net news, has an obligation to public life that goes beyond just telling the news and packaging of facts. As advocates of civic journalism contend, news organizations can become engaged intermediaries or civic catalysts, promoting democratic processes without advocating particular solutions. In this view, Net news has a central role to play in reviving civic life, cultivating citizenship, and improving public dialogue about important issues (Rosen, 1999). As a growing source of civic information—and activity—online news organizations appear to be addressing this public responsibility by giving consideration to the broader democratic promise of the Internet as a discussion forum or site of public deliberation.

A qualification should be added, however: This analysis only considered the 50 highest circulation newspapers, which have more resources and staff than smaller dailies that make up the bulk of the industry. A more complete picture of the civic affordances of online news would probably emerge in a larger sample. Additional analyses might also consider the entire newspaper site as the unit of analysis, rather than keeping to the Politics or Election sections as this study did, or focus on the Community news section for opportunities for civic engagement at the local level. Given the Web's evolving nature, the goal of this study was not to offer a definitive portrait of the structural aspects of the sites sampled but to explore the opportunities for interactivity and citizenship that exist online and assess the extent to which user options relevant to political participation either serve as invitations to, or function as forms of, direct civic involvement.

In the view of Internet optimists, one of the principal goals of online journalism is to "engage the unengaged" by allowing news consumers "to understand the meaning of the day's events in a personalized context that makes better sense to them than traditional media do now" (Pavlik, 1997). This study has conceptualized the interface mechanisms through which political engagement and enhanced understanding occur—whether in the form of media interaction, human interaction, or features that enhance information accessibility—as civic affordances. The significance of examining online news sites for their affordances is that it makes manifestly apparent the calls to civic action that Web interfaces present to users. Such calls are important to sustaining a vital public sphere because they give users the opportunity to enact their role as citizens rather than remain mere consumers of prepackaged news over which they have no control (see Bucy & Gregson, 2001). The function of civic affordances, then, is to encourage and promote democratic involvement while conveying information that forms the basis of democratic decision making. Of course, as Coleman (1999) aptly noted, "technological interactivity [alone] does not deterministically produce democratic interaction" (p. 70). Whether users avail themselves of the opportunities for engagement that are presented on Net news sites depends as much on the orientations and motivations of individual users as on the broader political culture in which online news organizations operate.

Another aspiration of digital journalism should be to construct a space for the user's public persona to reveal itself. As Rosen (1991) commented in an essay on making journalism more public, "the problem is not that citizens know too little or participate too rarely to qualify as a public. It is that no one can be a member of a public when not addressed as such by journalists, political leaders, public officials, intellectuals, and fellow citizens" (p. 269). Audiences need not be consulted on routine news decisions that are the rightful province of editors and producers; however, in the context of Net news, users should be afforded the opportunity to develop their unique civic identity through features and activities that invite involvement and deliberation. The more spaces in which citizens can assemble as a public—whether online or offline—and the more that citizens come to know their own minds, the better the chances of building what Elgin (1993) called "a more conscious democracy" (p. 9).

The finding from the quantitative analysis that forms of media interaction were much more prevalent than human interaction should not be surprising in light of previous studies that have documented this trend on both political and Net news sites. Opportunities to engage in the news as an active participant, whether through an online poll or quiz, multimedia download, informational interactive feature relating to the campaign, or self-guided slide show, were present on two thirds of the sections sampled. From a news perspective, such media interaction should not be regarded as merely providing a "façade of interaction," as it might with political campaign pages that have a pronounced need for message control (see Stromer-Galley, 2000). Rather, the ability to experience the story in different ways—visually, verbally, and interactively—arguably brings users "closer to the news" while promoting civic involvement.

Although still relatively scarce, the peer-to-peer communication that message boards, user forums, and other forms of human interaction promote is one of the most promising aspects of interactive news, performing the valuable service of enabling users to engage in democratic deliberation (see Bucy & Gregson, 2001). The downside to this is the time and resource-intensive nature of responding to user queries and monitoring certain types of human interaction, especially online discussions. In addition, as Murrie (2001, p. 31) pointed out, chat rooms raise a host of legal and editorial concerns for site management, including liability for user postings, ownership of discussion forum content, and decisions about how closely electronic discussions should be monitored. Even with their difficulties, however, user forums can benefit Net news organizations by priming interactive communication, which may have the potential to improve credibility ratings by enhancing perceptions of responsiveness (see Kiousis, 2001).

The title of this chapter addresses the contributions of Net news to cyber democracy. In fact, online newspapers have much to gain by recognizing the positive contributions that civically oriented news sites can make to democracy outside the cyber world.

ENDNOTES

1. Network television news responded with similar verve. In its special section devoted to the military engagement, titled "America at War," CBS News posted video reports about the military campaign, interactive updates, mini essays, photo diaries, and weather reports from Iraq, a message board for site visitors to "sound off," a personalized tribute to "fallen heroes" with photos and descriptions of soldiers killed in combat, even a Baghdad cam.
2. December (1997, p. 15) distinguishes between four different online functions: information delivery, communication, interaction, and computation.
3. Voter registration forms were categorized as a type of human interaction because they facilitate real-world political involvement (even if they don't provide it directly).
4. As the validity of these indices is conceptual rather than statistical, scale reliability analysis was not performed. Reliability in content analysis is generally assessed through intercoder reliability measures rather than scale reliability determinations (Singletary, 1994).

5. The eight newspaper sites with two forms of human interaction in their Politics or Election 2004 sections included: *The Washington Post, The Dallas Morning News, The Newark Star-Ledger,* the *Minneapolis Star-Tribune, The Cleveland Plain Dealer, The Kansas City Star, The Times Picayune,* and *The Indianapolis Star.* The eight papers with three or more forms of media interaction in the sections sampled were: the *Milwaukee Journal Sentinel, The Tampa Tribune, The Boston Globe,* the *New York Post,* the *Orlando Sentinel,* the *San Antonio Express-News,* the *Los Angeles Times,* and the *St. Petersburg Times.*

6. *The Times-Picayune,* a member of the Advance Internet network of online newspapers along with numerous other midsize dailies such as *The Cleveland Plain Dealer,* featured a similar set of user options.

7. Owing to the *Post*'s stature as the political newspaper of record, additional interactive mechanisms were offered through advertising boxes within the Politics section. Among other things, these ads promoted a free scrolling news bar for Web browsing software and the availability of a financial contribution searching service on the Federal Election Commission site.

REFERENCES

Barnhurst, K. G. (2002). News geography & monopoly: The form of reports on U.S. newspaper Internet sites. *Journalism Studies, 3*(4), 477–489.

Bradner, E. (2000, October). *Social affordances: Understanding technology mediated social networks at work.* Paper presented at the annual meeting of the Association of Internet Researchers, Minneapolis, MN.

Brown, M. (2000, October 2). Bringing people closer to the news. *Brandweek,* 26.

Bucy, E. P. (2004a). Second generation Net news: Interactivity and information accessibility in the online environment. *IJMM: The International Journal on Media Management, 6*(1&2), 102–113.

Bucy, E. P. (2004b). The interactivity paradox: Closer to the news but confused. In E. P. Bucy & J. E. Newhagen (Eds.), *Media access: Social and psychological dimensions of new technology use* (pp. 47–72). Mahwah, NJ: Lawrence Erlbaum Associates.

Bucy, E. P., & D'Angelo, P. (2004). Democratic realism, neoconservatism, and the normative underpinnings of political communication research. *Mass Communication & Society, 7*(1), 3–28.

Bucy, E. P., D'Angelo, P., & Newhagen, J. E. (1999). The engaged electorate: New media use as political participation. In L. L. Kaid & D. G. Bystrom (Eds.), *The electronic election: Perspectives on 1996 campaign communication* (pp. 335–347). Mahwah, NJ: Lawrence Erlbaum Associates.

Bucy, E. P., & Gregson, K. (2001). Media participation: A legitimizing mechanism of mass democracy. *New Media & Society, 3*(3), 359–382.

Civic catalyst: What's happening in Pew Projects. (2001, Summer). Washington, DC: The Pew Center for Civic Journalism.

Coleman, S. (1999). The new media and democratic politics. *New Media & Society, 1*(1), 67–74.

Davis, R. (1999). *The Web of politics: The Internet's impact on the American political system.* New York: Oxford University Press.

December, J. (1997). *The World Wide Web unleashed* (Rev. ed.). Indianapolis, IN: Sams.net Publishing.

Elgin, D. (1993). Revitalizing democracy through electronic town meetings. *Spectrum, 66*(2), 6–13.

Friedland, L. A., & Nichols, S. (2002, September). *Measuring civic journalism's progress: A report across a decade of activity.* Washington, DC: The Pew Center for Civic Journalism. Retrieved April 1, 2003, from http://www.pewcenter.org/doingcj/research/r_measuringcj.html

Gaver, W. (1991). Technology affordances. *Proceedings of the CHI'91 Conference on Computer and Human Interaction* (pp. 79–84). New York: ACM.

Gibson, J. J. (1979). *The ecological approach to visual perception.* Boston: Houghton Mifflin.

Katz, J. (1994, September). Online or not, newspapers suck. *Wired,* 50–58.

Kiernan, V., & Levy, M. R. (1999). Competition among broadcast-related Web sites. *Journal of Broadcasting & Electronic Media, 43*(2), 271–279.

Kiousis, S. (2001). Public trust or mistrust? Perceptions of media credibility in the information age. *Mass Communication & Society, 4*(4), 381–403.

Kurpius, D. D. (2000). Public journalism and commercial local television news: In search of a model. *Journalism & Mass Communication Quarterly, 77*(2), 340–354.

Kurpius, D. D. (2003). Bucking a trend in local television news: Combating market-driven journalism. *Journalism, 4*(1), 76–94.

Lasica, J. D. (1996, November). Net gain: Journalism's challenges in an interactive age. *American Journalism Review,* 20–33.

Li, X. (1998). Web page design and graphic use of three U.S. newspapers. *Journalism & Mass Communication Quarterly, 75*(2), 353–365.

Li, X. (2002). Web page design affects news retrieval efficiency. *Newspaper Research Journal, 23*(1), 38–49.

McMillan, S. J. (2002). Exploring models of interactivity from multiple research traditions: Users, documents, and systems. In L. Lievrouw & S. Livingston (Eds.), *Handbook of new media* (pp. 162–182). London: Sage.

Mohnkern, K. (1997). Visual interaction design: Beyond the interface metaphor. *SIGCHI Bulletin, 29*(2). Retrieved April 1, 2003, from http://www.acm.org/sigchi/bulletin/1997.2/vid.html

Murrie, M. (2001). *Local Web news: Case study of nine local broadcast Internet news operations.* Washington, DC: Radio and Television News Directors Foundation.

Norman, D. A. (1988). *The psychology of everyday things.* New York: Basic Books.

Norman, D. A. (1999). *The invisible computer: Why good products can fail, the personal computer is so complex, and information appliances are the solution.* Cambridge, MA: MIT Press.

Pavlik, J. V. (1997, July/August)). The future of online journalism. *Columbia Journalism Review.* Retrieved August 5, 2004, from http://archives.cjr.org/year/97/4/online.asp

Pew Research Center for the People and the Press. (2000, June 11). *Internet sapping broadcast news audience.* Retrieved July 23, 2000, from http://people-press.org/reports/display.php3?ReportID =36

Rosen, J. (1991). Making journalism more public. *Communication, 12*(4), 267–284.

Rosen, J. (1999). *What are journalists for?* New Haven, CT: Yale University Press.

Schultz, T. (1999). Interactive options in online journalism: A content analysis of 100 U.S. newspapers. *Journal of Computer Mediated Communication, 5*(1). Retrieved June 16, 2003, from http://www.ascusc.org/jcmc/vol5/issue1/schultz.html

Shneiderman, B. (1982). The future of interactive systems and the emergence of direct manipulation. *Behavior and Information Technology, 1*(3), 237–256.

Shneiderman, B. (1998). *Designing the user interface: Strategies for effective human-computer interaction* (3rd ed.). Reading, MA: Addison-Wesley.

Singer, J. B., & Gonzalez-Velez, M. (2003). Envisioning the caucus community: Online newspaper editors conceptualize their political roles. *Political Communication, 20*(4), 433–452.

Singletary, M. (1994). *Mass communication research: Contemporary methods and applications.* New York: Longman.

Stromer-Galley, J. (2000). Online interaction and why candidates avoid it. *Journal of Communication, 50*(4), 111–132.

14

Internet Newspapers' Public Forum and User Involvement

Xianyi Ye
Louisiana State University

Xigen Li
Southern Illinois University Carbondale

Internet is a new medium that has the potential to improve communication between journalists and audience, thus advocating democracy through user participation. However, media organizations do not necessarily exploit this opportunity effectively. Based on the assumption that there is a connection between state of democracy and interactive communications stimulated by media organizations, examination of channels that may foster interactive communications appears to be imminent. The goal of this study is to investigate online newspapers' public forum as a tool to engage audience in public discourse.

Public journalism advocate Merritt (1998) said, telling the news is not enough to ensure democracy. The idea of a deliberative democracy requires active citizens and intense political dialogues (Barber, 1984). Public journalists suggest public dialogue is helpful to maintain a healthy civic climate and such climate gives politics a chance to do its work (Rosen, 1996). But in large-scale societies, it is inevitable that producers and receivers of widely disseminated messages are separated (Schultz, 1999). Therefore, in recent years, scholars called for an "interactive journalism" that emphasizes audience participation and encourages and solicits feedback (Lawrence, 1993). Schultz (1999) argued that people in modern democratic societies should not be treated as passive consumers of mass media's manipulated, or at least commercialized, content. Instead, they should have the same chances to participate in public discourse as the information providers do.

The concept of *participation* denotes the sharing of decision making among all those involved in or affected by the area in which decisions are made (Picard, 1985). The sharing of thoughts turns people who live near one another into neighbors, and occupants into citizens (Yelvington, 1998).

PUBLIC FORUM FACILITATING
MANY-TO-MANY COMMUNICATION

A forum is a means of many-to-many communication that allows participants to actively speak before their fellows and to engage in group decision making (Tocqueville, 1937, p. 120). Tocqueville identified two venues to achieve a communication forum: meeting hall and the newspaper. A meeting hall is a true forum in that it allows participants to meet and to engage in face-to-face communication. Many-to-many communication is achieved in direct and immediate form. Participation in public affairs is at the fullest with this type of forum (1937, p. 199). However, a meeting hall forum suffers from severe barriers in space and time. Not all members may be able to participate, or the frequency of participation may be low. Participation may incur substantial private costs.

Newspapers provide another means of public forum. A newspaper can unite many members in daily communication, thereby maintaining the unity needed for a community. Newspapers overcome geographical barriers to communication because they do not require readers to meet at a common place. They also help people to identify the like-minded, and attract dispersed people to an issue of common interest (Tocqueville, 1945, p. 120). However, a traditional newspaper is not a true forum. It only allows one-to-many communication rather than many-to-many communication. It is a broadcast technology in which few speak and many listen. The act of reading a newspaper offers a less participative experience than attending a meeting. Although a newspaper is a social medium that is supportive to the public sphere, a newspaper cannot substitute for a meeting. Although it overcomes barriers of space, time, and cost, it does not facilitate many-to-many communication.

Scholars have analyzed the impact on political participation of a variety of media formats including broadcast television (Fishkin, 1991), cable television (Davidge, 1987), telephones (Laudon, 1977), and computer networks (Downing, 1989; McLean, 1989). Although conclusions have varied, many authors have lamented the technologies' lack of interactivity, bidirectionality, and broad accessibility (Dutton, 1992).

The Internet provides the possibility of achieving the many-to-many communication of a forum. The most common applications such as newsgroups allow participants to post messages in a common message area. Compared to a newspaper, the Internet allows far grater participation in many-to-many communication. Through Web-based discussions, people connect with one another without regard to age, gender, economic status, and geography. Due to these characteristics, the Internet was described as a "democratic cyberspace," the ideal place of virtual democratic community building and maintaining (Riley & Keough, 1998).

Technological development offers new possibilities of interactive media use and decentralization (Schultz, 1998). Because of the democratic nature of the Web, now anyone, from the "mightiest media conglomerate" to the "lone geek," can put up a home page and publish "unfiltered" information (Rieder, 1997). Therefore, the Internet creates a new space of information and a new platform of discussion, where the participants take part in the public discourse that is free from money and power (Schultz, 1998).

Participation is the most crucial component in the process of decision making. The stage of democracy can be determined by the amount of participation of citizens, the scope of activities in which participation is permitted, and the constraints on how participation is exercised (Picard, 1985). Internet offers the opportunity for involving audience in discussion with its interactive features. The public discussion on the Internet could significantly expand citizen participation and free people from many of the constrains they have to endure in civic participation through other venues.

Some literature on online democracy has addressed the topic of Internet as a public forum. Schneider (1996) noted that online forums provide space for public discussion but that unequal rates of participation raise questions about the equality of members in the forum. Myers (1994) examined the political uses of the Internet. His analysis related to the ability of forums to create greater "density" among political participants (p. 256). Klein's (1999) case study of a Boston-based interest group suggested that online forums allow communication between a group of people to be more responsive, more robust, and able to unite more people.

ACTIVE AUDIENCE AND ONLINE NEWSPAPER FORUMS

The Internet allows people to disseminate information and participate in discussion without regard to their location and background. However, none of the Internet forums that scholars looked at were affiliated with a media organization. The forum topics that drew attention of participants were usually narrow and disconnected and the scope of the discussions that people can participate in is relatively limited.

With a growing number of forums established by online newspapers, news media on the Internet are able to provide more flexible products that offer both information sources and interaction within and between users of various interests (Light & Rogers, 1999). Thus, the use of Internet forums obviously involves not only active participation in selecting and processing media messages, but also active participation in creating them as well (Singer, 1998). Journalists gain the opportunity to move away from just presenting material toward a situation where content can be negotiated with their audience (Light & Rogers, 1999). Meanwhile, audience gains the opportunity to be involved in the creation of news content.

Unlike traditional mass media with which people frequently act as a passive audience, the Internet returns various factors of control on communication back to the users involved (Plummer, 1997). The Internet changes the "I-will-publish, you-will-accept" pattern of news reporting ("A Two-Way Window," 2000). An online newspaper has a virtually unlimited newshole, which allows online stories to be electronically linked to archived, background stories. Moreover, audience can further discuss the issue with reporters or columnists through e-mail or live communication. With the comments and feedback from readers, journalists develop follow-up stories. Thus, online news publications have distinct advantages over hard copy versions (Henderson & Fernback, 1998). In the Internet environment, the most powerful attribute of user control is in reducing the effects of subjecting the audience to manipulation associated with issue framing, propaganda, and agenda setting by third parties so commonly evident in other mass media forms (Plummer, 1997).

Online newspapers, therefore, have great potential in maintaining and improving the stage of democracy. Internet, as a new era in which people will have power to express themselves and to be heard (Grossman, 1997), has potential to free the press from interior and exterior influence. Some observers argue that the Internet will bring far greater interest in government and move society toward being a huge, participatory democracy (Davis, 1999).

INTERACTIVE COMMUNICATION OF ONLINE NEWSPAPER FORUMS

New technologies, such as the Internet, have changed the relationship between newspaper readers and journalists, making the relationship more mutually interactive (Wanta & Upshaw, 1996). Whereas the unsynchronized e-mail has the potential to overwhelm reporters and editors, the synchronized online forum offers a better platform for user involvement with a relatively low demand for journalist response. Online forums are increasingly seen on the Web sites of the Internet newspapers.

Online newspapers provide live forum for discussion, where people can click into a conversation and participate by typing their comments and watching as they appear instantly on screen (Henderson & Fernback, 1998). According to Notess (1999), forums are powerful interactive tools that can manage discussion on multiple topics and subtopics. They especially widen opportunities for reader-to-reader communication. It is an excellent place for different groups to discuss their feelings and not to have them explained by the media (Oppenheimer, 1996). On the other hand, online newspapers can announce topics for discussion related to the current events. The discussion can be related to the content of the newspaper by offering links to news articles for discussion. Therefore, forums can ensure that people share some basic knowledge and background, and the online discussions have a better chance to achieve certain coherence. Some of the comments can be edited and used in the either print or online publication (Henderson & Fernback, 1998).

Although forums offer ample opportunities for active participation, encourage a dialogue with the readers, and help the paper deliver news of genuine interest to readers (Noth, 1996), studies on the forums provided by the Internet newspapers are scarce. Some earlier studies examining the status of the Internet newspapers discovered that most sites were failing to provide online discussion forum (Gubman & Greer, 1997). Schultz (1999) observed only one third of online newspapers ran discussion forums. He also found that journalists seldom visited their newspaper's forums (Schultz, 1998). The scope of these studies was quite limited. Online forums were only a part of the Internet newspaper operations that these studies looked into, and no studies looked further into the Internet tool that has the important implications for audience participation and public discourse. For example, Schultz's study only looks at the use of forum from journalists' perspectives but fails to examine the state of audience participation and the diversity of discussed issues in online forums, which are two key factors that determine the quality of forums. From a technology perspective, studying forums provided by the Internet newspapers is also a challenge. Online forum users are mobile and it is difficult to track actual user participation. Access to a broad range of the content of online forums on a continuous basis will require working closely with media organizations.

This study tries to explore forums of the Internet newspapers and user involvement from an empirical approach. It investigates diversity of the public forums of online newspapers, the topics that attract user participation, to what degree the forums engage readers and journalists, and how newspaper size affects diversity of public forums and user involvement. In the light of the previous discussion, this study attempts to answer the following research questions:

RQ1: How diverse are the public forums of online newspapers?

Diversity of the public forums of online newspapers refers to the extent that topics of the forum cover and the number of forums offered for a range of forum topics. A wider range of topics and a relatively even number of forums offered for the diverse topics denote a higher level of diversity.

RQ2: What forum topics are the most popular in attracting readers' participation?

Forum is a powerful tool that allows message exchange among participants. It is expected that the topics that attract most reader participation are those related to social events, prominent social issues, and the areas that users have an embedded personal interest.

RQ3: Do journalists take an active part in the forums of online newspapers?

Journalists won't gain significant benefit from the forums if they don't participate in the discussion. Without participation of journalists, the information or opinions flow only among readers and hardly influence the content of news stories or in-depth columns. *Journalist participation* in the forums will make a significant difference in how the public forums play a role in public discourse facilitated by media.

RQ4: Is there a difference in level of user involvement in public forums among online newspapers of different sizes?

Newspaper size is a factor that affects various aspects of media operation (Lacy & Simon, 1993; Majid & Boudreau, 1995; Picard & Rimmer, 1999). It is expected that large newspapers are more likely to offer more diversified public forums. But it is unknown whether the newspaper size affects user involvement in public forums. The answer to the question will provide understanding on the factors that affect user involvement.

METHOD

Sampling

To answer these research questions, a content analysis of U.S. online newspapers was conducted in May 2000. The population of the study is all U.S. daily newspapers published on the Internet. A daily newspaper with full online services is defined as a general circulation, mass-market newspaper that publishes a full range of regularly updated general news content online and in print at least 4 days a week. A list of online newspapers from the Web sites of *American Journalism Review* (2000) was used as the sampling frame. It is one of the most reliable and up-to-date lists of online newspapers (Schultz, 1999). The 1,126 online newspapers listed as U.S. general-circulation dailies with full online service were grouped according to their circulation in four categories. Circulation was measured by weekday circulation of the print edition, as reported in the *Editor & Publisher International Yearbook 2000.* The following circulation categories were used: less than 25,000, 25,001 to 50,000, 50,001 to 100,000, and more than 100,000. Thirty online newspapers were selected from each category through stratified random sampling. A total of 120 online newspapers were selected.

The categories used to select the sample for this study were different from the commonly used circulation categories defined by the Newspaper Association of America (under 50,000, 50,001 to 100,000, 100,001 to 250,000, and more than 250,000). The newspapers with a circulation less than 50,000 were oversampled for two reasons. First, if using NAA categories, 75% of samples would fall into the circulation category greater than 50,001, and 25% of samples were newspapers with circulation less than 50,000. Using NAA circulation categories will result in imbalanced distribution of newspaper sizes. In addition, the smaller newspapers are suspected to lack resources to explore interactive options effectively (Caruso, 1997; Schultz, 1999; Tankard & Ban, 1998). To include more small newspapers will give a more accurate account on how newspaper size affects use of interactive forums.

Operational Definitions

The measurement of key concepts in this study is based on several former studies using the similar measure instrument. They are Gubman and Greer's analysis of online sites of U.S. newspapers in 1997, Massey and Levy's study of English-language Asian Web newspaper in 1999, Schultz's examination of U.S. online newspapers in 1999.

Public Forum. A platform provided by the Internet newspapers for posting messages and opinions on a variety of topics. Forums vary in their breadth of topics and complexity of operation. In a typical discussion forum, the main topics are listed along with the date of the last message posted in that topic. Choosing one of the topics will either open a list of subtopics or go directly to the discussions (Notess, 1999). The readers read the postings that are publicly displayed on the Web site and add their own statements as well.

Forum Diversity. The study used the number of forum topics available and the number of forums offered for a range of forum topics as two components to measure forum diversity. The forum categories include:

1. General: No specific topic. This might happen especially when only one forum is offered overall. This type often has names such as "guestbook," "readers forum," or "opinion."
2. Media performance: The forums that are open for general comments or suggestions on the online newspaper that provides the forums.
3. Public affairs: The forum that discusses current news issues, politics, law/crime, religion, values/norms, and education. Examples are the presidential campaign 2000, state election, gun control, Congress members and their action, and so on.
4. Economy/business: This category includes all economic issues, such as stock market, job market, business strategies, and so on.
5. Science/technology/computer: All matters of technology and natural sciences. This category also includes medicine and health issues. If the discussions are from a political angle, they belong to public affairs. If the

discussions are from an economic angle, they fall into the economy/business forum.

6. Culture: Forums that deal with "popular" culture, including discussions about forms of art such as books, music, TV shows, movies, theater, fine arts, architecture, and cultural issues.

7. Sports: Forums that discuss professional and popular sports.

8. Hobbies/travel/leisure time/weather: Forums that deal with leisure time activities, including fashion, cosmetics, cooking, games, traveling, and those that do not belong to culture or sports forums.

9. Others: All topics that do not belong to any of the foregoing forums.

Participant. Refers to the readers who join and post their message on the online newspaper forums. Each of them has a pen name. Although a person can post a message by using different pen names, due to difficulty of identification one pen name is considered as one participant.

Journalist. Refers to the staff working in the newsroom, such as reporters, editors, and columnists. The clerks in newsroom and the staff in advertising and distribution service departments are not considered journalists.

The unit of study of the content analysis is 1 day's publication of an Internet newspaper. Through an observation of a week's publications of randomly selected 20 online newspapers 1 month before the coding period, the researcher found that forums provided by Internet newspapers tended to be relatively stable in terms of quantity and format. Although emphasis in discussion forums change often, the categories of topics do not. Therefore, only 1 day's content of a selected newspaper site was coded. After the coding period, 20 sites were double-checked and no significant changes were found in format and operation of the online forums.

Two coders performed the coding procedures. An intercoder reliability test for the variables was conducted with 10% of the sample, which was randomly selected. Holsti's r was used to calculate the intercoder reliability of the nominal variables. Pearson's correlation was used to calculate the intercoder reliability of the ratio variables. The value of r varied from .75 to 1.0 among the variables (see Appendix). The intercoder agreement averaged .91, which is higher than the 90% standard for content analysis (Wimmer & Dominick, 2003).

FINDINGS

This study found that 47 out of 120 online newspapers (39.2%) ran discussion forums. Compared with the forum numbers in Gubman and Greer's (1997) research (40%) and the figure in Schultz's (1999) study (33%), there was no significant change in the number of newspapers offering forums. Among those

TABLE 14.1
Effect of Circulation Size on Forum Number

Circulation	1–15		16–30		31 or More			
25,000 or less	9	27.3%	1	11.1%	0	0%	10	21.3%
25,001–50,000	5	15.1%	1	11.1%	1	20.0%	7	14.9%
50,001–100,000	9	27.3%	1	11.1%	1	20.0%	11	23.4%
100,001 or more	10	30.3%	6	66.7%	3	60.0%	19	40.4%
Column Total	33	70.2%	9	19.2%	5	10.6%	47	100.0%

TABLE 14.2
Effect of Circulation Size on Forum Diversity and Participation

Circulation	Mean of Forum Topics	Mean of User Participation
25,000 or less	2.30	1.33
25,001–50,000	3.23	22.73
50,001–100,000	4.83	9.83
100,001 or more	12.00	42.27
Total	5.59	19.04
One-Way ANOVA		
F value	9.48	2.52
df	3, 116	3, 116
Sig	.01	.06
Eta	.44	.25

providing forums, 19 out of 47 (40.4%) were newspapers with a circulation of 100,001 or more. The other three circulation categories did not vary much in the number of forums (see Table 14.1).

RQ1: How diverse are the public forums of online newspapers?

Although a few sites provided a variety of forums, a majority of newspapers (70.2%) had fewer than 15 discussion forums. Newspaper size had a significant effect on topic diversity of public forums ($F = 9.34$, $df = 3$, 116, $p < .01$). The larger the newspaper size, the more diverse the topics of the public forums. Of the 14 newspapers that had 16 or more forums, nine of them were from the largest circulation (see Table 14.1). The newspapers with a circulation more than 100,000 provided an average of 12 forums whereas the average of all four circulation categories was 5.59 (see Table 14.2). There were relatively small variations in mean of forum diversity among the newspapers with a circulation from below 25,000 to 100,000.

The online newspapers contained forums that covered a wide range of topics. These topics fell into nine categories, from public affairs and economic issues to sports, gardening, and movies. Out of 47 newspapers that offer public forums, the

TABLE 14.3
Number of Forum by Topics

Forum Topic	Number of Forums		Mean of Forum Topic	SD
Media performance	12	1.8%	.26	.67
Economy/business	17	2.5%	.36	.76
General	22	3.3%	.47	1.49
Science/technology/computer	42	6.3%	.89	1.46
Culture	52	7.7%	1.11	1.64
Others	58	8.7%	1.23	1.83
Hobbies/travel/leisure time	80	11.9%	1.70	2.77
Sports	174	25.9%	3.70	5.73
Public affairs	214	31.9%	4.55	4.62
Total	671	100%	14.28	2.10

number of forums under specific topics showed a clear dominance of two areas: sports ($M = 3.7$) and public affairs ($M = 4.55$). Other noticeable areas were leisure ($M = 1.7$), culture ($M = 1.11$), and technology ($M = .89$) (see Table 14.3).

RQ2: What forum topics are the most popular in attracting readers' participation?

Among the nine categories of forum topics, "Public affairs" and "Sports" were the most frequently discussed subjects. Of the 671 forums identified in this study, 214 forums (31.9%) were about "Public affairs," and 174 forums (25.9%) were about "Sports." The rest of forum topics had no more than 80 forums, with the least frequently discussed topic "Media performance" (1.8%) and the most frequently discussed topic "Hobbies/travel/leisure time" (11.9%) (see Table 14.3).

Although the online newspapers offered various forums, the readers didn't actually participate in the discussion actively. The study revealed that, on the specific day that data were collected, the average number of participants per forum was less than four (3.4). Two types of forums had participants more than the average: "Sports" (6.4) and "General forums" (4.5). The category "Public affairs" was in third place with 2.9 people participating in the discussion. Among all the participants, almost half of them (48.8%) showed up in the "Sports" forums and about a quarter (26.8%) in the "Public affairs" forums (see Table 14.4).

"Media performance" was the least interesting discussion topic to the readers. Similar to the number of forums, this topic again had the smallest number of participants (0.3) and only 0.2% of the forum participants posted messages in this category.

"Science/technology/computer," "Economy/business," and "Culture" were not popular topics either. "Science/technology/computer" had 0.67 participants and

TABLE 14.4
User Participation by Forum Topics

Forum Topic	Number of Participants		Participants per Forum
Media performance	4	0.2%	0.3
Economy/business	22	1.0%	1.3
General	99	4.3%	4.5
Science/technology/computer	28	1.2%	0.7
Culture	30	1.3%	0.6
Others	157	6.9%	2.7
Hobbies/travel/leisure time	217	9.5%	2.7
Sports	1,114	48.8%	6.4
Public affairs	613	26.8%	2.9
Total	2,284	100%	3.4

occupied 1.2% of participants. "Economy/business" had 1.3 participants (1.0%). As for "Culture," there were 0.6 participants (1.3%).

RQ3: Do journalists take an active part in the forums of online newspapers?

Of 47 newspapers that offered forums, only six sites had their reporters or editors participating in discussion. Rarely (two sites) did the online newspapers monitor their forums. For the other four sites, journalists participated only in the forums in one or two topic categories. *The Mercury News* (San Jose, California) featured several forums with an online columnist discussing news issues. The *Tribune* (Fort Pierce, Florida) and *The Courier-Journal* (Louisville, Kentucky) indicated that some of the forums on leisure time/hobbies/lifestyle were hosted. *The Star* (Kansas City, Missouri) advertised that journalists participated in some of the discussion about sports. *The Sun* (Baltimore, Maryland) and *The Christian Science Monitor* (Boston, Massachusetts) clearly indicated that the forum section was moderated.

RQ4: Is there a difference in level of user involvement in public forums among online newspapers of different sizes?

There was no difference in level of user involvement in public forums among online newspapers of different sizes ($F = 2.52$, $df = 3$, 116, $p > .05$). The average number of user involvement was 19.04. Means of user involvement of newspapers varied by sizes. The forums at the Web sites of the newspapers with a circulation over 100,000 had the highest level of user involvement ($M = 42.27$). However, newspapers with a circulation between 25,000 to 50,000 had higher user involvement ($M = 22.73$) than newspapers with a circulation between 50,000 to 100,000 ($M = 9.83$). Larger newspaper size did not necessarily lead to higher user involvement.

DISCUSSION

This study found about 40% of the online newspapers offered forums. Most of the forums remained inactive, with relatively few readers participating in the discussion. There was a relatively low user involvement in forums on public affairs, and few of the forums engaged journalists. There was a lack of discussion forums among smaller newspaper Web sites. Even many large newspapers rely primarily on a few simple feedback devices, such as e-mail, and they rarely develop advanced interactive forums. Although forums are widely accepted as the most meaningful form of user involvement, online media that offered public forums did not necessarily facilitate the discussion of public issues.

A few factors may contribute to the inactive public forums of online newspapers. First is the limitation in topics of the forums that newspapers can offer. The topics of forums are normally associated with the scope and coverage of the newspapers. National newspapers with a large circulation can afford to offer a wide range of forum topics. Readers are more likely to go to the Web sites of large national newspapers to engage in the forums with a national scope and diversity of topics. Diversity of forum topics may not be a uniform standard for all Internet newspapers. It would be a waste of resource for small newspapers to launch a large number of forums with few participants. Small newspapers could achieve diversity of forum topics differently from the large newspapers by offering a variety of forums about local matters.

Forum is a device that requires high user involvement. Schultz (1998) observed that the greater the number of communicators, the less time everyone has to listen to others. A large number of forums may result in insufficient participation as the number of users is relatively constant. Diversity of forum topics also calls for efficient organization of the messages and easy participation of users. Readers often get frustrated by the thousands of unorganized messages on the forums. The online newspapers have to provide an efficient platform to engage users in public forums.

The findings indicate that few forum topics dominate online forums of online newspapers. "Public affairs" is one of them. In this topic group, participants have opportunities to speak out on their political stance, their concerns about legislation and crime, their opinions on issues in the news, and their worries on educational system. Some Web sites had their news articles directly linked to the forum area and thus enabled readers to develop more serious dialogues with certain background information. Local matters were heavily discussed under the "Public affairs" topic. However, the average number of participants in public affairs per forum is lower than the overall average. This result suggests that although online newspapers usually offer forums on the topic of "Public affairs," readers are not as actively participating in the discussion of this topic as expected.

"Sports" was the second most popular forum. The average number of participants in the forum topic almost doubled that of the overall average. The finding indicates people prefer to talk about something relaxing (sports) than something serious (public affairs) in public forums. Oppenheimer (1996) suggested that in order to bring in more readers in the discussion, the media organizations should frame their materials in a way that can entertain audience, and encouraged them to entertain, inform, and help each other—then media can hold a crowd on the sidewalks of cyberspace. However, if the density of communication is growing from prattle, it is certainly a harmful factor to the serious public discourse.

Based on the findings, it is too early to say that forums are more egalitarian and democratic than traditional mass communication. The number of available forums and participants were low. The postings are sometimes trivial and repeated. The topic about "Public affairs" is not yet a readers' first preference. Therefore, the value of forum message is fairly limited, if measured by high standards of democratic deliberation.

The findings showed that forums were mostly unmoderated and that journalists rarely participated in the discussion. Online newspapers might view interactive forums merely as "reader playgrounds." Even when forums were hosted, these hosts were not the core staff of the media organization in many cases. Online staff usually are organizationally and often spatially separated from the newsrooms, which makes it even more unlikely that reporters, columnists, and editors will notice what is going on online (Noack, 1998). In fact, some journalists appeared horrified at the idea that readers want to engage in a discussion with them (Riley & Keough, 1998). Many traditional journalists see the online world as a place filled with unverified rumors, a place where traditional journalism standards count for nothing (Rieder, 1997).

Lack of journalists' participation may contribute to low user involvement in public discourse. Whereas forums offer a platform for the public to express opinions and concerns at their will, journalists' participation will help build the virtual community, keep discussion focused, and raise the level of quality discussion. The successful public discourse could never be achieved without the participation of the journalists. The public forums offered by online newspapers is not just a platform to gather newspaper readers, but also a field for the journalists to get ideas from readers and stimulate public discourse as the newspapers have been doing in the real world. A more active role of journalists in the public forums will benefit both journalism practice and public discourse.

The finding regarding the relationship between newspaper size and user involvement indicates public forums of large newspapers do not necessarily attract more readers than those of smaller newspapers. The finding asks for further investigation into the phenomenon. Large newspapers usually have forums with more diversified topics. But other factors such as what forums the newspapers actually offer, the way that users are allowed to participate in the forums, and the formation of a virtual community may also play an important role in user involvement. Although small newspapers may have less diversified forum topics, the more devoted readers may engage themselves more closely with the newspapers and participate more enthusiastically in the discussion of local issues that concern their immediate interest.

Further research can focus on both participants and platforms of forums. Studies that look at different aspects of forums could be conducted to discover how many forums are appropriate for an online newspaper, how to engage readers to participate in discussions, and in what format the public forums can be operated most efficiently. Studies could also be done to examine the content of forums such as quality and relevance of materials posted in the forums.

CONCLUSION

This study looked at public forums of the Internet newspapers and to what degree the forums engaged readers and journalists. A content analysis of 120 U.S. Internet newspapers found 39.2% of the Internet newspapers offered discussion forums. A majority of newspapers (70.2%) with public forums had less than 15 discussion forums. Newspaper size had significant effect on diversity of public forums. The findings suggest that the forums of the Internet newspapers have yet to be developed as an effective tool to advance public discourse and democracy deliberation. There was a relatively low user involvement in the public forums regardless of newspaper size. Although the topics on public affairs dominated public forums of the Internet newspapers, they attracted only a limited number of users. Smaller newspapers tended to fall behind the larger ones in establishing public forums. The larger newspapers, usually offering more forum topics, did not attain a significantly higher level in diversity of forum topics.

The Internet has the potential to be the greatest First Amendment tool in history. Public forums of the Internet newspapers, one of the innovative devices to get audience and journalists involved in public discourse, have attracted a number of users. However, it will take more time for both readers and journalists to adapt to the Internet forums, which might help promote discussion on issues of public concerns and allow newspapers to play a more effective role in advancing democracy. Today's online newspapers are merely at the starting point of pursuing this goal. The Internet newspapers are under the influence of many factors on which way to go to serve the public interest and advance democracy. The challenge of the future is to preserve the mass media as institutions of integration and public discourse and combine them with a new culture of interaction.

APPENDIX: INTERCODER RELIABILITY
OF CODED VARIABLES

Variables	Hosti's r
Discussion forum offered	.92
Forums Topic	
General forum	1.0
Media performance	.92
Public affairs	.83
Economy/business	.93
Science/technology/computer	1.0
Culture	1.0
Sports	.83
Hobbies/travel/leisure time/lifestyle/weather	.92
Other	.83
Forum Participants	
General forum	.83
Media performance	.92
Public affairs	.83
Economy/business	.92
Science/technology/computer	.92
Culture	.92
Sports	.75
Hobbies/travel/leisure time/lifestyle/weather	.83
Other	.83
Journalists' participation in forums	1.0

REFERENCES

American Journalism Review. (2000). Retrieved May 2000, from http://newslink.org/daynews.htm

Barber, B. (1984). *Strong democracy: Participatory politics for a new age.* Berkeley: University of California Press.

Caruso, D. (1997). Show me the money. *Columbia Journalism Review.* Retrieved May, 2000, from http://cjr.org/year/97/4/money.asp

Davidge, C. (1987). American's talk-back television experiment: QUBE. In W. H. Dutton, J. G. Blumler, & K. L. Kraemer (Eds.), *Wired cities* (pp. 75–101). Boston: C. G. Hall.

Davis, R. (1999). *The Web of politics: The Internet's impact on the American political system.* New York: Oxford University Press.

Downing, J. D. (1989). Computers for political change: Peacenet and public access data. *Journal of Communication, 39*(3), 154–162.

Dutton, W. H. (1992). Political science research on teledemocracy. *Social Science Computer Review, 140*(4), 505–522.

Fishkin, J. S. (1991). *Democracy and deliberation: New directions for democratic reform.* New Haven, CT: Yale University Press.

Grossman, L. K. (1997). *Reshaping political values in the information age: The power of the media. Vital Speeches of the Day.* New York: News Publishing Company.

Gubman, J., & Greer, J. (1997, July). *An analysis of online sites produced by U.S. newspapers: Are the critics right?* Paper presented to the Newspaper Division, Association for Education in Journalism and Mass Communication annual convention, Chicago.

Henderson, B., & Fernback, J. (1998). The campus press: A practical approach to online newspapers. In D. L. Borden & K. Harvey (Eds.), *The electronic grapevine: Rumor, reputation, and reporting in the new on-line environment* (pp. 113–121). Mahwah, NJ: Lawrence Erlbaum Associates.

Klein, H. K. (1999). Tocqueville in cyberspace: Using the Internet for citizen associations. *The Information Society, 15*(4), 213–220.

Lacy, S., & Simon, T. F. (1993). *The economics and regulation of United States newspapers.* Norwood, NJ: Ablex.

Laudon, K. (1977). *Communication technology and democratic participation.* New York: Praeger.

Lawrence, D., Jr. (1993). Why future is promising for newspaper industry. *Newspaper Research Journal, 14*(2), 11–17.

Light, A., & Rogers, Y. (1999, June). Conversation as publishing: The role of news forums on the Web. *Journal of Computer-Mediated Communication, 4*(4). Retrieved May, 2000, from http://www.ascusc.org/jcmc/vol4/issue4/light.html

Majid, R. A., & Boudreau, T. (1995). Chain ownership, organizational size, and editorial role perception. *Journalism and Mass Communication Quarterly, 72*(4), 863–872.

Massey, B. L., & Levy, M. R. (1999). Interactivity, online journalism, and English-language Web newspapers in Asia. *Journalism and Mass Communication Quarterly, 76*(1), 138–151.

McLean, I. (1989). *Democracy and new technology.* Cambridge, England: Polity.

Merritt, D. (1998). *Public journalism and public life: Why telling the news is not enough.* Mahwah, NJ: Lawrence Erlbaum Associates.

Myers, D. J. (1994). Communication technology and social movements: Contributions of computer networks to activism. *Social Science Computer Review, 12*(2), 250–260.

Noack, D. (1998, February 13). America's newsroom bend to the Internet. *Editor & Publisher, 131*(8), 13.

Notess, G. R. (1999, July/August). Communications and community on Web sites. *Online, 23*(4), 65–68.

Noth, D. P. (1996). *All the news that's fit to print out! It's the New York Times' full Web launch. Dom's Domain.* Retrieved March, 2000, from http://206.216.217.100:80/dom/#previous

Oppenheimer, T. (1996). Virtual reality check. *Columbia Journalism Review.* Retrieved May, 2000, from http://www.cjr.org/year/96/2/check.asp

Picard, R. G. (1985). *The press and the decline of democracy.* Westport, CT: Greenwood.

Picard, R. G., & Rimmer, T. (1999). Weathering a recession: Effects of size and diversification on newspaper companies. *Journal of Media Economics, 12*(1), 1–18.

Plummer, A. C. (1997, July). *Gathering of strangers in cyberspace: Public opinion on the Internet.* Paper presented to the Communication Technology and Policy Division, Association for Education in Journalism and Mass Communication annual convention, Chicago.

Rieder, R. (1997). A breakthrough in cyberspace. *American Journalism Review.* Retrieved April, 2000, from http://ajr.newlink.org/ajrbreakthru.html

Riley, P., & Keough, C. M. (1998, September). Community or colony: The case of online newspapers and the Web. *Journal of Computer-Mediated Communication, 4*(1). Retrieved October, 2005, from http://jcmc.indiana.edu/vol4/issue1/keough.html

Rosen, J. (1996). *Getting the connections right: Public journalism and the troubles in the press.* New York: The Twentieth Century Fund Press.

Schneider, S. (1996). Creating a democratic public sphere through a political discussion. *Social Science Computer Review, 14*(4), 373–393.

Schultz, T. (1998, August). *Mass media and the concept of interactivity: An exploratory study of online forums and reader e-mail.* Paper presented to the Newspaper Division, Association for Education in Journalism and Mass Communication annual convention, Baltimore.

Schultz, T. (1999, September). Interactive options in online journalism: A content anai,̣.
newspapers. *Journal of Computer-Mediated Communication, 5*(1), Retrieved February, ∠ʋʋ∿,
from http://www.ascusc.org/jcmc/vol5/issue1/schultz.html

Singer, J. B. (1998). Online journalists: Foundations for research into their changing roles. *Journal of Computer-Mediated Communication, 4*(1). Retrieved May, 2000, from http://www.ascusc.org/jcmc/vol4/issue1/singer.html

Tankard, J. W., & Ban, H. (1998, August). *Online newspapers: Living up to their potential?* Paper presented to the Newspaper Division, Association for Education in Journalism and Mass Communication annual convention, Baltimore.

Tocqueville, A. (1937). *Democracy in America* (Vol. 1). New York: Vintage Books. (Original work published 1835)

Tocqueville, A. (1945). *Democracy in America* (Vol. 2). New York: Vintage Books. (Original work published 1835)

A two-way window. (2000). *American Journalism Review Newslink.* Retrieved May, 2000, from http://ajr.newslink.org/ajrjd19.html

Wanta, W., & Upshaw, J. (1996, August). *Comparing consumer feedback channels: Newspapers versus television.* Paper presented to the Newspaper Division, Association for Education in Journalism and Mass Communication annual convention, Anaheim, CA.

Wimmer, R. D., & Dominick, J. R. (2003). *Mass media research: An introduction* (7th ed.). Belmont, CA: Wadsworth.

Yelvington, S. (1998). Discussions make medium interactive. *The Masthead, 50*(2), 12–13.

15

News of Priority Issues in Print Versus Internet Newspapers

Xigen Li
Southern Illinois University Carbondale

Internet newspapers present information in different ways from traditional media (Martin, 1998). The news media on the Internet are turning the traditional one-to-many communication process to many-to-many communication (Li, 1998). Availability of new technology for delivering news information and the variety of Web sites of newspapers due to different design approaches offer new ways that news of priority issues is presented on the Internet, and are probably altering media's function in setting the public agenda. This study examines whether different information delivery and access modes of the Internet newspapers have an effect on identifying news of priority issues, which is considered the starting point in setting the public agenda (Gormley, 1975).

AGENDA SETTING BY INTERNET NEWS MEDIA?

The research on agenda setting has been going on for decades (Kosicki, 1993). It started from how media set the public agenda and expanded in boundaries and scope. Media agenda refers to the priorities of issues in media content. Media agenda setting is the process whereby the news media lead the public in assigning relative importance to various public issues. Agenda-setting researchers expect media to affect people's perceptions of the importance of societal issues by influencing their awareness of issues and events. McCombs and Shaw (1972) argued that the more the media present a topic, the more the people think that the topic is important. The media accomplish this agenda-setting function not by directly telling the public that one issue is more important than another. Instead, the media signal the importance of certain issues by giving these issues preferential treatment, such as more frequent coverage and more prominent positions (Wanta, 1997; Zhu & Blood, 1997).

Numerous new concepts have been added to the original hypothesis as controlling, intervening, or moderating variables (Zhu & Blood, 1997). However, although the scope of agenda-setting research expanded significantly, it was mostly attached to the traditional media such as newspapers and television. With the development of media technology and expansion of the World Wide Web in the 1990s, the Internet newspaper emerged as a mainstream medium in delivering news information. Even though most newspapers have published on the Internet and more people have been getting news from the Internet, there has been a dearth of literature on the agenda-setting function of Internet newspapers (Althaus & Tewksbury, 2002; Wang, 2000).

NEWS INFORMATION FROM INTERNET MEDIA

The Internet newspapers provide news information similar to the traditional print newspaper. Journalists followed the same rules in selecting and publishing news stories. Most of the news content on the Internet is still produced by the staff of the newspapers and does not show significant difference from what appears on the print newspapers. Earlier studies found that the Internet newspapers were simple verbatim copies of the print versions (Gubman & Greer, 1997). Barnhurst (2002) found that the Internet newspapers reproduce the substance of their print editions in a way that relates similarly to readers. Newspaper stories online differ very little from those printed in the originating newspapers. The Internet versions do not usually add to or change the text of the stories. Staff members from the three newspapers that he studied confirmed that the print content tends to be duplicated each day online.

But unlike print media, the Web offers an unlimited storage of information and what is available on the Internet is usually more than that in the print version (Lapham, 1995). Compared to print newspapers, the articles were expected to be shorter, with an abbreviated "news item" style and linked with other online features (Neuberger, Tonnemacher, Biebl, & Duck, 1998). The key difference between the two is information delivery, that is, how information is structured and presented to the audience. Heeter, Brown, Soffin, Stanley, and Salwen (1989) observed in their study of electronic text news that news organizations tended to give relatively equal prominence to a larger variety of stories, and they usually presented audiences with an ability to shape their news flow. The Internet newspaper delivered through the World Wide Web is a quite different medium from electronic text because of the extensive use of graphics and hyperlinks. It is a medium with more features, more flexibility, and more freedom in processing news information than electronic text. Do the Internet newspapers give equal prominence to a large variety of stories? Has the ability to shape the news flow on the audience side grown stronger? The changes brought by the Internet newspaper since electronic text will have a profound effect on the function of agenda setting with the new medium.

The media agenda is often measured by how frequently and how prominently an issue is covered in the news, weighting factors such as column inches for press stories, or amount of air time for television, or position in newspaper or program (Gormley, 1975; Williams & Semlak, 1978). Graber (1993) noted that readers of traditional newspapers used importance cues provided by editors to guide their decisions in selecting news articles. Such cues included story location, headline or visual size, and story length. But interest in a topic could easily override the prominence criterion. Graber found that 72% of what was read came from the first section of the paper, the section that contained most of the national and international news and issues of social importance.

Whether these criteria can be used in Internet newspapers to measure priority issues requires a close examination. Applying the same procedures to the Internet newspaper may produce different results because the information structure and the way readers access information are different (Gunter, 2003). The attributes that make some issues prominent such as column inches, the size of type, and the position of stories in a newspaper may no longer be as evident in the Internet environment and may not be reliable identifiers of the story prominence in the Internet newspapers (Tewksbury & Althaus, 2000). Prominence cues based on the Internet environment may be used in addition to the cues used in traditional media.

WEB DESIGN AND INFORMATION ACCESS

As the technology of information delivery through the Web advances, more options are available for the Internet newspapers to construct their Web sites. There are three dimensions concerning Web design approach: information structure, presentation style, and navigation path (Li, 2002). *Information structure* refers to the manner that news information is arranged by an Internet newspaper. With the introduction of sections through a menu or tabs on a Web site, the news information can now be retrieved through nonlinear paths instead of linear order as in print newspaper (Vargo, 1998). Difference was observed when retrieving information by scrolling down or by using a Hyperlink (Oostendorp & Nimwegen, 1998). Three basic *presentation approaches* were used in Web design: graphic, textual, and balanced. The newspaper Web sites have the potential to become more graphic as their capacity to store and process information improves (Li, 1998). But on a graphic site that is appealing in its appearance (Chamber, 1998), it could take more time to access information because of the large file size of graphics. *Navigation* refers to how a Web site sets its path for readers to navigate and retrieve information, whether it allows readers to get the information sought immediately or through the shortest path (Niederst, 1999; Nielsen, 2000).

The changes brought by the Internet newspapers on how news information is delivered and how the audience accesses news information raise some concerns about public awareness on important social issues if more people get information from the Internet newspapers (Halleck, 2003). If publishers have less control in setting priority in an Internet newspaper, the news of priority issues may not be perceived by many in the audience (Davis & Owen, 1998).

PRIORITY ISSUES FROM THE INTERNET MEDIA

Tewksbury and Althaus (2000) conducted a study on the difference in knowledge acquisition among readers of the paper and online versions of a national newspaper. They found that online readers of *The New York Times* appeared to have read fewer national, international, and political news stories and were less likely to recognize and recall events that occurred during the exposure period. Tewksbury and Althaus' study is valuable in revealing the difference in knowledge acquisition among readers of a print paper and those who access information through an Internet newspaper, but it failed to look at two aspects that may affect the results. The first is the mode of readers, which is especially important for Web users. In a Web-viewing session, an individual could be either an information seeker or a Web surfer. An information seeker has a clear goal when accessing a Web site whereas a Web surfer may just be killing time without using much brain power (Hoffman & Novak, 1996). The second is due to the structural difference of Internet newspapers and the way that the information is accessed on different Internet newspapers. Tewksbury and Althaus only looked at one Internet newspaper. If the Internet newspaper did not provide an efficient path to access the news of social issues, it could result in fewer readers acquiring news of social issues. On the other hand, if the Internet newspapers construct sites with efficient access to news information and the readers were highly motivated information seekers, the readers of Internet newspapers could acquire as much news of social issues as readers of print newspapers.

Li (2002) examined the impact of Web design approaches on efficiency of news retrieval and found that Web sites with immediate access to the news content and a smooth news flow through an effective Web design were more likely to result in high efficiency in information retrieval. The findings suggest that Web design approaches affect how the news information is accessed and retrieved from Internet newspapers. But the study did not address the question of whether different information access modes created by different Web design approaches will influence the identification of the priority issues presented by the Internet newspapers.

When readers access news information from the Internet newspapers, if the prominence cues are not as evident as in print newspapers, they may try to find alternative cues in guiding their selection of news stories. Something identified by the print newspapers as priority issues may not be seen as so important in the Internet newspapers by readers. As the Internet newspapers with different Web designs offer various paths to access news information, the identified priority issues could be different between print newspapers and the Internet newspapers and among the Internet newspapers with different Web design approaches.

This study looks at how readers of print and Internet newspapers identify *priority news* differently due to the difference between print and Internet newspapers in presenting news information. This is not a study examining the complete process of agenda setting in the Internet environment. Instead, this study attempts to explore the first stage of media agenda setting, how the news of priority issues is identified by readers. This study expands the scope beyond Tewksbury and Althaus (2000) in three aspects. First, it looks at effects on identifying priority issues from the Internet newspapers due to different Web design. Second, it isolates the effects through the Internet readers that focus on information seeking instead of Web surfing. Third, with both the print and the Internet readers, this study compiles the actual news items identified from the two versions of the newspapers and a content analysis for a comparison of priority issues. Based on the literature and observed difference in Web design approach, information delivery, and access modes between print and Internet newspapers, the following hypotheses are proposed and will be tested:

H1a: Priority issues identified by Internet readers are noticeably different from those identified through content analysis.

H1b: Priority issues identified by Internet readers are noticeably different from those identified by readers of print newspapers.

H1 tests the effect of *access mode* on identifying priority issues. As prominence cues in the Internet newspapers are less evident and readers may try to find alternative cues in their selection of stories, the deviation between the priority issues identified by Internet readers and content analysis and between readers of the Internet and print newspapers is expected to be apparent.

H2: The priority issues identified by the Internet readers are less likely to be associated with those identified from content analysis of the print newspaper than those identified by the print newspaper readers.

H2 compares *level of association* between the Internet readers and content analysis and between the print newspaper readers and content analysis. It expects the former association is less than the later association. It is expected priority issues identified by the print newspaper readers who read the actual newspapers, are similar to those identified from content analysis, whereas priority issues identified by the Internet readers are substantially deviated from those identified from content analysis due to difference in information presentation and access.

H3: The Web design approach of Internet newspapers is associated with the distinctive patterns in priority issues identified from the three newspaper Web sites.

H3 tests whether *Web design approach* will lead readers to select priority issues differently. It examines the relationship between Web design approach and patterns in priority issues identified from the Internet newspapers. As information structure, presentation style, and navigation path affect the actual news items identified from the Internet newspapers, it is expected that patterns in priority issues identified from the Internet newspaper with different Web designs are distinctive from each other.

H4: The prominence cues that readers use to identify priority issues from Web sites are different from those that readers use to identify priority issues from traditional media.

The way to learn priority issues from print newspapers is to identify the prominence cues provided by the editors. On the Internet newspapers, as the prominence cues for priority issues are weakened due to Web environment, readers look for alternative cues to guide their selection of priority issues. H4 tests if a different set of *prominence cues* are used by readers of the Internet newspapers and to what degree such alternative cues go beyond the traditional criteria such as story prominence, headline type size, and story length.

H5: The way that news is presented on Web sites is likely to change readers' view of what the priority issues are.

If the priority issues identified from the Internet newspapers are noticeably different from the print newspapers, such difference could be the result that information was presented and accessed differently from print newspaper, and alternative cues from the Internet newspapers are used. H5 tests if the *information presentation* of the Internet newspaper and the alternative prominence cues used by readers change their view of what the priority issues are.

METHOD

A content analysis was employed to identify print newspapers' stories of priority issues set by newspaper editors. A between-group experiment was conducted to test the difference in news of priority issues identified by the readers of print and Internet newspapers and the prominence cues used in identifying the stories.

Selected Newspapers

Three U.S. newspapers, *The Washington Post, USA Today,* and the *Chicago Tribune,* were selected for study. These newspapers were selected because they are major national or metropolitan papers with the reputation and resources to report issues of social significance. Each newspaper also has large and diverse audiences. *The Washington Post* is considered an elite newspaper (Miller, Andsager, & Riechert, 1998). *USA Today* provides extensive coverage of issues of a national scope. The *Chicago Tribune* is a regional newspaper with national prominence (Powers & Andsager, 1999). The local newspaper is also the most important medium for the public to obtain political information. All three newspapers have sizable space devoted to international reporting with a section for World. For their Internet versions, these newspapers have the resources to hire professional Web designers to create and maintain updated Web sites.

Web Design of the Internet Newspapers

This study looked at the overall effect of Web design approach of the Internet newspaper on identifying news of priority issues. The Internet newspapers under study were distinctive in Web design. They all had a sophisticated design and varied in the three main elements, *information structure, presentation style,* and *navigation path* (Li, 2002). For information structure, *The Washington Post* had the shortest front page with a clear menu on the left listing sections in order of priority. *USA Today* had the longest main page with sections listed on the left without obvious order of priority. The *Chicago Tribune*'s menu did not reflect the issue of priority clearly, but the stories it presented on the front page bore a relatively visible order of priority. For presentation style, *USA Today* was the most graphic and the *Chicago Tribune* was the least graphic. All of the three Internet newspapers offered different navigation paths. Whereas *The Washington Post* and the *Chicago Tribune* imposed some restriction on navigation to keep readers on track, *USA Today* provided more links and options that may distract readers in identifying priority issues. Each newspaper was treated as a distinctive approach of Web design.

Content Analysis

The priority issues presented by the three print newspapers during the two non-event days (November 1 and 2, 2000) were identified and examined through a content analysis. A non-event day is a day that involves no national or international event that is so striking as to be covered by all media at the dominant position, such as the presidential election or a disaster of national or international scope such as Space Shuttle Columbia explosion. Content analysis was used in agenda-setting research in identifying priority issues (McCombs & Shaw, 1972). The measurement of story prominence is well accepted in terms of face and content validity. The content analysis examined the first 10 pages of Section A, and the front pages of the business and sports sections of each newspaper. Section A of a newspaper usually carries the news of the most importance. The front pages of the business and sports sections were included because they may contain stories of social significance such as a big event in national economy. They were also used as a manipulation check in the following experiment to see if subjects considered business and sports stories more important than the stories in Section A. A total of 164 news items was selected from the print versions of the three newspapers, including 61 news stories from *The Washington Post,* 42 stories from *USA Today,* and 61 stories from the *Chicago Tribune.*

A content analysis of the Internet newspapers was also considered. However, under the Internet environment, although news items were mostly presented as a list of stories in order, prominence cues, such as space, size of type, and position were no longer evident to produce enough variance for easy identification of what the news of priority issues are. The Internet newspapers carry the news content similar to or the same as that in print newspapers. A content analysis of the print newspapers will be sufficient to identify the news of priority issues determined by newspaper editors, the origin of media agenda.

The unit of analysis was one news item from a print newspaper. Each news item of the print newspapers was measured by its attributes that signaled prominence of the stories including total space, story position, page location, headline space, and headline type size. Weight coefficients were assigned to story position, page location, and headline type size to calculate story prominence. For example, a story at the top position of the page was adjusted using the coefficient 1.0, a story in the middle of the page, using .75, and a story at the bottom of the page, .50. A priority index was then computed for each news item.

Two coders participated in the coding. The coding of news content was conducted according to the prescribed procedures by Riffe, Lacy, and Fico (1998). Ten percent of the coding content was used for an intercoder reliability check. Scott's Pi was used to test the intercoder reliability for nominal variables; Pearson's correlation coefficient was used for ratio variables measuring headline and story space that required little subjective judgment in coding. The results of the test showed that intercoder reliabilities of all the variables were above the acceptance level .80.[1]

Computer Lab Experiment

A total of 124 students enrolled in a communication course at a southern U.S. university participated in the experiment as an in-class assignment. The subjects were randomly assigned to two groups. One group contained 64 students who read three print newspapers. The other group included 60 students who read the three newspapers' Internet version. The students ranged from sophomore to senior. About one third of the participants were non-communications majors, including a variety of academic areas on campus.

The experiment was conducted in computer labs. A total of six sessions over 2 days were held for the study. In the sessions for print newspapers, the subjects were given copies of one of the three newspapers one at a time. In the sessions for Internet newspapers, the subjects were asked to go to one of the three newspapers' Web sites.[2] For each newspaper, either print or Internet, the subjects spent 15 minutes to complete the following tasks: (a) Identify a total of six news items that they consider the most important from among the news stories on the Web site; (b) write down the headlines of the news items identified after finishing reading; and (c) rank order the news items identified according to their importance.

The subjects then answered several questions about how they identified the most important stories and the prominence cues used. To avoid carryover effects in the experiment in which subjects explored all three newspapers, the order of print newspapers or Web sites was counterbalanced according to Latin Square Design, that is, the first subject started with *The Washington Post,* the second subject started with *USA Today,* and the third started with the *Chicago Tribune* (Wimmer & Dominick, 2003). To ensure that subjects follow the procedures properly, two supervisors were present in the lab and monitored all sessions of the study. During the 2-day period when the Internet group studied the Web sites, the design of the three Internet newspapers remained unchanged whereas the news content was updated.

Measurement

All news items identified by the print and the Internet groups in their examination of the news content of the three newspapers were compiled. A priority rank measure was created to identify the rank order of all news items identified by the subjects. The top 10 stories from print and the Internet newspapers, which reflected news of priority issues with the highest agreement, were used for comparison between the groups and with what were identified through content analysis. Two aspects were measured to identify the top stories of priority news: percentage of the subjects who selected the story and the rank order a subject assigned to the story selected. A story that was selected by the highest percentage of the subjects and received the highest average rank was identified as the number one on the list of priority news. For example, for the story "Young Voters See Little in it for Them" in *The Washington Post* on November 2, 2000, 34% of the print readers selected it as the most important story; by integrating its rank order, the total score the story received made it rank number three of all stories selected by the print readers. Thirty percent of the Internet readers selected it as the most important story; by integrating its rank order, the story achieved number five of all stories selected by the Internet readers. The story was ranked number three by content analysis. Of all the stories identified through content analysis, the top 10 stories were considered news of priority issues and were used as a benchmark for comparison to those identified by the print and the Internet groups.

Confirm rate was used to measure relative level that print and the Internet readers agree on what prominence cues were used in identifying priority issues and whether the way that news was presented on Web sites changed readers' view of what the priority issues are. It was standardized to 100% for easy understanding. It was measured with a 5-point scale. The neutral point 3 indicated 0%, and a score of 5 (*strongly agree*), which produced a difference of 2 from the neutral point (3 = 0% confirm), would generate a confirm rate of 100%.

RESULTS

H1a, that priority issues identified by the Internet readers are noticeably different from those identified through content analysis, and H1b, that priority issues identified by the Internet readers are noticeably different from those identified by readers of print newspapers, are both supported. The rank order obtained through content analysis was used as a benchmark to test the relationship between priority issues identified from content analysis and those by the Internet readers. Differences in rank order between content analysis and the Internet readers were evident. The priority issues identified from the Internet readers were also clearly deviated from the print readers (see Table 15.1).

H2, that priority issues identified by the Internet readers are less likely to be associated with those identified through content analysis of the print newspaper than those identified by the print readers, is supported. Spearman's rho was used to test the rank order relationships. There was a significant difference in level of association between the Internet readers and content analysis and the level of association between the print readers and content analysis. Priority issues identified by the print readers of all three newspapers were highly correlated with those from content analysis: *The Washington Post*, $r_s = .72, p < .01$, *USA Today*, $r_s = .88$, $p < .01$, and the *Chicago Tribune*, $r_s = .62, p < .05$. Priority issues identified by the Internet readers of all three newspapers were much less associated with those from content analysis: *The Washington Post*, $r_s = .25, p > .05$, *USA Today*, $r_s = -.40, p > .05$, and the *Chicago Tribune*, $r_s = .26, p > .05$. No correlation was statistically significant (see Table 15.2).

The line charts (Figs. 15.1–15.3) of rank order of the 10 news items identified as priority issues from the three newspapers clearly displayed the deviation among what was identified through content analysis and what were identified by the print and the Internet readers. For all three newspapers, the rank order of the priority news identified by the print and the Internet readers oscillated to some degree against the line of content analysis. The content analysis and the print readers' pick of *The Washington Post* showed similar trend, whereas the Internet readers' pick showed clear deviation. The rank order line of *USA Today* by the print readers displayed a small oscillation against the line of content analysis, whereas that of the Internet readers deviated considerably from content analysis. The rank order lines of the *Chicago Tribune* by both print and the Internet readers deviated from content analysis, but not as considerably as the other two newspapers.

TABLE 15.1

**Rank Order of Priority Issues Identified Through Content Analysis
and by the Print and the Internet Readers**

Story Headline	Content Analysis	Print Readers	Internet Readers
The Washington Post			
Nominees Scour West for Votes	1	1	1
Few Drugs for the Needy	2	2	8
Young Voters See Little in it for Them	3	3	5
Space Station's Inaugural Crew	4	8	4
U.S. to Probe St. George's Police Force	5	7	3
Nominees Stump in Unusual Places	6	4	2
Supreme Court Hears of Birds and Watering Places	7	6	N.A.[a]
Election Won't End Budget Fight	8	10	6.5
Researchers Waiting to Plumb Abortion Pill	9	5	N.A.
Budget Is Shelved Until After Election	10	9	6.5
USA Today			
747 Hit Object, Crashed	1	1	6
Bush, Gore Target Seniors	2	3	4.5
Campaigns' RX Could Be Wrong Prescription	3	2	3
Battleground Voters Nearing Combat Fatigue	4	5	4.5
D.C. Hot Spot for ID Theft	5	6	N.A.
Relatives Grieve: I Lost Everything	6	N.A.	2
Investigators Scour Jet Wreckage for a Cause	7	4	7
Calif. Stop Sober One for Bush	8	8	1
Egyptair Relatives Dedicate Memorial	9	N.A.	N.A.
High Court Hears Arguments in Wetlands Case	10	7	N.A.
Chicago Tribune			
Mudslinging Spatters Mailboxes, Airwaves	1	N.A.	7
Another Bad Year for City Schools	2	1	3
Despite Pluses, Gore Struggles to Connect	3	3	1
DNC Sends Jackson to the Rescue	4	2	4
Chiapas Crisis a Critical Matter for Mexico's Fox	5	N.A.	N.A.
Questions Surface About Bush's Service	6	7	2
Jet Hits Object Before Takeoff; 70 Die	7	5	8
Ryan Gets Plenty of Takers Among Illinois First Foes	8	8	N.A.
Captain Is Questioned in Jet Crash	9	6	5
Both Sides Ratchet up Intensity in Mideast	10	4	6

Note. For content analysis, news items are ranked according to priority index; for the print and the Internet readers they are ranked according to percentage that readers select the items as the most important.

[a]N.A., item not identified by the group of readers among the top 10 stories.

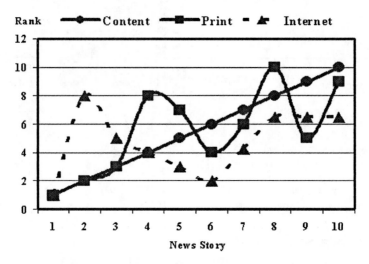

FIG. 15.1. Rank order of priority issues identified through content analysis and by the print and the Internet readers (*The Washington Post*). The rank order line of priority news identified by the print readers oscillates against content analysis, but not as greatly as the line of the Internet readers.

TABLE 15.2
Rank Order Correlations of Priority Issues Identified
Through Content Analysis and by Print and Internet Readers (*N* = 10)

Newspaper	Content Versus Print	Content Versus Internet	Print Versus Internet
The Washington Post	.72*	.25	.35
USA Today	.88*	−.40	−.38
Chicago Tribune	.62*	.26	.18

*$p < .05$.

H3, the Web design approach of Internet newspapers is associated with the differences in identifying priority issues from the three newspaper sites, is supported. Due to different Web design approaches of the three newspapers, the information delivery and access modes differed among the newspapers, which resulted in differences in identifying priority issues from the three newspaper sites. The line charts of rank order of priority news identified from the Internet readers and through content analysis and the print readers showed distinctive patterns among the three newspapers. The degree to which rank order lines of the Internet readers oscillated against the content analysis and the print readers varied among the three newspapers. Rank order correlations of priority news between content analysis and the Internet readers and between the print and the Internet readers also showed variations among the three newspapers.

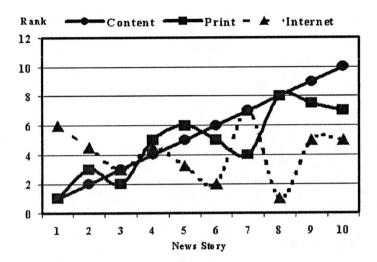

FIG. 15.2. Rank order of priority issues identified through content analysis and by the print and the Internet readers (*USA Today*). The rank order line of priority news identified by the print readers oscillates slightly against content analysis. The rank order line of the Internet readers oscillates considerably against content analysis.

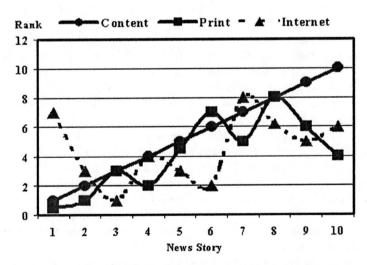

FIG. 15.3. Rank order of priority issues identified through content analysis and by the print and the Internet readers (*Chicago Tribune*). The rank order line of priority news identified by the print readers oscillates against content analysis. The rank order line of the Internet readers oscillates against content analysis more substantially.

TABLE 15.3
Prominence Cues in Identifying Priority Issues by the
Print Readers (N = 64) Versus the Internet readers (N = 60)

	Print Readers			Internet Readers		
Prominence Cues	Confirm	Mean	Differ	Confirm	Mean	Differ
Prominent position	67%	4.34	1.34*	78%	4.55	1.55*
Use large type	68%	4.36	1.36*	73%	4.46	1.46*
Story length	27%	3.53	0.53*	0%	3.00	0.00
Story with photo	61%	4.22	1.22*	42%	3.83	0.83*
Section importance	37%	3.73	0.73*	36%	3.72	0.72*
Immediate access	N.A.	N.A.	N.A.	73%	4.45	1.45*
No wait for display	N.A.	N.A.	N.A.	45%	3.91	0.91*
External link	N.A.	N.A.	N.A.	20%	3.40	0.40*

*One Sample t test, test value = 3 (neutral point, 0% confirm), $p \leq .01$.

H4, the prominence cues that readers use to identify priority issues from Web sites are different from those that readers use to identify priority issues from traditional media, is partially supported. A total of eight prominence cues were presented to the Internet readers for them to confirm after they identified the news items of priority issues from the Internet newspapers. Among them, five items were the prominence cues used in traditional media: prominent position, use of large type, story length, story with photo, and section importance. These five items were presented to the print readers for them to confirm after they identified the news of priority issues from the print newspapers.

The confirmation rate of these five items differs between print and the Internet readers. Prominent position (67% vs. 78%) and use of large type (68% vs. 73%) were strongly confirmed by both print and Internet groups. Story with photo was considered a prominence cue by the print readers (61%), but not as strongly by the Internet readers (42%). Section importance (37% vs. 36%) was weakly confirmed by both groups. Story length was weakly confirmed by the print readers (27%), but was not considered a prominence cue by the Internet readers (0%).

The other three items were specifically related to news access from the Internet newspapers. Immediate access (73%) was strongly confirmed as a factor in identifying priority issues from the Internet newspapers. No wait for display (45%) was also considered a notable factor. External link (20%) had a weak effect on identifying the priority issues from the Internet newspapers (see Table 15.3).

H5, the way that news is presented on Web sites is likely to change readers' view of what the priority issues are, is not supported. The confirm rate for a changed view of priority issues due to the way that news is presented was 4%, $p > .05$. The Internet readers saw the three traditional media, print newspaper, TV, and radio, slightly different from the Internet newspapers in how to identify priority issues. Confirm rate for that "the way to identify priority issues from

TABLE 15.4
Difference in Views on Priority Issues Between Internet Newspaper
and Traditional Media by the Internet Readers ($N = 60$)

Perception	Confirm	Mean	Differ	t	Sig
Different from newspaper	12%	3.24	0.24	1.60	0.12
Different from radio	35%	3.69	0.69*	4.43	0.01
Different way from TV	22%	3.43	0.43*	2.70	0.01
View changed by Web sites	4%	3.07	0.07	0.47	0.64

*One Sample t test, test value = 3 (neutral point), $p < .01$.

the Internet newspapers is different from print newspaper" was 12%, $p > .05$; different from radio, 35%, $p < .05$; different from television, 22%, $p < .05$ (see Table 15.4).

The fact that the Internet readers' view of priority issues was not changed by the way the news was presented on newspaper Web sites was also confirmed by the sections of Internet newspapers where the Internet readers selected priority issues. Subjects first looked at the Home Page, which was similar to the front page in print newspapers. More than 40% of the news items were identified from the home page, with *The Washington Post* 43%, *USA Today* 41%, and the *Chicago Tribune* 43%. The other sections that the Internet readers looked at most were World, Nation, and Latest News. The total news items from these four sections accounted for 73% from *The Washington Post,* 72% from *USA Today,* and 76% from the *Chicago Tribune.*

The result of the print readers is similar to that of the Internet readers regarding where the priority issues were identified. The total news items selected from Section A in print newspapers accounted for 79% from *The Washington Post,* 74% from *USA Today,* and 78% from the *Chicago Tribune.*

DISCUSSION

The findings suggest that Web design approach and information delivery and access modes of print and the Internet newspapers do have an effect on how priority issues are identified. Priority issues identified from the Internet newspapers are likely to deviate from those prioritized by print newspapers' editors and those identified by readers of the print newspapers.

Support of H1 indicates that information delivery and access through the Internet newspapers may produce a different list of priority issues. The variety of routes to access news information is the key factor for the difference in identifying priority issues from the Internet newspapers from those identified through content analysis and from print newspapers. The way that a story is accessed is undergoing a fundamental change from a simple linear route to nonlinear routes. The ability to shape the news flow has grown stronger for both editor and readers. The effect of a combination of factors will inevitably lead to different priority issues identified from the Internet newspapers.

Support of H2 confirms the agenda-setting function of the traditional media. The priority issues identified by print newspaper readers corresponded with those identified through content analysis. Rank order correlations between content analysis and the print readers were highly correlated. At the same time the finding suggests agenda setting may not work the same way in the Internet as with traditional media. The information delivery and access mode of the Internet newspapers produced a noticeably different list of stories of priority issues. What readers of Internet newspapers found to be important showed evident deviation from content analysis. If match of news of priority issues between the print readers and content analysis signifies high level of agenda-setting function, the deviation in priority issues between the Internet readers and content analysis demonstrated a weakened function of agenda setting under the Internet environment.

Support of H3 suggests that Web design approach does matter in identifying priority issues from the Internet newspapers.This study found rank order of priority issue varied among the three newspapers. The line chart showed clear deviation in the rank order patterns across the three newspapers. *The Washington Post* and the *Chicago Tribune* had low correlations between content analysis and the Internet readers, and between print and the Internet readers. *USA Today*'s negative correlations indicated the items identified by the Internet readers from *USA Today* appeared in a reverse order from what were identified through content analysis and by the print readers. Further examination is needed to find what factors caused the reverse order of the priority news from the Internet version. What was clear is that the distinctive Web design of the three Internet newspapers produced diverse patterns in priority issues identified from the two versions of the newspapers compared to content analysis. The difference in identifying priority issues was produced by Web design approach including information structure, presentation style, and navigation path. This study only looked at the overall effect of Web design approach of the Internet newspapers on identifying priority issues. To what degree that each of the elements contributed to the difference requires further investigations with all three elements properly manipulated. To further explore the effect of Web design on identifying priority issues, the major design elements could be measured to see how each contribute to the identification of priority issues.

The finding of H4 provides some insight for understanding the process to identify priority issues from the Internet newspapers. It suggests that the prominence cues used to identify priority issues in print newspapers are still useful in Internet newspapers. Although some of the prominence cues were no longer so evident on the Internet newspapers, such as story prominence and headline type size, they were still used to help readers select the most important news. The stories with special type treatment are most likely to be selected, especially when editors of the Internet newspapers give special weight to a story of the latest breaking news (Houston, 1999). But more aspects were involved when examining priority issues in the Internet. Story length was not considered as a factor by the Internet readers because the whole story would never appear on the front page. Stories presented on the front page with only headlines and abstracts might still be considered as important if prominence cues could be found. Two aspects that were exclusive for the Internet newspapers played important roles in identifying priority issues: immediate access and no wait for display. The confirmation of the two aspects suggests that the most important news items of the Internet newspapers appear as close to the home page as possible and are displayed without a long wait. The finding on these two added prominence cues reconfirms that Web design matters in identifying priority issues from the Internet newspapers.

The finding on H5 suggest that even though the way to access news information changed in the Internet, the way that news is presented has little effect on readers' view of what the priority issues are. The prominence cues associated with print newspapers were still used by readers of Internet newspapers. Web design approach that created diverse information structure, presentation style, and navigation path did not fundamentally change readers' view of priority issues in the Internet newspapers. Although readers had to adjust the way they identified priority issues from the Internet newspapers and looked for additional prominence cues from the Internet newspapers, their identification of the news of priority issues had some connection with what was considered news of priority issues by the editors. The lists of the priority issues identified by the Internet readers showed that the news stories selected as top priority issues captured the essence of social significance, which included the presidential election, domestic politics, the latest news development such as a plane crash, Mideast conflict, and the space station. The news items identified by the Internet readers may be different from content analysis and the print readers; what was represented by the substance of the stories from World, Nation, and Latest News conforms with the bigger frame of the media agenda.

This study was conducted a few days before the 2000 general election. Several news items regarding election appeared on the list of priority news. Were they selected because of their prominence or substance? The answer from this study was from both. Although people may have different tendencies when browsing news, for most people, prominence of the news attracts them first. This is the assumption that newspaper design is based on. For print newspaper readers, substance of the news practically comes after prominence. But they are integrated most of time. Those at the prominent position are usually the most important. For Internet newspaper readers, although they claimed they still used prominence cues in identifying priority news, because the prominence cues were not as evident as in print newspapers, substance played a more important role than story prominence in identifying priority news from the internet. Due to restriction of the specific period of this study, future studies could further test which factor plays a more important role in selecting priority news and the interaction of the two factors.

The finding could ease some of the concerns about public awareness of important social issues if more people get information from Internet newspapers. While Tewksbury and Althaus (2000) found that online readers of *The New York Times* read fewer national, international, and political news stories than print newspaper readers, this study found that an average of 73% of the news items identified from the Internet newspapers were from Main, World, Nation, Latest News, and Politics sections, which contained most of the issues of social importance. The selection was consistent with that of the print readers, 77% from Section A. The result is similar to Graber's (1993) findings from traditional newspapers. The different findings of this study from Tewksbury and Althaus may be due to the starting point of information processing: that is, information seeking instead of Web surfing. The Internet newspapers have changed information delivery and access modes. But information seekers, who have a clear goal in their information seeking, usually pay closer attention when they browse information and are more likely to identify the information related to their search. The substance of the news stories plus traditional and alternative prominence cues could still help them identify most of the priority issues from the Internet newspapers.

Has the agenda-setting function changed with different information delivery and access modes of the Internet newspapers? It may be too early to reach a conclusion. The media agenda that readers of the Internet newspapers identify may be somewhat different from what they may identify from traditional newspapers. It would be useful to analyze the substance of priority issues presented in the print and Internet versions of the news. On the other hand, the Web sites of the Internet newspapers are always changing. By the time this paper was written, there had been notable changes with two of the three Internet newspapers in a period of less than 2 years. The *Chicago Tribune* changed its home page from a one-screen compact design to a multiple page design with more options to access news information on its front page. *USA Today* changed its home page by reducing its scrolling length from 5.5 screens to 2 screens. These changes in Web design can affect how news information is presented and accessed and thus reduce or expand the difference of priority issues identified from the Internet newspapers and those presented by print newspapers.

The generalizability of this study is limited in several aspects. Only three newspapers were examined and the test period is short. As the effect of media agenda setting may not surface until a certain period of time lapses, whether the difference between the priority issues identified by the print and the Internet readers will remain for a longer period could not be answered by this study. A study over a longer period of time will be more helpful in revealing whether the information delivery and access modes of the Internet newspapers change the media's function of agenda setting. The subjects were instructed to identify the most important stories. Although the subjects were in a specific information-seeking mode, which was certainly different from Web surfing, the mode may be different from general information seeking and may affect how subjects read. The subjects participated in the study were drawn from college students. They bear the general characteristics of Internet users, but their actual media consumption habits may not be completely in line with the general audience of the Internet newspapers. Students may have been conditioned to consider certain information as important when reading print media. These habits may be carried over to Internet use. Internet newspapers are now updated more frequently. There are variations of content during the 24 hours due to content updates. The variation of the content that readers access and its effect on identifying priority news are important aspects in understanding how agenda setting works on the Internet. Other aspects worth exploring include the time spent online and its effect on identifying priority issues from the Internet newspapers, the interaction of using traditional media and the Internet newspapers in identifying priority issues, and changes of information structure, such as redesign of a newspaper Web site, and their effect on identifying priority issues.

CONCLUSION

This study partly confirms the findings of Tewksbury and Althaus (2000) that difference in layout and a reduction in importance cues may have independent effects on the stories that readers notice and read. The study found that the priority issues identified by the Internet readers were noticeably different from those identified through content analysis and by the print readers. The priority issues identified from the Internet readers varied in their relationship with content analysis and the print readers among the Internet newspapers with different Web designs.

However, the study revealed that the prominence cues used in print newspapers were still used by the Internet readers for accessing news information from the Internet newspapers. Two additional dimensions, immediate access and no wait for display, were found critical in the process of identifying the most important news items. Although rank order of priority issues between the Internet and the print readers and content analysis varied among the newspapers, about 73% of the news items were identified from the sections carrying national, international, and political news in the Internet newspapers. Although noticeably different from those identified by the print readers and content analysis, the priority issues identified by the Internet readers were still within the bigger frame of the media agenda. The subjects did not consider that the way that news was presented on Web sites changed their view of what the most important news was. It could be true that readers of the Internet newspapers noticed and read somewhat different stories from what appeared in print newspapers. However, it is unlikely that readers will read less news of social significance if they access news information from the Internet newspapers.

ENDNOTES

1. Intercoder reliability test results: Nominal variables: (a) page location 1.0; (b) headline type size .84; (c) story position .94. Ratio variables: (a) headline space .92; (b) story space .82; (c) picture size .88.
2. Three Internet newspapers: *The Washington Post,* http://www.washingtonpost.com; *USA Today,* http://www.usatoday.com; the *Chicago Tribune,* http://www.chicagotribune .com.

REFERENCES

Althaus, S. L., & Tewksbury, D. (2002). Agenda setting and the "new" news: Patterns of issue importance among readers of the paper and online versions of The New York Times. *Communication Research, 29*(2), 180–207.

Barnhurst, K. G. (2002). News geography & monopoly: The form of reports on US newspaper Internet sites. *Journalism Studies, 3*(4), 477–489.

Chamber, R. (1998, August). *Perceptions of graphics versus no graphics on WWW sites.* Paper presented at the Association for Education in Journalism & Mass Communication Convention, Baltimore, MD.

Davis, R., & Owen, D. M. (1998). *New media and American politics.* New York: Oxford University Press.

Gormley, W. T., Jr. (1975). Newspaper agendas and political elites. *Journalism Quarterly, 30,* 30–38.

Graber, D. A. (1993). *Processing the news: How people tame the information tide* (3rd ed.). Lanham, MD: University Press of America.

Gubman, J., & Greer, J. (1997, July 30–August 2). *An analysis of online sites produced by U.S. newspapers: Are the critics right?* Paper presented at the Association for Education in Journalism and Mass Communication, Chicago, IL.

Gunter, B. (2003). *News and the Net.* Mahwah, NJ: Lawrence Erlbaum Associates.

Halleck, D. (2003). Can new information technologies promote democratic deliberation? In J. Harper & T. Yantek (Eds.), *Media, profit, and politics: Competing priorities in an open society* (pp. 215–231). Kent, OH: Kent State University Press.

Heeter, C., Brown, N., Soffin, S., Stanley, C., & Salwen, M. (1989). Agenda-setting by electronic text news. *Journalism Quarterly, 66,* 101–106.

Hoffman, D. L., & Novak, T. P. (1996). Marketing in hypermedia computer-based environments: Conceptual foundations. *Journal of Marketing, 60,* 50–68.

Houston, F. (1999, July/August). What I saw in the digital sea. *Columbia Journalism Review, 38,* 34–37.

Kosicki, G. M. (1993). Problems and opportunities in agenda-setting research. *Journal of Communication, 43*(2), 100–127.

Lapham, C. (1995, July 1). The evolution of the newspaper of the future. *Computer-Mediated Communication, 7.*

Li, X. (1998). Web page design and graphic use of three U.S. newspapers. *Journalism and Mass Communication Quarterly, 75*(2), 353–365.

Li, X. (2002). Web design affects news retrieval efficiency. *Newspaper Research Journal, 23*(1), 38–49.

Martin, S. (1998). How news gets from paper to its online counterpart. *Newspaper Research Journal, 19*(2), 64–73.

McCombs, M. E., & Shaw, D. L. (1972). The agenda-setting function of the press. *Public Opinion Quarterly, 36,* 176–178.

Miller, M. M., Andsager, J. L., & Riechert, B. P. (1998). Framing the candidates in presidential primaries: Issues and images in press release and news coverage. *Journalism and Mass Communication Quarterly, 75*(2), 312–324.

Neuberger, C., Tonnemacher, J., Biebl, M., & Duck, A. (1998). Online—The future of newspapers? Germany's dailies on the World Wide Web. *Journal of Computer-Mediated Communication, 4*(1).

Niederst, J. (1999). *Web design in a nutshell: A desktop quick reference* (1st ed.). Beijing, China, and Sebastopol, CA: O'Reilly & Associates.

Nielsen, J. (2000). *Designing Web usability: The practice of simplicity.* Indianapolis, IN: New Riders.

Oostendorp, H. v., & Nimwegen, C. v. (1998). Locating information in an online newspaper. *Journal of Computer-Mediated Communication, 4*(1).

Powers, A., & Andsager, J. L. (1999). How newspapers frame breast implants in the 1990s. *Journalism and Mass Communication Quarterly, 76*(3), 551–564.

Riffe, D., Lacy, S., & Fico, F. (1998). *Analyzing media messages: Using quantitative content analysis in research.* Mahwah, NJ: Lawrence Erlbaum Associates.

Tewksbury, D., & Althaus, S. L. (2000). Differences in knowledge acquisition among readers of the paper and online versions of a national newspaper. *Journalism and Mass Communication Quarterly, 77*(3), 457–479.

Vargo, K. (1998, August). *Readers' response to digital news stories: Layers and links.* Paper presented at the Association for Education in Journalism & Mass Communication Convention, Baltimore, MD.

Wang, T.-L. (2000). Agenda setting online: An experiment testing the effects of hyperlinks in online newspapers. *Southwestern Mass Communication Journal, 15*(2), 59–70.

Wanta, W. (1997). *The public and the national agenda: How people learn about important issues.* Mahwah, NJ: Lawrence Erlbaum Associates.

Williams, W. J., & Semlak, W. D. (1978). Structural effect of TV coverage on political agendas. *Journal of Communication, 28,* 114–119.

Wimmer, R. D., & Dominick, J. R. (2003). *Mass media research: An introduction* (7th ed.). Belmont, CA: Wadsworth.

Zhu, J.-H., & Blood, D. (1997). Media agenda-setting theory: Telling what the public thinks about. In B. Kovacic (Ed.), *Emerging theories of human communication* (pp. 88–114). Albany: State University of New York Press.

16

Above the Fold: A Comparison of the Lead Stories in Print and Online Newspapers

Donica Mensing
Jennifer D. Greer
University of Nevada–Reno

What people read and hear in the news affects what they perceive as being important in the public realm (Dearing & Rogers, 1996; Erbring, Goldenberg, & Miller, 1980; Lippman, 1922; McCombs & Shaw, 1972). A variety of studies have demonstrated that media content influences what issues the public perceives as important, as well as their knowledge of and attitudes about the issues (Iyengar, 1991; McCombs, Shaw, & Weaver, 1997). Although many factors also influence the formation of public opinion, including predispositions, interpersonal communication, and demographic variables, mass media clearly impact the daily lives of most Americans.

This connection between what appears in the media and the "pictures in our heads" that Lippmann (1922) described has led to numerous studies of *news judgment*—the process that journalists use to determine what will appear in the news, and with what prominence. Analyzing how news judgment is exercised has been studied in depth by sociologists such as White (1950), Tuchman (1978), Gans (1980), and Fishman (1980). Although journalism as a whole shows a remarkable consistency in defining news (Manoff & Schudson, 1986), research shows that news judgment does vary between mediums for several reasons, including news cycles, news hole, deadlines, and the relative importance and availability of visual content (Neuman, Just, & Crigler, 1992). For example, Robinson and Sheehan (1983) found that news judgment varied between television and newspapers.

Understanding the implications of news judgment—in journalism overall and within each medium—has been an integral part of major communication theories including agenda setting, priming, and framing.

With online news becoming an increasingly popular form of news delivery, researchers have turned their attention to news judgment online and how that differs from judgment in other mediums. Most newspaper readers understand clearly that articles placed above the fold on the front page are the most important in that issue and that the story with the largest headline is the top story for the day. Online, however, these prominence cues can become more difficult to interpret. In an experimental study comparing the salience of public issues between print and online readers of *The New York Times,* researchers found that online readers appeared to read fewer national, international, and political news stories than readers of the print version; online readers also were less likely to recall events that occurred during the study period (Althaus & Tewksbury, 2002). Whether this occurred because online readers deliberately chose not to read national, international, and political news stories in the context of many other competing stories and features, or whether online readers couldn't discern the prominence cues that were more apparent in print, is a question for future research.

In theory, space in an online newspaper is unlimited, but because of the size of computer screens, space to prominently highlight important stories is much smaller online than in print. With advertisements and navigational buttons competing for space on the top screen, online editors are forced to make news decisions with even tighter space limitations than their print counterparts. In addition, the ability to post breaking news creates a 24-hour news cycle, meaning that news judgment has to be exercised constantly. Given these differences, it seems reasonable that news might be played differently online than in print, even within the same news organization. This study seeks to test that assumption, by systematically comparing the top stories in elite print dailies with the top stories that appeared in the same organizations' online editions at two points during the day. Specifically, the study compared the news judgment exercised in print and online by *USA Today, The New York Times,* and the *Los Angeles Times,* the three largest circulation general interest daily newspapers in the United States. Twenty-three days of stories that appeared "above the fold" in the print editions were compared with the top stories in the news organizations' online versions at noon and midnight on those days. This study examined whether the specific stories and, more broadly, topics covered, matched across the versions.

ONLINE NEWS AND NEWS JUDGMENT

Before examining the factors that influence news judgment and the few studies that have examined prominence differences by medium, it is helpful to examine how vital online news has become in recent years.

Demand for Online News

Respondents in a 2000 Pew study said they went online for news to get information unavailable elsewhere, for convenience, and to search for particular subjects. Since then, the percentage of Americans who go online regularly for news continues to grow, with 29% of all Americans now going online for news three times or more a week (Pew, 2004). Although the percentage that uses the Internet for news is lower than the percentage regularly watching local TV news (59%), network news (34%), or reading newspapers (42%), only online news use is increasing. A large majority of Internet users (72%) report that they have used the Internet to obtain news (Fallows & Rainie, 2004). Nearly half (47%) of Americans go online on any given day, and a quarter of those (24%) say they read news while they are online. The number of people who report "bumping" into the news inadvertently while they are online continues to increase, from 53% in 1996 to 73% in 2004 (Fallows & Rainie, 2004).

The mix of people who read online news is becoming more diverse over time, as the number of women and racial minorities using the Internet for news increases. For example, 22% of Hispanics reported using the Internet for news in 2002; that figure is now 32%, higher than for the U.S. population as a whole (Pew, 2004). Education, however, appears to be the most important factor in online news use. Half of all college graduates reported reading online news in the recent past, compared to only 18% of high school graduates and 8% of those who didn't finish high school. Overall, Internet news readers tend to be "young, affluent, and well-educated" (Pew, 2004, p. 8).

The most popular sources of online news are AOL/Yahoo (13%), network TV news Web sites (10%), local TV/newspaper sites (9%), national newspaper sites (6%), and online magazine/opinion sites (3%; Pew, 2004). Most online readers seek out weather-related information (76%), followed by science and health news (58%), politics (54%), and international news (54%; Fallows & Rainie, 2004). Like their print counterparts, online editors keep a watchful eye on trend reports such as these. User preferences are just one factor, however, that influences news judgment.

Factors That Influence News Judgment

To understand how, or whether, news might change when it is created for online distribution requires understanding what factors influence the creation of news. Graber (1997) provides an overview of some of these factors, which include government control and regulation, ownership, audience and advertiser pressures, and characteristics of media personnel. The government, at least for now, is not regulating the content or production of online news any differently than it regulates newspapers. Ownership of news sites varies widely, from individuals like Matt Drudge (www.drudgereport.com) and Harry Knowles (www.aintitcool.com) to the largest traditional media corporations. Audience and advertiser pressures are certainly growing online, but the diversity of online choices may dilute this pressure somewhat.

Whereas Graber describes news personnel in general as "upwardly mobile, well-educated white males whose political views are liberal" (1997, p. 102), the characteristics of online and print media personnel may differ, even within the same traditional media organizations. Singer, Tharp, and Haruta (1998) found that print and online newsrooms were staffed separately in 45% of the newspapers they surveyed, with all of the large papers (circulation greater than 250,000) having completely independent online staffs.

Besides the demographics, training, personality, and professional socialization of news personnel, other factors that affect news judgment include intraorganizational norms, professional role conceptions, and the pressures of internal and external competition (Graber, 1997, p. 102). For news sites, organizational norms and professional role conceptions are still developing. Singer et al. (1998) found that online journalists at newspapers expressed concern about their inability to get print staffs to take them seriously and the constant need to balance credibility and profitability. A number of online journalists also said they did not report directly to editorial supervisors, but to advertising, marketing, or production managers. Clearly, the purpose and role of online journalists are still in flux within many organizations.

Clyde and Buckalew (1969) determined that news editors use the elements of conflict, proximity, and timeliness most frequently to determine the newsworthiness of a story. Corrigan (1990), in a study of leads on the front pages of four newspapers, found that 98.8% of the stories had leads with news value. These values were prominence (54%), vitality/conflict (51.9%), timeliness (45.4%), significance (24%), proximity (24%), human interest (19%), and consequences (4%). Some argue that non-news stories are becoming more prominent as the desire to be entertaining and to produce profits exerts greater influence over news decisions (McChesney, 1999; Sharkey, 1994).

Because of these traditional elements and shared pressures, studies show that news judgment across major media is remarkably similar. Foote and Steele (1986) found the lead story shared by the three major television networks 43% and by two of the networks 91% of the time. Riffe, Ellis, Rogers, Van Ommeren, and Woodman (1986) also found the same kinds of stories and story types reported across media types.

Although news elements are similar across media, differences by medium can lead to differences in news judgment, as noted by Neuman, Just, and Crigler (1992). For example, visual elements are more necessary for a compelling broadcast story than a print story. Television producers must choose stories based on available video, thus leading to differing decisions by print and broadcast news producers about what stories to feature on any given day.

The production process by which news is selected, prepared, and distributed explains much of the similarity in news judgment across a wide variety of media organizations. The time pressure of frequent, unwavering deadlines demands that the creation and selection process for news be efficient, quick, and predictable. Bagdikian (1971) studied gatekeeping at eight different newspapers and observed that the typical newspaper editor could scan and discard stories in 1 to 2 seconds.

Because most newspapers today produce, essentially, a single edition, stories are packaged with an aim to be printed at the same time every day. News events that break at certain points in the news cycle are more likely to be included in the day's news than events that break at other times, for example, just after deadline. On the television side, the lure of "live coverage" also means that the timing of events influences news decisions in ways that differ from that of newspapers (Tuggle & Huffman, 1999).

With online news, however, the news cycle is continuous. News judgments are made more frequently with many online news sites instituting policies to either update news online as warranted or at specific times throughout the day (Alves & Weiss, 2004; Outing, 1999). In the early days of online, news sites would often hold stories to avoid scooping the print edition, but a sizable number of newspapers now break news first in whatever medium is available, which often is the online product. Many observers have noted that online news is similar to that of wire services, where the deadlines and time pressure have no ebb and flow (Stepp, 2001).

A newspaper's news hole also influences what news is selected for publication. Because print space is costly, only a tiny portion of available news on any given day can fit within the pages of a newspaper. News sites, in contrast, have no space constraints. Stories, photos, and supporting documentation all can be provided without regard for the amount of space they might take on a server. However, usability studies (Nielsen, 1997) indicate that many people do not scroll past the first few screens of text, thus constraining the visual space within which to fit stories even more severely than the front page of a newspaper. What is scarce is the time and attention of readers, as well as the time and resources of the staff. Online news stories and headlines must be written in a compressed and pithy format to fit both the space and time constraints of reading news on a computer screen (deWolk, 2001).

In one of the few studies comparing news judgment online and in print, Singer (2001) compared gatekeeping in the different versions of six Colorado newspapers. She found, at the time, that online sites had fewer stories overall than do newspapers. The stories that were missing online were primarily nonmetro stories, giving online papers a more local focus than their print counterparts. Online papers also had fewer political stories and very few politically related opinion columns, editorials, or letters to the editor. Online products had a higher percentage of staff-generated stories, used the wires less, and had fewer visual elements than their print counterparts.

In a 2000 study of five Iowa newspapers preceding the Iowa caucuses, Singer (2002) compared print and online content, finding "no evidence that any of these papers created daily news content specifically for the Web" (p. 68). Singer found that 1,149 stories ran online and in print with no alteration to the print stories, whereas just 72 stories and collections of briefs ran with some degree of alteration. Preceding the caucus, other content, including transcripts and campaign calendars, was provided online that was not included in the print edition. But most of this was supplemental content that could not be economically printed as opposed to additional stories (Singer, 2002).

As online newspapers become a permanent addition to most traditional newspaper companies, they may continue to develop their own identities and traditions or they may begin to look more like their print parents. Online editors can get immediate feedback from readers—as measured by hits, page views, and other devices—creating a TV-ratings like pressure for the online editors that the print editors don't face. Whether these differing pressures, conditions, and time cycles create significant differences in news judgment, even within the same news organizations, is the subject of this study.

RESEARCH QUESTIONS

Other than Singer (2001, 2002), few studies have examined how news is presented online and in print by the same news organizations. Singer compared local papers, which for the most part have small online staffs and limited resources for Web production, especially in 1999. This study, in contrast, seeks to eliminate the variable of staff size and resources by focusing solely on three large newspapers that serve a national audience and have generous resources and large online staffs. Within this context, the study asks whether news decisions made in print mirror or diverge from those made for online. Because ownership, organization, and professional socialization are consistent across the print and Web versions of newspapers, news judgment could be quite similar. Other factors, however, including the production process and news cycle, suggest that at any given point during the day, the news promoted on a newspaper's Web site might be very different from that presented in the morning newspaper.

To explore these issues, the following research questions were posed:

RQ1: How often is the lead story in the print version of the three newspapers also the lead story or one of the top three stories in that day's online versions (at midnight and noon)? Does this frequency vary by newspaper title?

RQ2: How often is the lead topic in the print version of the three newspapers also the lead topic or a top three topic covered in that day's online versions (at midnight or noon)? Does this frequency vary by newspaper title?

RQ3: Do print and online versions (at midnight and noon) differ in their placement of topics? (How highly correlated is topic placement in the print and online versions?)

RQ4: Overall, did the print and online versions emphasize the same topics during the study period? Did this vary by newspaper title?

METHOD

Population and Sample

Research indicates that there is a significant correlation between the features on a news site and the circulation size of the corresponding newspaper (Greer & Mensing, 2004; Mensing, 1996). Based on the assumption that the largest circulation newspapers are most likely to afford separate editors and producers for their online operations (Singer et al., 1998) and that large national newspapers are more likely to experiment with different content on their Web version than the print version (Fredin, 1997), large newspapers were chosen to test whether news judgment varies between a newspaper and its corresponding Web site. Therefore, the three largest daily circulation, general-interest newspapers in the United States were chosen as the population for this study: These newspapers are *USA Today,* the *Los Angeles Times,* and *The New York Times.* The last two titles also are considered among the top four opinion-leading newspapers in the United States (Krantz, 1994).

Paper copies of the national editions of the three papers were obtained every weekday during the study period. Because *USA Today* has no weekend editions, Saturday and Sunday editions of the *Los Angeles Times* and *The New York Times* were not used in this study. The study began at 12:01 A.M. January 31, 2000, and ended at noon on March 2, 2000. The data collection period included 23 days, or 69 data collection points as three versions of the papers were examined for each title.[1]

Procedure

For each title, the front page of the online version was first downloaded just after midnight, Pacific Time, every evening. This time period captured the point in the process when the online site was most likely to resemble the print product, as most online news staff load the next day's content late in the evening when the national edition of the print paper is published. Next, the paper copies of the day's newspaper were obtained in the morning. Then, the front page of the Web site was downloaded shortly after noon, Pacific Time. This period was chosen because it occurs about half way through the print version's news cycle.

For each title, three code sheets were filled out daily, one for each version of the paper. Coders identified the top three stories for each version based on *proximity to the top of the page, font size,* and *placement.* For print versions, the lead story was determined by the size of font, with the largest font ranked as the top story for the day. If two stories had the same font size, the story in the far right corner of the page was chosen as the lead story. This decision was made because print newspaper designers place the dominant element on a page in these two right columns either at the very top or just below a smaller story stripped across the top. Designers are taught that point on the page is where the reader's eye falls first. Stories stripped across the top were only counted as the lead story if it had a larger font than the story directly below it to the right of the page. For the second and third top stories, coders identified them by their proximity to the top story and font size.[2] Typically, print front pages only had three stories with headlines "above the fold."

For the online version, the headline of the lead story was in the largest font on the first screen. In cases where font size was equal, the story closest to the top of the screen was ranked as the lead story. Second and third top stories were determined by examining font size and proximity to the top story.[3]

Variables

Once the top three stories were identified, coders recorded their headlines and determined the story topic from a list of 13 topic categories (presidential primary, government news, international, entertainment, etc.).

The top three stories for the print and online versions of each front page were compared to look for matches in *specific story, story topic,* and *story type.* The matches were made by comparing the lead story in the print product with the lead stories online at the midnight before the morning paper was delivered and at noon the day the print paper was delivered. Story matches did not have to have the exact same wording in the headline or the lead paragraph, which occurred only in rare instances. Stories were counted as a match if they were about the same news event. Therefore, updates of stories were counted as a match, but stories that covered a substantially new angle of an ongoing story (such as the presidential primary) were not. Coders recorded whether no match was present, whether the lead print story matched the online version at midnight only, whether the lead print story matched the online version at noon only, or whether the lead print story matched both online versions examined. The same process was followed for topic matches.

One coder completed coding for the online versions after being trained by the primary author. The author then double-checked this online coding, coded the print versions, and recorded the matches in specific story and topics for all three versions.[4] Because the variables were coded as nominal data, only frequency calculations, simple cross-tabulations and Spearman's Rho were used for analysis.

FINDINGS

The three daily data collections for each of the papers over the 23-day study period could have produced 621 "Top 3" stories for examination. However, because of technical problems with capturing the Web editions, researchers were unable to complete two data collections at midnight (one for *USA Today* and one for the *Los Angeles Times*), reducing the total number of stories analyzed to 615 (207 in print, 207 online at noon, and 201 online at midnight).

Sample Demographics

Of the 13 topics examined, crime/accident news, the U.S. presidential primary, and international news dominated. Table 16.1 shows the topic distribution of all top three stories examined in print and online for the three newspaper organizations.

Coverage Differences by Title

Because *newspaper title* is used as an independent variable in the following analyses, it is helpful to examine overall differences among the titles in *topic* and *type of news covered*. For the *topic of the lead story,* significant differences were found by

TABLE 16.1
Distribution of Topics for All Newspapers,
Print and Online Combined

News Topic	Number of Stories (% of Total)
Crime/accidents	131 (21.65%)
Presidential primary	125 (20.66%)
International	108 (17.85%)
Government news	84 (13.88%)
Economic	55 (9.09%)
Technology	40 (6.61%)
Medical	22 (3.63%)
Sports	13 (2.15%)
Entertainment	9 (1.49%)
Science	9 (1.49%)
Weather	7 (1.16%)
Lifestyle	7 (1.16%)
Education	5 (0.83%)
Total	615 (100%)

TABLE 16.2
Comparison of Lead Print Story With Lead Online Story

	No Match	Match Midnight	Match Noon	Match Both Times
The New York Times	6 (26.1%)	15 (62.2%)	1 (4.3%)	1 (4.3%)
USA Today	17 (73.9%)	4 (17.4%)	2 (8.7%)	0 (0.0%)
Los Angeles Times	14 (60.9%)	2 (8.7%)	7 (30.4%)	0 (0.0%)
Total	37 (53.6%)	21 (30.4%)	10 (14.5%)	1 (1.4%)

newspaper titles ($\chi^2 = 56.16$, $df = 16$, $p < .001$). Overall, *The New York Times* was more likely to feature news about the presidential primary and international news than the other papers, but significantly less likely to feature news about crime and accidents. *USA Today* was more likely to feature technology news than the other papers, but less likely to feature the presidential primary and international news. The *Los Angeles Times* featured less governmental and economic news than the other papers, but more crime and accident stories.

RQ1: How often was the lead story in print also the lead story online?

To analyze this research question, the lead story in print was compared with the lead story in the two online versions (midnight and noon) of the newspaper for that date. More than half of the lead print stories (37 or 53.6%) were not placed as the lead story in either of the online versions. Twenty-one (30.4%) of the lead print stories matched the lead online stories at midnight, 10 (14.5%) matched online at noon, and only one (1.4%) matched both times. As Table 16.2 shows, significant differences did emerge by newspaper title ($\chi^2 = 27.44$, $df = 6$, $p < .001$). Lead print stories in *The New York Times* were most likely to match with the paper's online version at midnight, whereas *USA Today* and the *Los Angeles Times* rarely matched their print and online versions at any time. When the matches did occur for these two papers, they were most likely to be at midnight for *USA Today* and at noon for the *Los Angeles Times*.

Next, the lead print story was examined to see if it matched any of the top three online stories featured in the Web editions. This examined whether the stories were not only carried over as the lead online story but as any top three story on the site during the same day. As expected, matches between stories emphasized in the print and online versions increased in this analysis. Less than one third (21 or 30.4%) of the lead print stories had no match in the top three stories online. Twenty-four (34.8%) matched at midnight, 12 (20.3%) matched at noon, and 10 (14.5%) matched top online stories in both Web versions. As Table 16.3 shows, significant differences emerged by newspaper title ($\chi^2 = 29.29$, $df = 6$, $p < .001$). *USA Today* was most likely not to match its lead print story with its top three online stories, whereas the *Los Angeles Times* was most likely to place the lead print story in a prominent position in its online versions at midnight, noon, and at both times. *The New York Times* was most likely to emphasize its lead print story online at midnight.

RQ2: How often did the top topics in print match the top topics online?

The same matching technique used for the aforementioned stories was repeated for topics. About half the time (32 or 46.4%), the topics in the lead story did not match. The lead print topic matched with the lead online topic at midnight 16 (23.2%) times, with the lead online topic at noon 13 (18.8%) times, and at both 8 (11.6%) times. Table 16.4 shows that significant differences in the occurrence of topic matching did emerge by newspaper title ($\chi^2 = 26.61$, $df = 6$, $p < .001$). Again, topics of the lead stories were most likely to match in *The New York Times,* with most of those matches occurring at midnight or at both times. *USA Today*'s top online Web topics looked least like the paper's print page, with nearly two thirds of the lead story topics not matching. More than half of the lead topics covered in the print version of the *Los Angeles Times* weren't covered in the top spot on that paper's online versions, but when matches did occur, it was most likely at noon.

Finally, the lead print story topic was compared with any top three story topics from the two online versions. This final type of matching analysis showed the highest rates of similarity among the three versions, as would be expected. Less than a quarter (16 or 23.2%) of the lead print story topics didn't occupy a prominent position in the online versions. Another 17 (24.6%) matched at midnight only, 14 (20.3%) matched at noon, and 22 (or 31.9%) matched at both times. As Table 16.5 shows, significant differences again emerged by newspaper title ($\chi^2 = 16.37$, $df = 6$, $p < .01$). *USA Today* was most likely not to match, whereas

TABLE 16.3
Comparison of Lead Print Story With Top Three Online Stories

	No Match	*Match Midnight*	*Match Noon*	*Match Both Times*
The New York Times	4 (17.4%)	14 (60.9%)	2 (8.7%)	3 (13.0%)
USA Today	15 (65.2%)	3 (13.0%)	3 (13.0%)	2 (8.7%)
Los Angeles Times	2 (8.7%)	7 (30.4%)	7 (30.4%)	5 (21.7%)
Total	21 (30.4%)	24 (34.8%)	12 (20.3%)	10 (14.5%)

TABLE 16.4
Comparison of Lead Print Topic With Lead Online Topic

	No Match	*Match Midnight*	*Match Noon*	*Match Both Times*
The New York Times	4 (17.4%)	10 (43.5%)	2 (8.7%)	7 (30.4%)
USA Today	15 (65.2%)	4 (17.4%)	4 (17.4%)	0 (0.0%)
Los Angeles Times	13 (56.5%)	2 (8.7%)	7 (30.4%)	1 (4.3%)
Total	32 (46.4%)	16 (23.2%)	13 (18.8%)	8 (11.6%)

TABLE 16.5
Comparison of Lead Print Topic With Top Three Online Topics

	No Match	Match Midnight	Match Noon	Match Both Times
The New York Times	2 (8.7%)	8 (13.0%)	3 (13.0%)	10 (43.5%)
USA Today	11 (47.8%)	3 (13.0%)	3 (13.0%)	6 (26.1%)
Los Angeles Times	3 (13.0%)	6 (26.1%)	8 (34.8%)	6 (26.1%)
Total	16 (23.2%)	17 (24.6%)	14 (20.3%)	22 (31.9%)

The New York Times was most likely to match story topics at both times and the *Los Angeles Times* was most likely to match at noon.

RQ3: Did print and online versions differ in their placement of topics?

To examine this question, the 13 topics were analyzed in terms of their rankings on the page among the different versions of the paper. For example, if presidential primary news was covered, coders noted its position on the page (first, second, or third story). Rank-order correlation (Spearman's rho) was used to examine, by date, how correlated the placement of each topic was between the print and online versions of the newspapers.

The ranking of only two topics was significantly correlated between the versions of the news outlets. Stories on the presidential primary were ranked similarly between the printed newspaper and the online version at midnight ($r = .617$, $p < .001$) and between the printed version and the online version at noon ($r = .615$, $p < .01$). The online versions were not significantly correlated, however. The ranking of economic news also was highly correlated between the printed newspapers and the online version at midnight ($r = .819$, $p < .01$), but no correlation was found between the ranking of the printed version and the online version at noon.

To examine rankings of these topics another way, chi-square analyses were run on the ranking of each topic (first, second, or third story) by version of the news outlet. It should be noted that this analysis could not control for rankings by date, as could the Spearman's rho analysis. Of the six topics that had enough stories for meaningful analysis, no difference in ranking was found for stories on the presidential primary, the economy, crime and accidents, and technology. Significant differences in ranking among versions were found for other government news ($\chi^2 = 10.43$, $df = 4$, $p < .05$) and for international news ($\chi^2 = 14.73$, $df = 4$, $p < .01$). For government news, print versions placed 64.5% of the stories on this topic in the lead position, compared with 20.8% of the government news that appeared in the online newspapers at noon and 47.6% that appeared online at midnight. For international news, the picture was reversed. Traditional print versions placed only 4.2% of their international stories in the lead story position, compared with 41.0% of the international stories that took the lead online at noon and 33.3% online at midnight.

TABLE 16.6
Comparison of Lead Story Topics Between Print and Online Editions

	Print	Online Midnight	Online Noon	Total
Presidential primary	25 (36.2%)	19 (28.4%)	12 (17.4%)	56 (27.3%)
Crime/accidents	5 (7.2%)	21 (31.3%)	21 (30.4%)	47 (22.9%)
Government news	20 (29.0%)	10 (14.9%)	5 (7.2%)	35 (17.1%)
International	1 (1.4%)	11 (16.4%)	17 (24.6%)	29 (14.1%)
Economic	6 (8.7%)	2 (3.0%)	7 (10.1%)	15 (7.3%)
Technology	3 (4.3%)	3 (4.5%)	4 (5.8%)	10 (4.9%)
Medical	5 (7.2%)	1 (1.5%)	3 (4.3%)	9 (4.4%)
Sports	2 (2.9%)	0 (0.0%)	0 (0.0%)	2 (1.0%)
Education	2 (2.9%)	0 (0.0%)	0 (0.0%)	2 (1.0%)
Total	69 (100%)	67 (100%)	69 (100%)	205 (100%)

RQ4: Did print and online versions emphasize the same topics?

Whereas the previous three research questions examined the matches and correlations in coverage in a date-sensitive manner, this research question examines the bigger picture. It tests not whether the coverage is exactly the same for each of the three versions of the newspaper examined for each day but whether the online versions emphasized the same topics that the print versions did over the 23-day study period. To examine this, cross-tabulations were run on versions of the newspaper by topic of the lead (No. 1 ranked) story. As Table 16.6 shows, significant differences emerged among the topic of the lead stories based on the version of the newspaper examined ($\chi^2 = 52.27$, $df = 16$, $p < .001$). The print versions of the newspapers over the month studied were significantly more likely to place the presidential primary and other government news in the lead story slot, whereas crime and accident and international news were rare as the lead print story. In contrast, both online versions (midnight and noon) were more likely to feature crime and accidents. But the online versions differed in the lead story selection as well. Online versions at noon were less likely to feature the presidential primary and other governmental news and more likely to feature international news (which could be expected given that the Asian and European news cycles would be at or near their close about that time).

Next, the cross tabulations examining the topics covered among the three versions were run for each newspaper. No significant differences emerged for *The New York Times* for any of its top three topics. However, for the second-ranked story, *USA Today* was significantly more likely to feature the presidential primary online at midnight (seven stories or 31.8% of the stories collected for that version) than in its print version (two or 8.7%). Accidents and crashes dominated in *USA Today's* second story spot online at noon (nine or 39.1% of the stories), whereas other technology news, absent in the second story spot online, was the most frequently occurring topic in that spot in the print version (five or 21.7% of the print stories, $\chi^2 = 35.11$, $df = 20$, $p < .05$). The lead story topic differed significantly for the *Los Angeles Times* ($\chi^2 = 33.97$, $df = 12$, $p < .001$). The presidential primary was rarely the lead story topic online at noon for that title (three or 13.0% of the stories), whereas it was much more likely featured as the lead topic in the print (eight or 34.8%) and online midnight (six or 27.3%) versions. Other government news also was common in the print version (seven or 30.4% of the lead stories) but was virtually absent online (in only one story in either Web version). In contrast, international and crime and accident stories dominated that paper's online versions.

DISCUSSION

The findings show that the selection of lead stories can vary significantly between print and online products produced by one newspaper company. More than half of the most prominent print stories in the three newspapers were not included as lead stories online (Table 16.2). The common conception of online newspapers as shovelware, primarily duplicating content from the print side, overlooks the significant differences generated by editing decisions and production differences. The editorial decisions that online news editors make hourly lead to different choices for top stories. Because lead stories are most likely to catch readers' attention, these differences in news judgment could influence the messages received by readers of the different editions.

Differences at Midnight

When the print and online versions shared a lead story, it was generally at midnight. This seems predictable, given that many online papers have systems for uploading stories from the print side as the presses roll in the late evening. In the morning, online news staffs begin the process of adding new content, so that by noon, the online front page can look starkly different from that morning's print edition. Although expected, this finding underscores the differences between the two publishing formats, with online newspapers responding to readers who expect frequent updates and fresh news. This also makes the midnight comparison the most instructive when comparing differences in news judgment, because, presumably, that is the time when both editions are working with the same material and deadlines.

Even with the same content and roughly the same time constraints, more than two thirds (68%) of the online headlines failed to match the print headlines at midnight. This may overstate the case somewhat, because on some days the *Los Angeles Times* had not yet uploaded the next day's stories when the data collection was made at midnight. For *The New York Times* and *USA Today*, however, the midnight collection time on the West Coast captured the 3 A.M. East Coast front page. Even then, one third of *The New York Times* online top stories differed from the print stories at midnight, as did more than 80% of the stories in *USA Today* and its online edition. One possible explanation for these differences is that online editors are using explicitly different criteria, based on their understanding of audience interests, which leads them to highlight different stories. Other explanations are that online newspapers have turned into breaking news wire services, with the latest headline taking prominence because of timeliness, as opposed to other criteria.

Differences at Noon

Because studies consistently show that online papers have much greater readership during the day than at night (Mori, 2003), focusing on the differences between the print paper and the noon online edition most closely approximates readers' experiences. Only 11 of the 69 lead print stories examined (16%) were identical between the print and online noon editions. Thus, people who read only the online version of a newspaper during the day would not read the same lead story as print readers about 85% of the time. The online reader would not be exposed to prominent placement (in any of the top three online spaces) of the lead print story about 65% of the time. Because of the constrained nature of the computer screen and the design of online newspapers, the top three online stories often take up the opening screen of the computer, requiring readers to scroll to see additional stories.

Given this prominence cue, print readers and online readers of the same newspaper could, over time, develop very different perceptions of the day's news. Although it is obvious that different media choices give people different views of the world, the purpose of this study—to investigate whether the choice of an online medium would give a different picture than that of print even within the same news organization—demonstrates that the online medium does have its own individual characteristics that distinguish its content from the print version. This observation could partially explain the differences Althaus and Tewksbury (2002) found when they compared the recall and recognition of news events between print and online readers of *The New York Times.*

Differences Between Newspaper Titles

Similarities between the print and online versions clearly exist, but in varying degrees for each paper. *USA Today* was the least likely to have similar content between the lead stories in print and online. On nearly three quarters of the days studied, the lead story in *USA Today* was not the lead story in the online edition, either at noon or midnight. And 65% of the time, the lead print story wasn't included in the top three stories online. *The New York Times* tended to match fairly closely at midnight, but out of the 23 days studied, only twice did the lead story in print match the lead story in the noon online edition. This pattern held true even when comparing the lead print story with the top three online stories: Only five matches were found between the lead print story and any of the top three online stories at noon. The *Los Angeles Times* most often matched at noon, but this may be due partly to the production cycle of the paper and the midnight data collection time. As noted earlier, for a few of the data collection points at midnight, the *Los Angeles Times* had not yet uploaded the next day's news stories. But this demonstrates that once the site posted the day's stories, its front page remained relatively stable at least until noon.

The time zone issue is clearly a limitation in this study that should be addressed in future studies by collecting data at a consistent time within each time zone. Future studies could also examine why the newspaper companies differed in the degree to which their online and print editions matched. Examining editing routines, newsroom production practices, and online staff characteristics could explain the story play differences found in this study.

Differences in News Topics

The question then becomes whether there are patterns in the differences in news judgment between the two types of media. As Table 16.6 shows, significant differences were found in the types of topics covered in print and online. The print versions were much more likely than the online versions to give prominent play to the presidential primary and other governmental news, two traditional news stories long covered in print. In contrast, when online versions had the highest readership—at noon—they were more likely to have news of crime/accidents and international stories. Given the immediacy of the ratings pressure that makes online journalism more like broadcast than print, it may be that news judgment in an online environment is more likely to resemble the broadcast preference for timely breaking news, rather than the more analytical stories and topics of print newspapers.

One explanation for the larger volume of crime and accident news could be the extensive coverage in the *Los Angeles Times*. An Alaska Airlines jet crashed just off the California coast early in the study period, and this was covered heavily in Los Angeles. The greater focus on international news may be due to the news cycles in the Asian and European markets, or the fact that many of these stories are breaking news at the time, thus giving them a high value for timeliness. Although international stories might not be considered of high enough news value for the print editions, in the breaking news environment of online news, they become prominent. It is also a possibility that online news staff are considering their audiences, which can be much more global than the geographically based readership of most print versions.

CONCLUSION

The invention of television and the development of broadcast news changed the daily news experience of citizens (Robinson & Sheehan, 1983; White, 1982) as well as the way politicians, officials, interest groups, and citizens interacted with and responded to the news. The challenge for today's scholars is to discern and document how the Internet is shaping and changing the news experience once again. The fact that readers who focus primarily on either print or online newspapers are likely to encounter different lead stories is significant not just for the reader, but also for what it tells us about the changing nature of news, and the implications this has for communication theories such as agenda setting. Scholars have used the prominence of news stories as an important variable in tracing media effects (Dearing & Rogers, 1996). If prominence systematically changes online, understanding the patterns and reasons for the change will be critical to understanding the changing news environment.

Online editors at larger newspapers such as those studied here often make hourly news judgments, a situation far different from the once-a-day judgments of the print side (Alves & Weiss, 2004). As Singer (2001, 2002) discovered, online staff do shape news selection differently than do print staff, and this selection has significant implications for what the public perceives as important news. Why this occurs is likely due to a number of factors, including the organizational structure of the print and online news rooms, differences in orientation and relationships between online staff and print staff, technological factors, news flow, and deadlines (Boczkowski, 2004). Another possible factor is the information that online editors have about what readers find most interesting. Because user logs provide managers with accurate and detailed statistics about how many people click on each story online, they have immediate feedback about what stories are the most popular. Managers who pay attention to this user feedback have discovered how to manipulate attention to different stories by experimenting with various page placements, as well as by drawing attention to particular stories in e-mail newsletters and other forms of communication with readers (W. Grueskin, personal communication, April 16, 2004). This knowledge may prompt online editors to select stories that they know are more likely to attract readers, potentially diverging from the traditional news values print editors use when selecting news.

For the time period covered in this study, editors of online newspapers appeared to highlight more international stories, and more stories about crime and accidents, than did their print counterparts. By contrast, print editors tended to feature more stories about government and politics, as well as more top stories about health, education, technology, and sports. It appears that breaking news stories fill the front pages of online sites, whereas more analytical stories, and a greater diversity of stories, are chosen for the front pages of print newspapers. If online news develops a pattern of focus on breaking news, it may become more difficult for the trend stories, think pieces, and perspectives to be found—and read—online. Many journalism critics have focused on the tendency of journalism to be event oriented. Online journalism has the potential to exacerbate this tendency, a possibility that, again, would need further research.

As citizens increasingly turn to online news sources for information, it becomes more important to understand how these sources differ and to catalog and anticipate what impacts these differences might have on news audiences, news producers, and news sources. As online readers encounter different types of stories online and pursue their individual interests more easily because of the format of online sources, disparate pictures of the world could develop between readers of the different mediums (Sunstein, 2001). Older media models based on gatekeeping and agenda setting may no longer apply to a changing news environment (Williams & Delli Carpini, 2004). Further research to identify trends over time in differences between various types of traditional and online news outlets, as well as what causes these differences, will help us better understand changes in the news environment occurring as a result of technological innovations, economic changes, and cultural shifts.

ENDNOTES

1. Because of coder error, data for February 15 was unavailable.
2. No teasers for inside stories were selected, except in the case of large photographs that dominated above the fold and were accompanied by captions that provided some significant information about the story.
3. In both print and online, agate information (sports scores, economic news, and weather statistics) were excluded.
4. No data on intercoder reliability were recorded during the initial collection period. To demonstrate reliability of the instrument, the codesheet and protocol were tested with a similar set of data as a class project. In that study, 39 sets of three versions of a newspaper were each recorded by two or more coders. Intercoder reliability on the instrument in the subsequent study ranged from 82.4% to 100%, with an average reliability of 91.3%. This suggests solid reliability for the instrument used in this study.

REFERENCES

Althaus, S., & Tewksbury, D. (2002). Agenda setting and the "new" news: Patterns of issue importance among readers of the paper and online versions of *The New York Times*. *Communication Research, 29,* 180–207.

Alves, R., & Weiss, A. (2004). Many newspaper sites still cling to once-a-day publish cycle. *Online Journalism Review.* Retrieved July 22, 2004, from http://ojr.org/ojr/workplace/1090395903.php

Bagdikian, B. (1971). *The information machines.* New York: Harper & Row.

Boczkowski, P. (2004). *Digitizing the news.* Cambridge, MA: MIT Press.

Clyde, R. W., & Buckalew, J. K. (1969). Inter-media standardization: A Q-analysis of news editors. *Journalism Quarterly, 46,* 349–351.

Corrigan, D. M. (1990). Value coding consensus in front page news leads. *Journalism Quarterly 67,* 653–662.

Dearing, J. W., & Rogers, E. M. (1996). *Agenda-setting.* Thousand Oaks, CA: Sage.

deWolk, R. (2001). *Introduction to online journalism.* Needham Heights, MA: Allyn & Bacon.

Erbring, L., Goldenberg, E. N., & Miller, A. H. (1980). Front-page news and real-world cues: A new look at agenda-setting by the media. *American Journal of Political Science, 24,* 16–49.

Fallows, D., & Rainie, L., (2004). The Internet as a unique news source. *Pew Internet & American Life Project.* Retrieved July 6, 2004, from http://www.pewinternet.org/PPF/r/130/report_display.asp

Fishman, M. (1980). *Manufacturing the news.* Austin: University of Texas Press.

Foote, J. S., & Steele, M. E. (1986). Degree of conformity in lead stories in early evening network TV newscasts. *Journalism Quarterly, 63,* 19–23.

Fredin, E. S. (1997, September). Rethinking the news story for the Internet: Hyperstory prototypes and a model of the user. *Journalism & Mass Communication Monographs, 163,* 1–47.

Gans, H. (1980). *Deciding what's news: A study of CBS Evening News, NBC Nightly News, Newsweek and Time.* New York: Vintage Books.

Graber, D. A. (1997). *Mass media and American politics* (5th ed.). Washington, DC: Congressional Quarterly Press.

Greer, J., & Mensing, D. (2004, Spring). U.S. news web sites better, but small papers still lag. *Newspaper Research Journal, 25*(2), 98–113.

Iyengar, S. (1991) *Is anyone responsible? How television frames political issues.* Chicago: The University of Chicago Press.

Krantz, Michael. (1994, April). Still setting America's agenda. *Mediaweek, 4,* 17.

Lippmann, W. (1922). *Public opinion.* New York: The Free Press.

Manoff, R. K., & Schudson, M. (Eds.). (1986). *Reading the news.* New York: Pantheon Books.

McChesney, R. W. (1999). *Rich media, poor democracy.* Chicago: University of Illinois Press.

McCombs, M., & Shaw, D. L. (1972). The agenda-setting function of mass media. *Public Opinion Quarterly, 36,* 176–187.

McCombs, M., Shaw, D., & Weaver, D. (Eds.). (1997). *Communication and democracy: Exploring the intellectual frontiers in agenda-setting theory.* Mahwah, NJ: Lawrence Erlbaum Associates.

Mensing, D. (1996). *The economics of online newspaper sites.* Unpublished master's thesis, University of Nevada, Reno. Retrieved May 2001, from http://unr.edu/homepage/dmensing

Mori Research. (2003). *Online dayparting: Claiming the day, seizing the night.* Retrieved June 12, 2003, from http://www.moriresearch.com

Neuman, W. R., Just, M. R., & Crigler, A. N. (1992). *Common knowledge: News and the construction of political meaning.* Chicago: The University of Chicago Press.

Nielsen, J. (1997). *How users read on the Web.* Retrieved August 2001, from http://www.useit.com/altertbox/9710a.html

Outing, S. (1999). Newspaper stories online in 30 minutes or less. *Editor & Publisher Online.* Retrieved August 2001, from http://www.mediainfo.com/ephome/news/newshtm/stop/st110399.htm

Pew Research Center for the People and the Press. (2004). *News audiences increasingly politicized.* Retrieved July 6, 2004, from http://people-press.org/reports/display.php3?PageID=839

Riffe, D., Ellis, B., Rogers, M. K., Van Ommeren, R. L., & Woodman, K. A. (1986). Gatekeeping and the network news mix. *Journalism Quarterly, 63,* 315–321.

Robinson, M. J., & Sheehan, M. A. (1983). *Over the wire and on TV: CBS and UPI in Campaign '80.* New York: Russell Sage Foundation.

Sharkey, J. (1994). Judgment calls. *American Journalism Review, 16*(7), 18–26.

Singer, J. (2001). The metro wide web: Changes in newspapers' gate-keeping role online. *Journalism & Mass Communication Quarterly, 78,* 65–80.

Singer, J. (2002). Information trumps interaction in local papers' online caucus coverage. *Newspaper Research Journal, 23*(4), 91–96.

Singer, J., Tharp, M., & Haruta, A. (1998, August). *Superstars or second-class citizens? Management and staffing issues affect newspapers' online journalists.* Paper presented at the 1998 conference of the Association of Educators in Journalism and Mass Communication, Chicago.

Stepp, C. S. (2001, June) Whatever happened to competition? *American Journalism Review, 23*(5), 22–31.

Sunstein, C. (2001). *Republic.com.* Princeton, NJ: Princeton University Press.

Tuchman, G. (1978). *Making news: A study in the construction of reality.* New York: The Free Press.

Tuggle, C. A., & Huffman, S. (1999). Live news reporting: Professional judgment or technological pressure? *Journal of Broadcasting and Electronic Media, 43,* 492–505.

White, D. M. (1950). The "gate keeper": A case study in the selection of news. *Journalism Quarterly, 24,* 383–390.

White, T. H. (1982). *America in search of itself: The making of the president, 1956–1980.* New York: Harper & Row.

Williams, B., & Delli Carpini, M. X. (2004). Monica and Bill all the time and everywhere: The collapse of gatekeeping and agenda setting in the new media environment. *American Behavioral Scientist, 47,* 1208–1230.

About the Contributors

Robert B. Affe (JD, New York University) is director of the Telecommunications Management Institute and senior lecturer in the Department of Telecommunications at Indiana University, Bloomington. His professional interests span programming, advertising, and commercial free-speech issues.

Erik P. Bucy (PhD, University of Maryland) is an associate professor in the Department of Telecommunications and adjunct associate professor in the School of Informatics at Indiana University, Bloomington. His research focuses on the social impact of information technology, the effects of compelling images in the news, and normative theories of media and democracy.

Zhanwei Cao (PhD, University of Texas at Dallas) is a consumer credit risk officer at Bank of America. Her current research includes business value of information technology, telecommunications economics, and strategic performance analysis.

Jinmyung Choi is a doctoral student in the College of Communication and Information Sciences at the University of Alabama. His research focuses on media effects and entertainment theory.

Hsiang Iris Chyi (PhD, University of Texas at Austin) is an assistant professor in the Departments of Journalism and Communication at the University of Arizona. She has conducted extensive research on the economics of online newspapers in the United States and in Hong Kong. Her research interests include communication technology and media economics.

Renee duPlessis (MMC, Louisiana State University) holds multidisciplinary expertise in media planning, buying, and client management in the advertising industry. Her clients range from Fortune 500 companies in large markets to independently owned and operated businesses all over the country.

Jennifer Greer (PhD, University of Florida) is academic chair and associate professor at the Reynolds School of Journalism at the University of Nevada, Reno. Her research focuses on new media, political communication, and the effects of these forms of communication on audiences.

Dominic L. Lasorsa (PhD, Stanford University) is an associate professor of journalism at the University of Texas at Austin. His research focuses on political communication and news media use.

Xigen Li (PhD, Michigan State University) is an assistant professor in the School of Journalism at Southern Illinois University Carbondale. His research focuses on news media and the Internet, impact of media technology on news content, and international communication.

Carolyn Lin (PhD, Michigan State University) is a professor in the Department of Communication Sciences at the University of Connecticut. Her research interests include the economics and sociocultural impact of communication technology and advertising.

Wilson Lowrey (PhD, University of Georgia) is an assistant professor in the Journalism Department of the College of Communication and Information Sciences at the University of Alabama. His research focuses on the sociology of media and media work, and on the impact of new technologies on journalism.

Donica Mensing (PhD, University of Nevada) is director of the graduate program and an assistant professor at the Reynolds School of Journalism at the University of Nevada, Reno. Her research focuses on impacts of the Internet on news and democracy.

Michael Salwen (PhD, Michigan State University) is a professor in the School of Communication at the University of Miami. He is the author of numerous journal articles in media effects and is the author of several books. He is associate editor of *Journalism & Mass Communication Quarterly.*

Mark Tremayne (PhD, University of Wisconsin–Madison) is an assistant professor in the School of Journalism at the University of Texas at Austin. His research focuses on the Web and the changes it brings about for journalism and mass communication.

Xianyi Ye (MMC, Louisiana State University) is a System Analyst and Project Leader in Allied Technology Group Inc. (ATG). Her team is responsible to design, develop, and maintain the web application for the U.S. Department of Education, which is ranked the top 10 most-visited government Web sites and has over 60,000 web pages.

Qian Zeng (MMC, Louisiana State University) is a biostatistician at Boston Scientific Corporation. Her main interest is in statistical analysis and Internet communication.

Author Index

Subject Index

LEA'S COMMUNICATION SERIES
Jennings Bryant/Dolf Zillmann, General Editors

For a complete list of titles in LEA's Communication Series, please contact Lawrence Erlbaum Associates, Publishers, at www.erlbaum.com.

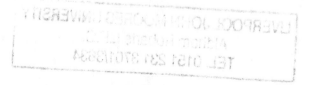

Internet Newspapers

The Making of a Mainstream Medium